PUBLICATIONS OF THE NEW CHAUCER SOCIETY

THE NEW CHAUCER SOCIETY

Studies in the Age of Chaucer, the yearbook of The New Chaucer Society, is published annually. Each issue contains a limited number of substantial articles, reviews of books on Chaucer and related topics, and an annotated Chaucer bibliography. Articles explore such concerns as the efficacy of various critical approaches to the art of Chaucer and his contemporaries, their literary relationships and reputations, and the artistic, economic, intellectual, religious, scientific, and social and historical backgrounds to their work.

Manuscripts, in duplicate, accompanied by return postage, should follow the *Chicago Manual of Style*, thirteenth edition. Unsolicited reviews are not accepted. Authors receive free twenty offprints of articles and ten of reviews. All correspondence concerning manuscript submissions for Volume 16 of *Studies in the Age of Chaucer* should be directed to the Editor, Lisa J. Kiser, Department of English, Ohio State University, 164 West 17th Avenue, Columbus, OH 43210-1370. Subscriptions to The New Chaucer Society and information about the Society's activities should be directed to Christian Zacher, Center for Medieval and Renaissance Studies, Ohio State University, 306 Dulles Hall, 230 West 17th Avenue, Columbus, OH 43210-1311.

Studies in the Age of Chaucer

Studies in the Age of Chaucer

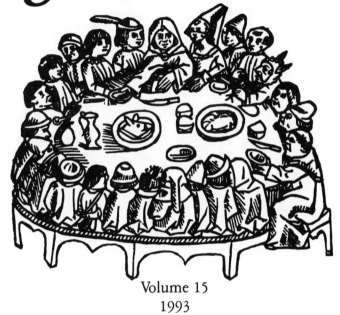

Volume 15
1993

EDITOR

LISA J. KISER

PUBLISHED ANNUALLY BY THE NEW CHAUCER SOCIETY

THE OHIO STATE UNIVERSITY, COLUMBUS

The frontispiece design, showing the Pilgrims at the Tabard Inn, is adapted from the woodcut in Caxton's second edition of *The Canterbury Tales*.

ISBN 0-933784-17-1

ISSN 0190-2407

CONTENTS

Studies in the Age of Chaucer

THE PRESIDENTIAL ADDRESS
The New Chaucer Society
Eighth International Congress
August 1–4, 1992
The University of Washington
Seattle

The Presidential Address

Old, *New*, and *Yong* in Chaucer

Alfred David
Indiana University

Allas! I wepynge, am constreyned to bygynnen vers of sorwful matere, that whilom in florysschyng studie made delitable ditees. For lo, rendynge muses of poetes enditen to me thynges to ben writen, and drery vers of wretchidnesse weten my face with verray teres. . . . They that weren glorie of my youthe, whilom weleful and grene, conforten nowe the sorwful wyerdes of me, olde man.

[*Boece*, book 1, metrum 2, lines 1–13][1]

THE EPIGRAPH AND TITLE FOR *The Strumpet Muse* came from the first prosa of *Boece*, where Philosophy drives away the muses, whom she calls "thise comune strompettis," from the bedside of the sick Boethius. The strumpet muse became the heroine of that book, both compromising with and holding out against the powerful pressures of morality up to the very last. Being young and easy, I paid no attention to the first metrum of *Boece*, where the muses are pictured in a different light, and this is the epigraph for my talk today: the muses, who once inspired the flourishing studies and works of green and glorious youth, now comfort white-haired old age with tears shed over verses about human miseries.

That image hardly fits conventional notions of Chaucer's muse or of his old age. When he alludes to his age, as he does in *The Envoy to Scogan*, he

---

[1] All citations of Chaucer's works are from Larry D. Benson, gen. ed., *The Riverside Chaucer*, 3d ed. (Boston: Houghton Mifflin, 1987).

is usually playful. He seems to be making fun of lugubrious versifying when he tells his friend that he is forgotten "in solytarie wildernesse," and he protests that his muse "rusteth in my shethe stille in pees." Obviously the *Envoy* displays Chaucer's colt's tooth; Scogan would be quite right to say, as Chaucer suggests he might, "Lo, olde Grisel lyst to ryme and pleye!" And yet this playful poem takes a melancholy and reflective turn: "While I was yong, I put hir forth in prees; / But al shal passe that men prose or ryme; / Take every man hys turn, as for his tyme." The lines suggest that, though the time may not be yet, Chaucer's turn will not last much longer.

The melancholy strain, which humor lightens but certainly does not cancel in this late short poem, is present from the very first. Even in Chaucer's gayest performances, the pain is never far below the surface. More often it is entirely explicit. In her brilliant essay, "'Voice Memorial,'" Louise O. Fradenburg draws out some of the implications of the fact that, as she puts it, "Chaucer's poetry. . . is at nearly all points deeply concerned with the experience of loss."[2] I want to follow up that insight by examining the word *old* in its oppositions with its antonyms *new* and *yong*. In these related terms we can detect patterns of coping with disillusionment, grief, and pain.

If one asks where are the "delitable ditees" Chaucer composed in the glory of his youth, they are probably all lost. None of the surviving shorter poems really fits that formula or Chaucer's own reference in the *Retraction* to "many a song and many a leccherous lay." The most common type among the surviving lyrics is the complaint, which laments the losses of pity, good government, or the former age. The closest we can come to an early work glorying in youth is the A fragment of *The Romaunt of the Rose*, the only part of the Middle English translation that is probably by Chaucer. Inside the garden of Mirth all the carolers are beautiful young folk. Mirth, the French text says, has no beard or moustache, just a bit of down, lines rendered by Chaucer as: "Of berd unnethe hadde he nothyng, / For it was in the firste spryng" (*RR* 833–34). Seasonal imagery strikes the keynote in the opening setting of the poem, where every bush and hedge wants to adorn itself in new foliage (line 56), and the earth has grown so proud that she wants a new dress (line 64). The same kind of imagery describes the physical appearance and the floral decoration of the costumes and garlands worn by the company, among whom all is young, new, and fresh. The

[2] Louise O. Fradenburg, "'Voice Memorial': Loss and Reparation in Chaucer's Poetry," *Exemplaria* 2 (1990): 172.

couples are lovers, seen most attractively in the portrait of Youth, who is not quite twelve, and her consort, innocently kissing "As it two yonge dowves were" (line 1298). Yet one cannot completely forget about Youth's opposite, the complementary portrait of Elde, excluded from the garden yet menacing it on the other side of the wall. That portrait contains the somber passage on time, which seems to be spoken in a threatening voice, different from that of the twenty-year-old narrator's (lines 369, 388–90):

> The tyme that passeth nyght and day, . . .
> The tyme eke that chaungith all,
> And all doth waxe and fostred be,
> And alle thing distroieth he.

The youthful garden world in Guillaume de Lorris is sheltered from but also shadowed by time.

It is perhaps not simply due to the accident of the death of the young duchess that Chaucer's first important poem should have been an elegy. The bereavement is for the loss of Blanche but, more than that, for the loss of illusion brought about by a new awareness of time, which is marked by the tale of Ceyx and Alcyone and by the striking clock that awakens the dreamer at the end. In the figure of "goode faire White" (*BD* 948), Blanche represents all the carolers in the Garden of Mirth: Youthe, Beaute, Courtesie, and Franchise. It is as if they, too, were dead, and "Be God, hyt ys routhe!" (line 1310).

Chaucer's first narrative poem feels disturbingly different from the *Roman* and the poems of Machaut and Froissart, the works from which it borrows so liberally. The opening passage about the narrator's melancholia and insomnia, though parts of it have been lifted almost verbatim from the beginning of Froissart's *Paradys d'amour*, is much longer and heavier. The narrator's eight-year sickness hints at the conventional lover's malady, which is explicitly the cause of Froissart's distress, but in Chaucer's poem the cause of the sickness is deliberately left vague and mysterious.

What chiefly makes the beginning of Chaucer's poem different from his French sources is the tale of Ceyx and Alcyone in the induction to the dream. The framing of that tale gives us the earliest occurrence of *old* in a surviving original work by Chaucer. The narrator picks up the book of fables "That clerkes had in olde tyme, / And other poetes, put in rime" (*BD* 53–54). This conjuring up of "olde tyme," preserved in old books composed by old clerks, will become a Chaucerian *topos* with an effect here

7

altogether different from that of the many mythological allusions in the works of Machaut and Froissart. There the allusions normally serve as analogues to the woes of disconsolate lovers but without introducing any dimension of time. It is as though the woeful Achilles, Troilus, Alcyone, and other bereft or unrequited ancient lovers existed in the same dimension of time with the poet Froissart or Machaut's patrons, the way the well of Narcissus exists within the garden of Mirth.

In Machaut's *Dit de la fontainne amoureuse*, the tale of Ceyx and Alcyone is told as part of a much longer complaint by the Duke of Berry; the point (reached after 150 lines) is that the duke wants Morpheus to send a spirit to express his suffering to his lady. But Chaucer's framing device gives the tale, and thereby his own poem, a new dimension of time and focuses not on some present lover's grief, for which a cure may be possible, but on grief for an irremediable sorrow of long ago: "This was the tale: There was a king. . . ." Thus the sad tale over which the narrator falls asleep opens up naturalistically and dramatically the time that is personified in the portrait of old age in the *Roman*. The sleepless narrator who retells the story seems much older than twenty. The story told to him by the Black Knight, so new to the dreamer, turns out to be an old one, a variant of the story over which the dreamer fell asleep.

Long ago Bertrand Bronson suggested that the knight is the dreamer's surrogate or double.[3] Like the narrator in the induction, the knight is self-absorbed in his grief. According to the rules of the genre, he should belong to the company of Mirth, and he is "ryght yong . . . , / Of the age of foure and twenty yer" (lines 454–55). The knight resembles Mirth in having "Upon hys berd but lytel her" (line 456). But instead he turns out to be Sorrow, the last of the personifications excluded from the garden in the *Roman* (lines 595–97):

> For whoso seeth me first on morwe
> May seyn he hath met with sorwe,
> For y am sorwe, and sorwe ys y.

It is as though the figures in Guillaume's dream had merged; the portrait of sorrow superimposes itself on that of youth.

In French courtly narrative as well as in Christian poetry, protagonists are conventionally consoled by the promise of a future end to sorrow. Unhappy

---

[3] Bertrand Bronson, "*The Book of the Duchess* Reopened," *PMLA* 67 (1952): 871.

lovers as well as Christian sinners receive the advice dispensed by the God of Love: if they heed his commandments and cling to Hope and Swete-Thought, all will eventually be well in a new life. However, the notion that the Black Knight has been somehow consoled by his conversation with the dreamer is, I feel, another fiction constructed by a few twentieth-century critics. That the dreamer-poet is consoled through the act of putting the dream in rhyme is self-evident. He constructs a new version of the old tale of Ceyx and Alcyone by which his personal grief is assuaged. The dream, however, holds out no more promise of comfort or restoration to the knight than the fable did to Alcyone; what it does offer is "solas" to the dreamer and perhaps to the poet and his audience, that is to say, both pleasure and consolation by means of true tears shed over imagined ones. Moreover, that sorrow is tempered by a whimsical humor, which stems from a consciousness that this is only a fiction, a fantasy, which can produce a snoring god of sleep or a dream horse in a dream bedchamber.

I have said that the death of the duchess implies sorrow for the death of a literary tradition celebrating Youth, Beauty, and the rest of the courtly virtues. *The Book of the Duchess* may also express nostalgia for a historical moment when these carolers had for a brief period seemed to come alive at the English court. In 1360 the young Froissart first visited England, where he stayed on as Queen Philippa's secretary. Chaucer himself was twenty or younger. A new generation had grown up who, like Arthur's court in *Sir Gawain and the Green Knight*, were still "in her first age." Of Edward III's sons, the Black Prince was thirty; Lionel, twenty-two; John, twenty; and Edmund, eighteen; the last three became Knights of the Garter in 1360. Gaunt had married Blanche of Lancaster the year before. The Peace of Brétigny was signed in 1360, bringing an influx of young French hostages, including the twenty-year-old Duke of Berry, whose departure from France was the occasion of Machaut's *Fountain*. By the end of the 1360s the atmosphere had changed. The English had failed to reap the financial windfall promised to them by the Treaty of Brétigny, and Edward III was slipping into his long dotage. Chaucer's first mistress and master, Elizabeth of Ulster and Prince Lionel, and the young Duchess of Lancaster were dead.

Nostalgia for a lost courtliness, or rather for a lost illusion of courtly manners and courtly ethos, pervades the poetry of Chaucer's middle period. In *Troilus and Criseyde* that loss is projected back into the distant past through the pretense that the narrator has translated the ancient history of Lollius. In the Proem to *Troilus*, Chaucer invokes the "rendynge muses" from the first metrum of *Boece* (*TC* 1.1–7):

> The double sorwe of Troilus to tellen,
> That was the kyng Priamus sone of Troye,
> In lovynge, how his aventures fellen
> From wo to wele, and after out of joie,
> My purpos is, er that I parte fro ye.
> Thesiphone, thow help me for t'endite
> Thise woful vers, that wepen as I write.

The "sorwful matere" of Boethius becomes specifically "the double sorwe of Troilus." The "woful vers," corresponding to the "drery vers of wrecchednesse" in the metrum, weep the author's tears. The sad tale is ostensibly told not to console the speaker for some personal loss, though we may wonder about what lies behind his "unliklynesse" (1.16), but to comfort unhappy young lovers in his audience. The narrator does not actually tell us that he is old, but his tone throughout implies a generation gap between himself and his audience, to whom he occasionally tries to explain the alterity of his material: "Ye knowe ek that in forme of speche is chaunge / Withinne a thousand yeer" (2.22–23).

A distinction should be made between seasonal and generational change, which is part of a constant cycle of life, a regular replacement of the old by the new and vice versa, on the one hand, and, on the other, linear historical change such as that in language and culture alluded to by the narrator in the passage I have cited from the Proem to book 2. The former is given both great natural beauty in the structure and imagery of the poem and a moral force, particularly in Troilus's Boethian song at the end of book 3, where the rotation of day and night and of the seasons is attributed to love. A sense of regular renewal animates the temple scene in which the besieged Trojans celebrate their ancient spring rite. Chaucer emphasizes the traditional nature of the feast of Palladion by referring to the "olde usage" (1.150) and "observaunces olde" (1.160). The time is April, "whan clothed is the mede / With newe grene, of lusty Veer the pryme" (1.156–57). The focus in the temple is on youth, "so many a lusty knyght, / So many a lady fressh and mayden bright" (1.165–66). Troilus is leading "His yonge knyghtes...up and down" (1.184). What catches the eye, however, is the figure in black, the bright star behind the black cloud, who, like the Black Knight, evokes simultaneous associations of youth and of sorrow, but Criseyde's mourning, unlike the knight's, contains the promise of change in her interception and return of Troilus's look.

As the poem progresses, however, such "observaunces olde" come to

10

seem little more than vestiges of tradition in a society that in many respects resembles English society in Chaucer's day. There is a sense of crisis and tension eroding long-standing values. The first reference to the towns-people describes the general indignation over Calchas's treason, which threatens to lead to reprisals against his innocent daughter. We learn as a result of one of Pandarus's elaborate lies something about these earlier troubles: Aeneas and Antenor, the future traitors, and one of their agents had tried to take away Criseyde's property (2.1471–75). For the time being, these scoundrels are held in check by men like Hector and Deiphebus, who still believe in chivalry, justice, and the rights of widows.

Pandarus's lies, by which he manipulates Deiphebus, his niece, and everyone else, even Troilus, express not simply his unique personality but, in the context of the whole poem, a new *mentalité* that pervades the town. Though he is not a villain like Antenor and, at least in his own mind, believes that he acts unselfishly, he has little regard for truth and believes that the means justify the end. Ironically, the word "old" is always on Pandarus's lips. He constantly supports his arguments with references to "olde lered," "bokes olde," "olde stories." In this respect Pandarus antici-pates those Canterbury pilgrims whom Anne Middleton writes about as "Chaucer's 'New Men,'" who are concerned to validate their discourse with reference to established values: "The newness of a new man's ethos will be disguised and diffuse in his story, characteristically — and paradoxically — appearing as an earnest and insistent honoring of old ways and the received high culture."[4] There could hardly be a better description of Pandarus.

With regard to values, the young prince, like his brothers Hector and Deiphebus, clings to old ways. The problems so many readers have with Troilus — his passivity, his timidity, his fatalism — come from the literalness with which he observes the code of courtly love and the seriousness with which he takes the feudal obligations he believes he owes to his lord, the God of Love, and to his lady. Riding beneath Criseyde's window, "so fressh, so yong, so weldy" (2.636), he blushes and modestly casts down his eyes in a reversal of the temple scene. Jill Mann and Gayle Margherita have made me aware of the feminization of Troilus in this passage, which dramatizes the reversal in courtly love of traditional male and female roles.[5] For Pandarus,

---

[4] Anne Middleton, "Chaucer's 'New Men' and the Good of Literature in the *Canterbury Tales*," in Edward W. Said, ed., *Literature and Society: Selected Papers from the English Institute* (n.s., vol. 3 [1978]), (Baltimore, Md.: Johns Hopkins University Press, 1980), p. 7.

[5] Jill Mann, *Geoffrey Chaucer*, Feminist Readings Series (Atlantic Highlands, N.J.: Humanities Press, 1991), p. 166. Gayle Margherita's essay "Historicity, Femininity, and Chaucer's *Troilus*" is forthcoming in *Exemplaria* 6.2 (1994).

who often preaches about the rules of love to Troilus and Criseyde, these roles and rules are part of an entertaining, aesthetically pleasing rhetorical game at which he excels, but oaths and protestations are only words, which entail no real or lasting commitment, and he can joke about them even as he is playing at enforcing them.

The parliamentary decision to exchange Criseyde for Antenor best reveals the change overtaking Troy: a seemingly pragmatic and opportunistic reasoning replacing chivalric principle. The parliament scene is the most clearly political in the poem, satirizing the institution of which Chaucer himself would soon become a member. Hector is not simply overruled by the commons for sticking by outdated principle — "We usen here no wommen for to selle" — but ridiculed: "O Ector, lat tho fantasies be!" (4.182, 193). Hector's fantasies are no other than the rules of chivalry, worn down by a long and costly war. And so Criseyde, a woman without strategic value, is sold to bring home the new man, Antenor.

In the subsequent exchange between Pandarus and Troilus, the associations of *new* turn bitter. Reasoning like the parliament, Pandarus advises Troilus to exchange Criseyde. Citing Zanzis (a wise old clerk scholars have failed to identify), Pandarus argues "The newe love out chaceth ofte the olde; / And upon newe cas lith newe avys" (4.415–16). The natural order of the sun and moon, which Troilus in his song had used as an example of the eternal binding power of love, now becomes a rationalization of mutability in all human affairs (4.421–24):

> For also seur as day comth after nyght,
> The newe love, labour, or oother wo,
> . . . . . .
> Don olde affecciouns alle over-go.

Perhaps these words are said, as the narrator cautions, "for the nones alle" (4.428), but in fact Pandarus loves the excitement of change, news, and game with which his hood is always full. His words are always "for the nones."

Troilus bitterly rejects the idea that he "shulde love another / Al fresshly newe" (4.456–57). Ironically, however, in the Greek camp Zanzis and Pandarus prove to be right. The new love does drive out the old, and the pain of that exchange is heightened by the imagery of the natural cycles. The season is of course spring, and Diomede, "as fressh as braunche in May" (5.844), visits Calchas's tent, recalling an earlier visit by Pandarus "In May, that moder is of monthes glade" (2.50). And like Pandarus, "This Diomede al fresshly newe ayeyn / Gan pressen on" (5.1010–11). The day on which Criseyde has promised to return happens to be that of the new moon. At night from the wall Troilus tells his sorrow to the moon, whose "hornes olde" (5.652) he has seen in the morning: "Ywis, whan thow art horned newe, / I shal be glad, if all the world be trewe!" (5.650–51). The moon thus becomes the symbol not of orderly change in nature but of Criseyde's "slydynge of corage" (5.825) and Troilus's invisible horns.

The fear of the *new* becomes unbearable; Troilus takes comfort in rereading "The lettres ek that she of olde tyme / Hadde hym ysent" (5.470–71) and revisiting old familiar places. But the old books provide Troilus not with the solace of fiction but with the bitterness of truth. Cassandra reiterates the word *old* as if to torment her brother in telling him that to understand his dream he needs to listen to "a fewe of olde stories": how Fortune has overthrown "lordes olde"; the strife about which "olde bokes tellen us"; about Tideus's descent from Meleager, "or ellis olde bookes lye"; and finally, after all these "gestes olde," about Diomede (5.1459, 1461, 1478, 1481, 1511, 1512). Indeed, the violent history of Thebes, full of betrayals, not only proves Criseyde's infidelity as revealed in Troilus's dream: it proves that the ideals of fealty, chivalry, and love held by men like Hector, Deiphebus, and Troilus are fantasies. Interpreted rightly, the old books and stories, including Lollius's old book, hold out no true comfort or solace to the narrator or to the "yonge, fresshe folkes" (5.1835) in his audience. The only consolation promised is that of Christ: "What nedeth feynede loves for to seke?" (5.1848). In context, "feynede" means false, but it also means imagined, fictional, love as it is feigned in old fables and stories. Yet the human need to seek out such feigned loves in old books persists.[6]

The General Prologue to *The Canterbury Tales* extends the opposition between old and new to Chaucer's own time. With the exceptions of the Knight, the Parson, and the Plowman, the pilgrims resemble the Monk, one of Middleton's new men, in their progressivism: "This ilke Monk leet olde thynges pace, / And heeld after the newe world the space" (*GP* 175–76).

---

[6] The primary meanings of *feyned* are "false, insincere, counterfeit"; but a secondary sense, "fictional," is possible in *Mars* 173: "This is no feyned mater that I telle"; and an ironic double sense, "falsify / make up a fiction," is strongly implied in *GP* 736, "Or feyne thyng, or fynde wordes newe." In *The Canterbury Tales* what the narrator denies is exactly what Chaucer is doing.

New, like *worthy*, echoes through *The General Prologue* with ironic resonance, as it does in the phrase about the Monk's "newe world." The new world is reflected particularly in the equipment of the guildsmen: "Ful fressh and newe hir geere apiked was" (line 365). The mutually profitable alliance of the professionals, the Physician and his apothecaries, is actually of long standing, but Chaucer expresses it in a negative construction: "For ech of hem made oother for to wynne — / Hir frendshipe nas nat newe to bigynne" (lines 427–28). The Wife of Bath's shoes, which are suggestively "ful moyste and newe" (line 457), counteract any notion of undue wear and tear inflicted by five husbands, not to mention "oother compaignye in youthe" (line 461). The Pardoner, "for jolitee" (a word glossed as "pleasure,"[7] but an ambiguous term if we think of the "joly Absolon"), is bareheaded, displaying shoulder-length hair: "Hym thoughte he rood al of the newe jet" (lines 680–82). Expressions like "newe world" and "newe jet" betray a consciousness of many of the pilgrims that costume, customs, work, government, science, agriculture, and so forth are changing and that it is important to keep up with the new age. We tend to regard the Prioress's table manners, the Clerk's desire for twenty volumes of Aristotle, the Franklin's concern about his mews and fishponds, and the Summoner's drunken Latinity as traits of individual character, but they also express social and intellectual fashion and the desire to belong to the brave new world of the 1380s.

Except for the churls, however, the new men advertise their tales as old stories, and it is worth reminding ourselves that even in writing fabliaux Chaucer was reviving an old genre that had flourished in France during the thirteenth century and declined in the fourteenth. When we come to the links and the tales, the significant opposition is between *old* and *yong*. In *The Knight's Tale*, the two young Theban knights and especially Emilye (*KnT* 1035–37),

> that fairer was to sene
> Than is the lylie upon his stalke grene,
> And fressher than the May with floures newe —

are reminiscent of the dancers in the Garden of Mirth. But one of Chaucer's most fascinating innovations in Boccaccio's tale is his introduction of Old Father Time himself (lines 2443–49):

---

[7] Norman Davis et al., eds., *A Chaucer Glossary* (Oxford: Clarendon Press, 1979); John H. Fisher, ed., *The Complete Poetry and Prose of Geoffrey Chaucer* (New York: Holt, Rinehart, and Winston, 1977).

> . . . the pale Saturnus the colde,
> That knew so manye of aventures olde,
> Foond in his olde experience an art
> That he ful soone hath plesed every part.
> As sooth is seyd, elde hath greet avantage;
> In elde is bothe wysdom and usage;
> Men may the olde atrenne and noght atrede.

This praise of Elde takes on an ironic, even shocking force as Saturn proceeds to boast of his powers: drowning, strangling, hanging, rebellion, poisoning, "maladyes colde, / The derke tresons, and the castes olde," and so forth (lines 2456–69). The trick he finds in his old experience is to send the fury, whose eruption from the earth causes the death of Arcite at the moment of his triumph. Saturn's speech may contain further irony. Chaucer would have remembered very well Reason's story of his castration in the *Roman*, where she uses the rude word *coillons* that so greatly offends the lover. Is the cold god's boasting about his destructive powers at some level connected to his impotence?

In *The Strumpet Muse*, I argued that *The Miller's Tale*, and especially the portrait of Alisoun, provides a reply, even an antidote, to the pessimistic and Boethian strains in *The Knight's Tale*. The fabliau generally sides with the young wife against the old husband. At least initially John gets no sympathy for marrying Alisoun: ". . . she was wylde and yong, and he was old" (*MilT* 3225). By the end the sely old carpenter has come to seem a victim of the ruthless pleasures of youth. The images in the portrait of Alisoun assert more strongly than those in the portrait of Emilye the energy, potency, and fertility of whatever is new and young. Alisoun is a more blissful sight "Than is the newe pere-jonette tree," brighter "Than in the Tour the noble yforged newe" (lines 3248, 3256). The image of the coin, however, implies that Alisoun is not simply a child of nature but, like Criseyde, an object of exchange between men. The new man Chaucer will use the metaphor of purse as lady to charm the new king, Henry IV, into getting his pension paid. *The Reeve's Prologue* and *Tale* are a Saturnian response to the Miller. The Reeve holds a bitter, grumbling sermon on the impotence of old age, then unleashes a sardonic tale of animalistic potency in which the young clerks perform "vengeance and pleyn correccioun" (*KnT* 2461) upon the surrogate Miller.

Chaucer's most profound treatment of *old* and *young* comes with the Wife of Bath and the Pardoner. The prototype of the Wife is La Vieille in the *Roman*, and in her *Prologue*, the Wife, like the *vekke*, expresses her antagonism toward everything old, including the old age that is overtaking her. When she is tongue-lashing her old husbands, "old" is the epithet prefixed to the other insults by which she addresses them: "Sire olde kaynard," "Sire olde lecchour," "olde dotard shrewe," "olde barel-ful of lyes" (*WBP* 235, 242, 291, 302). Thus she is all the more painfully aware that age has crept up on her, and of course she hates it. We do not know how long it has been since her fifth husband died — evidently for once she was left without a "hole for to sterte to" — but she feels that her charms were not greatly diminished even when, at the age of forty, she married Jankyn, for, in that respect she does not differentiate the last marriage from the rest (lines 605–608):

> As help me god, I was a lusty oon,
> And faire, and riche, and yong, and wel bigon,
> And trewely, as myne housbondes tolde me,
> I hadde the beste *quoniam* myghte be.

There is pathos in the shift from the past tense to the present in the next lines: "For certes, I am al Venerien / In feelynge" (lines 609–10). She attributes the antifeminism of the authorities she contests throughout her *Prologue* to age and impotence (lines 707–10):

> The clerk, whan he is oold, and may noght do
> Of Venus werkes worth his olde sho,
> Thanne sit he doun, and writ in his dotage
> That wommen kan nat kepe hir mariage!

It is touching that the old hag's defense of old age in her curtain lecture, compared to 68 lines on "gentilesse" (citing Dante, Valerius Maximus, Seneca, and Boethius) and 30 on poverty (citing Seneca and Juvenal), comes to a mere 10 lines and cites no authorities at all, though she claims that "auctours shal I fynden, as I gesse" (*WBT* 1212). "Thogh noon auctoritee / Were in no book," says the hag, echoing the *Wife's Prologue*, noble folk "Seyn that men sholde an oold wight doon favour" (lines 1208–10). On the surface *The Wife of Bath's Tale* has little to say in favor of old age. Nevertheless, much of its force and delight derive from the fact that the *Tale* is an old fable; the Wife of Bath knows this, just as well as the Franklin knows that his *Tale* belongs to a type made by "Thise olde gentil Britouns in hir dayes" (*FranP* 709). As a new woman, the Wife, like the

16

Franklin, though without his pomposity, gives her *Tale* a literary introduction, informing her audience that it takes place "In th'olde dayes of the Kyng Arthour, / Of which that Britons speken greet honour" (*WBT* 857–58).

The Pardoner's rejection of age, in contrast, is decidedly bitter and sarcastic. His effort to appear "al of the newe jet" is an affectation of youth, as is his tongue-in-cheek compliment to the Wife's eloquence: "I was aboute to wedde a wyf; allas!" (*WBP* 166). With mock courtesy he invites her to "teche us yonge men of youre praktike" (line 187), thereby indirectly calling her an old woman. Not that the Pardoner expects people to take him for a young man, but his affectation of youth and the flaunting of his appetites in his *Prologue*, like his sexual ambiguity, turn him into an ambiguous young-old man.[8] The tale is the expression of his true impotence, his desire of a desire that has failed. As Carolyn Dinshaw points out in her profound analysis of the Pardoner's performance, frenetic use of language and gesture is his means of generating pleasure from lack, a lack of which his eunuchry is the ultimate symbolization: "Myne handes and my tonge goon so yerne / That it is joye to se my bisynesse" (*PardP* 398–99).[9] Yet all joy is denied in the wish, hauntingly articulated by the old man in the tale, expressing the ultimate oedipal desire (*PardT* 729–31):[10]

> And on the ground, which is my moodres gate,
> I knokke with my staf, bothe erly and late,
> And seye, "Leeve mooder, leet me in!"

Unlike the old hag in *The Wife of Bath's Tale*, the old man in the *Pardoner's* can find no one, not even in fiction, to exchange "youthe" for "age."

The configurations of *old*, *new*, and *yong* in those works I have discussed indicate that there is a deep structure of values in Chaucer's works, which

---

[8] On the Pardoner as a young-old man, like the personification of Death in Thomas Mann's *Death in Venice*, see my "Criticism and the Old Man in Chaucer's *Pardoner's Tale*," *CE* 27 (1965–66): 44.

[9] "He uses language as he does his relics and his documents, as a partial object, as a substitute for his literal or figuratively absent genitals"; Carolyn Dinshaw, *Chaucer's Sexual Poetics* (Madison: University of Wisconsin Press, 1989), p. 176.

[10] Ibid., p. 179. I do not, however, agree that this death wish, expressed as an erotic desire to return to Mother Earth, "figures a more complex self-understanding" in the Pardoner, though it can certainly deepen our understanding of the tragic and destructive effects of gendering.

17

sometimes contradicts explicitly stated values. In *The Parliament of Fowls* he had written with fondness of old books (lines 22–25):

> . . . out of olde feldes, as men seyth,
> Cometh al this newe corn from yer to yere,
> And out of olde bokes, in good feyth,
> Cometh al this newe science that men lere.

The rhetorical balance of "olde" and "newe" in this oft-cited passage would seem to express a balance between reverent regard for past tradition and curiosity about new ideas and forms of expression that grow naturally out of that intellectual soil, a balance which has often been seen as Chaucerian. A survey of the occurrences of *old*, as the antonym of *new* in Chaucer's works, however, reveals quite a different semantic range and associations. Old books, as well as other literary items possessing antiquity — "olde stories," "olde Roman gestes," "old ensamples," "olde clerkes," "olde wise" — carry favorable connotations, even as learned baggage in the mouths of charac- ters like Pandarus or Chauntecleer. There are notable exceptions, like the stanza at the end of *Troilus* denouncing "payens corsed olde rites" and "the forme of olde clerkis speche / In poetrie, if ye hire bokes seche" (*TC* 5.1849, 1854–55). On the other hand, the laudatory mention of "newe science" in the *Parliament* is a vague and rare tribute to modern learning. According to the cynical advice of the Manciple's mother, it is safest not to write anything at all: "My sone, be war, and be noon auctour newe / Of tidynges, wheither they been false or trewe" (*ManT* 359–60).

New carries traditionally favorable connotations whenever it refers to the world of nature in springtime, though in the fifth book of *Troilus* such images have a painful ambiguity, connecting changes in nature to the change in Criseyde's heart. In other contexts *new* frequently has ironic negative connotations of "newfangelnesse," of status recently acquired, old loves forsaken, or old values disregarded. Even as an adverb *newe* often has a comic or satiric bite, as when Pandarus "gan newe his tong affile" (*TC* 2.1681) or "poked evere his nece new and newe" (3.116), or when January "was shave al newe in his manere" (*MerT* 1826), or the Pardoner urges the pilgrims to take pardon "Al newe and fressh at every miles ende, / So that ye offren, alwey newe and newe" (*PardT* 928–29). The oppositions between *old* and *new* are most keenly felt in *Troilus*. Significantly, *new(e)* occurs

18

forty-six times there, compared to sixty-five occurrences in all of *The Canterbury Tales*.[11]

In contrast with the opposition between *old-new*, that between *old(e)-yong(e)* is far more pervasive in *The Canterbury Tales*, where *yong* occurs eighty-one times, compared to only eight occurrences in *Troilus*. *Yong*, when it is not purely descriptive or formulaic in stock phrases like "yong or oold," rarely has negative valence except for the "yonge folk" in *The Pardoner's Tale* and in *The Tale of Melibee*. *The Merchant's Tale* is a special case; there, both *old* and *yong* are used by the narrator with withering sarcasm: ". . . whan a man is oold and hoor; . . . / Thanne sholde he take a yong wyf and a feir" (*MerT* 1269–71).

Old versus *new* applies chiefly to things and actions; *old* versus *yong* applies primarily to persons. The old clerks have, in effect, become things in being dead. Even the worthy Petrarch "is now deed and nayled in his cheste" (*ClP* 29). There is a world of difference between respectful allusions to "olde clerkis" and the Wife's scornful reference to "the clerk whan he is old." In the frame story, in the fabliaux, and in the romances *old* usually conveys pejorative, *yong* favorable connotations, as in "olde housbondes" and "yonge wyves." In tales of "moralitee and hoolynesse" *old* can signify patient poverty, as in Griselda's "olde povre fader" (*ClT* 222) or wisdom as in "hooly olde Urban" (*SNT* 185), the pope in *The Second Nun's Tale*, or it can be a term of abuse when applied to the villainesses in *The Man of Law's Tale*, the "olde Sowdanesse" and "olde Donegild" (*MLT* 414, 896). Their daughter-in-law, Custance, is the Emperor's "yonge doghter" and "yonge child" (lines 447, 1105). Griselda's youth, too, is emphasized at the beginning, and both *The Man of Law's Tale* and *The Clerk's Tale* end by focusing on the heroines' young children. The child Maurice succeeds Custance's father as emperor. Griselda calls out, "O tendre, o deere, o yonge children myne!" (*ClT* 1093). We see the contrasting value of *new* in the "stormy peple": ignorant of the identity of their "newe markysesse," "evere untrewe," and "Delitynge evere in rumbul that is newe," they are "glad, right for the noveltee, / To han a newe lady of hir toun" (lines 942, 995–97, 1004–1005).

The passage about the "stormy peple" is Chaucer's addition, a conser-

---

[11] These and the figures below are taken from Akio Oizumi, *A Complete Concordance to the Works of Geoffrey Chaucer*, 10 vols. (Hildesheim and New York: Olms-Weidmann, 1991). In *Troilus* there are 39 occurrences of *old(e)*; in *The Canterbury Tales*, 162 occurrences, 24 of which come in *The Wife of Bath's Prologue* and *Tale*, which edges out *The Tale of Melibee* for the highest incidence.

vative reflex that reveals again a distrust of things valued simply because they are new. But in *The Clerk's Tale*, as in most of the other tales, youth is not a value wept over as irreplaceable or as irretrievably lost or betrayed in some garden planted by God or by Mirth or by January. Its strength and vitality endure in a new generation and everywhere in the generative power of language. The words by which Griselda describes her children also describe the "tendre croppes" and the "yonge sonne" of the powerful reverdie that opens *The Canterbury Tales*. The young sun in Aries grows old in Capricorn (*FranT* 1245–51):

> Phebus wax old, and hewed lyk laton,
> That in his hoote declynacion
> Shoon as the burned gold with stremes brighte;
> But now in Capricorn adoun he lighte,
> Where as he shoon ful pale, I dar wel seyn.
> The bittre frostes, with the sleet and reyn,
> Destroyed hath the grene in every yerd.

But romance looks Janus-like in both directions, backward, to the glory of youth, "whilom weleful and grene," and forward to the imagined Noel, the new birth (lines 1252–55):

> Janus sit by the fyr, with double berd,
> And drynketh of his bugle horn the wyn;
> Biforn hym stant brawen of the tusked swyn,
> And "Nowel" crieth every lusty man.

Chaucer's works, especially *Troilus and Criseyde*, express disenchantment and regret over change and loss. There are heartrending verses of sorrowful matter, but the "solas" of *Troilus and Criseyde* comes from the pleasure of feigning the ancient world after the image of the modern one so that not only Chaucer's audience but we, too, may imagine that we are experiencing identity with its fiction and feeling both its pleasure and its pain. Other than in a chronological sense, *The Canterbury Tales* is a more youthful work than *The Book of the Duchess* or *Troilus*, nor should that seem a paradox. "Lewed peple loven tales olde" (*PardP* 437) says the Pardoner. By feigning a frame in which young and old, lerned and lewed indulge themselves and one another in the fascination and pleasure of feigning, there is an imagined recovery of loss in the power to manipulate and control imagined worlds. "Olde Grisel lyst to ryme and playe." Philosophy might not approve, but it seems a good way for an old poet to make his ending.

THE BIENNIAL CHAUCER LECTURE
The New Chaucer Society
Eighth International Congress
August 1–4, 1992
The University of Washington
Seattle

Perpetual Motion: Alchemy and the Technology of the Self

Lee Patterson
Duke University

Science searches for perpetual motion. It has found it; it is itself.

Victor Hugo

BECAUSE THE CONGRESS for which this article was delivered as a lecture had as its special theme the current state of Chaucer criticism, I shall begin, conventionally enough, by surveying the critical history of my chosen text, *The Canon's Yeoman's Introduction, Prologue*, and *Tale*.[1] I had better confess right away, however, that this choice was largely deter-

---

[1] The Ellesmere manuscript rubricates the text as a *Prologue* (lines 554–719) followed by a two-part *Tale, Prima Pars* (lines 720–971), and *Pars Secunda* (lines 972–1481). It is printed this way by Walter W. Skeat and F. N. Robinson and by Larry D. Benson, whose text in *The Riverside Chaucer* (3d ed., Boston: Houghton Mifflin, 1987) I cite throughout. Yet many editors have found this disposition unsatisfactory, including Skeat (*The Works of Geoffrey Chaucer* [Oxford: Clarendon Press, 1900], 5.421). A number of critics have pointed out that the Yeoman's three-part performance structurally mimics the tales of the Wife of Bath and the Pardoner: a dramatic *Introduction* (lines 554–719), a confessional *Prologue* (lines 720–971), and an illustrative *Tale* (lines 972–1481); see Judith Sherer Herz, "The Canon's Yeoman's *Prologue* and *Tale*," *MP* 58 (1961): 233 n. 4; Samuel McCracken, "Confessional Prologue and the Topography of the Canon's Yeoman," *MP* 68 (1971):289–91; Derek Pearsall, *The Canterbury Tales* (London: Unwin, 1985), pp. 107–108; and Robert Cook, "The Canon's Yeoman and His Tale," *ChauR* 22 (1987–88): 28–40. In *Chaucer's Poetry: An Anthology for the Modern Reader* (New York: Ronald Press, 1958), E. Talbot Donaldson printed the text as *Introduction, Prologue*, and *Tale*, and I follow that pattern.

mined by the thought that the comparative dearth of criticism would make my task less daunting. But while I was right that the amount of publication on this text is relatively modest, I was wrong in thinking that it would make my job easier. For the quality of the criticism is extremely high, with a lot of hard-earned scholarship and little of the critical zaniness that provides a lecturer with easy laughs. As with so much else of value in contemporary Chaucer criticism, *Chaucer and the French Tradition* established the terms of critical discussion. There Professor Muscatine dismissed as unproductive the debate about Chaucer's biographical relation to alchemy, arguing instead that the Canon's Yeoman offered a prophetic warning directed against the "blind materialism" that leads to a "complacent faith in science that despises God." "In the light of later history," he concluded, "the poem is reactionary."[2]

In the next decade this reading was deepened and extended, especially in the indispensable articles that Joseph Grennen distilled from his 1960 doctoral dissertation.[3] Grennen demonstrated that Chaucer's knowledge of alchemy was extensive and detailed,[4] that both the character of the Yeoman and the structure of his narration were represented in terms derived from alchemical literature,[5] and — above all — that his discourse had to be read in

[2] Charles Muscatine, *Chaucer and the French Tradition* (Berkeley: University of California Press, 1957), pp. 213–21.

[3] Joseph Grennen, "Jargon Transmuted: Alchemy in Chaucer's *Canon's Yeoman's Tale*" (Ph.D. diss., Fordham University, 1960); "The Canon's Yeoman and the Cosmic Furnace: Language and Meaning in the 'Canon's Yeoman's Tale,'" *Criticism* 4 (1962): 225–40; "Chaucer's 'Secree of Secrees': An Alchemical 'Topic'," *PQ* 42 (1963): 562–66; "Chaucer's Characterization of the Canon and His Yeoman," *JHI* 25 (1964): 279–84; "The Canon's Yeoman's Alchemical 'Mass,'" *SP* 62 (1965): 546-60; "Chaucer and the Commonplaces of Alchemy," *C&M* 26 (1965): 306–33; and "Saint Cecilia's 'Chemical Wedding': The Unity of the *Canterbury Tales*, Fragment VIII," *JEGP* 65 (1966): 466–81.

[4] This in opposition to Pauline Aiken, "Vincent of Beauvais and Chaucer's Knowledge of Alchemy," *SP* 41 (1944): 371–89, who argued that Chaucer's knowledge was restricted to the elementary account provided by one of Vincent of Beauvais's encyclopedias. For a similarly low opinion of Chaucer's alchemical knowledge, see Dorothee Finkelstein, "The Code of Chaucer's 'Secree of Secrees': Arabic Alchemical Terminology in 'The Canon's Yeoman's Tale,'" *Archiv* 207 (1970): 260–76. Edgar Duncan had earlier argued that Chaucer understood the details of alchemical processes ("The Yeoman's Canon's 'Silver Citrinacioun'," *MP* 37 [1939–40]: 241 –62), although the complexity of Duncan's account makes it difficult to believe that Chaucer was as fully informed as he assumes. Grennen's well-taken point, however, is that Chaucer understood the characteristic forms of the *discourse* of alchemy if not its practice.

[5] In "Chaucer and the Commonplaces of Alchemy," Grennen says, "I doubt that there is a single feature of the Canon's Yeoman's *Prologue*, or of the first section of the tale (Prima Pars), which can not be seen as an imaginative re-shaping of the details of alchemical theory and experiment *as* these were set down in written treatises" (p. 308). A similar point was made by Edgar H. Duncan, "The Literature of Alchemy and Chaucer's *Canon's Yeoman's Tale*: Framework, Theme, and Characters," *Speculum* 43 (1968): 633–56.

conjunction with that of the Second Nun. When read this way, according to Grennen it revealed alchemy as a "profane parody of the divine work of Creation and an unwittingly sacrilegious distortion of the central mystery of the Christian faith."[6]

Grennen and others were assiduous in detailing the oppositions between the two tales: the fires of Christian suffering that prove Cecilia's purity versus the fires of alchemy that discolor the Yeoman; Cecilia's "bisynesse" versus the obsessive "werkynge" of alchemy; the odor of sanctity versus the goatish stink of brimstone; the clear-sighted Cecilia versus the bleary-eyed alchemists; the good end achieved by Christian martyrs versus the inconclusiveness of the alchemical quest; the "leveful bisyness" with which the Second Nun relieves her "ydelnesse" versus the leaden despair from which the Yeoman cannot free himself; the rootedness of Cecilia in the faith versus the endless questing of the vagabond alchemists; the verbal simplicity of *The Second Nun's Tale* versus the knotty intricacy of the Yeoman's discourse; the clarity of Christian doctrine versus the "elvyssh nice lore" of alchemy; the spiritual conversion of sinners versus the failed transmutation of fallen matter; Urban's salvific refuge in the suburbs versus the Canon's guilty lurking; the martyrdom of Valerian and Tiburce versus the "mortification" of the "brothers" mercury and sulfur; Almachius's idolatrous worship of a stone versus the alchemists' quest for the philosopher's stone; Christian sapience versus worldly science; saintly charity versus alchemical cupidity; revelation versus reason; divinity versus demonism; God's divine work versus the Canon's diabolical labor.[7] Grennen argued that these oppositions were controlled by a conceptual distinction between the simplicity and integrity of *The Second Nun's Tale* and the confused complexity — the "multiplicacioun" — of *The Canon's Yeoman's Tale*. As he said:

[6] Grennen, "Saint Cecilia's 'Chemical Wedding,'" pp. 466–67.

[7] For these and other comparisons, see Grennen's articles (n. 3 above) and John Gardner, "*The Canon's Yeoman's Prologue* and *Tale*: An Interpretation," *PQ* 46 (1967): 1–17; Bruce L. Grenberg, "The *Canon's Yeoman's Tale*: Boethian Wisdom and the Alchemists," *ChauR* 1 (1966–67): 37–54; K. Michael Olmert, "*The Canon's Yeoman's Tale*: An Interpretation," *AnM* 8 (1967): 70–94; Glending Olson, "Chaucer, Dante, and the Structure of Fragment VIII (G) of the *Canterbury Tales*," *ChauR* 16 (1981–82): 222–36; Bruce A. Rosenberg, "The Contrary Tales of the Second Nun and the Canon's Yeoman," *ChauR* 2 (1967–68): 278–91; Bruce A. Rosenberg, "Swindling Alchemist, Antichrist," *CentR* 6 (1962): 566–80; John Scattergood, "Chaucer in the Suburbs," in Myra Stokes and T. L. Burton, eds., *Medieval Literature and Antiquities: Studies in Honour of Basil Cottle* (Cambridge and Wolfeboro, N.H.: D. S. Brewer, 1987), pp. 145–62.

It is no accident that the term "multiplye" is the keynote of the *Canon's Yeoman's Tale*, but it is to be understood against the background of unity and integrity which the legend of St. Cecilia displays. On the simplest and most abstract level the two poems lay out the theme of "unity vs. multiplicity."[8]

The third stage in our understanding of this text was the development of Muscatine's sense that it censured a dangerous modernity. For example, James Dean has argued that the two tales describe "a degeneration from Cecilia's bright age [of primitive Christianity] to the modern era;"[9] for A. V. C. Schmidt, the Yeoman is "a figure more startlingly 'modern' in his rootlessness and 'alienation' than any of the characters depicted in the *General Prologue*, . . . [a man who] connects more readily with the creations of a Pinter or a Beckett than with any of Chaucer's own."[10] Even those critics who read *The Canterbury Tales* in frankly materialist terms agree that the Canon and his Yeoman have a negative valence on the scale of Chaucerian values. For Stephen Knight, alchemists symbolize the cash nexus at its most destructive — "the whole world of mercantile practices is [here] gathered in by the ideological imagination and directed towards the everlasting bonfire" — and for Britton Harwood the critique of alchemy stands for Chaucer's refusal to represent productive capital.[11] In sum, Muscatine's thirty-six-

---

[8] Grennen, "Saint Cecilia's 'Chemical Wedding,'" pp. 472–73; see also Traugott Lawler, *The One and the Many in* The Canterbury Tales (Hamden: Archon Books, 1980), pp. 125–46. As Grennen says in "Chaucer and the Commonplaces of Alchemy": "To say that the word 'multiply' is an important word in alchemy is to understate the case. There is hardly a treatise in which it does not figure prominently, and it is frequently made the discriminant by which an alchemical author may evaluate the performance of other workers in alchemy (that is, by defining the sense in which *they* may be said to be 'multipliers')" (pp. 320–21). The history of the term shows that it means two completely opposite things: (1) to intensify a substance through sublimation and (2) to proliferate needlessly and confusingly the materials or, especially, words used in the alchemical work. It signifies, in short, an intensification into singularity, purity, and essence (identity) and a proliferation into multiplicity and heterogeneity (difference).

[9] James Dean, "Dismantling the Canterbury Book," *PMLA* 100 (1984): 751.

[10] A. V. C. Schmidt, ed., *The* General Prologue *to the* Canterbury Tales *and the* Canon's Yeoman's Prologue *and* Tale (New York: Holmes and Meier, 1976), pp. 38–39.

[11] Stephen Knight, *Geoffrey Chaucer* (Oxford: Basil Blackwell, 1985), p. 150; Britton J. Harwood, "Chaucer and the Silence of History: Situating the *Canon's Yeoman's Tale*," *PMLA* 102 (1987): 338–50. In an article I came upon only after having written the lecture on which this essay is based, Sheila Delany also reads the *Tale* as a "vitriolic attack" on a modernizing alchemy: "Run Silent, Run Deep: Heresy and Alchemy as Medieval Versions of Utopia," in *Medieval Literary Politics: Shapes of Ideology* (Manchester: Manchester University Press, 1990), p. 16.

year-old assessment of the text's politics as reactionary seems beyond challenge.[12]

After a beginning like that, you know that a challenge is coming. But I want to come at the question a bit obliquely. Given the penetration of the criticism, it is curious indeed that what I take to be three fundamental questions have yet to be asked. First, if this is a tale that represents all that must be rejected, why is it introduced into *The Canterbury Tales* with such a powerful sense of urgency and belatedness? At the beginning of the pilgrimage the order of tale-telling had been upset by the importunate Miller; now, as we near the end, Chaucer seems willing to revise his text again — or at least to *stage* an act of revision — to allow voice to a rebellious Yeoman. The end approaches, yet something of such importance remains to be said that Chaucer draws our attention to it by an ostentatious interruption. Second, if we dispense with unfounded biographical speculation, why alchemy? Alchemy was not a particularly pressing or widespread social problem of the day,[13] and its introduction here seems inconsistent with Chaucer's usual avoidance of specialized vocabularies.

Finally, what is the point of the little drama that introduces the Yeoman's

---

[12] There are partial exceptions to this critical consensus. Scattergood says that the tales of both the Second Nun and the Canon's Yeoman are about the confrontation between unorthodox belief and authority: "...new ideologies constantly present a challenge to the establishment" ("Chaucer in the Suburbs," p. 160); and David Raybin draws an analogy between the alchemist and the poet as artists in "'And Pave It Al of Silver and of Gold': The Humane Artistry of *The Canon's Yeoman's Tale*," in Susanna Greer Fein, David Raybin, and Peter C. Braeger, eds., *Rebels and Rivals: The Contestive Spirit in* The Canterbury Tales (Kalamazoo, Mich.: Medieval Institute Publications, 1991), pp. 189–212.

[13] A comprehensive survey of the widely varying medieval attitudes toward alchemy is provided by Will H. L. Ogrinc, "Western Society and Alchemy, 1200–1500," *Journal of Medieval History* 6 (1980): 103–32. Ogrinc mentions documents of 1329 and 1350 revealing Edward III's interest in alchemy (pp. 118–19), and the 1374 case of William Shuchirch, a canon in the royal chapel of Windsor, gave rise to John M. Manly's speculations about Chaucer's personal involvement (*Some New Light on Chaucer* [New York: Henry Holt, 1926], pp. 235–52). However extensive this royal interest may have been, it ceased in 1403 when Henry IV issued a proclamation banning alchemy, doubtless because of a fear of counterfeiting. But Henry VI patronized alchemists in 1452 and again in 1456–57 in the hope of easing his money troubles (see Ralph Griffiths, *The Reign of Henry VI: The Exercise of Royal Authority, 1422–1461* [Berkeley: University of California Press, 1981], pp. 386, 787–88), and both George Ripley's *The Compound of Alchemy* (1470–71) and Thomas Norton's *Ordinal of Alchemy* (1477) were dedicated to Edward IV. As for Chaucer's contemporary poets, Langland linked alchemy with necromancy and arts of "gynful speche" (see B 10.213–19 in William Langland, *Piers Plowman: The B Text*, ed. George Kane and E. Talbot Donaldson [London: Athlone Press, 1975], p. 419), while for Gower alchemy was legitimate — "This craft is wroght be weie of kinde" (4.2508) — but difficult (*Confessio Amantis* 4.2457–2632).

Prologue? When the Yeoman — who is a personal servant, perhaps even an apprentice[14] — begins to reveal himself to the Host, the Canon protests (*CYP* 695–96):

> Thou sclaundrest me heere in this compaignye,
> And eek discoverest that thou sholdest hyde.

The Canon here accuses the Yeoman of violating two of the prohibitions central to the strict discipline of London society: that a man should not slander his superior, that an apprentice should not reveal trade secrets.[15] These were serious transgressions, which makes it all the more remarkable that the Host should encourage the Yeoman in his misconduct: "'Ye,' quod oure Hoost, 'telle on, what so bityde. / Of al his thretynge rekke nat a myte!'" (lines 697–98). The result is not only to force the Canon out of the pilgrimage but to emancipate the Yeoman: he arrived as a servant but has now been willy-nilly transmuted into one of those vagabonds, those men without masters, who so disturbed the governors of late-medieval England.[16] Here then, fast upon the Second Nun's dutiful hagiography, is an

[14] The title "yeoman" is not unambiguous. In a rural context it designated a non-*gentil* landholder (Christopher Dyer, *Standards of Living in the Later Middle Ages* [Cambridge: Cambridge University Press, 1989], p. 14), while in the city it referred to a lesser member of a company, craft, or mystery (including an apprentice) who was not entitled to wear its livery (see Sylvia Thrupp, *The Merchant Class of Medieval London* [Ann Arbor: University of Michigan Press, 1977 (1948)], pp. 12–14, 28–29). In these contexts it was a catchall term for a man of middling status (Dyer, p. 15; Thrupp, pp. 217–18; see also J. C. Holt, *Robin Hood*, rev. ed. [London: Thames and Hudson, 1989], pp. 117–24). But it also designated, as in the case of the Knight's Yeoman in *The General Prologue*, a personal servant (see Benson's note in *The Riverside Chaucer*, p. 802): it was the English term that translated the *valettus* of the noble household (Kate Mertes, *The English Noble Household, 1250–1600* [Oxford: Basil Blackwell, 1988], p. 26). Here the term probably means "servant," but we are also encouraged to think of apprenticeship when the Yeoman says that he has dwelt with the Canon for "seven yeer" (*CYT* 720), the minimum term for apprentices (A. H. Thomas, ed., *Calendar of Plea and Memoranda Rolls, 1364–1381* [Cambridge: Cambridge University Press, 1929], p. xxxiii). When he goes on to complain that, despite this service, "of [the Canon's] science am I never the neer" (line 721), he echoes the frequent complaints by apprentices of the failure of their masters to teach them their craft; see, for example, the cases cited in A. H. Thomas, ed., *Calendar of Select Pleas and Memoranda of the City of London, 1381–1412* (Cambridge: Cambridge University Press, 1932), pp. 120–21, 135, 145, 167, 180, 193, 199, 253, 274, 284, 293, 303, 311. My thanks to Caroline Barron for bringing these sources to my attention.

[15] See the note to this passage by John Reidy in Benson, ed., *The Riverside Chaucer*, p. 949.

[16] The contemporary fear of vagabondage and of "an unduly mobile" working class has recently been well described in relation to Chaucer's Miller, and with reference to previous discussions, by Ralph Hanna III, "Pilate's Voice / Shirley's Case," *SAQ* 91 (1992): 796–97.

insurrectionary moment that is allowed a certain space — a tolerance that might make us hesitant to consign the Yeoman to the outer darkness of the ideologically incorrect.

Any rehabilitation of *The Canon's Yeoman's Prologue* and *Tale* must rely on Grennen's sense that it is about "multiplicacioun" and on Muscatine's that it is about modernity. But these themes need not be seen as unconditionally negative, as that which must be rejected for a Chaucerian poetic to be itself. On the contrary, I shall propose that the Canon's Yeoman's performance is a final, extravagant instance of Chaucer's lifelong interest in the way subjectivity seeks to represent itself in language, and, further, that as an innovative tale of the last moment, as both literally and metaphorically the dernier cri, it expresses Chaucer's awareness of *himself* as a modern poet oriented toward a dynamic future. The bitterly self-canceling *Manciple's Tale* and the austerely transcendental *Parson's Tale* await, but before they arrive the Canon's Yeoman will have his fascinating say. Alchemy, as both verbal discourse and social practice, serves as the best vehicle for this saying because, I shall argue, it functioned in late-medieval culture as one of the sites where the modernizing impulse took root, as a place where modernity came to know itself as endowed with both urgency and belatedness, both eager anticipation of what is to come and panic-stricken fear that all might be lost.

I

If the characteristic topic of *The Canterbury Tales* is character — if, as Marshall Leicester has put it, Chaucer's subject is the subject[17] — then *The Second Nun's Tale* is striking, even unique in its avoidance of the topic. Both Cecilia and her author lack all signs of personality: they are mere agencies, empty vessels for a power beyond. Like the Virgin Mary, Cecilia is the vehicle by which God enters the world: Christ became man "withinne the cloistre blisful of [Mary's] sydis" (*SNP* 43), and so too his conversionary power passes unimpeded through a saint uncontaminated by either sexual attachments or psychological complexity. The Second Nun shares this self-effacement. Of all the *Canterbury Tales* this is the most nearly anonymous: the only indication of the teller is provided by the rubrics, which in fact vary widely among the manuscripts.[18] Unlike the Prioress she accompanies, the

---

[17] H. Marshall Leicester, *The Disenchanted Self: Representing the Subject in the* Canterbury Tales (Berkeley: University of California Press, 1990), p. 15.

[18] See the notes by Florence H. Ridley in Benson, ed., *The Riverside Chaucer*, pp. 942–43.

Second Nun turns away from the conflicted world of contemporary piety to the homogenized simplicity of the primitive church, and her *Tale* is derived not from the modest, even suspect vernacularism of miracles of the Virgin but from a timeless Latin legacy.[19] In her *Prologue* she represents herself in terms derived from monastic *accidia*, and just as she conceives of herself in the vocational terms defined by the church, so she presents her *Tale* as a mere "translacioun" (line 25).

So simplified a conception of the self entails a language conceived in equally simple terms for its expression. An exemplary instance is provided by the scene of Valerian's conversion, in which an "oold man" appears with a book written in golden letters, reads three lines—an English version of Ephesians 4:5-6 (*SNT* 207-209),

> O Lord, o feith, o God, withouten mo,
> O Cristendom, and Fader of alle also,
> Aboven alle and over alle everywhere

—and receives Valerian's immediate assent. Conversion by reading is a familiar medieval event, finding its archetype in the garden at Milan and being restaged in a variety of later medieval texts.[20] What these scenes usually stress, however, is the complexity of the process and its attendant perils. Augustine's conversion is located within an elaborate sequence of imitations, some of which are dangerous rather than salvific, models to be read *in malo* rather than *in bono*. But *The Second Nun's Tale* effaces the complexity of the transactions between text and reader, providing instead a scene of pure immediacy that celebrates the perfect unity the passage from Ephesians describes—unity between the author (St. Paul) and his words, between words and meaning, between meaning and audience. This linguistic immediacy is affirmed in the *Prologue* with the etymologies of "Cecilia," where the very sound of the saint's name—her phonic image—is thought to embody her sanctity. This belief in the unbreakable connection

[19] For the sources of the *Tale* see Sherry Reames, "A Recent Discovery Concerning the Sources of Chaucer's *Second Nun's Tale*," *MP* 87 (1990): 337-61, and the previous studies by Reames cited there.

[20] On the theme of conversion by reading, see Pierre Courcelle, *Recherches sur les Confessions de saint Augustin* (Paris: E. Broccard, 1950). Recent studies of medieval reading include Susan Noakes, *Timely Reading: Between Exegesis and Interpretation* (Ithaca, N.Y.: Cornell University Press, 1988), and Robert S. Sturges, *Medieval Interpretation: Models of Reading in Literary Narrative, 1100-1500* (Carbondale: Southern Illinois University Press, 1991).

between words and their significance also allows the Second Nun to claim, however impossibly, that her translation contains not just "the sentence" but actually "the wordes" of the original (*SNP* 81).

If both linguistic and psychological self-presence are everywhere in *The Second Nun's Tale*, the Canon and his rebellious Yeoman display the difference between outer role and inward desire, and between language and meaning, that are more typically Chaucerian. Like the Friar and the Monk, the Canon is a churchman whose religious identity is a public phenomenon manipulable for private purposes; like the Reeve and the Manciple, the Yeoman is a servant whose social obligations are discarded under the pressure of his own psychological needs. This return to a Chaucerian norm is marked by the fact that the Canon and his Yeoman are granted descriptions that match those of the other pilgrims in *The General Prologue*,[21] descriptions that are here, too, mediated through the eyes of a credulous pilgrim-narrator.[22] Not until the narrator has carefully described the Canon's clothing and "hadde longe avysed" himself is he prepared to pronounce that this is indeed "som chanoun" (*CYP* 572, 573), and the rhetoric of wonder so habitual in *The General Prologue* now reemerges in his pleasure in—of all things—the Canon's perspiration: "But it was joye for to seen hym swete!" (line 579).[23]

From this kind of introduction it is only a short step to the fully dramatic contretemps between Canon and Yeoman, and an even shorter step to the Yeoman's claustrophobically subjectivized discourse. Our best aids in understanding his performance are the previous tales of the Wife of Bath and the Pardoner, tales that represent what we now take to be among the grandest of Chaucerian achievements.[24] Whatever else Chaucer is up to

[21] As has been noted by, for instance, Grennen, "Chaucer's Characterization," p. 280.

[22] For this strategy in *The General Prologue*, see Donaldson, *Chaucer's Poetry*, pp. 1038–41.

[23] Indeed, this account is almost a parody of *The General Prologue*, since the narrator figures out the Canon's identity only in slow motion, a dim-wittedness all the more marked because the Canon's dress would have made him instantly recognizable; see Marie P. Hamilton, "The Clerical Status of Chaucer's Alchemist," *Speculum* 16 (1941): 103–108.

[24] Again, critics have long noted the tight parallels among the three texts—parallels obscured by Ellesmere's misleading rubrics *Prima Pars* and *Pars Secunda*—although they have rarely seen this continuity of interest as allowing the Yeoman or his *Tale* to function as anything other than negative examples; see n. 1 above. It should also be pointed out that, at least in the Ellesmere order, all three of these confessional performances are preceded by hagiographical narratives that celebrate female virtue: the Wife of Bath by the Man of Law, the Pardoner by the Physician, and the Canon's Yeoman by the Second Nun. *The Canon's Yeoman's Prologue* and *Tale* may seem like an interruption, but a place has already been prepared for them: they are at once unexpected and inevitable.

here, he is again demonstrating his virtuosity in showing how a person struggles toward self-understanding in a language that is at once unpropitious and appropriate. Just as the Wife of Bath manipulated a masculinist rhetoric of femininity to express a dream of liberation, just as the Pardoner deployed a penitential discourse that he simultaneously cherished and despised, so the Yeoman toils to represent himself in an alchemical jargon as unstable as the shifting selfhood he seeks to discover.

If *The Second Nun's Tale* is underwritten by linguistic immediacy, *The Canon's Yeoman's Prologue* and *Tale* are a discourse of radical deferral. What he says of alchemy is equally true of his tale-telling: "... evere we lakken oure conclusioun" (*CYP* 672), "For alle oure sleightes we kan nat conclude" (*CYT* 773), and we "Concluden in multiplicacioun" (line 849)—the last a phrasing that plays on the double meaning of the word "multiplication" (as simultaneously dispersal and concentration) to express deferral both alchemically and verbally.[25] Not surprisingly, both *Prologue* and *Tale* lack coherent narratives. The *Prologue* keeps promising to arrive at the *Tale*—"Passe over this; I go my tale unto" (*CYT* 898)— but keeps inserting more alchemical lore. And the *Tale* is constantly derailed by exclamatory interruptions, and then when told turns out to be not a formally organized narrative, with beginning, middle, and end, but a paratactic concatenation of one virtually identical trick after another, a series that could go on forever.[26]

We can hardly be surprised, then, that the *Tale*'s closure fails by excess, that the troublesome final fifty-four lines provide not one but three endings. First a cryptic alchemical recipe from Arnold of Villanova is glossed by an equally cryptic saying of Hermes. This process of explanation by substitution is then ostentatiously repeated in the dialogue between Senior Zadith and master Plato (lines 1448–71).[27] Senior asks for "the name of the privee stoon" (line 1452), and Plato responds, "Titanos"; Senior asks that Titanos be identified, and Plato says, "Magnasia" (line 1455); Senior—complaining that Plato is proceeding *"ignotum per ignocius"* (line 1457)—asks that Magnasia be identified, and is told that "it is a water that is

---

[25] See n. 8 above.

[26] See the comment by Peter Brown, "Is the *Canon's Yeoman's Tale* Apocryphal?" *ES* 64 (1983): 487: "The worst fault of *pars secunda* is pointless repetition, almost as if it were written as an exercise in creating a Chaucerian tale out of the material available in the prologue and *prima pars*. The narrator is right when he says 'it dulleth me to ryme' (1093)."

[27] For the source of this dialogue, see Edgar H. Duncan, "Chaucer and 'Arnold of the Newe Toun,'" *MLN* 58 (1942): 31–33, and Finkelstein, "The Code of Chaucer's 'Secree of Secrees.'"

maad... / Of elementes foure" (lines 1459–60); Senior asks for the "roote... / Of that water" (lines 1461–62), whereupon Plato abruptly terminates the conversation by invoking Christ's decision that the secret of the stone should be revealed only to an unknown someone whom he will arbitrarily designate: "...*where it liketh* to his deitee / Men for t'enspire, and eek for to deffende / *Whom that hym liketh*..."(lines 1469–71; italics added). This divine willfulness, an arbitrariness that refuses to be constrained by human desires or deserts, thus forecloses alchemical effort without denying the possibility of alchemical success.

The quest for alchemical truth thus leads to the negative knowledge that we now call the "logic of the supplement." A synonym is offered to identify an unknown term but is then discovered to be itself in need of identification. As the process continues, the disclosure of an original meaning becomes the multiplication of meanings; as each signified is revealed to be only another signifier, the act of revelation becomes itself a concealment. The explanation is at once confirmatory (it restates the truth again) and disruptive (by restating the truth in different words, it causes us to wonder whether there is indeed *a* truth).[28] By insisting that the process is foreclosed by an arbitrary act of divine will, the Yeoman shows that what is in doubt is not the existence of the alchemical truth but the efficacy of explanation. The truth can be known, but it cannot be said.

"Thanne conclude I thus" (line 1472), says the Yeoman, in his third try at closure, that since God will not allow philosophers to name ("nevene" [line 1473]) the means by which the stone may be obtained—since the truth cannot be represented in language—the whole enterprise is impossible. "And there a poynt" (line 1480): brought to recognize that further speech is useless, the Yeoman ends with a metaphor drawn from writing. This "lewed man" (line 787) wants to endow his vibrantly oral performance with the fixity of script, to remove it from the fluid world of speech, with its endless opportunities for continuation, revision, and rebeginning, and to locate it in the more stable world of textuality. Yet readers of this very text know that even writing is disturbingly mobile.[29]

---

[28] Derridean supplementation is most explicitly prefigured in alchemical discourse by "multiplication," which as we have seen signifies both an uncontrollable expansion and a purification that grasps the essence—or, in alchemical terms, the quintessence.

[29] Indeed, the *Tale*'s antepenultimate line—"Thogh that he multiplie terme of his lyve"— is ambiguous: it can mean "even though he practices alchemy for his whole life," or, by referring to the idea of the quintessence, "even though he increases the length of his life." That the ambiguity turns on a pun on the word "multiplie" is almost inevitable.

Each of the Yeoman's three conclusions says that the truth of alchemy cannot be said. This sense of verbal insufficiency—a central topic of Chaucer's writing since the stammering Black Knight of *The Book of the Duchess*—controls the Yeoman's performance as a whole. When he first enters the pilgrimage, his language is a tissue of double meanings. "Trusteth me," he says to the Host about the Canon (*CYP* 601–14),

> And ye hym knewe as wel as do I,
> Ye wolde wondre how wel and craftily
> He koude werke, and that in sondry wise.
>
> . . . .
>
> If ye hym knewe, it wolde be for youre prow.
> Ye wolde nat forgoon his aqueyntaunce
> For muchel good, I dar leye in balaunce
> Al that I have in my possessioun.
> He is a man of heigh discrecioun;
> I warne yow wel, he is a passyng man.

There is not a line in this passage that does not contain an unexploded time bomb, especially the last— "I warne yow wel, he is a passyng man"—which signifies in ways that even the shifty Yeoman cannot predict. Nor is he prepared to acknowledge the mutability of his own language, for when the Host invites him to partake of the socially incorporative act of confession, the Yeoman responds with a blandly unthinking commitment to truthtelling: "Swich thyng as that I knowe, I wol declare" (line 719).

This desire for straightforward declaration is everywhere visible in the Yeoman's discourse. He insists on the simplicity of both his motives and his message. He speaks only "To th'entente that men may be war therby, / And for noon oother cause, trewely" (*CYT* 1306–1307), and the lesson is, "Lat every man be war by me for evere!" (*CYT* 737). At pivotal moments he summarizes his account with sound bites of proverbial wisdom (lines 746–48, 962–63, 967–69, 1476–78):

> For unto shrewes joye it is and ese
> To have hir felawes in peyne and disese.
> Thus was I ones lerned of a clerk.

36

> But al thyng which that shineth as the gold
> Nis nat gold, as that I have herd told.
>
> He that semeth the wiseste, by Jhesus,
> Is moost fool, whan it cometh to the preef;
> And he that semeth trewest is a theef.
>
> For whoso maketh God his adversarie,
> As for to werken any thyng in contrarie
> Of his wil, certes, never shal he thryve.

Even the chaotic inventory of alchemical lore is reduced to a jingle (lines 822–29):

> The firste spirit quyksilver called is,
> The seconde orpyment, the thridde, ywis,
> Sal armonyak, and the ferthe brymstoon.
> The bodyes sevene eek, lo, hem heere anoon:
> Sol gold is, and Luna silver we threpe,
> Mars iren, Mercurie quyksilver we clepe,
> Saturnus leed, and Juppiter is tyn,
> And Venus coper, by my fader kyn!

"By my fader kyn!": the emphatic tag reveals the schoolboy character of this inventory. We can well believe the Yeoman when he tells us that he was taught the list "By ordre, as ofte I herde my lord hem *nevene*" (line 821; italics added): here alchemy is reduced to a simple, mnemonic verse. Yet his painful fumbling in the labyrinth of alchemical terminology— "termes... so clergial and so queynte" (line 752)—reveals not only a mind overwhelmed by its own contents but one that has invested this esoteric vocabulary with a magical, incantatory force: "For, as I trowe, I have yow toold ynowe / To reyse a feend, al looke he never so rowe" (lines 860–61).

A doomed commitment to intelligibility and explicitness—to sorting the world into clear categories—is also visible in the *Tale*. There the canon is a monstrous figure of unmitigated evil—a "feend" (line 984) of "infinite falsnesse" (line 976), the "roote of al trecherie" (line 1069), a "cursed man" (line 1259), the "roote of alle cursednesse" (line 1301), and so forth—while the priest is simply a dim-witted dupe: "O sely preest! O sely innocent! / With coveitise anon thou shalt be blent!" (line 1076–77). But again, at the same time as the Yeoman reduces alchemical deception to the simplest of

37

con games, he also endows it with an immense weight of religious significance. The canon becomes a figure of apocalyptic size, a heresiarch or even
an Antichrist who threatens "Cristes peple" (line 1072), including the
"worshipful chanons religious" (line 992) who may have a Judas in their
midst: "God kepe us from his false dissymulynge!" (line 1073). Alchemy is
both simpleminded and heavy with consequence, both a shabby fraud and
the ultimate portent. This extravagant polarization bespeaks a desire for
clear understanding and an inability to achieve it: just as alchemy seeks in
vain to identify the stone, so the Yeoman equally vainly tries to identify — to
"nevene" — alchemy itself.

The same impossible dream of accurate naming also drives the Yeoman's
account of himself. Just as the Wife of Bath presented herself as a nightmare of the misogynist imagination, just as the Pardoner presented himself
as an extravagant parody of sinfulness, so the Yeoman offers himself up as a
simple if extravagant exemplum of the wasted life: "Lat every man be war
by me for evere!" (line 737). His most impressive act of self-objectification
is his famous color changes. In the course of the *Tale* he applies to himself
the terms of an elementary alchemical experiment, a kind of technologiz-
ing of the self. For a man who is "nat wont in no mirour to prie" (*CYP* 668),
he is well informed about his leaden appearance; and when he tells us that
"my chekes wexen rede" (*CYT* 1095), he describes himself as passing
through the stages of alchemical transmutation, turning from the lead of
despair to the rosy gold of hope.[30]

The Yeoman's theatrical self-allegorization is consistent with the melo-
dramatic quality of his whole performance. There is no accusation we can
make of him that he does not make of himself. He creates himself as a
spectacle of deprivation, an absolutist of desire, a hunger artist. He displays
the spiritual vacuity that is his most secret self with an ostentation that is
anything but secret. Here Chaucer goes beyond *The Pardoner's Prologue*
and *Tale* and conducts the ultimate experiment in the dynamics of self-
representation. For the desperation that lurks behind the Pardoner's bra-
vado is by the Yeoman eagerly displayed. His cards are on the table, his
depths on the surface, and he demands that we solve the mystery of a man
without a mystery.

And this is the demand he also lays upon himself. If his theatricality
makes us question the reliability of what we hear, his garrulity shows him to
be just as unconvinced by what he says. In his befuddled candor he reveals

[30] For similar accounts of the spiritual and physical changes of the alchemist, see Noel
Brann, "Alchemy and Melancholy in Medieval and Renaissance Thought: A Query into the
Mystical Basis of Their Relationship," *Ambix* 30 (1985): 127–48.

all, including the fact that self-revelation offers no consolations. The Yeoman can never quite say what he means, never capture the evil of the trickster alchemist, or the truth of alchemy, or the truth about himself. He can only supplement what he has already offered—just as the *Tale* is itself an ostentatious supplement to *The Canterbury Tales* as a whole. He wants "to tellen al" (*CYP* 716) but always falls short: "We mowen nat, although we hadden it sworn, / It overtake, it slit awey so faste" (lines 681–82). His performance proceeds "*ignotum per ignocius*," his language multiplying itself—proliferating uncontrollably—yet never finally grasping the essence it seeks. The more he talks about the self that so fascinates him, the more dispersed it becomes, leaving him a cipher, an absence, a desire—a being who seeks rather than an object sought.

II

Although alchemy is, as the distinguished historian of science David Lindberg has said, "one of the least studied and most poorly understood of all aspects of medieval science,"[31] a nonspecialist like myself can begin to understand at least some of the reasons why Chaucer chose it as the vehicle for the Yeoman's performance.[32] For one thing, the discourse of alchemy raises the problem of the verbal representation of truth with a special intensity and sophistication. There is hardly an alchemical treatise that does not comment on the obscurity of alchemical language, and especially on the failure of alchemical denomination: "O doubtful names which are like the true names," laments an ancient treatise, "what errors and anguish you have provoked among men!"[33] The theme is continuous throughout

[31] David C. Lindberg, *The Beginnings of Western Science: The European Scientific Tradition in Philosophical, Religious, and Institutional Context, 600 B.C. to A.D. 1450* (Chicago: University of Chicago Press, 1992), p. 287.

[32] The primary texts are available in two collections: Lazarus Zetzner, ed., *Theatrum chemicum*, 6 vols. (Strasbourg: Zetzner, 1659–61), and Jean Jacques Manget, *Bibliotheca Chemica Curiosa*, 2 vols. (Geneva, 1702; repr. Bologna: A. Forni, 1976). As we shall see, alchemical texts present enormous difficulties—in their huge number, their language, their uncertain literary relationships, their authorship, and, above all, their meaning. Fortunately, despite Lindberg's caveat, there have been major advances in the study of this material in recent years, including a number of annotated translations. I have also relied on the excellent recent work of Chiara Crisciani, Robert Halleux, William Newman, and Barbara Obrist. Their writings are cited in subsequent notes.

[33] This passage from the Greek *Book of Crates* is the epigraph to Maurice P. Crosland, *Historical Studies in the Language of Chemistry* (Cambridge, Mass.: Harvard University Press, 1962). As Crosland says, "There would be some justification for the view that alchemical literature was a conspiracy between successive generations of writers to use a maximum number of words to give a minimum of information" (p. 36)—a view shared by many alchemical writers themselves.

the medieval history of alchemy: the twelfth-century text known as *Morienus* claims that "it is only the multitude of terms which causes the masters of this operation to err"; in the thirteenth century Albertus Magnus complains that the alchemists "hide their meaning through metaphors, which was never the practice of philosophers"; in the fourteenth century the English master John Dastin says that "although I have worked hard enough to recognize the path of truth in this science, I have found only figurative expressions and what seems rather strange"; and a fifteenth-century English poem complains that alchemical lore "ys but a poesie of Phylosofrys words derke."[34] Alchemical writers typically open their treatises with a denunciation of the obscurity of others and a promise—always unfulfilled—to speak plainly that which has elsewhere been enigmatic. Hence one alchemical writer said that he had torn his book from the gibberish of other treatises as a rose is picked from thorns: there soon developed a fashion of titles like *The Lily Torn from Thorns*.[35] Not surprisingly, there also developed a vigorous genre of alchemical dictionaries that promised to decipher the mysteries of figurative language.[36]

The treatises offer two explanations for the obscurity of alchemical discourse: the "envy" of philosophers who wish to keep the secret to themselves, and—which is really the same thing, but seen from the other side—the need to protect the secret from profanation. But there is another, usually unacknowledged reason that gets to the heart of the dilemma of alchemical discourse. In a sixteenth-century English treatise entitled "An Apology for the Obscurity of Alchemical Books and the Secrecy Observed by the Professors of This Art," an anonymous writer offers both the conventional rationale for alchemical obscurity—these matters are darkly described to hide them from the foolish—but then adds a more original

---

[34] Lee Stavenhagen, ed. and trans., *A Testament of Alchemy: Being the Revelation of Morienus to Khalid ibn Yazid* (Hanover, N.H.: University Press of New England, 1974), p. 16; Robert Halleux, "Albert le Grand et l'alchimie," *Revue des sciences philosophiques et théologiques* 66 (1982): 73 n. 122 (cited from *De mineralibus* 3.1.7); Wilfred R. Theissen, ed. and trans., "John Dastin's Letter on the Philosopher's Stone," *Ambix* 33 (1986): 79, 83; F. Sherwood Taylor, "The Argument of Morien and Merlin: An English Alchemical Poem," *Chymia* 1 (1948): 27 (line 47).

[35] Lynn Thorndike, *A History of Magic and Experimental Science* (New York: Columbia University Press, 1934), 3.93.

[36] See Dorothea Waley Singer, ed., *Catalogue of Latin and Vernacular Alchemical Manuscripts in Great Britain and Ireland Dating from Before the XVI Century*, 3 vols. (Brussels: Maurice Lambertin for the Union Académique Internationale, 1928–31), items 386–413 for texts entitled *Synonyma alchemica*, and items 415–438A for treatises that list the names and symbols of the planets and metals as keys with which to decode alchemical treatises.

explanation: "...thus much j finde by groaping at the matter, that nothing staieth a clearke more, then doeth the bare letter."[37] What is invoked here is a clerical inability *not* to gloss, an unwillingness to rest content with what Chaucer once called "the naked text."[38] Arrested by the bareness of the letter, the glossator augments it with a labyrinthine accretion, with the result that a truth originally "named openly of euery man" is now obscured within its own clarification.

There are, then, two antithetical reasons for alchemical obscurity: it is both a deliberate encrypting undertaken to hide the truth and an unintended complexity caused by the effort to reveal the truth.[39] Either the secret cannot be spoken at all, or it must be so often respoken that it becomes lost within its own explanation. Not surprisingly, the anonymous author's own effort at revelation falls prey to echolalia: trying to "shewe what...the thinge is," he succeeds only in piling up citations from his learned predecessors and finally sinks into an all-too-familiar cento of alchemical jargon. It is relevant to note here that the word *jargon* derives from the Arabic *jargun*, a chemical term for a kind of zircon; so, too, the word *gibberish* comes from the name of the famous Arabic mystic and chemist Jabir ibn Hayyan, to whom was ascribed a large number of alchemical texts. As these etymologies imply, the problem with alchemy is above all linguistic. The dilemma that confronts the author of this sixteenth-century treatise is one common to virtually all alchemical writing, which claims to know the truth but to be unable to say it. And the problem becomes most insistent when it becomes time to identify what the *Turba philosophorum* calls "the stone which we call by all names."[40] In his *Pretiosa margarita novella* of 1330, Petrus Bonus of Ferrara admits that "our Stone has really no proper name of its own," that it "has as many names as

---

[37] The text is found in Bodleian Library MS Ashmole 1408, lines 135–50; the citation is derived from Robert M. Schuler's fascinating article, "The Renaissance Chaucer as Alchemist," *Viator* 15 (1984): 318.

[38] In *Prologue* G to *The Legend of Good Women*, line 86; that the phrase "naked text" probably means "without gloss" is suggested by *Romaunt of the Rose* 6556; see also *A Treatise on the Astrolabe*, Prol. 26.

[39] For medieval instances of the argument that the figurative writing used by alchemy is necessary to make clear what would otherwise be obscure, see the citations from the works of Petrus Bonus and Arnold of Villanova in Barbara Obrist, *Les débuts de l'imagerie alchimique (XIVe–XVe siècles)* (Paris: Le Sycomore, 1982), pp. 50–51.

[40] Arthur Edward Waite, ed., *The Turba Philosophorum* (London: George Redway, 1896; repr. New York: Samuel Weiser, 1973), p. 44. The *Turba* was written in Arabic around 900 and appeared in Latin at the beginning of the fourteenth century.

there are things, or names of things."[41] One dictionary actually provides about 600 names, while another text says that there are no fewer than 10,000.[42]

This overwhelming complexity calls up as an antidote assertions of unity. According to Petrus,

> our whole Magistry is one Stone, which is self-sufficient, is not mixed with anything else, proceeds from one root, becomes several things, and yet again is restored to its unity.[43]

The alchemical project relies on a radically monist view of the world. According to *The Visions of Zosimus*, a founding text of Western alchemy composed probably about 300 B.C.E., all natural generation, including animal, vegetable, and mineral, proceeds from "one single nature reacting on itself, a single species."[44] Some 900 years later, the *Tabula smaragdina*, a kind of alchemical decalogue ascribed to Hermes of Thoth or Hermes Trismegistus, asserts that

> what is below is like what is above, and what is above is like that which is below, for the performing of the marvels of the one thing. And as all things were from one thing, by the mediation of one thing: so all things were born of this one thing, by adaptation. . . . Thus was the earth created.[45]

And the elixir or stone that alchemy seeks is not an element *within* nature but the quintessence, i.e., nature itself.

This monism was underwritten by a physics derived from Aristotle and then modified by Islamic science. For Aristotle, metals, like all other substances, consist of a prime matter "formed" according to the proportion in which the four basic qualities — heat, cold, dryness, and moistness — are mixed. Minerals and metals are created through the interaction of the sun with water and with earth, interactions that generate either vaporous exhalations, which are cold and moist, or smoky exhalations, which are hot

---

[41] Petrus Bonus, *The New Pearl of Great Price*, trans. Arthur Edward Waite (London: Vincent Stuart, 1894), p. 149.

[42] For 600 names see Crosland, *Historical Studies*, p. 24 n. 24; for 10,000 names see Robert Halleux, *Les textes alchimiques* (Turnhout: Brepols, 1979), p. 116.

[43] Petrus Bonus, *New Pearl*, p. 149.

[44] Cited by F. Sherwood Taylor, *The Alchemists: Founders of Modern Chemistry* (New York, Schuman, 1949), p. 60. The *Visions* are translated by Taylor in *Ambix* 1 (1937): 88–92.

[45] Taylor, *Alchemists*, p. 89.

and dry. When shut in and compressed, these exhalations form all minerals and metals. Islamic alchemists subsequently identified the vaporous exhalation with sulfur, which was cold and moist, and the smoky exhalation with mercury, which was correspondingly hot and dry. Since these two "spirits" were the constituent elements of all metals, transmutation could be accomplished by altering the proportions between them in any individual substance. Hence, as Albertus Magnus said, since "nature could transform sulphur and mercury into metals by the aid of the sun and stars, it seemed reasonable that the alchemist should be able to do the same in his vessel."[46] Just as the human body becomes ill from an imbalance of the four elements (the humors), so does a metal: it can be "cured" (that is, promoted from base to pure) by the addition of a medicine — an elixir — that readjusts the proportions of the four elements. In this sense the alchemist does not violate but perfects nature: George Ripley, a fifteenth-century Augustinian canon and the best-known English alchemist, advises the adept, "Where Nature did leave off, what tyme look ye begynn."[47] And the elixir that accomplishes this completion of nature's work is the philosopher's stone: it embodies the divine *pneuma* or *spiritus* from which the world is constituted, the quintessence that another late-medieval English text called "Gods Prevetie."[48]

The unity of nature is matched by the simplicity of alchemical doctrine: as Petrus Bonus warns, "If you once depart from the unity and truth of Nature, you are involved in the bewildering mazes of confusion and error."[49] According to Ripley:

> . . . though the Philosophers speake plurally,
> All is but one Thing, ye may me trowe,
> In kinde, which is our Base principally.[50]

[46] Ibid., p. 97.

[47] George Ripley, *The Compound of Alchemy* (1470–71), in Elias Ashmole, ed., *Theatrum Chemicum Britannicum: Containing Severall Poeticall Pieces of our Famous English Philosophers, who have written the Hermetique Mysteries in their owne Ancient Language* (London: N. Brooke, 1652; repr. Hildesheim: Georg Olms, 1968), p. 115.

[48] This is the brief treatise entitled "Pearce the Black Monk upon the Elixir," found in ibid., p. 274. As Taylor says, "In the belief of many alchemical authors there was a subtle spirit diffused throughout the world. That spirit is described as a *quinta essentia*, a fifth being, over and above the four elements, and . . . it was believed to exist in all earthly bodies and to be their active principle" (*Alchemists*, pp. 116–17).

[49] Petrus Bonus, *New Pearl*, p. 132.

[50] Ripley, in Ashmole, ed., *Theatrum Chemicum Britannicum*, p. 112. Pearce the Black Monk almost scornfully insists on the simplicity of alchemical doctrine: "Sun and Moone, Erth and Water; / And here ys alle that men of clatter" (ibid., p. 271).

Petrus says that "the art is one, and it is true. Were it stripped of all figures and parables, it would be possible to compress it into the space of eight or twelve lines."[51] And a *Rosarius* ascribed to John Dastin gives "seven artificial propositions" in which the whole of alchemy is contained.[52] Nature and alchemy are unified and self-identical: ". . . all true Phylosophers record and say the same," says Ripley, adding that "all our secrets of one Image must spryng."[53] So, too, the elaborate metaphoric language of alchemical treatises presupposes an underlying unity among a wide variety of apparently disparate activities. A typical example is an early-fourteenth-century alchemical *Visio* by John Dastin: it describes the convocation of the planets to celebrate the marriage of mercury and sulfur and the birth of the child who will redeem the impure planets/metals through death and resurrection — a unification of astrology, alchemy, and Christian myth typical of late-medieval and Renaissance alchemical writing.[54] Alchemy acknowledges little distinction between literal and metaphoric: if the conjunction of female mercury and male sulfur can be described in the language of sexual intercourse and marriage, then marital intercourse can also be described as a form of alchemy.

This assertion of the simplicity of alchemical doctrine and the unity of natural processes is designed to provide a point of stability for a discourse always threatening to lose itself in its own elaboration. Paradoxically, however, these claims to unity actually entail the overwhelming multiplicity they seek to counter. Once distinctions have been erased — between the metaphoric and the literal, the material and the spiritual, the scientific and the religious, the chemical and the marital, metals and stars — then praxis becomes impossible: staged movement toward a goal is undone by a process of endless substitution. When everything means everything else, then nothing means anything; when identity no longer exists, identifica-

---

[51] Petrus Bonus, *New Pearl*, p. 140.

[52] Thorndike, *History*, 3.94.

[53] Ashmole, ed., *Theatrum Chemicum Britannicum*, p. 123. For Pearce's similar assertion, see ibid., p. 271. The reference to the image invokes the elaborate illustrations that, beginning in the fourteenth century, occasionally accompany alchemical treatises: alchemical lore can be encapsulated in a single, immediately graspable picture, a representation that for all its cryptic implications embodies in its visibility the simplicity of alchemy itself. In *Les débuts de l'imagerie alchimique*, pp. 60–65, Obrist discusses how alchemical illuminations affirm an illuminationist epistemology.

[54] The *Visio* was translated in the sixteenth century as *Dastin's Dream* and can be found in Ashmole, ed., *Theatrum Chemicum Britannicum*, pp. 257–68. For another example see the early-fifteenth-century *Buch der heiligen Dreifaltigkeit*, discussed by Obrist, *Débuts de l'imagerie*, pp. 117–82.

tion is impossible. The very monism that seeks to stabilize alchemy subverts the procedures whereby it might achieve its goal. Walter of Odington's *Ycocedron*, written in the mid-fourteenth century, describes a world of ceaseless transmutation:

In nature the elements circulate and pass their properties on to one another. Fire impresses its heat on the air; the air pours its humidity rarefied by heat into water; water transmits frigidity to earth, drying it by the heat of the air; and the dried earth sends its dryness, chilled, moistened, and warmed, to fire. Thus fire recovers the heat which it has remitted to each of the other elements, and air its humidity, and water its frigidity, and earth its dryness.[55]

And Ripley envisions a world of "conversyon / Fro thyng to thyng, fro one state to another"; as he elsewhere says, "Thynges into thyngs must therfore be rotate, / Untyll dyversyte be brought to parfyt unyte."[56] But a world without difference forecloses the possibility of identification.

One way in which alchemical texts both register and seek to disarm the threat of semiotic anarchy is by claiming that they both do and do not contain the truth. While asserting their own indispensability, they also employ a language of spiritual understanding that implies that the truth they signify can be known only extratextually. The thirteenth-century *Aurora consurgens* recites a familiar litany of scriptural passages to assert that the prerequisite for understanding is conversion:

The letter killeth, but the spirit quickeneth [2 Cor. 3:6]. Be renewed in the spirit of your mind and put on the new man [Eph. 4:24], that is, a subtle understanding. If ye understand in the spirit, ye shall also know in the spirit. Let every one of you prove his own work [Gal. 6:4], whether it be perfect or defective. For what things a man shall sow, those also shall he reap [Gal. 6:8]. O how many understand not the sayings of the wise; these have perished because of their foolishness, for they lacked spiritual understanding and found nothing but toil.[57]

Alchemical understanding requires a *pre*understanding that obviates the need for instruction. Like the biblical exegete, but lacking his institutional support, the alchemist is placed in the uncomfortable position of having to know everything before he can know anything, to possess the truth before

[55] Thorndike, *History*, 3.130–31.
[56] Ripley, *Compound*, in Ashmole, ed., *Theatrum Chemicum Britannicum*, pp. 165, 137.
[57] Marie-Louise Von Franz, ed., *Aurora Consurgens*, trans. R. F. C. Hull and A. S. B. Glover, Bollingen Series, vol. 77 (New York: Pantheon Books, 1966), pp. 117–19.

he can learn what it is. Individual items of information are useless apart from a totalized knowledge that cannot be attained gradually but only possessed all at once.

Finally, as material as well as verbal structures, alchemical texts participate in the radically piecemeal world they describe and hope to unify. In discussing Petrus Bonus's *Margarita*, George Sarton provides an imaginary scenario for its composition:

> If [Bonus] had written out all the Latin alchemical, philosophical and mystical books available to him, cut the copies into small pieces, classified the innumerable fragments as plausibly as possible, and finally edited them in the new order thus obtained..., the final result would not have been very different from his compilation.[58]

Important alchemical texts such as the *Turba philosophorum* and the *Aurora consurgens* are largely compilations of disparate items, and many treatises are frankly florilegia, as their titles proclaim: one favorite is *Rosarius*—besides the *Rosarius philosophorum* there is the *Rosarius minor*, the *Parvum rosarium*, the *Rosarius novus*, the *Rosarius Phebi*, the *Rosa novella*, and the *Rosa aurea*, as well as the *Flos florum*, the *Flos regis*, and so forth.[59] Treatises are less singular documents than momentary coagulations of inherited materials, exhibiting in their emergence and reconfiguration the world of endless transmutation they represent.

Nor is this world stabilized by authorship. The list of alchemical authorities is almost as long as the names of the stone they seek. Petrus Bonus enumerates the sages of alchemy as Adam, Asclepius, Enoch, Hermes,

---

[58] George Sarton, *Introduction to the History of Science* (Washington, D.C.: Williams and Wilkins, 1948), 3.751–52. In fact, although Sarton's description is applicable to many treatises, it does misrepresent Bonus's carefully organized text: see Chiara Crisciani, "The Conception of Alchemy as Expressed in the *Pretiosa Margarita Novella*," *Ambix* 20 (1973): 165–81.

[59] Thorndike, *History*, 3.55–57. Halleux, in the most recent and penetrating survey of this material, describes alchemical treatises as "living texts, with manuscript traditions that are extremely unstable" (*Textes*, p. 90). Thorndike says that the typical alchemical treatise "consists of a congeries of familiar phrases and sanctified notions, drawn from the past literature of the subject" (*History*, 3.40); Taylor adds that "most alchemical works [are] a mosaic of quotations from earlier authors" (*Alchemists*, p. 111). Even granted the prevalence of the citational mode in medieval writing, the alchemical treatise is unusually subject to disruption and appropriation: as Thorndike says, "It was likely to be treated as common property which anyone could maul over, corrupt, amend, comment upon, or abbreviate to suit his times and fancy" (*History*, 3.40).

Moses, David, Solomon, John the Evangelist, Homer, Virgil, and Ovid; other names that are regularly invoked—only a few of which have any legitimacy at all—include Alchimo (the founding father, according to Albertus Magnus, although Zosimos gives credit to a fallen angel named Chemes), Hermes, Daedalus, Archelaos, Artefius, Mahrari, Cleopatra, Mary the Jew, Socrates, Plato, Aristotle, Galen, Apollonius of Tyre, Ptolomy, Balinas, Jabir, Senior Zadith, Morienus, Avicenna, Michael Scot, Pope Innocent III, Roger Bacon, Thomas Aquinas, Arnold of Villanova, and Raymond Lull. The problem of attribution opens up what Halleux calls an aporia: Arnold of Villanova is credited with 57 titles, of which perhaps 5 or 6—or perhaps none—are authentic; more than 80 treatises are attributed to Raymond Lull, who not only did not write any of them but was a firm opponent of alchemy.[60] In a fifteenth-century manuscript called the *Ars philosophorum* and ascribed to one Hugh of England, this invocation of authority reaches a kind of climax:

After the mynde of Hermes, Plato, Morien, Geber, Aristotill, Virgill, Albert, Avicen, Alphide, Innocent Bishope of Rome, freer Robert lumberd, freer bacon, Arnold of newe town, William frances, Tolomeus and other, hewe of england declareth thus and saith in mysty worde, Recipe an hogg and rost him and make good fyre to him.[61]

Evidently an alchemical barbecue cannot have too many cooks.

What all this adds up to is that alchemical discourse displays in a hyperbolic form unacknowledged characteristics that typified medieval textuality as a whole. Its extravagant use of the citational mode blurred textual boundaries by folding one text into another; it treated authorship as an ex post facto construction rather than a pretextual given; and, above all, it collapsed an apparently unalloyed truth ("seen as simple, intact, normal, pure, standard, self-identical") into a morass of multiplicity (seen as "derivation, complication, deterioration, accident").[62] Because the non-existence of the philosopher's stone lured alchemy into a quest without a goal, it was forced to discover the endlessness of writing, to confront the

---

[60] Halleux, *Textes*, pp. 97–109; see also Thorndike, *History*, 3.63–65. For an expert survey of the Lullian material see Michela Pereira, *The Alchemical Corpus Attributed to Raymond Lull*, Warburg Institute Surveys and Texts, vol. 18 (London: Warburg Institute, 1989).

[61] Singer, *Catalogue*, 1.17.

[62] The cited phrases are from Jacques Derrida, "Limited, Inc.," *Glyph* 2 (1977): 236.

nonidentity between language and that which it seeks to represent.[63] Alchemy's "gynful speche," as Langland called it, disclosed not the secrets of nature but the guilty secret of language.[64] And if the knowledge that alchemical writing provided is less about nature than about culture, its exorbitance placed it in an ironic relation to the official genres of medieval writing. In effect, it may be seen as unwittingly encouraging a certain disenchantment, a certain awareness, in Marshall Leicester's words, that the late Middle Ages was "a culture whose cover is blown."[65]

I am suggesting, then, that alchemy was an instance not of all that had to be left behind for modernity to flourish but instead a site where modernizing values could take root. According to traditional accounts of alchemy, there is nothing surprising in this: if we assume that modernization is driven by rationalization and that the supreme instance of rationalization is the scientific revolution of the seventeenth century, then alchemy can be understood as preparing the way. To cite the title of one history, alchemy can be seen as the *Prelude to Chemistry* and hence to modern science as a whole.[66] And indeed, alchemy *did* function in the Middle Ages as one of the places where a sophisticated and coherent physical theory was allied to the pragmatism of the workshop. Many alchemical treatises are divided into two parts, labeled *theorica* and *practica*, and if these two activities were never as close as a genuinely scientific method would prescribe, alchemy was at least able to imagine the possibility of their relationship.[67]

[63] For other discussions of alchemical language see Michel Butor, *Répertoire* (Paris: Editions de Minuit, 1960), pp. 12–19, and Chiara Crisciani, "*Experientia* e linguaggio nella tradizione alchemica," in *Atti del XXIV Congresso Nazionale di Filosofia* (Rome: Società Filosofica Italiana, 1974), 2.357–64. I have not been able to consult James Dauphiné, "De 'L'Ésprit de l'or': Langage et alchimie au moyen âge," in James Dauphiné, *Ésotérisme et littérature* (Nice: C.E.M., 1987), pp. 29–48.

[64] See n. 13 above. Certainly its critics frequently revert to the theme of alchemical language: in the bull of 1317 that outlawed alchemy because of its links to counterfeiting, Pope John XXII said that alchemists are "men [who] dissimulate their falsity with words," that they "admire those who speak about this business" even though they cannot perform what they promise. The bull *Spondet quas non exhibent* is printed, translated, and discussed by Halleux, *Textes*, pp. 124–26. Despite this prohibition, John may himself have patronized alchemy: see Ogrinc, "Western Society and Alchemy," pp. 114–15.

[65] Leicester, *The Disenchanted Self*, p. 28. For a somewhat similar argument about alchemy, see John Reidy, "Alchemy as Counter-Culture," *Indiana Social Studies Quarterly* 24 (1971–72): 41–51.

[66] John Read, *Prelude to Chemistry: An Outline of Alchemy*, 2d ed. (Cambridge, Mass.: Harvard University Press, 1966 [1936]).

[67] In part this capacity was a function of alchemy's mixed heritage: on the one hand is a metallurgical interest expressed in a tradition of very pragmatic recipe books (see Pierre

But this kind of account of alchemy's modernity is finally not adequate. For alchemy was founded on the very Aristotelian physical theory that needed to be set aside for modern science to arise.[68] If we are looking for the roots of either scientific theory or methodology, they are unlikely to be found in alchemy. As one historian has said:

Throughout the possibly 2,000 years of its history, alchemy undergoes no appreciable change and has contributed surprisingly little of worth to the corpus of chemical theory or fact, especially considering the length of its history and the diverse, scientifically rich cultures through which it has passed so largely unaffected.[69]

Moreover, beginning around 1300, alchemical texts come more and more to appropriate the mode and manner of religious discourse.[70] They are often highly allegorical in form, inviting the reader to apply to them the same interpretive techniques as were used in the exegesis of the Bible; they insist that the alchemist must possess moral purity and spiritual piety if he is to be successful; and they typically present God or Christ as the keeper of the alchemical secret that can be revealed only to the worthy. In other words, many alchemical treatises present alchemy less as a secular pursuit opposed to the otherworldliness of Christian doctrine than as another form of piety.

If alchemy is progressive, then, its dynamism cannot be understood in the usual terms by which scientific progress is measured. On the contrary, alchemy's contribution to modernization was ideological and social rather

---

Cézard, "L'alchimie at les recettes techniques," *Métaux et civilisations* 1 [1945]: 5–10, 41–45), on the other a quasi-mystical belief in a dynamic universe. That these two traditions were at work in Arabic alchemy as early as the ninth century is shown by Brian Stock, "Science, Technology, and Economic Progress in the Early Middle Ages," in David C. Lindberg, ed., *Science in the Middle Ages* (Chicago: University of Chicago Press, 1978), pp. 15–16.

[68] Lindberg, *Beginnings of Western Science*, provides a balanced survey of current opinions regarding the degree of continuity between medieval and modern science and concludes that the "new science" of the seventeenth century "produced a radical conceptual shift, which destroyed the [Aristotelian] foundations of natural philosophy as practiced for nearly two thousand years" (p. 361). The absence of a genuine chemistry in the Middle Ages—and indeed until Lavoisier's work at the end of the eighteenth century—is discussed by Robert P. Multhauf, "The Science of Matter," in ibid., pp. 369–90.

[69] Trent Eglin, "Introduction to a Hermeneutics of the Occult," in Harold Garfinkel, ed., *Ethnomethodological Studies of Work* (London: Routledge and Kegan Paul, 1986). p. 134.

[70] The "spiritual turn" of alchemical theorizing around 1300 has been best discussed by Barbara Obrist, "Die Alchemie in der mittelalterlichen Gesellschaft," in Christoph Meinel, ed., *Die Alchemie in der europäischen Kultur- und Wissenschaftsgeschichte* Wolfenbütteler Forschungen, vol. 22 (Wiesbaden: Harrassowitz, 1986), pp. 33–59.

than intellectual.[71] As we have seen, the alchemical secret of secrets, forever out of material reach, brought within conceptual reach the idea that truth itself is linguistically inaccessible. This knowledge is one of alchemy's most profound accidents — a metaphysical spin-off, a modernism or even post-modernism *avant la lettre*. But there were other, more explicitly ideological spin-offs as well. Alchemy's challenge to medieval culture can be found most profoundly in its commitment to an applied science — a technology — capable of transforming the material conditions of human life. Beginning toward the end of the thirteenth century and gathering force throughout the next century, alchemy was attacked by the ecclesiastical authorities. The reasons for its censure were many. Clerics were forbidden alchemy because it violated their vows of poverty, because it brought them into contact with money, and because it was a mechanical rather than a liberal art. The charge of necromancy was also frequently invoked: since alchemy could not produce its goal by natural means, it must have had recourse to demons. But the most important argument was that alchemy presumptuously claimed to be able to improve a God-given nature by the application of human art.[72] As we have seen, alchemical theory argued that all metals

[71] The peculiar nature of alchemy's progressivism supports, I believe, a larger and very important point made by Brian Stock, one worth quoting in full: "The reasons why the Middle Ages contributed decisively to the advent of modernity, that is, to the conjunction of science, technology, economics, and mental attitudes that we associate with the modern world, cannot be found by means of a number of tried historiographical approaches, even though each has added its share of insights to the process of modernization as Weber understood it. These methods include: the internalist history of science and technology, the unmodified Weberian sociology of religion, the mere pushing back of modernity into the Middle Ages, or any sort of functionalism, which reduces cultural change to a superstructure of economic and social transformations. However, if this criticism of earlier schemes is accepted, then it follows that the essential changes of the Middle Ages may not have taken place in science or technology as such, *but rather in more subtle mutations in the cultural and religious environment*, which not only prepared the way for the reception of modern attitudes, but, more importantly, began the debate, which continues down to our own day in the less developed world, on whether this sort of rationalization was a good thing" ("Rationality, Tradition, and the Scientific Outlook: Reflections on Max Weber and the Middle Ages," in Pamela O. Long, ed., *Science and Technology in Medieval Society*, Annals of the New York Academy of Sciences, vol. 441 [New York: New York Academy of Sciences, 1985], p. 14; italics added).

[72] The argument that alchemy is impossible because art cannot improve nature entered the tradition as early as the twelfth century, when Aristotle's incomplete *Meterologica* was supplemented with three chapters from Avicenna's *Kitâb al Shifâ* (a lucid explanation of this process is provided by Halleux, "Albert le Grand et l'alchimie"). The incapacity of art to improve nature is the central point of attack of the *Contra alchimistas*, written in 1396 by Nicolas Eymeric: see Sylvain Matton, "Le Traité *Contre les Alchimistes* de Nicolas Eymeric," *Chrysopoeia* 2 (1987): 93–136. In defending alchemy, both Albertus Magnus and the

aspire to the condition of gold, and would in time attain to it; but alchemy could speed up the process, could bring about in a moment what nature needed eons to achieve. As John Dastin said, "Art imitates nature, and in certain respects corrects and supersedes it, as weak nature is helped by the efforts of the physicians."[73] Alchemy also had a medical side, which in its most extravagant form asserted—as in a claim made by Roger Bacon in 1266—that the elixir is able to restore the bodies of human beings to the perfection of Adam and Eve before the Fall.[74] This claim strikingly prefigures the words of *Francis* Bacon, for whom the goal of human knowledge is "a restitution and reinvesting (in great part) of man to the sovereignty and power... which he had in his first state of creation."[75]

What these claims assert is nothing less than the capacity of human beings to transform the material conditions of their lives: they assert, in other words, the power of technology. In an important essay William Newman has shown that "the alchemists of the Middle Ages developed a clearly articulated philosophy of technology, in which human art is raised to a level of appreciation difficult to find in other writings until the Renaissance."[76] And this philosophy is deeply at odds with official attitudes: despite the major advances in technological practice that were

---

canonist Oldrado da Ponte (d. 1335) argued that alchemical art follows nature but does not surpass or complete it: see Pearl Kibre, "Albertus Magnus on Alchemy," in James A. Weisheipl, ed., *Albertus Magnus and the Sciences* (Toronto: Pontifical Institute of Mediaeval Studies, 1980), pp. 187-202, and Thorndike, *History*, 3.49. This is essentially the argument found in the second part of the *Roman de la Rose*, ed. Félix Lecoy (Paris: Champion, 1966), 2.16035-118 (the later reputation of Jean de Meun as an alchemist, which derived from this passage, is expertly surveyed by Pierre-Yves Badel, "Alchemical Readings of the *Romance of the Rose*," in Kevin Brownlee and Sylvia Huot, eds., *Rethinking the* Romance of the Rose [Philadelphia: University of Pennsylvania Press, 1992], pp. 262-85).

[73] Theissen, "John Dastin's Letter," p. 84; see also the comment by Ripley quoted in part II of this essay.

[74] William Newman, "Technology and Alchemical Debate in the Late Middle Ages," *Isis* 80 (1989): 433. See also Von Franz, ed., *Aurora consurgens*: "For the first Adam and his sons took their beginning from the corruptible elements, and therefore it was needful that the composed should be corrupted, but the second Adam, who is called the philosophic man, from pure elements entered into eternity" (p. 129).

[75] Cited by George Ovitt, Jr., *The Restoration of Perfection: Labor and Technology in Medieval Culture* (New Brunswick, N.J.: Rutgers University Press, 1987), p. 86.

[76] Newman, "Technology and Alchemical Debate," pp. 424-25. See also Delany, "Run Silent, Run Deep," p. 11. The figure who is often taken to represent Renaissance humanism at its most exalted, Leonardo da Vinci, admired medieval alchemy precisely for its technological capacities: it "processes the simple products of nature, since nature is not capable of this, having no organic instruments to do what man can do with his hands" (cited by Ogrinc, "Western Society and Alchemy," p. 112).

made throughout the period, technology *as an ideology* was always regarded with suspicion if not outright hostility.[77] In part this negative
attitude was a function of a familiar and pervasive otherworldliness, but in
part it reflected the recognition that technological change was an agent for
social change. As several alchemical writers pointed out, and as princely
patrons of alchemists were all too aware, what would happen to social
hierarchy if gold were available to everyone?

We can recognize the alchemical impulse toward social change in the way
alchemy functioned as an intellectual practice. Although several powerful
authorities, including Albertus Magnus, recognized the legitimacy of alchemical investigations, and although the study of both natural and
artificial metals had been initially included as a legitimate area of study
within the university, by the early fourteenth century alchemy was beginning to be banned from curricula.[78] In 1332 the University of Paris included in its *Chartularium* a statement that "it is forbidden to all *sub poena
excommunicationis* to teach or learn alchemy any longer, and all writings
on the subject are to be burned."[79] Yet alchemical writing continued to
flourish, as the vast number of fourteenth- and fifteenth-century manuscripts attests. For alchemy allured as an intellectual tradition and practice
that may have imitated but nonetheless stood to the side of — and so could
not be controlled by — the official institutions of medieval intellectual
culture.[80] The genuinely attested authors of these texts — men such as Paul
of Taranto, Constantine of Pisa, Arnold of Villanova, Petrus Bonus of
Ferrara, and John of Rupescissa — were lower clerics or friars who did their
intellectual work outside the university. And the men to whom texts were
misattributed — men such as Ramon Lull — were very much outsiders: al-

[77] This point is demonstrated in the important book by Ovitt, *The Pursuit of Perfection*,
countering the claims made by Lynn White and others. Ovitt's account is nuanced and
supported by Elspeth Whitney, *Paradise Restored: The Mechanical Arts from Antiquity
Through the Thirteenth Century*, Transactions of the American Philosophical Society, vol. 80,
pt. 1 (Philadelphia: American Philosophical Society, 1990).

[78] See Obrist, "Die Alchimie in der mittelalterlichen Gesellschaft," pp. 51–55. This is in
contrast to its earlier welcome: Chiara Crisciani, "La *quaestio de alchimia* fra duecento e
trecento," *Medioevo* 2 (1976): 119–68.

[79] Ogrinc, "Western Society and Alchemy," p. 116.

[80] Several alchemical texts are written in such a way as to accommodate alchemy to the
discourse of university learning: see Constantine of Pisa, *The Book of the Secrets of Alchemy*,
ed. and trans. Barbara Obrist (Leiden: E. J. Brill, 1990), and Crisciani, "The Conception of
Alchemy as Expressed in the *Pretiosa Margarita Novella*." The aspiration of alchemy to be
considered a genuine philosophy is discussed by Chiara Crisciani and Claude Gagnon,
Alchimie et philosophie au moyen âge: Perspectives et problèmes (Montreal: L'Aurore, 1980).

though Lull disapproved of alchemy, his autodidactic intellectual history and his visionary utopianism made of him exactly the sort of man alchemists aspired to be. Perhaps also relevant here is Lull's position as a Franciscan tertiary, since there seems to have been something of a Franciscan alchemical tradition.[81] Elias of Assisi was reputed to have been deposed from the generalship of the Franciscans in 1239 because of his interest in alchemy,[82] and Franciscans such as Paul of Taranto, Roger Bacon, John of Rupescissa, and (probably) Arnold of Villanova certainly promoted it. They were at least in part motivated by what Friedrich Heer has called "a spirit of ecstatic impatience":

...objects must be "radically" transformed by working outwards from their roots, their essential substances, and man must "radically" transform himself to match, by renouncing those arbitrary authorities by which the old, unregenerate world was governed.[83]

This sense of self-transformation—of a self-creation that bespeaks a far more profound technology of the self than the Yeoman's superficial changes of color—is given expression in the quasi-autobiographical nature of alchemical writings. Alchemical texts had always tended to ground their doctrinal materials in a structure of personal experience by presenting the theory as the teachings of a master to a disciple.[84] By the end of the fourteenth century this rhetorical maneuver had developed toward a more fully articulated autobiographical form: examples are the *Liber de intentione alchimistarum*, which describes the various methods the author has discovered in his journeys;[85] the *Sedacina*, written about 1378 by an English Carmelite named William Sedacerius;[86] and the *Liber de consideratione quinta essentiae*, written in 1351–52 by John of Rupescissa (and

---

[81] See Reidy, "Alchemy as Counter-Culture," pp. 46–47; Chiara Cristiani, "Nota sull'alchimia 'francescana' nel sec. XIII," *Atti del XXV Congresso nazionale di filosofia* (Rome: Società Filosofica Italiana, 1980). The Franciscan authorities issued at least three pronouncements against alchemy, in 1272, 1287, and 1289; the Dominicans issued five, in 1273, 1287, 1289, 1313, and 1323.

[82] Thorndike, *History*, 3.347.

[83] Friedrich Heer, *The Medieval World: Europe, 1100–1350*, trans. Janet Sondheimer (New York: New American Library, 1963), p. 303.

[84] This is true even of the first Arabic treatise to be introduced to the West, the so-called *Morienus*, translated by Robert of Ketton (or Chester), archdeacon of Pampelona, in 1144.

[85] Pereira, *Alchemical Corpus*, p. 8.

[86] Thorndike, *History*, 3.629–30.

translated into English in the next century).[87] By the early fifteenth century elaborate fictive alchemical autobiographies began to appear, romantic accounts of the long journeys and lifetimes of effort that were spent in alchemical quest.[88] What these texts demonstrate is that what is sought is less the philosopher's stone than the name and status of philosopher. Although alchemical study was incapable of making gold, it could produce alchemists; and although it was unable to change the material world, mastering its elaborate theory could change the self-identity of the alchemist. What alchemy provided, in short, was a way to be an intellectual. And with the translation of these texts into the vernacular—a process that begins in the late fourteenth century[89]—we can see alchemy as one of the forces that undermined the clerical monopoly upon learning.

III

Given this account of alchemy as a verbal and social practice, several answers to my opening questions now seem possible. For one thing, we are encouraged to take seriously the act of emancipation that induces the Canon's Yeoman's performance while recognizing the limits within which it is contained. Throughout both *Prologue* and *Tale* the Yeoman makes clear his desire for the "clergial" learning that his master possesses but is denied to a "lewed man" like himself. What drives him, we can now see, is not the private avarice of the multiplier but the social ambition to become a philosopher. This recognition can also help us understand the ambivalences of his attitude both toward the ecclesiastical establishment and toward religiosity as a whole. On the one hand he represents churchmen as either venal or foolish, either tricksters like the canon or dupes like the greedy priest. One might even speculate that the otherwise unmotivated

[87] John of Rupescissa, *The Book of Quinte Essence*, ed. F. J. Furnivall, EETS, o.s., vol. 16 (London: Tuebner, 1856).

[88] See Pereira, *Alchemical Corpus*, chap. 3. Less extravagant examples in English include Norton's *Ordinal of Alchemy*, Ripley's *Compound of Alchemy*, and the unwittingly hilarious *Breviary of Naturall Philosophy*, written in 1557 by Thomas Charnock (available in Ashmole, ed., *Theatrum Chemicum Britannicum*, pp. 291–303). These autobiographical texts multiply in the sixteenth century, one of the most interesting being the *De chemico miraculo* ascribed to the fourteenth-century Bernard Trevisan. An English translation, written by Edward Barlow in 1579, can be found in MS Ashmole 1487.

[89] Robert Halleux, "L'Alchimie," in *La littérature française aux XIVᵉ et XVᵉ siècles*, vol. 8, pt. 1, of *Grundriss der Romanischen Literaturen des Mittelalters*, ed. Daniel Poirion (Heidelberg: Carl Winter, 1988), 1.336–45.

appearance of the "worshipful chanons religious" serves to show that even virtuous clerics harbor, as he says, a hidden Judas. Yet the Yeoman's whole performance is also saturated with religious anxiety and a desire to endow his world with a meaning that derives from the ultimate source of all meaning. If the Yeoman prefigures a disenchanted rationalism eager to dominate the natural world, he also bespeaks a yearning, heightened by the possibility of loss, for the value-laden, animated universe of traditional religion—a contradiction at the heart of alchemy itself. We should also notice that the Yeoman's rebelliousness takes a typically moderate Chaucerian form, whereby a politically charged confrontation is displaced into a less incendiary form. By relocating the Yeoman's attack on his master into a context of intellectual rather than nakedly political rivalry, Chaucer avoids the political implications of his behavior and makes it part of a larger process of cultural emancipation.

Moreover, by recognizing that Chaucer was himself an agent of this cultural emancipation, we can begin to understand the personal relevance of the Yeoman's performance, and especially of his sudden appearance. The analogy between the poet and his alchemical Yeoman is unavoidable, not only because of the appearance here of the loaded word "elvyssh" by which Chaucer had earlier described himself, and not only because both alchemy and poetry are transformative arts (a parallel made explicit in the discussion of alchemy in the *Roman de la Rose* which in part underwrites the Canon's Yeoman's performance).[90] What is more important is that Chaucer himself is both a *grant translateur*—a layman who made Latin and French texts available in English—and an amateur natural philosopher whose relation to his learned materials is not dissimilar to the Yeoman's. In *A Treatise on the Astrolabe*, which translates the technical details of astronomy into, as he puts it, "naked wordes in Englissh" (*Prologue* 26–27), Chaucer apologizes for being only "a lewd compilator of the labour of olde astrologiens" (lines 61–62). Like the Yeoman, Chaucer is no clerk, yet he is not only a writer informed by "clergial" learning but also, in his public life as Controller of Customs and Clerk of the King's Works, a layman who held positions previously reserved to clerics. And like the Yeoman, Chaucer is socially indefinable: neither courtier nor merchant nor clerk, he participates in all three social formations without fully according with any.[91]

---

[90] The connection between alchemy and poetry is most fully discussed by Raybin, "'And Pave It Al of Silver and of Gold.'" An excellent discussion of the connection between the passage in the *Roman* and *The Canon's Yeoman's Prologue* and *Tale* is provided by John M. Fyler, "Domesticating the Exotic in the *Squire's Tale*," *ELH* 55 (1988): 11–12.

[91] This point is well made by Derek Brewer, "Class Distinctions in Chaucer," *Speculum* 43 (1968): 290–305.

This social indefinability lies behind Chaucer's interest in what I have elsewhere called a socially undetermined subjectivity. If we are to specify in what consists the undeniable modernity of Chaucer's poetry—its demonstrable capacity to speak to subsequent ages with special directness and force—then it will be found, I submit, in the foregrounding of an emancipated selfhood existing apart from social determinants. That such a selfhood is a fiction is less important than that it has become—in the form of the ideology of individualism—the enabling fiction of modern culture. The capacity to imagine the world as different from what it is, the willingness to place upon oneself the responsibility to make history rather than to receive it as a preordained whole—these depend in the first instance on the capacity to imagine oneself as other and more than an integer in a fixed social order, as an autonomous self capable of a variety of social identities.

Philosophers of modernity since at least Hegel have asserted that the first step in moving from the closed immobility of traditionalism to the open dynamism of modernity is to endow the self with autonomous desire: the transformation of institutions requires and entails the transformation of individuals. "The right of the subject's particularity," said Hegel, "his right to be satisfied, or in other words, the right of subjective freedom, is the pivot and center of the difference between antiquity and modern times."[92] Modernization is bound up with the development of a kind of empathy that allows people to put themselves in the place of others, "to identify... with a role, time, or plan different from [one's] own."[93] But we have also been taught that such transformations also entail an overwhelming sense of loss, whether called alienation (Marx) or anomie (Durkheim) or disenchantment (Weber). As Marshall Berman has said:

To be modern is to find ourselves in an environment that promises adventure, power, joy, growth, transformation of ourselves and the world—and at the same time, threatens to destroy everything we have, everything we know, everything we are. . . . To be modern is to be part of a universe in which, as Marx said, "all that is solid melts into air."[94]

[92] Hegel, *Philosophy of Right*, no. 124Z, cited by David Kolb, *The Critique of Pure Modernity: Hegel, Heidegger, and After* (Chicago: University of Chicago Press, 1986), p. 20.

[93] See Daniel Lerner, "Modernization, I: Social Aspects," in David L. Sills, ed., *Encyclopedia of the Social Sciences* (New York: Macmillan and Free Press, 1968), 10.391. This aspect of modernity has been recently discussed in detail under the rubric of self-reflexivity by Anthony Giddens, *Modernity and Self-Identity: Self and Society in the Late Modern Age* (Stanford, Calif.: Stanford University Press, 1991).

[94] Cited by David Harvey, *The Condition of Postmodernity* (Oxford: Basil Blackwell, 1989), pp. 10–11.

Throughout his work Chaucer persists in challenging the efficacy of objective systems of value, persists in seeing meaning as located less in society than in the self. Whether it be the critique of the reified honor world of *The Knight's Tale*, the relocation in *The Pardoner's Tale* of the drama of salvation from the external forum of judgment to the inner world of contrition, or *The General Prologue*'s rewriting of estates satire into an asocial discourse of personal psychology—everywhere we look Chaucer turns from a traditionalist objectivism to a subjectively centered modernity. We can also see how this turn accords with his own refusal to assume authorial jurisdiction over his texts and his tolerance for open rather than closed forms. To return to my opening account of the critical tradition, I would gratefully note that Chaucer allows Chaucerians to stay in business by handing over his work to a future conceived as dynamic and appropriative rather than by acquiescing in the reproduction of the past.

Yet so sunny a picture of "our" Chaucer is of course incomplete. For if the Canon's Yeoman represents Chaucerian modernity, he is an appropriately irresolute spokesman. His mode of arrival expresses through its sense of anticipation and novelty modernity in its positive mode and yet also modernity's negativity in its belatedness, in the Yeoman's fear that something crucial has already passed him by, that the new will be old before he can join it. Hence too his strangely unspecifiable guilt, a guilt we can now perhaps recognize as generated by the feeling that modernity itself may be a sin. And we should not forget that the interruption provided by the Canon's Yeoman is just that—a blip on the screen—and that *The Canterbury Tales* will end with the Parson's relentless objectification of the self by means of the clerical discourse of the seven deadly sins. The Canon's Yeoman stands in relation to *The Canterbury Tales* as a whole as alchemy stands in relation to medieval culture—a strange phenomenon on the margin. We may look to this phenomenon when we are feeling skeptical about the binarisms to which our own modernity is bound, but we should also remember that we would not see it—or recognize it for what I believe it is—were they not in force.[95]

---

[95] This article had its beginning in a classroom session of an NEH Seminar for College Teachers that Anne Middleton and I codirected in the summer of 1988. It became an essay in the spring of 1990, when I spent a month at the University of California Humanities Research Institute at Irvine in a group organized by Stephen Nichols. Versions were subsequently delivered to the Southeastern Medieval Association and to the Center for Literary Study at the Hebrew University of Jerusalem. In the course of this history the essay has gone through almost as many changes as the alchemical opus that is its subject. Whatever approximation to gold it may have achieved is due to the ministrations (and skepticism) of many friends, including David Aers, Jon Whitman, and Howard Bloch.

Studies in the Age of Chaucer

Deflection in the Mirror: Feminine Discourse in *The Wife of Bath's Prologue* and *Tale*

Lynne Dickson
Rutgers University

> I hate hym that my vices telleth me,
> And so doo mo, God woot, of us than I.
>
> *The Wife of Bath's Prologue* 662–63[1]

RECENT CRITICISM HAS STUDIED the degree to which Chaucer's Wife of Bath expands beyond the antifeminist tradition from which her character is drawn. For the most part, critics interested in gender concur that Alison of Bath represents a momentary imagining of something other than the prototypical woman of antifeminist satire.[2] In many ways her

---

[1] All citations of Chaucer's works are from Larry D. Benson, gen. ed., *The Riverside Chaucer*, 3d ed. (Boston: Houghton Mifflin, 1987).

[2] Lee Patterson, for example, finds that, "once having achieved maistrye, the Wife abandons it in the interest of a larger purpose, whether it be marital harmony or the pleasure of the reader. As a wife she withdraws into gentle submission; as a speaker she replaces the complex self-promotions of her *Prologue* with a *Tale* that offers itself as pure entertainment"; Lee Patterson, "'For the Wyves Love of Bathe': Feminine Rhetoric and Poetic Resolution in the *Roman de la Rose* and the *Canterbury Tales*," *Speculum* 58 (1983): 680. Similarly, Barbara Gottfried finds that, "even as she attempts a deconstruction of patriarchal literature in an experiential revision of it, the Wife necessarily falls short of the goal of overcoming authority because she can define herself only in relation to that authority"; Barbara Gottfried, "Conflict and Relationship, Sovereignty and Survival: Parables of Power in the *Wife of Bath's Prologue*," *ChauR* 19 (1985): 202–24. Other recent studies that concern the construction of the Wife of Bath are Elaine Tuttle Hansen, "The Wife of Bath and the Mark of Adam," *Women's Studies* 15 (1988): 399–416; Jill Mann, *Geoffrey Chaucer*, Feminist Reading Series (Atlantic Highlands, N.J.: Humanities Press International, 1991); Priscilla Martin, *Chaucer's Women: Nuns,*

character emerges as something beyond the terrifyingly reductive under-standing of woman as oversexed harpy. Yet these critical studies also find that, much as her character may (consciously or unconsciously) complicate, challenge, or subvert the pat notions of this clerical tradition, Alison of Bath is ultimately returned to and remains an affirmation (albeit a trou-bling one) of the antifeminist *topos*.[3] It is, however, that which transpires before this "return," the not-so-affirmative and highly digressive narrative before she reaches the "happily ever afters" of both her *Prologue* and *Tale*, that provides the ground to see, or at least to see gestures toward, a notion of the feminine that problematizes the demarcations of the antifeminist type.

This article concludes that both Wife of Bath texts challenge the mis-ogyny of the patristic tradition known as antifeminism in two complemen-tary ways. First, the *Prologue* and *Tale* work to disrupt any purely masculine or paternalistic response to antifeminism that a reader may have. By juxtaposing and layering both feminine and masculine responses to this misogynist discourse, the texts expose the inadequacies of a purely mas-culine response and ask their readers to respond instead as complex sexual beings. Second, *The Wife of Bath's Prologue* and *Tale* reiterate the tyranny of a purely patriarchal mode of understanding by dramatizing the degree to which Alison's efforts to articulate a feminine position are threatened and constrained by the weight of this culturally sanctioned tradition. Rather than resting at such a critique, however, the texts gesture toward a discursive alternative to patriarchy: a feminine community of readers and speakers.

This feminine community is shadowed in the illusory "wise wyves" to whom Alison appeals in the *Prologue* and is manifested in the community

---

Wives and Amazons (London: Macmillan, 1990), pp. 52–65; Barrie Ruth Straus, "The Subversive Discourse of the Wife of Bath: Phallocentric Discourse and the Imprisonment of Criticism," *ELH* 55 (1988): 527–54.

[3] The strict definition of medieval antifeminism, or antifeminist satire, as Hope Phyllis Weissman has pointed out, "refers to those writings which revenge themselves upon woman's failure to conform to male specifications by presenting her as a nagging bully and an avaricious whore." Weissman correctly extends this definition to include antifeminist images "which celebrate with a precision often subtle rather than apparent, the forms women's goodness is to take"; Hope Phyllis Weissman, "Antifeminism in Chaucer's Characterization of Women," in George D. Economou, ed., *Geoffrey Chaucer* (New York: McGraw-Hill, 1975), p. 93. However, as Alison of Bath is specifically drawn from the literary genre of antifeminist satire, a genre initiated by such writers as St. Jerome, Theophrastus, and Jean de Meun (sources for much of Chaucer's text), it is within the strict definition of antifeminism that I am writing. Katharina Wilson and Elizabeth M. Makowski also provide an excellent study of misogamous literature in *Wykked Wyves and the Woes of Marriage* (New York: SUNY Press, 1990).

of authoritative women in the *Tale*. However, while Chaucer's texts present a persuasive imagining of such a feminine discourse community, ultimately the *Prologue* and *Tale* do not construct this community as a real alternative to patriarchal discourse; rather, the feminine community of readers and speakers is given only illusory and fleeting status. Feminine discourse remains a possibility that the text is willing to admit, but only in imaginary terms; feminine speech is ultimately left unaffirmed, imagined but not actualized. To better understand the dynamics of Chaucer's representation of feminine discourse, how it may or may not have been constrained by the status of actual medieval women's access to literary authority, this article opens with a discussion of and some conjectures about discourse communities of women in the medieval period.

I. Medieval Feminine Discourse: Actual and/or Imaginary

In 1399 Christine de Pizan writes *L'Épistre au Dieu d'Amour* and thus initiates the *querelle des femmes*, a debate over Jean de Meun's antifeminist portrait of women in his section of the *Roman de la Rose*. In so doing, she becomes one of the first women to open a space for women to resist patriarchal discourse, at least in literary terms.[4] While Christine articulates many of her objections to misogyny in the letters and poems that compose the debate, her objections find perhaps their most mature articulation in her *Book of the City of Ladies* (ca. 1405).[5] This book opens with the quasi-

---

[4] Joan Kelly, "Early Feminist Theory and the *Querelle des femmes*, 1400–1789," *Signs* 8 (1982): 11. Christine's *Épistre au Dieu d'Amour* provoked the series of letters and poems known as the *querelle de la rose*. As Kelly points out, this minor debate was the foundation for the *querelle des femmes* which lasted for centuries; ibid., pp. 10–11. I would only add to Kelly's point that women were not the only ones who took offense at antifeminist discourse. Christine, for example, managed to enlist the support of Jean Gerson, chancellor of the University of Paris, in the *querelle*. In this sense, rather than simply asserting that Christine opened a space for women, perhaps we should define gender more broadly, finding that she opened a space for a feminine voice to resist antifeminist thinking.

[5] Susan Schibanoff argues for Christine's progress "from immasculated reader to woman reader" over the course of her works beginning in 1399; "Taking the Gold Out of Egypt: The Art of Reading as a Woman," in Elizabeth Flynn and Patrocinio Schweickart, eds., *Gender and Reading: Essays on Readers, Texts, and Contexts* (Baltimore, Md.: Johns Hopkins University Press, 1986), p. 100. Kevin Brownlee also argues for Christine's authorial development in *RR* 79 (1988): 199–221. For more on Christine see Sylvia Huot, "Seduction and Sublimation: Christine de Pizan, Jean de Meun, and Dante," *RomN* 25 (1985): 361–73; Glenda McLeod, *Virtue and Venom: Catalogs of Women from Antiquity to the Renaissance* (Ann Arbor: University of Michigan Press, 1991), pp. 111–39; Maureen Quilligan, "Allegory and the Textual Body: Female Authority in Christine de Pizan's *Livre de la cité des dames*," *RR*

autobiographical narrator, Christine, who, after reading Matheolous's popular antifeminist *Lamentations*, finds herself dejected and overwhelmed. Matheolous's text prompts Christine to wonder whether so many men can be right about the evil of women:

They [antifeminists] all concur in one conclusion: that the behavior of women is inclined to and full of every vice. Thinking deeply about these matters, I began to examine my character and conduct as a natural woman and, similarly, I considered other women whose company I frequently kept, princesses, great ladies, women of the middle and lower classes, who had graciously told me of their most private and intimate thoughts, hoping that I could judge impartially and in good conscience whether the testimony of so many notable men could be true.[6]

Here Christine's text indicates that antifeminism was a matter of concern not only to herself but also to the medieval women with whom she habitually kept company. Yet, despite her sense that the women she knows do not match the image drawn in antifeminist texts, Christine concludes:

It would be impossible that so many famous men . . . could have spoken falsely on so many occasions. . . . This reason alone, in short, made me conclude that although my intellect did not perceive my own great faults and, likewise, those of other women because of its simpleness and ignorance, it was however truly fitting that such was the case. . . . And I finally decided that God formed a vile creature when He made a woman.[7]

In this passage Christine illustrates how the myths of patriarchy become internalized by the feminine subject, despite what her experience has shown. The narrator's dejection, moreover, is so oppressive that it can be alleviated only by the appearance of the three visionary ladies: Reason, Rectitude, and Justice. These visionary women explain to Christine that the antifeminist portraits of women are not drawn by an objective hand but rather are produced by a biased male subjectivity. Christine's text thus

---

79 (1988): 222–48; Karen Sullivan, "At the Limit of Feminist Theory: An Architectonics of the Querelle de la Rose," *Exemplaria* 3 (1991): 435–66; Earl Jeffrey Richards, Nadia Margolis, and Christine Reno, eds., *Reinterpreting Christine de Pizan* (Athens and London: University of Georgia Press, 1992).

[6] Christine de Pizan, *The Book of the City of Ladies*, trans. Earl Jeffrey Richards (New York: Persea Books, 1982), p. 4.

[7] Ibid., pp. 4–5.

undermines the authoritative stance of misogynist discourse and presents a productive counter-discourse to misogyny.

Tellingly, Reason also presents Christine with a mirror, offering her a more positive self-image. Christine, in turn, extends a similar mirror of feminine virtue to her readers; this mirror is her *Book of the City of Ladies* — the first history of women.[8] Throughout this book medieval women could find representations of the feminine that resisted the definition that discourses like antifeminism would thrust on them. Despite the frequent Griselda-like features of the women in the terrain of her text, Christine authorizes women, as well as women's discourse.[9] The very production of her book, however, written about women and addressed to women, constitutes one of her most significant validations of women and feminine discourse communities. Certainly the discourse community she initiated has been a significant one; those who argued on the women's side of the *querelle des femmes* of 1400 to 1789 heralded Christine as the founder of their debate and garnered much of their force from her writing. Finally, then, Christine's role as a historical literary figure is perhaps best emblematized in the now-familiar image of her presenting her book to Queene Isabeau — a presentation she makes not only to the queen but also to the circle of women in the court, a circle that extends to and embraces women of future generations.

Yet, while Christine has been located as one of the first literary defenders of women, one wonders whether women's resistance to patriarchal discourse was registered elsewhere in medieval culture. Given that Christine kept company with and presented her book to other women, it seems only logical to suppose that some other medieval women took umbrage at the production of misogynist discourse. Surely some medieval women were frustrated by their exclusion from centers of learning and literacy, particularly when such alienation in an increasingly literate and nation-state–centered culture would mean alienation from the production of power.

Indeed, thirteenth- and fourteenth-century women appear to have had less power than those of preceding centuries. The dominance of universities as centers of learning led to a decline in the education of women.[10] This

[8] Quilligan, "Allegory and the Textual Body," p. 223.

[9] Something should be said about the critical controversy surrounding Christine's text; while some criticize how she ultimately affirms women's subservience, others are currently discussing how Christine emerges as a feminist thinker within the confines of her cultural moment. See citations in n. 4 above.

[10] Patricia H. Labalme, ed., *Beyond Their Sex: Learned Women of the European Past* (New York: New York University Press, 1984), p. 17. Angela Lucas also provides a useful discussion of medieval women and letters in part 3 of her *Women in the Middle Ages: Religion, Marriage, and Letters* (New York: St. Martin's, 1983), pp. 137–79.

decline was exacerbated by a corresponding reduction in the quality of education to be found in medieval nunneries.[11] The Salic Law of 1329, a law that prohibited women from inheriting the French throne, is symbolic of the diminished legal and ideological power of medieval women. Generally, in previous centuries women had enjoyed the maintenance of their feudal estates after their husband's deaths or in their absence, but by the twelfth century "public power was gradually being recaptured from the great aristocratic families by kings and princes."[12] The aristocracy adjusted readily to the centralization of power by maintaining itself through patrimony; such adjustments, though, were clearly at the expense of aristocratic women. The rise in misogynist texts in the period is surely a partial consequence of the perceived patriarchal need to exclude women from economic power.[13]

One of the more interesting developments that paralleled women's reduced power and learning was an alteration in the representation of the Virgin Mary. While Mary had long been represented spinning or weaving, beginning in the first half of the thirteenth century, the attributes of study, lecture, and the book were increasingly attached to this female icon. This depiction of Mary found its authority in the legendary tradition that at the moment of the Annunciation she was reading passages from Hebrew scripture, but the notion of a literate Mary also seems to correspond to a renewed female desire for literacy. As one critic notes, the shift from the

Virgin as spinner to the Virgin as reader. . . coincides with the introduction of the universities which excluded women from their doors. Women, therefore, with images, created a subliminal and subversive iconography of disobedience, an iconography honoring themselves as participants in the forbidden learning.[14]

[11] Eileen Power remains the authority on the lives of medieval nuns. For her analysis of education in convents see *Medieval English Nunneries* (Cambridge: Cambridge University Press, 1922), pp. 237–83. Power concludes that "the majority of nuns during this period [fourteenth and fifteenth centuries] knew no Latin"; ibid., p. 246. "In the fifteenth and sixteenth centuries the Bishops almost invariably sent their injunctions to the nuns in English"; ibid., p. 247. For an abbreviated version of Power's discussion, see the collection of her notes in *Medieval Women*, ed. M. M. Postan (Cambridge: Cambridge University Press, 1975), pp. 89–100.

[12] Jo Ann McNamara and Suzanne Wemple, "The Power of Women Through the Family in Medieval Europe, 500–1100," in Mary Erler and Maryanne Kowaleski, eds., *Women and Power in the Middle Ages* (Athens: University of Georgia Press, 1988), p. 96.

[13] Ibid., pp. 96–97.

[14] Julia Bolton Holloway, Constance S. Wright, and Joan Bechtold, eds., *Equally in God's Image: Women in the Middle Ages* (New York: Peter Lang, 1990), pp. 47, 55. While articles

In addition to this shift in the representation of the Virgin Mary, medieval women's desire for literacy and access to learning is articulated in their tenacious hold on the reading and preaching figure of Mary Magdalene.[15]

The reading female icon can often be found in books of hours and psalters of the period, many of which were owned by women. As Susan Groag Bell's "Medieval Woman Book Owners" has demonstrated, laywomen in the medieval period "frequently bought and inherited religious as well as secular books."[16] Scholars have noted, moreover, a distinct rise in documented ownership of books by women of the fourteenth and fifteenth centuries, the very moment in which women's public power was in decline. In addition to images of a reading Mary, these books often contained illuminations that featured the female reader-owner as central.[17] I find it highly suggestive that medieval women commissioned books in which they were depicted reading. Such illustrations, while perhaps a reflection of the actual reading habits of these women, are also evocative of

---

in this book are signed, the introduction and linking sections are unsigned; I have chosen, therefore, to cite the book's title rather than the editors when I refer to a linking section. The notion of the book holding Mary as a code for female literacy is also implied in Sibylle Harksen, *Women in the Middle Ages*, trans. Marianne Herzfeld (New York: Abner Schram, 1975). In her description of plate 63, *The Virgin from a Representation of the Annunciation*, Harksen writes, "The woman of the fourteenth century, anxious for some erudition, is symbolized here by the Virgin reading a book." For various images of the Virgin with books see ibid., plates 22a, 42, 63, 73, 77, 108. Susan Groag Bell also notes the rise in depictions of Mary as an avid reader in her excellent article "Medieval Women Book Owners: Arbiters of Lay Piety and Ambassadors of Culture," in Erler and Kowaleski, eds., *Women and Power in the Middle Ages*; originally printed in *Signs* 7 (1982): 168.

[15] *Equally in God's Image*, p. 5. Given the confines of this article, I do not take up the subtleties of meaning surrounding the oddity that a feminine desire for literary access gets coded into a devotional icon sanctioned by the church. This notion certainly merits further consideration; for now I simply quote Bell's reasoning that, "because women's public participation in spiritual life was not welcomed by the hierarchical male establishment, a close involvement with religious devotional literature, inoffensive because of its privacy, took on a greater importance for women"; Bell, "Medieval Women Book Owners," p. 160. In this sense women's association with devotional literature, and coding a desire for greater access to literate culture into a religious icon, fits into a general narrative of resisting patriarchal hegemony.

[16] As Bell explains, about 75 percent of books owned by medieval women were religious in nature, and 60 percent of the books owned by women were religious and in the vernacular; "Medieval Women Book Owners," p. 160. The opening section of my article is deeply indebted to Bell's work. I would add to her findings, however, that, while ownership of books implies literacy, it does not necessarily prove it. Without regressing into the notion that women in the medieval period were neither sophisticated readers nor writers, I would simply suggest that the desire to own illuminated books may suggest a cultural desire for female literacy rather than (or in addition to) being proof of it.

[17] *Equally in God's Image*, p. 20; Bell, "Medieval Women Book Owners," p. 168.

their need to construct the image of a reading self.[18] The reduplication of a literate self may suggest reality, but also can be the figure of a desired reality—literary access, and perhaps a community of feminine readers.

Certainly efforts to maintain and create a community of feminine readers are implicit in the documented passing of books between women—most generally mother to daughter. Mothers often left books to daughters in their wills; books also tended to be included in a young bride's trousseau.[19] Such woman-to-woman transmission of books suggests a feminine investment in passing literacy along, of maintaining a community of women readers.[20] Bell cites the moving example of a Dutch book of hours inscribed with the names of six generations of women; such a manuscript surely conveyed great symbolic value to its recipient.[21] It is crucial to note that, while most of the books owned by women were devotional, their content varied richly, and they spoke to medieval women's lives in a variety of ways ranging from daily tasks to devotional aspirations.[22] Illuminations, in particular, coded feminine experience into these devotional books.

For the purposes of the argument I am developing, one of the most fascinating female-owned manuscripts is the Psalter of the Countess of Leicester. In one of the illuminations in this Psalter, St. Anne teaches the Virgin Mary to read (fig. 1). Roughly dated at 1300, this English illumination puts in sharp focus the desire for a transmission of written authority between medieval women. In fig. 1, St. Anne holds her cloak open both to reveal and to shelter her daughter as she looks at the alphabet book. This pose registers the female need to be sheltered in the quest for the rudiments of literacy and, furthermore, that the protection of learning is handed down from one female generation to the next. The womblike position of Mary, drawn as the mirror image of St. Anne in miniature, seems to underscore the mother-daughter transmission of the text. St. Anne, moreover, does not instruct Mary with a text that is already written (and thus already inscribed by a patriarchal culture) but rather gives her an alphabet book—a building block to form her own text. This image, then, might be taken as a paradigm for a female community of readers. The geometric

---

[18] Bell asserts, for example, that the image of the Virgin Mary "as a constant reader was surely based on the reality of their patron's lives"; "Medieval Women Book Owners," p. 173.

[19] Ibid., pp. 156–57; Power, *Medieval Women*, p. 85.

[20] Even if such reading was generally done by a woman alone in silent devotion, it presented her with an alternative to the monolithic interpretations of her husband, her father, or the church.

[21] Bell, "Medieval Women Book Owners," p. 157.

[22] Ibid., p. 161.

Fig. 1. Saint Anne teaching the Virgin, who is holding an alphabet book, to read. English, ca. 1300. *Psalter*, Bodleian Library, Oxford, MS Douce 231, fol. 3. Courtesy of the Bodleian Library, Oxford.

patterns that begin in the pages of the book and repeat on the interior of St. Anne's cloak and again beside and behind her are conventionally gothic, yet together they form a figural pattern for a desire to repeat the scene at the center of the image.

The pattern for the repetition and expansion of women sharing access to literacy would find yet another dimension when the Countess of Leicester held the book in her hands. Thus, while Christine's work is most surely seminal in women's investigation and redefinition of antifeminism, I want to add that the period also offers artifacts that register a similar desire for women's access to literature and for a discourse community of women. As I move on to Chaucer's Wife of Bath, a fictional figure who, like Christine, takes on antifeminism, I consider how Chaucer's texts register and / or resist the apparent desire among medieval women for a community of female readers and listeners.

II. Alison and Audiences

In the section above I argued that the notion of a feminine discourse community appears to have occupied the imagination of at least some medieval women and, I would add, perhaps some medieval men as well.[23] Entering the debate on Christine's side, Jean Gerson contributed his *Traité against the Roman de la Rose*, a letter to Pierre Col, and three sermons.[24] Furthermore, the many sculptures of Mary with a book in her hands or the illuminations of women reading might certainly have come from a man's pen or chisel. As I argue in this section, Chaucer is perhaps the best example that the medieval period offers of a man invested in revising and

[23] In the opening, historical section of this article I use the expedient biological terms male and female. In the rest of the article I adopt the terms masculine and feminine to signify the culturally constructed nature of gender identity — identity of which Chaucer's texts seem to be acutely aware. My specific use of the phrase "masculine discourse," moreover, means those monolithic and culturally sanctioned discourses expressive of patriarchal desires (such as antifeminism). By "feminine discourse" I mean those discourses that are plural, open, and placed in opposition to masculine (patriarchal) hegemony. I hope that it is adequately clear from my discussion that both men and women participate in the production of feminine and masculine discourses. In my discussion of Jean de Meun, I occasionally use more essentialist terms to signal his complicity with such structures.

[24] For a convenient translation of the documents in the debate see Joseph L. Baird and John R. Kane, eds., *La Querelle de la Rose: Letters and Documents* (Chapel Hill: North Carolina Studies in the Romance Languages and Literatures, 1978).

resisting antifeminist discourse.[25] His text, like Christine's some ten years later, partly opens a space for feminine discourse. The Wife herself, as critics have noted, is a speaking subject who mimics and thus partly destabilizes antifeminist discourse. Through the persona of the Wife, and in the textual call for a complex gendered response from the reader, Chaucer asks his audience not only to rethink antifeminism but also to reconsider the sorts of dichotomized and essentialist notions of gender upon which discourses like antifeminism rely.

Perhaps it is best to begin with the antifeminist text represented so clearly in the Wife's *Prologue*: Jankyn's "book of wikked wyves." In this text, Alison tells us, "...ye fynde / That womman was the los of al mankynde" (*WBP* 719–20), a truism the book demonstrates by a series of examples of "wikked" women that range from Eve to Clytemnestra. We are told that Jankyn would bring out this book in an effort to control his older, boisterous wife. He would "lough alwey ful faste" (line 672) as he read in this book. His laughter, of course, would be shared by the masculine audience, which would very likely be delighted to recognize the sources from which Jankyn's book is drawn (largely Valerius, Theophrastus, and St. Jerome). Yet the *Prologue* does not rest at dramatizing the masculine relationship to the antifeminist *topos*; rather, Chaucer's text also exhibits the feminine response to such discourse. Alison says, "Who wolde wene, or who wolde suppose, / The wo that in myn herte was, and pyne?" (lines 786–87). These lines suggest a textual recognition that, while antifeminist satire is used by men and enjoyed by men, it torments the female reader or listener. At such moments masculine jocularity becomes a fully inappropriate response, and the text seems to demand a feminine-identified response from its reader audience.

The complexities of gender identity are, in fact, scripted into *The Wife of Bath's Prologue* and *Tale* from the outset. In the most basic of terms, Chaucer's male-authored text presents a compelling feminine speaker (a speaker whose gendered voice seems so authentic that too frequently she is

[25] My line of thinking in this section has been greatly advanced by the work of Carolyn Dinshaw, *Chaucer's Sexual Poetics* (Madison: University of Wisconsin Press, 1989), esp. pp. 3–27, 113–31, who notes "the suppleness of Chaucer's ideas of gendered poetics" and finds, moreover, that Chaucer positions himself as feminine and thus makes "extraordinary and difficult attempts to envision fully the place of the Other in patriarchal society—to imagine even the pleasures and pains of a woman's body" (p. 10). As Dinshaw notes a bit later, "...women can and do read like men, and—perhaps more importantly—men don't have to read like men" (p. 12).

treated more like a real person than a fictional construct). This feminine speaker, moreover, respeaks the patently patriarchal discourse of antifeminism. Chaucer ventriloquizes antifeminism through Alison; this gendered complexity raises the question whether the Wife, in a powerful profeminist gesture, takes on and parodies a patriarchal voice or whether she is simply revealed as the very object of a discourse she can only attempt to master. Critics have argued both, but the best conclusion is probably that Chaucer's text dramatizes the irresolvable antagonism between such constructions of the feminine and the female subject.

For whom, then, does Chaucer present this gendered problematic? Recent Chaucer criticism has studied (albeit inconclusively) his historical audience. Analyses in the "Symposium on Chaucer's Audience" in the *Chaucer Review* in 1983 range from Richard Firth Green's considerations of the number of women in a courtly audience (surprisingly few) to R. T. Lenaghan's study of specific readers of Chaucer's poetry and how poetic jocularity establishes a masculine fellowship that overcomes social hierarchy. Susan Schibanoff, however, presents one of the most productive interpretations of Chaucer's audience in her analysis of the Ellesmere and Egerton manuscript glosses. Generally, she argues that in the Ellesmere glossator we find someone open to the "new" (private) reader whom Chaucer endorses, a figure, Schibanoff argues, manifested most clearly in the Wife of Bath. Equally significant is how the Egerton glossator's angry marginalia register resistance to the sort of feminized reading the Wife represents; such marginalia document the threat that the notion of a feminine discourse community presented to patriarchal hierarchies.[26]

In addition to considering the conflicting responses of Chaucer's historical audience, the Chaucer critic must also contend with the labyrinth of internal audiences that the text presents; the host, the pilgrims and the implied readers (both masculine and feminine) scripted into the text all

---

[26] As Susan Schibanoff writes: "In the Egerton glossator's struggle with the Wife to control scriptural text, there is evidence of the late-medieval conflict over whether interpretation of 'auctoritee' would remain in the hands of the clergy or pass, as it later did, into the hands of the laity. It is also important to realize, however, that the Egerton glossator's opposition to new reading of Scripture would include vigorous resistance to female textuality. We have only recently begun to understand that one of the particular threats of translation and hence "laicization" of Scripture was that it would make the text accessible to female readers"; "The New Reader and Female Textuality in Two Early Commentaries on Chaucer," *SAC* 10 (1988): 105. This is surely connected to how the feminine desire for literary authority was registered in the figure of Mary with the book and the illuminations of women reading in books of hours and psalters.

insist on a plurality of possible responses.[27] This, taken in conjunction with the text's equally kaleidoscopic layering of speakers, presents a *mise en abîme* effect in which both speaker and audience are constructed as multiple, conflicted, and indeterminate entities.[28] The gendered layering in the categories of speaker and spoken-to arguably establishes a textual desire to resist the sort of overdetermined bifurcation of gender that discourses like antifeminism present.

Consider the effect of Alison respeaking the commonplaces of antifeminism in section 2 of her *Prologue*.[29] From the perspective of the clerical audience, the Wife's ventriloquism would elicit laughter because she closely resembles the "wikked wyves" etched in that very discourse (though this laughter would perhaps border on nervousness, given Alison's ability to bend patristic texts to her meaning). However, the effect on this constructed masculine audience could also be one of guilt as Alison for over fifty lines sustains an accusatory "Thou saist" that seems directed more at those laughing listeners than at her three old (and dead) husbands. A few lines of this harangue are worth quoting (lines 248–57):

> Thou seist to me it is a greet meschief
> To wedde a povre womman, for costage;
> And if that she be riche, of heigh parage,
> Thanne seistow that it is a tormentrie
> To soffre hire pride and hire malencolie.
> And if that she be fair, thou verray knave,
> Thou seyst that every holour wol hire have;
> She may no while in chastitee abyde,
> That is assailled upon ech a syde.
>   Thou seyst som folk desiren us for richesse, ...

---

[27] See Paul Strohm, "Chaucer's Audience(s): Fictional, Implied, Intended, Actual," *ChauR* 18 (1983): 137–45.

[28] Hansen has been very useful to my thinking here. As she writes, ". . . the form of the *Canterbury Tales* (as 'pluralized discourse') may seem to undermine a masculine teleology and even suggest the open-ended plural, anti-authoritarian, 'irrational' qualities of what in the late twentieth century has been called *ecriture feminine*"; "The Wife of Bath and the Mark of Adam," p. 413.

[29] It seems standard by now to divide this text into three distinct sections. In section 1 the Wife discusses virginity and marriage and takes on the ranks of ecclesiastical authorities. Section 2 focuses on her three good, old husbands, and in it Alison respeaks the commonplaces of antifeminism. In section 3 Alison tells of her fourth and fifth husbands, the fifth being Jankyn.

Although Alison claims that these words are what she would say to her old husbands, her anaphora has the effect of pointing an incriminating finger at its masculine listeners; the audience cannot help but feel indicted.[30]

The text also complicates a pat masculine response when Alison discloses that her Dame taught her to feign that Jankyn had enchanted her in order to persuade him to marry her. The Wife adds: ". . . I folwed ay my dames loore, / As wel of this as of othere thynges moore" (lines 583–84). This reference would, from the masculine listener, again elicit laughter. Alison's literary Dame, after all, is La Vieille from Jean's *Roman de la Rose*, and the advice Alison tells of is plucked directly out of his text. Yet the text simultaneously offers that, if clerks are in some sort of masculine coterie of readers, a feminine discourse community is also implied when Alison says she was taught by her Dame. Again, the text complicates a pat masculine response and seems to ask its reader to consider events from multiple-gendered positions.

It is important at this point to note that, despite the early appeals to the masculine "Lordynges" and "Sire," as well as Alison's attention to her clerical audience, the Wife specifically appeals to a feminine auditor at several moments in the text: "Now herkneth hou I baar me proprely, / Ye wise wyves, that kan understonde" (lines 224–25). Alison also tells of a community of women with whom she converses—her "gossib," Alisoun; her niece; and another worthy wife. The feminine voice of the text, then, appeals to an apparently absent feminine discourse community.[31] In such moments the text seems to ask its masculine audience to listen from a feminized perspective.

Perhaps the most important episode that elicits a pluralistic-gendered response comes between Alison and the Pardoner. Earlier in her *Prologue* Alison is, rather freely, glossing the texts of the Apostle Paul; in the middle of such glossing, the Pardoner breaks into her monologue (lines 160–65):

[30] Through the figure of Alison the text seems to register that her speech cannot truly be accepted by masculine listeners. As Patterson notes, the text's understanding of masculine listening is articulated in the version of the story of Midas that appears in *The Wife of Bath's Tale*. The Wife's rendering of the Midas story "argues that men, their listening, obstructed by the carnality symbolized by their ass's ears, will naturally prefer the immediate self-gratifications of antifeminism to the severer pleasures of self-knowledge"; "'For the Wyves Love of Bathe,'" p. 657.

[31] The "wise wyf" community would potentially be manifest in the few other women on the pilgrimage, the Prioress and the Nun. As Power has discussed, widows and wives in difficult circumstances often entered into nunneries; *Medieval English Nunneries*, pp. 38–41. However, the fact that neither the Prioress nor the Nun responds directly to Alison's discourse suggests that she is the only "wise wyf" on the pilgrimage.

"Right thus the Apostel tolde it unto me,
And bad oure housbondes for to love us weel.
Al this sentence me liketh every deel" —
    Up stirte the Pardoner, and that anon;
"Now, dame," quod he, "by God and by Seint John!
Ye been a noble prechour in this cas."

In this moment we can read the Pardoner as sarcastically breaking into Alison's discourse, suggesting that her "noble preaching" is inappropriate for a feminine speaker. The term "noble," a word that certainly does not describe Alison's estate, perhaps underscores that she has crossed the appropriate boundaries of feminine discourse. Further, because the Pardoner comfortably calls on the very sort of ecclesiastical authorities (God and St. John) that Alison is striving to reinterpret from a feminine perspective, and because he effectively redirects her speech, we could say that his interruption dramatizes the impact of a masculine presence on a feminine speech act. Indeed, after the interruption Alison no longer "confronts the ranks of biblical and ecclesiastical authorities"[32] but rather shifts to ventriloquize antifeminist satire. This episode, however, simultaneously demands another possible perspective. For Lee Patterson, for example, the Pardoner's description of the Wife as a "noble prechour" signals that he responds to Alison as "both professional colleague and sexual challenge."[33] We are presented, then, with the compelling image of a collegial relationship between the Pardoner, a figure whose sexuality, as Carolyn Dinshaw has argued, escapes the "clear and straightforward gender categories of masculine and feminine," and Alison, a figure who resists the overdetermined notion of the feminine constructed by antifeminist discourse.[34] The symmetry between these figures rests on the fact that they both resist any clear male-female definition, and this mutual resistance is crucial to understanding how the two figures interact. The text, then, repeatedly reveals the inadequacy of the strict male-female dichotomy articulated in *topoi*-like antifeminism; it is inadequate because the production of the text's meaning is contingent on the audience's ability to adopt both masculine and

---

[32] R. W. Hanning, "Roasting a Friar, Mis-taking a Wife, and Other Acts of Textual Harassment in Chaucer's *Canterbury Tales*," *SAC* 7 (1985): 16; Hanning describes the various sections of the *Prologue*.

[33] Patterson, "'For the Wyves Love of Bathe,'" p. 678.

[34] The Pardoner's sexuality has been the subject of critical controversy for some time. For an excellent discussion of how the Pardoner resists the heterosexual terms of gender identification, see Dinshaw, *Chaucer's Sexual Poetics*, chap. 6.

feminine perspectives. *The Wife of Bath's Prologue* offers a kaleidoscope of gender possibilities that critiques the essentializing and generalizing that so characteristically surround the feminine but that also define the masculine.[35]

III. The Omnipresence of Patriarchy

It has become a critical commonplace to note that through Alison we are led to understand that the overdetermined, antifeminist stereotype of woman is a masculine construct. As she states (lines 688–92):

> . . . it is an impossible
> That any clerk wol speke good of wyves,
> But if it be of hooly seintes lyves,
> Ne of noon oother womman never the mo.
> Who peyntede the leon, tel me who?

The text here recognizes that the negative, derogatory things said about women are formulated by a masculine clergy. Alison's question, "Who peyntede the leon?" specifically points out that the very way in which the feminine gets "peyntede" is a matter of perspective. This recognition is reiterated in her later suggestion that aged clerks condemn women as unfaithful only because they're too old to enjoy sex (line 707). Such an assertion locates misogyny in the subjectivity of impotent clerks and thus further discredits the notion of antifeminism as objective "truth."

Yet, despite how such moves welcome a more subjective sexual response by exposing that seemingly monolithic discourse is also merely subjective, Chaucer's text also dramatizes how Alison's discourse is still inevitably constrained and delimited by the omnipresence of these monolithic and patriarchal modes of understanding. Despite her character's ability to articulate the subjective nature of patriarchy, it remains an inescapable and shaping presence for Alison. From the beginning of her *Prologue* the Wife

---

[35] Hansen's recent work has been indispensable to my thinking in this regard. In "The Wife of Bath and the Mark of Adam" she wisely discusses the negation of the Wife in the text and finds that "the Wife of Bath and woman's foregrounded difference, a result of gender, gives way to a subground of sameness, as all of the speakers in the poem are constrained by the gender roles, suffer the anxiety of sexual difference, and have (or present) only an unstable sense of "self," riddled with contradiction" (p. 411). Hansen concludes that a feminist reading of Chaucer's text ultimately discloses "the fact that males are also constrained and constituted by gender" (p. 414).

is shown to be highly conscious of her masculine audience. She often addresses "lordynges" and "sires"; also, the very frequency of her verbal addresses to "yow" suggests that Alison tailors her speech to accommodate her listeners. The number of questions Alison directs to the reader-listeners in this section further suggests an acute awareness of her audience (lines 59–62):

> Wher can ye seye, in any manere age,
> That hye God defended mariage
> By expres word? I pray yow, telleth me.
> Or where comanded he virginitee?

These questions are open to various responses from variously identified listeners but specifically call on patristic listeners to substantiate their antifeminist claims. While the text may disturb the masculine community by such a call, the question is already answered implicitly by the various antifeminist texts upon which Chaucer draws. It seems fitting, then, that, rather than being an effective rhetorical strategy, these questions run rampant throughout the first section of Alison's *Prologue* and seem to exceed their rhetorical value. Such excess could signal that, as much as Alison may try to put her audience on the defensive, she ultimately exhibits a greater anxiety about their potentially superior knowledge. As suggested above, this anxiety finds its root in the text's ready awareness of its audience beyond the pilgrim listeners: the clerical generators of anti-feminism. As E. T. Hansen has usefully pointed out, part of the difficulty of Alison's speaking situation is that there is no single authority against whom she can argue. Rather, the Wife must

defend herself against a much vaguer force of social disapproval, powerfully un-named and unnameable, and her later attempts to meet specific arguments are self-defeating efforts to pin down and triumph over that generalized, mystifying, and hence invincible hostility that she meets from all sides.[36]

The cumulative effect of the questions suggests the worry of a feminine speaker trying to confront the suffocating omnipresence of patriarchal discourse.

Indeed, Alison repeatedly attempts to confront or disarm her audience, only to expose her anxiety about such confrontations. Her inability to

[36] Ibid., p. 402.

sustain a position against antifeminists is again demonstrated in her carefully worded discussion of the uses of the genitalia (lines 119–24):

> Glose whoso wole, and seye bothe up and doun
> That they were maked for purgacioun
> Of uryne, and oure bothe thynges smale
> Were eek to knowe a femele from a male,
> And for noon oother cause — say ye no?
> The experience woot wel it is noght so.

Alison takes on "whoso wole" say that the genitalia are made only for "office" (for the "purgation of urine" and to distinguish between male and female) and insists that we all know from "experience" that the genitalia have other uses. She hints that they are for sexual pleasure, and, indeed, that is exactly what we expect her to assert (given what we know of her sexual appetite). Yet instead she begins to tailor her utterances to accommodate the ecclesiastical authorities (lines 125–28):

> So that the clerkes be nat with me wrothe,
> I sey this: that they maked ben for bothe;
> That is to seye, for office and for ese
> Of engendrure, ther we nat God displese.

To appease the "clerkes," Alison, rather than asserting that the genitalia are primarily for sexual pleasure, concedes that they are both for "office" (practical employment) and "ese" (pleasure, delight). However, as Barbara Gottfried has discussed, she retreats even from this compromised assertion by determining "ese" in line 128 as "ese / of engendrure," meaning for the use of procreation, sanctioned fornication. In this passage we see that, while Alison began boldly to assert that sex is pleasurable, she cannot, in the context of her speaking situation, articulate that which her experience has proved true.[37] Alison's ability to speak freely is constrained by the presence of her patriarchal audience, as well as the invisible but omnipresent authority of the "clerkes."

The overall momentum of Alison's attack on antifeminism, while at

[37] Gottfried similarly finds that Alison "hedges" in this passage, writing that "she baits her audience and 'the clerkes' by seeming to prepare them for a compromise that will incorporate both the orthodoxy of 'office' and her sure knowledge of 'ese'"; "Conflict and Relationship," p. 210.

times aggressive and persuasive, largely remains shaped by the weighty presence of patriarchal hegemony. The Wife, for example, frequently tries to make an argument against patristic beliefs but ends up retreating into the specifics of her experience. Toward the end of her *Prologue* she descends from respeaking antifeminism to discussing her more painful relationships with her fourth husband and Jankyn. Rather than maintaining her attack, Alison makes the disabling move of showing her vulnerability to her opposition; consider her often-remarked-on lament regarding her age: "The flour is goon; ther is namoore to telle" (line 477). Despite textual signals that Alison tries to control and disempower the antifeminist *topos*, it ultimately overwhelms her. The sheer length of her *Prologue* and the fact that she loses her train of thought six times support the reading that Alison experiences considerable discomfort with her speaking situation. One of the *Prologue*'s strategies, then, seems to be to expose the tyranny of masculine discourse; it oppresses even a figure like Alison. This revelation is complemented by the text's method of hailing its reader as more complicated and open than the oppressively monolithic audience that Alison cannot escape.[38]

IV. Seeking a Community of "Wise Wyves"

A more interesting reaction to Alison's uneasiness with her patriarchal audience (more interesting, that is, than her only moderately successful attempts to disarm her listeners) is her attempt to imagine an alternative speaking situation, a speaking situation in the context of a community of women. The first hint that Alison seeks such a context is her address to "Ye wise wyves" (line 225), a constituency that significantly is not represented by anyone on the pilgrimage other than Alison herself. She says, "Now herkneth hou I baar me proprely, / Ye wise wyves, that kan understonde" (lines 224–25).[39] The Wife's specific use of "wise wyves" would seem to be a

[38] I find the pilgrims, with a few exceptions such as the Pardoner, to be overwhelmingly masculine listeners who are placed in opposition to the more complicated sexual beings hailed by the text as its readers. In an argument similar to mine above, Schibanoff finds that "Chaucer uses his old readers [the pilgrims] to define and highlight the characteristics, from an author's point of view, of new reading"; "The New Reader and Female Textuality," p. 103.

[39] Straus reads this moment in useful, though slightly different, terms. She argues that the Wife's "insertion of addresses to women inside addresses to men exposes the major requirement of phallocentrism — that masculine discourse enclose feminine discourse"; "The Subversive Discourse of the Wife of Bath," p. 530. Straus further finds that, "having undertaken to speak of serious matters, as if a man speaking to men, the Wife speaks as if to women, but still addresses men; thus she crosses the boundaries of public and private in multiple ways, and in a manner that indicts the very distinctions between authority and experience and between masculine and feminine discourses" (p. 533).

rewriting or at least reevaluation of the antifeminist category of "wikked wyves"; the alliteration of the *w*'s creates a verbal echo that suggests a deliberate association between the two phrases. However, the difficulty of such a rewriting and reimagining is also articulated in this passage (lines 224–34):

> Now herkneth hou I baar me proprely,
> Ye wise wyves, that kan understonde.
> Thus shulde ye speke and bere hem wrong on honde,
> For half so boldely kan ther no man
> Swere and lyen, as a womman kan.
> I sey nat this by wyves that been wyse,
> But if it be whan they hem mysavyse.
> A wys wyf, if that she kan hir good,
> Shal beren hym on honde the cow is wood,
> And take witnesse of hir owene mayde
> Of hir assent.

The text quickly blurs the categories of "wise" and "wikked" wives and thus permits only a fleeting image of such a constituency. While the Wife of Bath seems to be imagining a community of women with whom she can speak, within the space of three lines the "wise wyves, that kan understonde" become the prototypical antifeminist stereotype of lying, adulterous women.[40] Furthermore, the Wife of Bath seems to erase her audience of "wise wyves" in the line "I sey nat this by wyves that been wyse," admitting the possibility that "wise wyves" may behave foolishly. In such moments the text suggests that efforts to conceive of an alternative notion of the feminine are largely restricted by the oppressive weight of antifeminism — ironically, the very discourse from which Alison is drawn. Yet still, in applying the epigraph "wise wyves" to this category of women, Alison appends a term to, and thus partly redefines, the antifeminist type. Talkative, aggressive, and sexually charged women are not, to her mind, wicked but rather are wise. One feature of their particular wisdom, moreover, is in getting other women to substantiate what they say; a "wys

[40] This appeal to "wise wyves" is especially interesting given the fact that, as Richard Firth Green has pointed out, there would be few, if any, women in Chaucer's actual audience (provided we accept the theory that the poet would present his work orally at court); "Women in Chaucer's Audience," *ChauR* 18 (1983): 146–53.

wyf" will "take witnesse of hir owene mayde / Of hir assent"; wise women will speak with each other and share a feminine consensus.[41]

In part, the text's efforts to conceive of a productive feminine community of speakers and listeners are contingent on its ability to redefine the feminine as it has been constructed by antifeminist satire. While such redefinition generally remains coded rather than explicit in the text, *The Wife of Bath's Prologue* does disrupt boundaries that traditionally defined the antifeminist type. Such disruption is perhaps figured in the ways Alison does not match the stereotypical figure on which she is modeled. Alison is closely based on La Vieille, the Old Woman in Jean de Meun's antifeminist *Roman de la Rose*, but she does not exactly mirror her literary predecessor. For example, Alison's speaking situation departs significantly from the specifics of La Vieille's monologue.[42] In contradistinction to Chaucer's text, Jean's text obviously delights in a masculine response. Indeed, Jean seems to reward his patriarchal audience with extended jokes about and ammunition against La Vieille. The pleasure of the masculine audience is only increased by the fact that it is La Vieille who, in her endless and explicit comments about how women should enjoy many men, fool all men, and do their best to extract money from men, provides the evidence against herself.

Furthermore, unlike Alison, La Vieille does not dramatize the difficulty of feminine speech in a masculine context. Rather, she is oblivious to how her speech is perceived and discredited by patriarchy:

Then the Old Woman grew quiet and sighed, to hear what he wanted to say, but she delayed hardly at all; for, when she saw that he was being careful to listen to her and remain quiet, she took up her subject again, thinking, "Whoever says nothing agrees to everything. Since he is pleased to hear all that I say, I can say everything without fear."[43]

[41] Frequently Alison proudly claims the very traits of the antifeminist type, traits that ecclesiastical authorities condemn as female faults. She has been "the whippe" in her marriages (*WBP* 175) and boasts that no man can "swere and lyen as a womman can" (line 228); again the wise wife is connected with the forceful use of language, even if transgressive. In gesturing toward a community of "wise wyves," Alison, in part, celebrates the very qualities that antifeminists denounce as vices.

[42] One clear connection between La Vieille and Alison, for example, would be La Vieille's assertion that "I know everything by practice. Experiments, which I have followed my whole life, have made me wise in love"; Jean de Meun, *The Romance of the Rose*, trans. Charles Dahlberg (Princeton, N.J.: Princeton University Press, 1971), p. 222. All quotations from the *Roman* are from this translation.

[43] Ibid., p. 225.

La Vieille assumes that her listener's silence indicates complete agreement. Jean's text thus has a good laugh at the old woman's expense; she is too naïve and too foolish to recognize how she would sound to a patriarchal audience — an audience partly figured in the relationship between Bel Acueil or Fair Welcoming, and the Lover-narrator.[44] If Jean's masculine reader has failed to laugh at La Vieille's foolishness here, the next line, in which Bel Acueil tells the narrator how he viewed La Vieille as she spoke, dramatizes and thus ensures the desired response; he says, "Then she began her babbling again and spoke like a false old woman, a serf." Jean's reader is asked not to identify with the experience of the Old Woman but rather to censure her babbling lies.

La Vieille's gestures toward a female audience, moreover, serve only to underscore the antifeminist definition of woman:

A wise woman will gather the fruit of love in the flower of her age. The unhappy woman loses her time who passes it without enjoying love. And if she disbelieves this advice of mine, which I give for the profit of all, be sure she will be sorry when age withers her. But I know that women will believe me, particularly those who are sensible, and will stick to our rules and will say many paternosters for my soul, when I am dead who now teach and comfort them. I know that this lesson will be read in many schools.[45]

Far from suggesting the writer's effort to understand the desires of a feminine other, Jean's presents La Vieille's speech as proof of inevitable and deliberate female inconstancy for his masculine listeners. The passage confirms the antifeminist position that women by definition conspire to be deceitful and whorish. The text, therefore, repeatedly figures forth the threat of feminine speech to masculine order; and generally, like most

---

[44] While Bel Acueil, or Fair Welcoming, is given a masculine gender in the original French, this listener represents a facet of the Lady whose Love (Rose) the Lover-narrator is seeking. Communication between the Lover and Fair Welcoming seems to be aided by their masculine (perhaps homoerotic?) fellowship. Within the confines of this discussion I do not take up the possible gendered complexities of Jean's text — though they merit discussion. It seems that the traditional view of Jean as the bourgeois "rewriter" of the courtly Guillaume de Lorris is undergoing critical reevaluation. Nadia Margolis calls for a reevaluation of Jean, asserting that "more research needs to be done on the extent of Christine's debt to the *Rose*"; "Elegant Closures: The Use of the Diminutive in Christine de Pizan and Jean de Meun," in Earl Jeffrey Richards, ed., with Joan Williamson, Nadia Margolis, and Christine Reno, *Reinterpreting Christine de Pisan* (Athens: University of Georgia Press, 1992), p. 121.

[45] Jean de Meun, *The Romance of the Rose*, trans. Dahlberg, p. 232.

other medieval misogynist discourses, Jean's text defines woman as a "bundle of verbal abuses."[46]

Therefore, although Alison may follow in her literary dame's footsteps in some ways, her character also departs significantly from the character in Jean's text. While Alison may encompass La Vieille's garrulous, oversexed qualities, she argues against antifeminism, dramatizes the problems of speaking as a woman, and appeals to a community of "wise wyves." Thus Alison's character extends beyond the overdetermined figure of La Vieille. It is where the image of Alison does not completely mirror La Vieille's image, where her character distorts the antifeminist type, that we see Chaucer's text gesturing beyond the overdetermined concepts of the feminine found in antifeminist discourse.

Chaucer's text seems to endorse the notion of a discursive alternative to an oppressive patriarchy. Several hundred lines after her "wise wyfe" speech, the Wife discusses her "gossib," Alisoun (line 530). The Wife is particularly interested in recounting how she would speak to Alisoun (lines 531–38):

> She knew myn herte, and eek my privetee,
> Bet than oure parisshe preest, so moot I thee!
> To hire biwreyed I my conseil al.
> For hadde myn housbonde pissed on a wal,
> Or doon a thyng that sholde han cost his lyf,
> To hire, and to another worthy wyf,
> And to my nece, which that I loved weel,
> I wolde han toold his conseil every deel.

The Wife's habit of telling more to her friend Alisoun than to the parish priest indicates that she would say more in a different speaking situation than she is willing or able to in the "confession" that constitutes her *Prologue*.[47] Also, Alison's expansion of the category of her friend Alisoun

---

[46] For an analysis of the intersection between the medieval alignment of the feminine with false language see Howard Bloch, "Medieval Misogyny," *Representations* 20 (Fall 1987): 1–24. Bloch asserts that the "reproach against women is a form of reproach against language itself" (p. 3). "Because of the inadequacies of language she embodies, she is in some fundamental sense, always already a deceiver, trickster, jongleur" (p. 5). It is this view that Jean's text seems to confirm.

[47] Chaucer's text, it is important to note, does not erase the threat of feminine speech to a masculine discourse community. It acknowledges here, for example, that when Alison speaks with other women she betrays her husband.

to include another "worthy wyf" and her "nece" reiterates and underscores the desire for a discourse community of women. One way to understnd the Wife's desire at this point is to see her as trying to duplicate her mirror image, an effort suggested by the very fact that her friend's name, "Alisoun," echoes her own. Furthermore, as Mary Carruthers has demonstrated, "gossib" did not carry the modern definition of a woman who engages in meaningless prattle but rather signified that Dame Alys was the godparent of the Wife of Bath's child.[48] Women listed by Alison in this passage are intimately related or even identical to her (as in "worthy wyf"), suggesting that this community of women is conceived of as some reduplication of the Wife herself.

The doubled conception of these women, of course, points to the disturbing absence of such a community; there are no other speaking, acting wise wives — neither on the pilgrimage nor elsewhere in Alison's *Prologue*. Alison repeatedly tells of events in which, despite her efforts to actualize a community of women, she is the sole actor, a solitary "wise wyf." Generally, whenever the Wife of Bath tries to locate and sustain the notion of an empowered community of women, as indicated by the pronouns "us," "we," or "oure," her effort breaks down. For example, the aggressive "And lat us wyves hoten barly-breed" (line 144) is quickly reduced to a first-person-singular assertion, "I wol persevere; I nam nat precius" (line 148). Alison, it seems, is speaking and acting alone; she can construct a community of "wise wyves" only through playing with mirrors.

The text also asserts the Wife's desire for a community of women when she narrates how she persuaded Jankyn to marry her. She explains that she told Jankyn that he had enchanted her and that this was a trick that her "dame taughte" her, adding, ". . . I folwed ay my dames loore, / As wel of this as of othere thynges moore" (lines 583–84) (suggesting whole discourses — or the desire for whole discourses — that only women are privy to). While "Dame" on the most obvious level probably refers to Alison's mother, it is also interesting to consider that this name may refer to Alison's literary "Dame," La Vieille. The method of manipulating men by feigning enchantment is clearly described by La Vieille in the *Roman*, and thus it is truly La Vieille (a fiction produced by antifeminist satire) who has "taught" Alison this technique.[49] The implied fictionality of Alison's "Dame" sug-

---

[48] See Mary Carruthers, "'Clerk Jankyn at Hom to Bord / with my Gossib,'" *ELN* (March, 1985): 15.

[49] La Dame says that a woman should tell her lord, "I think you must have cast a spell over me; you have sung me a wicked song"; Jean de Meun, *The Romance of the Rose*, trans. Dahlberg, p. 235.

gests that the "loore" to which Alison refers is also only fictional; again, the community of "wise wyves" remains unactualized, illusory, and elusive.[50] The coded reference to La Vieille at this point, moreover, perhaps hints that, despite the appeals Alison makes to feminine discourse, she is always partly defined and thus constrained by her connection to the antifeminist *topos*. While the Wife briefly muses about her "dames loore," she shortly reminds herself that she is currently speaking in a masculine context: "But now, sire, lat me se what I shal seyn" (line 585).

V. What the *Tale* Reflects

The community of "wise wyves" to which Alison's character gestures, then, is a projection of her mirror image forward — a reduplication of the Wife that works to escape the demarcations of the antifeminist type. The mirror production of the self that is not defined by patriarchy in Chaucer's text seems to register much the same desire as those reading selves drawn in the books of hours and psalters owned by medieval women. *The Wife of Bath's Prologue*, along with the above-discussed cultural artifacts, seems to suggest that, owing to the realities of medieval culture, a medieval feminine discourse community was necessarily conceived of as perhaps nothing more than the mirror image of the self.

Surely the actualization of such a community was desired; consider how Alison relishes the possibility of feminine authorship (lines 693–96):

> By God, if wommen hadde writen stories,
> As clerkes han withinne hire oratories,
> They wolde han writen of men moore wikkednesse
> Than al the mark of Adam may redresse.

While in her *Prologue* the Wife can only muse on such a possibility, the *Tale* arguably manifests such feminine discourse. As Susan Crane has demonstrated, the Wife shifts from antifeminist satire, a genre in which

[50] Drawing lines between the fictional and the actual in *The Wife's Prologue* is problematic because Alison herself is not an actual speaking woman but a fictional construct. However, that she specifically locates her behavior in a literary (not actual) past does seem to point to a textual recognition that, to redefine or undefine the feminine, one must imagine something outside the cultural norms, and further points to the difficulty of getting outside culturally constructed thinking.

there is no possibility for women's power, to a modified romance genre.[51] The *Tale* is not a standard romance; it "lacks chivalric or military adventures and features a crucially knowledgeable and capable female character."[52] Generally, it highlights women's power by allowing the courtly ladies (rather than the king) to decide the knight's punishment for raping a young maiden, and thus perhaps fits best into the definition of a romance subgenre, the Breton lay.[53] In terms of the specific interest of this discussion, the shift to the *Tale* is also a shift that allows the Wife again to envision a discourse community of women. While many critics have heretofore viewed the *Tale* as a sort of wish fulfillment for Alison, it seems more accurate to find that it provides a literary context more accommodating to the notion of feminine discursive power — power the Wife conceives of as self-reduplication, distortion of the antifeminist type, and a viable women's audience.

However, such an actualization of feminine power, the *Tale* suggests, requires masculine permission. After Arthur passes a death sentence on the knight, the ladies and the Queen in the *Tale* (*WBT* 895-99)

> So longe preyeden the kyng of grace
> Til he his lyf hym graunted in the place,
> And yaf hym to the queene, al at hir wille,
> To chese wheither she wolde hym save or spille.
>   The queene thanketh the kyng with al hir myght,....

The ladies must plead with the King, and it is only after such a request that they are allowed to do with the knight as they please. Furthermore, the women must thank the King profusely, and it appears that, if they are grateful that the knight's life has been spared, they are equally pleased with the provisional power they will enjoy in deciding his fate. Women, the *Tale*

---

[51] My conception of *The Wife of Bath's Tale* owes a considerable debt to Susan Crane, "Alison's Incapacity and Poetic Instability in the *Wife of Bath's Tale*," *PMLA* 102 (1978): 20–28.

[52] Ibid., p. 23.

[53] Critics variously conceive of the *Tale* as a romance or a lay. Peter Brown and Andrew Butcher find that the *Tale* conforms to the lay definition in three distinct ways: a lay is generally oral; tends to be associated with female authorship, as with Marie de France; and is often used for an inversion of traditional romance values — stressing the feminine point of view in sexual encounters, as well as the foregrounded role of fairies in the genre; *The Age of Saturn: Literature and History in the* Canterbury Tales (Oxford and New York: Basil Blackwell, 1991), p. 546.

reminds us, must always be aware of the patriarchal boundaries circum-scribing their experience.

But permission granted, for the duration of the *Tale*, the text permits Alison to conceive of an empowered female community. Quite early in the *Tale* we are offered a potential image of the reproduction of Alison's mirror self. Notably, the image is offered from the knight-rapist's inadequate perspective (lines 991–99):

> Wher as he saugh upon a daunce go
> Of ladyes foure and twenty, and yet mo;
> Toward the whiche daunce he drow ful yerne,
> In hope that som wysdom sholde he lerne.
> But certeinly, er he cam fully there,
> Vanysshed was this daunce, he nyste where.
> No creature saugh he that bar lyf,
> Save on the grene he saugh sittynge a wyf—
> A fouler wight ther may no man devyse.

If the old hag is a reduplication of Alison of Bath, as signaled by the word "wyf," so are the more than four-and-twenty dancing ladies. This representational moment characterizes the Wife as composed of multiple and conflicting images of the feminine. She is the old hag—foul and wise—as well as the many desirable dancing ladies. D. W. Robertson has argued that, in seeing the dancers absorbed into the hag, "we have not witnessed a magical transformation, no miracle, but simply a shift in point of view."[54] However, as much as this moment may explain how a given viewer sees the Wife and reiterate the subjectivity inherent in gender constructions, it also suggests the possibility of seeing Alison as from a perspective that (unlike the knight-rapist's masculine "either-or") is open to a plural, undetermined representation of the feminine.[55] The representation desire assigned to Alison, a character specifically modeled on a stereotype, articulates a desire to resist the labels assigned by patriarchy.

The notion of gendered plurality enters again at the end of the *Tale* when the knight-rapist, now schooled in feminine desire, is told to choose

---

[54] D. W. Robertson, "The Wife of Bath and Midas," *SAC* 6 (1984): 12.

[55] H. Marshall Leicester reads this moment in terms of how Alison would like to be seen. Leicester finds that Alison is recovering images of her lost youth and that "her memory swirls and dances with all the women she has been until they vanish away . . . and leave her all alone as she has become"; "Of a Fire in the Dark: Public and Private Feminism in the *Wife of Bath's Tale*," *Women's Studies* 11 (1984): 166.

whether the old hag will be foul, old, and faithful or young, beautiful, and potentially unfaithful. He permits the hag to define herself, saying, "I do no fors the wheither of the two" (line 1234). Predictably, the text shows that Alison has the hag opt to be both fair and good—a possibility never articulated in antifeminist satire.[56] According to antifeminist discourse, there are no women who are both fair and true. However, as H. M. Leicester has insightfully noted, magic is required for these transformations to take place.[57] The necessity of magic undercuts this possibility and insists that the Wife's attainment of a community of "wise wyves" and even her very desire to redefine the antifeminist type remain illusory and untenable.

Yet at times the text nearly substantiates such a community. Consider the courtly ladies assembled to decide the knight's fate (lines 1026–29):

> Ful many a noble wyf, and many a mayde,
> And many a wydwe, for that they been wise,
> The queene hirself sittynge as a justice,
> Assembled been, his answere for to heere; . . . .

Alison narrates this moment, and it seems to be the image of women who are both "wise" and "many." The text underscores this image, repeating "many" three times; we are particularly informed that a "wydwe" (like Alison) is wise. Alison, the solitary "wise wyf" who fights to speak in the *Prologue*, seems here to be assembling her own ideal audience. This group of ladies is specifically assembled to hear the old hag's (the Wife's) answer to what women want: "Wommen desiren to have sovereynetee" (line 1038). This feminine response, however, is mediated through the figure of the masculine knight-rapist. Thus the *Tale* recalls the sort of deliberate and gendered layering foregrounded in the *Prologue*. This time, however, the layering is in reverse; here, in a direct reversal of Alison respeaking the commonplaces of antifeminist satire, the knight respeaks the desire for feminine power. Not only is the reader reminded of the gendered complexity of human experience and identity, but the knight is compellingly close to a figure for Chaucer himself, working to respeak the desires of a feminine other.[58]

---

[56] *WBP* 257–75, lines that reproduce the commonplaces of antifeminist satire, argue that ultimately every kind of wife will be untrue.

[57] Leicester, "Of a Fire in the Dark," p. 167.

[58] One is tempted at this point to consider the rape charges brought against Chaucer. A more fruitful discussion of Chaucer and the notion of rape, however, is to be found in Dinshaw, *Chaucer's Sexual Poetics*, introd.

Unlike the *Prologue*, this speech is offered to an audience, the femininity of which the text is at pains to underscore: "...ne was ther wyf, ne mayde, / Ne wydwe that contraried that he sayde" (lines 1043–44). The old hag, in this context, can easily insert herself into the discourse; the feminine community validates the hag's claim and forces the knight to make good on his promise to do the first thing the hag requires of him, which is to marry her. Further, the knight-rapist is turned into the (now somewhat feminized) audience to whom the hag can preach her lengthy curtain lecture. The knight listens quietly to her lecture, and her persuasive redefinition of the terms of "gentillesse" and "poverte" seems analogous to the text's redefinition of the antifeminist type.

Ultimately, though, the duration of the hag's speaking power is only as long as the duration of the courtship. The hag, having been given sovereignty, immediately concedes her power and, as Alison tells us, "obeyed hym in every thyng / That myghte doon hym plesance or likyng" (lines 1255–56).[59] In a strange affirmation of masculine desire, the *Tale* ultimately rewards the concession of masculine "maistrie" with the very thing patriarchy wants to begin with: a passive, nonthreatening female who obeys. The image of the undefined and plural hag who speaks to a receptive audience is abruptly reduced to a disturbingly Griselda-like figure. The text here seems bent on defeating the very possibility of feminine discourse that the *Tale* narrates. And, indeed, as we come to the end of the *Tale*, it is increasingly clear that the *Tale*'s imagining of a feminine discourse community, unlike the pervasiveness of antifeminist satire, is just that: an envisioning of Alison's mirror image that collapses once the mirrored funhouse of feminine power comes to a close.

The image of the plural feminine figure that escapes definition and that speaks to other women, is left as illusory—alluded to, but far from actualized. Alison's closing and cursing rage, then, would seem to be the consequence of the return to the conditions of masculine discourse that ultimately circumscribe the *Tale* (lines 1261–64):

> And eek I praye Jhesu shorte hir lyves
> That noght wol be governed by hir wyves;
> And olde and angry nygardes of dispence,
> God sende hem soone verray pestilence!

[59] This formulation comes from Crane, who writes about the *Tale*, "A heroine's strength lasts only for the temporal and fantastic space that delays her submission and demonstrates the capabilities of her suitor"; "Alison's Incapacity and Poetic Instability," p. 24.

Yet even if the text here dramatizes the harsh return to a masculine context that inevitably constructs not only Alison but Chaucer as well, it is likely that some readers, whether new or old, masculine or feminine identified, could not now hear her diatribe against men as he or she would have before entering the textual complexities inherent in *The Wife of Bath's Prologue* and *Tale*. The reader must hear this outburst with the self-conscious knowledge about his or her masculine and / or feminine modes of reading that the text continually points up. In this sense, while Chaucer may grant the feminine only illusory status, his text perhaps opens a space for feminine discourse to emerge — a space perhaps analogous to the three pages Alison tears from Jankyn's "book of wikked wyves." In the very act of representing a desire for feminine discourse, Chaucer surely helped re-shape feminine experience. Yet still, given the illusory status to which the feminine community is confined in *The Wife of Bath's Prologue* and *Tale*, it seems that those feminine readers and thinkers who sought actual models and modes of feminine discourse (and surely, as those illuminations suggest, there were more than some) would have to wait for Christine to write and hail feminine readers, who, as the *querelle des femmes* testifies, did more than play with mirrors.[60]

[60] This article could not have been written without the intellectual generosity of Susan Crane, who read drafts and commented insightfully on the project through its evolution; I thank her for providing me with the feminine discourse community that I needed to write this article. This article also benefited from a particularly lively discussion of Wife of Bath criticism at the 1992 meeting of the New Chaucer Society. I also thank the two anonymous readers, who were very helpful with later revisions.

The Cock and the Clock:
Telling Time in Chaucer's Day

Linne R. Mooney
University of Maine

The sonne fro the south lyne was descended
So lowe that he nas nat, to my sighte,
Degreës nyne and twenty as in highte.
Foure of the clokke it was tho, as I gesse,
For ellevene foot, or litel moore or lesse,
My shadwe was at thilke tyme, as there
Of swiche feet as my lengthe parted were
In six feet equal of proporcioun.
Therwith the moones exaltacioun—
I meene Libra—alwey gan ascende
As we were entryng at a thropes ende;....

The Parson's Prologue 2–12[1]

W ITH THESE WORDS, in the *Prologue* to *The Parson's Tale*, near
the end of *The Canterbury Tales*, Geoffrey Chaucer emphasizes that it was
four o'clock in the afternoon of a mid-April day, nearing the end of the day
and the end of the pilgrimage, by referring to the time as calculated in
three different manners: by angle (or height) of the sun, by shadow length,
and by position of the zodiac. For us moderns "foure of the clokke," at line
5, is the only reference that immediately connotes time of day. In Chaucer's

---

[1] All citations of Chaucer's works are from Larry D. Benson, gen. ed., *The Riverside
Chaucer*, 3d ed. (Boston: Houghton Mifflin, 1987). For a discussion of the astronomical
reading of these lines, see J. C. Eade, *The Forgotten Sky: A Guide to Astrology in English
Literature* (Oxford: Clarendon Press, 1984), pp. 137–41.

91

time people calculated time of day by a number of methods, depending on their learning, their occupation, or their proximity to time-telling devices. Apparently even those like Chaucer learned in the various methods sometimes found them confusing: Chaucer makes an error in the passage just quoted when he says that Libra is the moon's exaltation; in fact, Taurus is the moon's exaltation, while Libra is Saturn's.[2]

People in the fourteenth century had inherited from the classical world a number of methods for telling time. Through examining two almanacs, or calendars, written by Chaucer's contemporaries and Chaucer's own references to time, I have discovered that many of these methods for telling time were still in use and that at least the two almanac writers and Chaucer were in the habit of citing the time by several methods consecutively, as if to compare them. What is more surprising is the evidence that these writers give of the growing preeminence of clock time among the methods as early as the last quarter of the fourteenth century, when historical and archaeological data suggest that there were still relatively few clocks in England.

The two almanac writers are John Somer and Nicholas of Lynn, who compiled calendars in 1380 and 1386, respectively, to cover the seventy-six years from 1387 to 1462.[3] Their astronomical calendars presented information about times of sunrise and sunset, about conjunctions of sun and moon, and about the height of the sun at midday, as well as other astronomical or astrological data on month-by-month calendars of saints' days and other religious festivals, together with tables of eclipses and other tables of astronomical, astrological, or medical importance. Chaucer was clearly acquainted with these astronomical calendars and their use, since he proposed to include tables from them in the unfinished or now lost Part 3 of his *Treatise on the Astrolabe* (lines 77–86):

The thirde partie shal contene diverse tables of longitudes and latitudes of sterres fixe for the Astrelabie, and tables of the declinacions of the sonne, and tables of longitudes of citees and townes; and tables as well for the governaunce of a clokke,

---

[2] An exaltation is a degree in a sign of the zodiac in which a planet is thought to have its greatest power to influence earthly affairs. The exaltations are as follows: moon, 3 degrees in Taurus; Mercury, 15 degrees in Virgo; Venus, 27 degrees in Pisces; Sun, 19 degrees in Aries; Mars, 28 degrees in Capricorn; Jupiter, 15 degrees in Cancer; Saturn, 21 degrees in Libra; Dragon's Head, 3 degrees in Gemini; and Dragon's Tail, 3 degrees in Sagittarius. See Eade, *Forgotten Sky*, pp. 64–65.

[3] For Nicholas of Lynn's *Kalendarium* see the edition of Sigmund Eisner, The Kalendarium *of Nicholas of Lynn*, Chaucer Library (Athens: University of Georgia Press, 1980).

as for to fynde the altitude meridian; and many anothir notable conclusioun after the kalenders of the reverent clerkes, Frere J. Somer and Frere N. Lenne.

One finds in the calendars evidence of the many different ways one could reckon the time of day — or night — in fourteenth-century England. In the tables incorporated in and accompanying the calendars, the day may variously begin at midnight, at sunrise, at sundown, or at noon of the preceding or stated day. Hours may be variously computed as artificial or common and reckoned in sequences of twelve or twenty-four hours or backward for the hours before noon and forward for those after noon.

The most confusing aspect of time in the calendars, both for us moderns and, apparently, for Chaucer's fourteenth-century audience, is the question, When did the day begin?[4] Chaucer's, Somer's, and Lynn's society had inherited a number of methods for determining this. From Judeo-Christian tradition and from the Roman calendar they had received the method of beginning the day at sunrise. In the Roman calendar we see this method in use in the assigning of planets' or gods' names to the days of the week — Saturn-day, Sun-day, Mon-day — based on the planet thought to govern the first hour of the day, i.e., the first hour after dawn. In Somer's "Kalendarium" we find this method of time telling outlined in the "Table for Knowing Which Planet Rules in Each Hour" (see fig. 1).[5] There the twelve hours of the day are set forth in the top half of the table and the twelve hours of the night in the bottom half, showing which planet rules each hour of each of the seven days and nights: Dies dominici begins with Sol ruling the first hour of the day; Dies Lune, with Luna ruling the first hour; Dies Martis, with Mars ruling; dies Mercurii, with Mercurius ruling; Dies Jovis, with Jupiter ruling; etc.

In Chaucer's writing, the most obvious example of this method of time telling can be found in the hours chosen for prayer by Palamon, Emelye, and Arcite in Part 3 of *The Knight's Tale*: Palamon goes to the temple of Venus to pray for aid on "The Sonday nyght, er day bigan to sprynge, . . . / (Although it nere nat day by houres two. . .)" (lines 2209, 2211), the second hour before dawn on a Monday being governed by Venus; Emelye prays to Diana, goddess of the moon, in "The thridde houre inequal that

---

[4] For discussion of a court case of 1387 arguing when the day began, see Leonard C. Hector, "The Beginning of the 'Natural Day' in the Late 14th Century," *Journal of the Society of Archivists* 2 (1961): 87–89.

[5] My edition of Somer's "Kalendarium," with St. John's College, Cambridge, MS K.26 as base text, is forthcoming in the Chaucer Library series of the University of Georgia Press.

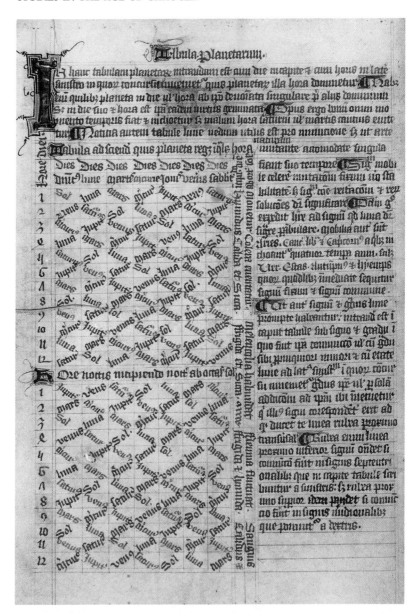

Fig. 1. "Tabula ad Sciendum quis Planeta Regnat in Qualibet Hora" ("Table for Knowing Which Planet Rules in Each Hour"). From John Somer, "The Kalendarium" (1380), Trinity College, Cambridge, MS R.15.18, fol. 16v. Reprinted by permission of the Master and Fellows of Trinity College, Cambridge.

Palamon / Bigan to Venus temple for to gon" (lines 2271–72), that is, in the first hour after dawn on the Monday, the hour whose ruling planet gives the day its name; and Arcite prays to Mars "The nexte houre of Mars folwynge this" (line 2367), or three hours later, the fourth hour of a Monday being ruled by Mars.

Also inherited from Jewish and Christian tradition was the method of calculating the day beginning at sundown.[6] The Jewish Sabbath, for example, begins at sundown on Friday. The Christian practice of observing Vigils — e.g., Christmas and Easter eves, the *evenings* before Christmas and Easter — illustrates this tradition as well, each of these feasts beginning at sundown of the preceding calendar day. In the calendars of Lynn and Somer this method would have applied to the calculation of saints' days, though neither writer specifically makes this point in his canons: it was probably so well known to their audiences as to be unnecessary. Both indicate the eves of major feast days as "Vigilia." Chaucer uses this method for calculating the beginning of the day when he tells us in *The Parliament of Fowls* that it was St. Valentine's Day as he dreamed at night (lines 85–87, 309).

Using either of these methods, one might still speak of the twelve hours of the day and the twelve hours of the night, those of the day giving their names to the daily monastic or liturgical offices Prime, Terce, Sext, and None, originally celebrated at the first, third, sixth, and ninth hours of the day.[7]

Since sunrise and sunset vary with the seasons, however, calculating the day to begin with either would result in days of fewer than twenty-four hours in one six-month period, more than twenty-four in the other (and this would be particularly noticeable in northern latitudes). Therefore, astronomers from antiquity onward had used as the boundary between one day and the next the far less variable solar meridian, or moment when the sun reaches its zenith, its highest point. The usual astronomical day began at noon of the *stated* calendar day. Somer uses this method for calculating the date in his "Eclipse Tables," as he explains in some detail in the canons:

There follow...figures of the eclipses, above which is written the time of the beginning of the eclipse, which will be on that day before sunset or before the midnight immediately following, in so many hours and minutes after noon...if

---

[6] See C. R. Cheney, *Handbook of Dates for Students of English History* (London: Royal Historical Society, 1961), p. 9, n. 1.

[7] David Knowles, *The Monastic Order in England...*, *940–1216*, 2d ed. (Cambridge: Cambridge University Press, 1963), pp. 714–15.

the hours and minutes there should be less than twelve. But, however, if they should be more than twelve, it will begin that same night in the case of an eclipse of the moon or on the following day in the case of an eclipse of the sun, so many hours and minutes after midnight... after twelve hours have been taken away from them.[8]

This method of calculating astronomical time posed a problem for writers of astronomical calendars like Somer and Lynn, because their month-by-month tables showed saints' days on the same page as astronomical data like dates and times of the conjunctions and oppositions of sun and moon. Since the usual astronomical day began at noon on the *stated* day and the Christian saints' days began at sundown of the *preceding* day, the two systems overlapped for only approximately six of the twenty-four hours (from noon to sundown). Therefore, we find in the calendars of Somer and Lynn a recalculated astronomical day beginning at noon of the day *preceding* the stated calendar date; the two systems thus overlapped for approximately eighteen of the twenty-four hours (from sundown to noon). Lynn uses this method of dating for all the astronomical data in his calendar, including the eclipses.[9] Somer, confusingly, employs the recalculated dating for his cycles of conjunctions on the month-by-month calendar, while he shows usual astronomical time — that is, each eclipse occurring one date later — for his "Eclipse Table."

None of these four methods corresponds to our modern method of calculating the date, beginning the day at midnight. This last method may have been used by the common people in calculating the day of the week and the day of the month, and was clearly becoming increasingly popular as clocks became more common.[10]

---

[8] From the version of St. John's College, Cambridge, MS K.26, fol. 27. Unless otherwise noted, translations are mine.

[9] See Lynn, *Kalendarium*, pp. 14–16, 142–63.

[10] Hector describes a case of 1387 before the Court of Common Pleas, revolving around the time that day begins: "At first sight Clopton's arguments might seem to suggest that for purposes of dating the practice of the 14th century Chancery was to reckon the day from dawn to dawn. But if this was notoriously so, there would have been no room for Thirning's objection that the writ antedated Katherine's death. Clopton's concern was to show that there was a permissible system of dating under which his clients' writ could be held good, and to leave it to be presumed that that system had been used to date it. Thirning, for his part, contended that the date changed at midnight. But neither side claimed that the system it championed was that followed in the Chancery. This may mean only that the problem was a new one.... There is, however, a bare possibility... that practice varied within the Chancery itself, some clerks favouring the 'common course' advocated by Clopton, others the more modern view advanced by Thirning." Hector, "The Beginning of the 'Natural Day,'" pp. 88–89.

Before turning to clocks, however, I should point out that there were still more problems with the telling of time, even after one had settled the question of when the day began. First, there were no time zones—time zones are a modern invention, created at the instigation of the American transcontinental-railroad men a little over a century ago—so, in Chaucer's day, time of day varied with the times of sunrise, meridian, and sunset, which changed with longitude and latitude: a certain hour might occur in Norwich as much as half an hour before it struck in Bristol. While this posed no problem for intercity communication in those days of slow travel and immovable timepieces, it did pose problems for the composers of calendars. Both Somer and Lynn included detailed instructions for converting their tables, calculated for Oxford, to usable figures in other longitudes and latitudes.[11] Chaucer, too, included instructions for finding the latitude of one's position as canon 23 of Part 2 of his *Treatise on the Astrolabe*. In addition, Lynn also included instructions for calculating meridian altitudes for each of the four years in the leap-year cycle.[12]

Second, for those systems calculating from sunrise or sunset, there might be confusion over when the day began or ended. Astronomical time calculates sunrise as the moment when the sun appears over the artificial horizon (discounting geophysical variations in the earth's surface), and sunset when it disappears below the opposite artificial horizon. This period marks the *dies artificialis*, or artificial day. But, as we all know, we have what we would call "daylight," light enough to see and work by, for quite a while longer than that. The longer day, including both morning and evening twilights, was termed the *dies vulgaris*, or common day.[13] Lynn paid lip service (or quill service) to this method of calculating the day by including on his calendar pages, besides the figures for sunrise and sunset, columns of figures for the beginning and end of twilight (determined by the sun's

[11] Lynn's sixth canon, "Canon ad sciendum horam inequalem diei artificialis," *Kalendarium*, pp. 192–95. Somer gives instructions in his long introductory canon for "The Kalendarium."

[12] Lynn's first canon, "Canon pro gradu solis inveniendo in signis omni die," *Kalendarium*, pp. 184–87.

[13] In 1370 rules for the governance of masons at work on York Minster took into account this longer common day. From Michaelmas until the first Sunday in Lent they were to be "ilka day atte morne atte yare werke . . . als erly als yai may see skilfully by day lyghte for till wyrke," and they were to "stande yar trewly wyrkande atte yair werke all ye day aftyr, als lang als yai may se skilfully for till wyrke, yf yt be alle werkday." *The Fabric Rolls of York Minster*, Surtees Society, vol. 35 (London: George Andrews, 1859), from the "Ordinacio cementariorum," p. 181.

being less than 20 degrees below the horizon).[14] Chaucer speaks of activities occurring during evening twilight, calling it the beginning of the night, in *The Franklin's Tale* when, after the meeting between Dorigen and Aurelius at which she gives her rash promise, her friends rejoin her and (lines 1015–19)

> ...sodeynly bigonne revel newe
> Til that the brighte sonne loste his hewe;
> For th'orisonte hath reft the sonne his lyght—
> This is as muche to seye as it was nyght—
> And hoom they goon in joye and in solas, ...

And in his *Treatise on the Astrolabe* he included in Part 2 a canon (number 9) "To knowe the quantite of the day vulgar, that is to seyn fro spryng of the day unto verrey nyght."[15]

Third, a major source of confusion lay in the difference between calculating "common hours" and "artificial hours." Common hours were those determined by astronomical calculation: the length of time between sunrise and sunset was divided into twelve equal portions, each representing one hour of the day, and the time between sunset and sunrise was divided equally into twelve portions, the hours of the night. The hours of the day would be longer in summer (nearly ninety of our minutes in England around the summer solstice) and proportionally shorter in winter.[16] These common hours were used in either system that began the day at sunrise or sunset, in all astrological calculations (e.g., to determine which planet governed), and in reckoning time by shadow length. An hour was calculated as the time it took the sun to ascend or descend 15 degrees in its arc, however that arc might change with seasonal changes in the tilt of the earth's axis. Chaucer draws attention to the difference between these common, or unequal, hours and artificial, or equal, hours (calculated as 15

---

[14] On the calendar pages Lynn's last column before the four cycles of conjunctions and oppositions is headed "Quantities of each of the twilights of morning and evening." *Kalendarium*, pp. 65, 71, 77, 83, 89, 95, 101, 107, 113, 119, 125, 131.

[15] Benson, ed., *The Riverside Chaucer*, p. 672.

[16] Note that both the Rule of St. Benedict and the *Regularis Concordia Anglicae nationis monachorum sanctimonialiumque* of ca. 972, observed by the early English monastic community, took into account the variation in length of day in regulating the monastic schedule. According to the *Regularis Concordia*, Prime was to be celebrated at about 6:45 A.M. in winter, 6:00 A.M. in summer; Vespers, at about 4:15 P.M. in winter, 6:00 P.M. in summer; and Compline, at about 6:15 P.M. in winter, 8:00 P.M. in summer (see Knowles, *Monastic Order*, app. 18, pp. 714–15).

degrees on the equinoctial arc) when he says that Chauntecleer of *The Nun's Priest's Tale* is a more accurate time teller than a clock, because he crows at each 15-degree ascension of the equinoctial (lines 2853–58):

> Wel sikerer was his crowyng in his logge
> Than is a clokke or an abbey orlogge.
> By nature he knew ech ascensioun
> Of the equynoxial in thilke toun;
> For whan degrees fiftene weren ascended,
> Thanne crew he that it myghte nat been amended.[17]

Both Somer and Lynn include directions for converting time measured in unequal hours to "artificial time," our modern time with hours of fixed length regardless of length of day or night.[18] Lynn also includes canons for use of his "Shadow-Length Table" explaining how to convert shadow length to artificial time, and the Canterbury pilgrims' Host Harry Bailly must have used tables like Nicholas's in determining that it was time that the Man of Law began his tale (*MLP* 1–14):

> Oure Hooste saugh wel that the brighte sonne
> The ark of his artificial day hath ronne
> The ferthe part, and half an houre and moore,
> And though he were nat depe ystert in loore,
> He wiste it was the eightetethe day
> Of Aprill, that is messager to May;
> And saugh wel that the shadwe of every tree
> Was as in lengthe the same quantitee
> That was the body erect that caused it.
> And therfore by the shadwe he took his wit
> That Phebus, which that shoon so clere and brighte,
> Degrees was fyve and fourty clombe on highte,

[17] Chaucer may here be alluding to the notorious inaccuracy of the early clocks. For discussion of the astronomical aspects of this passage, see John North, *Chaucer's Universe* (Oxford: Clarendon Press, 1988; repr. 1991), pp. 457–58.

[18] Lynn's fifth canon, "Canon ad sciendum horas de clok cum die artificiali," and sixth canon, "Canon ad sciendum horam inequalem diei artificialis," *Kalendarium*, pp. 188–95. He includes his "Shadow-Length Table" on the calendar, pp. 68–69, 74–75, 80–81, 86–87, 92–93, 98–99, 104–105, 110–11, 116–17, 122–23, 128–29, and 134–35. In the long introductory canon to his "Kalendarium," Somer explains how to convert common hours to artificial hours.

> And for that day, as in that latitude,
> It was ten of the clokke, he gan conclude, ... [19]

Finally, in systems that counted hours from noon to noon, there was possible confusion over the counting of hours ante meridiem. Originally, these had been counted backward, as "one hour before the meridian" or "two hours before the meridian" (equivalent to our eleven o'clock and ten o'clock in the morning).[20] For those who counted hours of the day from sunrise to sunset yet began the date at noon, this method of numbering hours ante meridiem served well, since one might speak of its being two hours before the meridian of such-and-such a date, referring to the date that began at the meridian. By the fourteenth century, however, it was more common to count the hours ante meridiem in order from one to twelve as we do. And this change, with the change from common to artificial lengths of hours, might be due to the advent of clocks in England, beginning in the late thirteenth century.

Both calendar authors, and Somer in particular, appear to have tried to avoid confusing their readers with these various methods for computing time by spelling out in their canons or even at the headings of the tables themselves what methods of computing and reckoning were used for each table. First, on his "Table for Knowing Which Planet Rules in Each Hour,"[21] Somer draws attention to his method of reckoning the day from sunrise by noting at the heading to the table that it works "by beginning the day from the rising of the sun," even though he has already made this clear in the canon for use of this table (these words are squeezed into the top right-hand corner of the table, fig. 1, and the same point is made again for hours of the night in the words "The hour of the night beginning from the setting of the sun" halfway down the table, above the hours of the night). Second, he explains clearly that it is the *artificial* time one can find by using a quadrant, given his table for the sun's height at midday.[22] Third, he emphasizes in the canons that he is giving "clock time" (that is, time

---

[19] For discussion of Chaucer's calculations here, Benson, ed., *The Riverside Chaucer*, pp. 854–55. See also Eade, *Forgotten Sky*, pp. 123–26; North, *Chaucer's Universe*, pp. 116–30.

[20] E.g., Lynn's counting of hours ante meridiem in reverse order, as explained by Eisner in *Kalendarium*, p. 15.

[21] See fig. 1.

[22] Somer's canon reads: "Afterwards is written the sun's altitude at midday, with which you will thus easily be able to find the artificial time on a quadrant: put the perpendicular side of the quadrant. . . . And you will find the clock time uniformly on the quadrant in this manner." Somer, "Kalendarium."

reckoned in twelve sequential hours from midnight to noon and again from noon to midnight) for the rising and setting of the sun.[23] Fourth, in the canons for his table of eclipses, which reckons the day from noon of the date given, he gives instructions for converting to clock time, although he does not there designate it as "clock time."[24]

Somer's determination to clarify these points may be taken as evidence of the time-telling methods which he could assume his audience knew and which of them was most commonly used. The first example shows that reckoning of hours for a given day from sunrise (inherited from the classical world) was by the end of the fourteenth century sufficiently unusual to require specific designation both in canons and on the table itself. The second example demonstrates that Somer felt a need to make clear the distinction between "artificial hours" and "common hours" but assumed that his audience understood what was meant by those terms. Both of these examples mark a shift toward modern reckoning of time, and the third and fourth examples, in one of which he explains that he is giving clock time and in the other gives instructions for converting to clock time, show still more clearly that the method of reckoning time by clocks that counted hours consecutively from midnight to noon and noon to midnight was considered by Somer to be the one with which his lay audience would be most familiar, the one with which other methods were to be compared or brought into accord through computation. It will be noted, too, in the examples of Chaucer's astronomical periphrasis that I have quoted above, in the *Prologue* to *The Parson's Tale* (lines 2–12), and in the *Prologue* to *The Man of Law's Tale* (lines 1–14), he gives the equivalent clock time for the astronomical time he describes.[25] And, as I have suggested above, this evidence of the acceptance of "clock time" virtually as a norm in late-fourteenth-century England is the more surprising since clocks had been introduced into England only at the end of the previous century and were still relatively scarce.

The first weight-driven clocks, probably introduced to England in the 1280s, were no more than systems of gears and weights constructed to ring a

---

[23] Somer's canon reads, "Joined with this [is] the moiety of the artificial day [or semidiurnal arc], showing how many times the clock will strike in its last striking before the setting of the sun." Ibid.

[24] See n. 8 above.

[25] For other examples of Chaucer's use of astronomical periphrasis, see Chauncey Wood, *Chaucer and the Country of the Stars* (Princeton, N.J.: Princeton University Press, 1970), pp. 70–102.

bell the number of times to correspond to the hour in twelve-hour sequences[26] — in twelve-hour sequences rather than twenty-four probably because it was difficult and time-consuming to count the number of rings from thirteen to twenty-four.[27] There were no clock faces, no dials, and no way to tell the time between hours. These bell clocks were introduced first to monastic communities, where their ringing might keep the inmates to the *horarium*, or regulated daily schedule centered around the offices Prime, Terce, Sext, None, Vespers, Compline, Nocturns, and Matins.[28] In monastic communities they probably replaced a less accurate person who had rung the bell to call the order to prayer. Nevertheless, the early bell clocks were themselves notoriously inaccurate.[29] In his study of the St. Alban's clock, John North cites a "document of 1302 from Ely abbey, a Benedictine foundation," explicitly stating that "the monks were to assemble at the proper times with its help, wherefore [their clock] must be kept in good order."[30]

[26] See *clok(ke)* in Hans Kurath, Sherman M. Kuhn, and Robert E. Lewis, eds., *Middle English Dictionary* (Ann Arbor: University of Michigan Press, 1954–), pt. C.3, p. 337. David S. Landes discusses the earliest European clocks, including the water-driven clocks that were predecessors to the weight-driven ones, in *Revolution in Time: Clocks and the Making of the Modern World* (Cambridge, Mass.: Harvard University Press, 1983), pp. 53–82. As Landes points out, Dante's reference to mechanical clockworks in *Paradiso* 24, written 1316–21, establishes that weight-driven clocks were not only known in Italy by the early fourteenth century but well enough known for Dante to assume that his audience would understand his simile. Ibid., p. 57.

[27] John North, *Richard of Wallingford*, 3 vols. (Oxford: Clarendon Press, 1976) 2.338–39, reviews the history of striking clocks, noting how difficult it would be "to make a mechanism capable of sounding the *unequal* hours" and explaining that the introduction of striking clocks "seems almost to have been a necessary condition of chroniclers' recording the time in equal hours." He also notes that there were clocks that struck twenty-four hours, whose supposed invention in 1373 is recorded forty years later in the *Eulogium historiarum* by a monk of Malmesbury.

[28] Knowles, *Monastic Order*, pp. 714–15.

[29] See R. T. Gunther, *The Astrolabes of the World: Based upon the Series of Instruments in the Lewis Evans Collection in the Old Ashmolean Museum at Oxford, with Notes on Astrolabes in . . . Other Public and Private Collections* (London: Holland, 1976), p. 535. Note that the phrase "running like clockwork" or, more generally, "like a clock" to refer to steady regularity is relatively modern, first recorded in Harriet Beecher Stowe's *Uncle Tom's Cabin* (*Clock*, no. 4, *OED* 2.510). Chaucer may also be alluding to the inaccuracy of the early abbey clocks when he notes that Chauntecleer's crowing was more accurate (*NPT* 2853–58), as quoted above and mentioned in n. 17 above.

[30] John North, *Richard of Wallingford*, 3 vols. (Oxford: Clarendon Press, 1976), 2.363. North's source for this information is an ordinance issued by Bishop Orford in 1302, cited by C. F. C. Beeson, *English Church Clocks, 1280–1850*, Antiquarian Horological Society, Monograph no. 5 (London and Chichester: Phillimore, 1971), p. 15: "The convent should rise at the agreed-upon hours of night and day by the clock (*orelogium*), which we direct to be kept in an appropriate and secure place in the church and to be kept in sound condition by the monk, for performing the daily offices which are not fulfilled either by anticipating the time or by prolonging it."

Our word *clock* comes from the Middle Dutch or Northern French *clocke* or *cloke* (Southern French *cloche*), from earlier Anglo-Saxon *clucge* and still earlier Celtic *cloc* (OIr.), *clag* (Gael.), or *cloch* (Cornish and Welsh), meaning "bell," and we still speak of "telling" (or counting) time or of an hour "striking."[31]

The first use of the word "clock" in England was in a Latin court roll of 1371, where we are told that a bell for perpetually indicating the hours of day and night is called by the common name "clok."[32] Two of the earliest English uses of the word "clock" occur in the Latin canons to the calendars of Somer and Lynn.

By the fourteenth century in English the word "horologe" was apparently reserved for designating any timepiece with a face or dial—in the earliest records apparently of the sundial type—but with the advent of what we would call clocks, weight-driven timepieces with both faces and a ringing device, the two terms "clock" and "horologe" seem to have been coming together, "clock" emerging as the single term to designate either form of timepiece. The term *orloge* or *horologe*, derived from Old French *orloge* or *oriloge*, and earlier from Latin *horologium* (literally "hour-teller")[33] is first used in English in Chaucer's *Parlement of Fowles* (line 350); it next appears in the lines quoted above from *The Nun's Priest's Tale*, where Chauntecleer's crowing is said to keep more accurate time than an "abbey orlogge."[34] John Wycliffe uses the word "oriloge" in 1382, as does Reginald Pecock in 1449, clearly to designate a sundial,[35] but Chaucer seems to be using the term in 1386 in *The Nun's Priest's Tale* to refer to a clock as we know it, with face and ringing mechanism, because he clearly associates it with an audible telling of the hour and with location at an abbey.

Here and elsewhere in his writings, Chaucer reminds us of other methods for time telling used by the common people both before the advent of clocks and afterward when they were beyond the range of the bells. In *The Parlement of Fowles* he reminds us that the cock is the clock of small villages ("orloge . . . of thorpes lyte," line 350), as we are again reminded in the praise of Chauntecleer's time-telling ability in *The Nun's Priest's Tale* just cited. In *The Reeve's Tale*, where the miller's cottage in Trumpington is too far from Cambridge for the bells to be heard, Aleyn and the miller's daughter are

---

[31] *Clock*, *Oxford English Dictionary* (Oxford: Oxford University Press, 1933; repr. 1971), 2.510. See also Landes, *Revolution in Time*, p. 68.

[32] H. Playford and J. Caley, eds., *Rotulorum Originalium in Curia Scaccarii Abbreviatio*, 2 vols. (London: Record Commission, 1805–10), 2.314 (Edward III).

[33] *Orloge*, *MED*, pt. O.3, p. 296.

[34] See *NPT* 2853–54.

[35] *Orloge*, *MED*, pt. O.3, p. 296.

wakened by the third crowing of the cock: "This joly lyf han thise two clerkes lad / Til that the thridde cok bigan to synge" (lines 4232–33), when Aleyn says, "The day is come" (line 4237).[36] By contrast, Alison and Nicholas of *The Miller's Tale* lie within the city of Oxford where they can hear the bells: "And thus lith Alison and Nicholas, . . . / Til that the belle of laudes gan to rynge, / And freres in the chauncel gonne synge" (lines 3653–56). Such dependence of the laity on the church bells for time telling is confirmed in documents of Chaucer's lifetime: at York in 1370 the masons building the minster were not to stop work for their midday meal on days between Michaelmas and Lent "till itte be hegh none smytyn by þe clocke."[37]

Given the ambiguity of meaning for the words "clock" and "horologe," it is difficult to tell from the early records of clocks in England whether the writer intends to designate the weight-driven gears for ringing a bell or the same device with added dial (and sometimes other visual representations of time as well, as will be described below). The earliest reference to a clock in England comes in 1283 from the Priory of Austin Canons, in Dunstable, Bedfordshire; the Annals of the Priory indicate that in that year a "horologium" was constructed to surmount the rood screen (*supra pulpitum*), just as, more than a century later, in 1423, a large clock with frame measuring 34 × 39 × 48 inches was set *supra pulpitum* in Bourges Cathedral.[38] By 1284 there must have been a bell clock at Exeter Cathedral, for a Patent Roll entry of 1318 confirms an earlier grant of 1284 to a bell founder, Roger de Ropford, his wife, and his heirs, in which repair of the cathedral clock (*horologium*) is mentioned.[39] By 1286 there was an "horologe" in St. Paul's

---

[36] The third crowing of the cock was thought to signal one hour before dawn.

[37] *The Fabric Rolls of York Minster*, p. 181. From the "Ordinacio cementariorum," G.c.100, b, observance of which was sworn to by Robert de Patrington and twelve other masons before the chapter on October 31, 1370. A similar set of rules for the masons, "Ordinance made for the masons and others working on the building," ibid., acta cap. 1343–68, 77, a, pp. 171–73, in Latin, names the ringing of bells for sacred offices as the timing device by which they are to be regulated (e.g., "until the striking of the bell of the Blessed Virgin Mary," "thus they should work until the first striking of the bell for vespers," and "until the striking of the bell of the abbey of the Blessed Virgin Mary which is called the Longbell"). This suggests that the bell clock had been installed between 1352 and 1370. The Middle English document also attests to yet another way of measuring time: the time it would take a man to walk a mile, a "mileway," in several references to the men not pausing in their work for sleep or drink after their dinners for longer than a "mileway" (e.g., "and yai sall noghte cese no lefe yair werke in slepyng tyme, passande ye tyme of a mileway, no in drynkyng tyme after none, passande ye tyme of a mileway." Ibid., p. 182.)

[38] See Beeson, *English Church Clocks*, pp. 13–14.

[39] Ibid., p. 14.

Cathedral, London, for the building or repair of which the *horologiarius* Bartholomew was paid for three quarters' and eight days' work.[40] The bursarial accounts for Merton College, Oxford, in 1289–90 indicate expenses for installing or maintaining a clock (*orologium*) in the college.[41] Norwich Cathedral had a weight-driven clock as early as 1290, referred to as the "old clock" (*antiquum horologium*) when the new clock was built in 1322. This new Norwich "horologe," built by the *horologiarius* Roger of Stoke in 1322, may have had dials for phases of the sun and moon, though we have no very detailed description of its workings or appearance.[42] Other early English clocks were to be found at Ely Abbey in 1291 (as noted above);[43] at Christchurch Cathedral, Canterbury, in 1292; and at Salisbury Cathedral in 1306. In the late 1320s work began on the St. Alban's clock, described more fully below, and by the time Chaucer was writing his *Treatise on the Astrolabe* and *Canterbury Tales* in the 1380s and 1390s there were clocks of some sort at Colchester, Essex (1357?); Durham Cathedral (1360); York Minster (1371); Ripon Minster (1379); Salisbury Cathedral (1386); Ottery St. Mary in Devon (1390); and Wells Cathedral (1392).[44] The *compotus* roll of the Bridgewater town receiver in 1373–75 records as its last entry in the expense list, "*Et* liberante clokkemakyr iiii pounds x shillings," suggesting that there may have been a clock at the convent of Franciscan friars in that town, where Somer entered the brotherhood.[45]

By the second half of the fourteenth century clocks were also to be found in royal residences: in 1351–52 a clock was installed in the Great Tower of Windsor Castle; by 1366 there was a clock at Sheen, in Surrey; in 1366 Edward III had one installed in his new castle at Queenborough, on the Island of Sheppey in Kent; and in 1368 a clock was installed at Kings Langley Manor.[46] Sufficient records survive for C. F. C. Beeson to describe the construction and installation of the bell clock at Windsor:

Carpenters began work on a room for the clock in December 1351 and were more or less permanently on the job until June 1352. The clock was made in London and

[40] Ibid., pp. 14–15.

[41] Ibid., p. 15.

[42] Ibid., pp. 15, 16–18. Beeson's fig. 2, p. 17, is a photograph of the page from the Sacrist's Roll of 1324–25 which deals with the building of the "new" clock.

[43] See n. 30 above.

[44] Beeson, *English Church Clocks*, pp. 20–22.

[45] Thomas Bruce-Dilks, ed., *Bridgewater Borough Archives, 1191–1377*, Somerset Records Society, vol. 48 (London: Butler & Tanner, 1933), p. 222.

[46] Beeson, *English Church Clocks*, pp. 19–21.

delivered to Windsor in April with various accessories, e.g., 12 lbs of large wire, 6 lbs of copper wire, a great cord, 6 little cords, 2 lines, iron work and a hammer weighing 160 lbs, 7 iron bars, a staple for a weight, 2 copper bolsters for a pulley, etc. A large bell was transported from Aldgate to Windsor and 99 lbs of iron work were used to set it up in the Tower.

Three Lombards, the clockmakers who made the clock, arrived at Windsor with their tools on the 8 April 1352 and stayed for 6 + ½ weeks boarding at the table of Stephen Chesebury. By Whitsun the clock seems to have been finished in working order and the Lombards left on 24 May, and presumably returned to Italy. . . . The battlement or roof of the clockhouse was covered with lead (*cooperture orologii*) in May 1352. In December 1353 the clock was enclosed in a protective case or cupboard.[47]

English records of 1391 suggest that Henry Bolingbroke owned a "clokke," perhaps in his London residence, that might be carried from place to place, for he paid "John Clockmaker. . . 8 pence for one basket bought by him to carry a clock from London to Bolingbroke."[48]

Many of these early records refer to clocks of the ringing-bell variety. The records do not usually clarify for us whether they had faces or dials showing the hour and minutes. Very few clocks survive for modern assessment, e.g., the works of the bell clock of 1386 from Salisbury Cathedral;[49] the works, face, and automata of the Wells clock of 1392;[50] and the clocks of Hampton Court and Exeter Cathedral from the sixteenth century.[51]

The Wells clock may be considered as representative of these early abbey clocks. It had four dials: the outer dial, two series of numbers one to twelve in roman numerals, counting the semidiurnal hours one to twelve twice; the next inner dial, counting one to sixty for the minutes between hours;

---

[47] Ibid., pp. 19–20.

[48] Lucy Toulmin-Smith, ed., *Expeditions to Prussia and the Holy Land Made by Henry, Earl of Derby in the Years 1390–1 and 1392–3*, Camden Society, n.s., vol. 52 (London, 1894), pp. 19–20.

[49] Illustrated in G. H. Baillie, Courtenay Ilbert, and Cecil Clutton, eds., *Britten's Old Clocks and Watches and Their Makers: A History of Styles in Clocks and Watches and Their Mechanisms*, 9th ed. (London: Methuen, 1982), p. 11, pl. 3.

[50] The face and some automata are illustrated in Henry C. King, with John R. Millburn, *Geared to the Stars: The Evolution of Planetariums, Orreries, and Astronomical Clocks* (Toronto: University of Toronto Press, 1978), p. 46, fig. 4.3. The works, now in the Science Museum in London, are illustrated in Muriel Goaman, *English Clocks* (London: Connoisseur and Michael Joseph, 1967), p. 35, pl. 17.

[51] The Hampton Court clock is illustrated in King, *Geared to the Stars*, p. 51, fig. 4.9, and in Goaman, *English Clocks*, facing p. 29, colorpl. 2; the Exeter clock is illustrated in King, *Geared to the Stars*, p. 45, fig. 4.2, and in Goaman, *English Clocks*, facing p. 28, colorpl. 1.

the third dial, with numbers one to thirty, counting the days of the moon; and the inmost dial, with a cutout circle for illustration of the moon in its changing phases, which rotated once in a lunar day, a pointer at the outer edge of the moon circle indicating the day of the moon on the third dial.

Automata, set above the clock face and connected with the clockworks, are thought to be part of the original clock. They are four mounted knights who revolve around a central axis at each striking of the quarter hour, two in one direction and two in another, so that they appear to joust with one another. One of the horsemen appearing from the left opening, hinged at his waist, falls backward as he is struck by his opponent's lance, and is automatically restored to his upright position after reentering through the right opening. The ringing mechanism for this clock is also an automaton, described by Henry C. King in *Geared to the Stars*:

Higher in the triforium, to the right of the knights, is a seated wooden figure nicknamed "Jack Blandifer," believed to be largely original and therefore late fourteenth-century. At the hours and quarters Jack taps with his heels two bells under his seat and at the hour strikes with a hammer a third bell suspended in front of him. With each stroke at the hour he also slightly turns his head. Automatons also accompany the outside dial. They take the form of two knights in armour, each about 1.20 m. high and carved from solid oak. At the quarters each figure rotates slightly on a vertical spindle to strike a bell with his axe.[52]

Automata of this sort, large figures called "jacks" that moved to ring a bell for the hour or quarter hour, were primarily a feature of clocks of the fifteenth century and later, and those at Wells may have been added after the 1392 date of the clock itself. Other early jacks were connected to the clocks at St. Paul's Cathedral, already described, and St. Mary Steps, in Exeter.[53]

According to King, the Wells clock is unusual among clocks of this size in that its second dial shows minutes, and in fact the second dial was added to the clock in the seventeenth century.[54] Other large clocks of that period usually showed the sun's position in the zodiac, sometimes accompanied by an indication of the month and day, on the second plate. So, apparently,

[52] King, *Geared to the Stars*, p. 46.

[53] Goaman, *English Clocks*, pp. 38–39. Later examples of such automata are those known as Gog and Magog built for St. Dunstan's-in-the-West Church, in Fleet Street, London, in 1671 (ibid., pp. 39–40) and those on the Carfax clock tower in Oxford, still ringing the hour and quarters.

[54] King, *Geared to the Stars*, p. 46.

did the Norwich Cathedral clock and the St. Alban's Abbey clock, described by John Leland in 1546 as being "second to none in all Europe."[55] This was the astronomical clock of Richard of Wallingford at St. Alban's, begun in the 1330s when Wallingford was abbot and completed by the *horologiarius* Laurence of Stoke sometime in the abbacy of his successor, Thomas de la Mare, who was abbot between 1349 and 1396. John Capgrave, in his *Abbreuiacion of Cronicles*, remembers Wallingford at his death principally for his design of the St. Alban's clock:

This ȝere [1336] deyed Richard Walingforth, abbot of Seynt Albones, a studious man in astronomie. Be his avis was mad þat grete horologe, þat standith þere, with many meruelous meuyngis of astronomye.[56]

For "meruelous meuyngis of astronomye," Wallingford's huge clock showed the motions of the sun, moon, and stars and the ebb and flow of the tide, besides the time of day. It may also have run an automated wheel of fortune, as suggested by praise of its carving in the *Gesta Abbatum* of St. Alban's:

. . . by the skill of Master Laurence of Stoke, eminent horologiarius, and one of his fellow monks, William Walsham — who in the work of their hands and in subtlety of carving surpassed all the craftsmen of the district — the upper dial and wheel of fortune.[57]

Leland's description of the clock reinforces this possibility:

One may observe the course of the Sun, the Moon, or the fixed stars, or again, one may regard the rise and fall of the sea, or lines with an almost infinite variety of figures and demonstrations.[58]

---

[55] North, *Wallingford*, 2.365.

[56] Peter J. Lucas, ed., *John Capgrave's* Abbreviacion of Cronicles, EETS, o.s., vol. 285 (1983), p. 159, lines 13–16.

[57] North, *Wallingford*, 2.366, quoting H. T. Riley, ed., *Gesta Abbatum Monasterii Sancti Albani a Thoma Walsongham, Regnante Ricardo Secundo, ejusdem ecclesiae praecentore, compilata*, 3 vols., pt. 4 of *Chronica Monasterii S. Albani*, Rerum Britannicarum Medii Aevi Scriptores (London: Longmans, Green, Reader & Dyer, 1867), 3.385.

[58] North, *Wallingford*, 2.366, quoting John Leland, *Commentarii de scriptoribus Britannicis*, ed. Anthony Hall, 2 vols. (Oxford: Sheldonian, 1709), 2.404–405.

Horologes are associated with abbeys like St. Alban's in the passage quoted from *The Nun's Priest's Tale*, but they may also have found their way into the castles and palaces of the nobility by the 1390s, as suggested by the references to "clocks" at Windsor Castle, Sheen, Queenborough Castle, Kings Langley Manor, and Bolingbroke and Westminster palaces mentioned above.[59]

The calendars of Somer and Lynn help us moderns better understand Chaucer's references to time. But perhaps what is most interesting about the calculation of time in the calendars is not that they employ side by side so many different systems for telling time, inherited from various classical, Christian, and scientific traditions, but that they so often take pains to explain to their readers how to convert these different systems to "clock time." The trouble they take over this suggests that, although clocks were still relatively rare — and, in our sense of the word, of a timepiece with face or dial, extremely rare — in Chaucer's time, nevertheless by the end of the fourteenth century "clock time" was apparently fast superseding the older methods for telling time. And just as we have learned to expect Chaucer to express his age's interest in and knowledge of astronomy,[60] he also demonstrates that he is highly learned in respect to the telling of time: taught in the various conflicting methods for telling time, demonstrating in his writings his facility with them all and his awareness of their comparative usefulness and accuracy, and yet reflecting, too, in his works the movement toward acceptance of the new time, calibrated by that new and increasingly influential instrument, the clock.

[59] Beeson, *English Church Clocks*, pp. 19–21.
[60] See North, *Chaucer's Universe*.

Jerome's *Prefatory Epistles* to the Bible and *The Canterbury Tales*

Brenda Deen Schildgen
University of California, Davis

The voice of books informs not all alike.

Thomas à Kempis, *Imitation of Christ*

...the lerned man mygte / feele in o wise in the same sentence / and the unlerned in an other maner....

St. Jerome, *Prefatory Epistles*[1]

ALTHOUGH MUCH ATTENTION HAS BEEN DIRECTED to the influence Augustine's *De doctrina Christiana* may have had on medieval interpretive theory and literary practice, particularly in regard to Chaucer's *Canterbury Tales*,[2] less attention has been paid to Jerome's theory of

---

[1] *Jerom in his Prolog on the Byble* 8. All quotations from *Jerom in his Prolog* are from Conrad Lindberg, *The Middle English Bible: Prefatory Epistles of St. Jerome* (Oslo, Bergen, Tromsö: Universitetsforlaget, 1978). Lindberg's edition includes the Latin version of the *Prefatory Epistles* as well as two Middle English versions—the first translation attempt and a later revised version. For this discussion I have used the later Middle English version, dated, according to Lindberg, in the 1380s; it is a less literal rendition of Jerome's *Prefaces*.

[2] Sancti Aurelii Augustini, *Opera*, pt. 4, *De doctrina Christiana*, ed. Joseph Martin, in *Corpus Christianorum series Latina*, vol. 32 (Turnholti: Typographi Brepols Editores Pontificii, 1962), pp. 1–167; subsequent quotations from *De doctrina Christiana* are from Augustine, *On Christian Doctrine*, trans. D. W. Robertson (New York: Bobbs-Merrill,1958). See also D. W. Robertson, *A Preface to Chaucer: Studies in Medieval Perspectives* (Princeton, N.J.: Princeton University Press, 1962). A forthcoming two-volume collection of essays on *De doctrina Christiana* (South Bend, Ind.: Notre Dame University Press, 1992) explores the large range of hermeneutical implications of Augustine's treatise. Brian Stock's forthcoming *Augustine and the Birth of the Medieval Reader* includes a chapter on *De doctrina Christiana* and its impact on reading habits in the Middle Ages.

111

biblical interpretation as represented in his *Prefatory Epistles* to various sections of the Bible and the influence that theory may have had on literary interpretive attitudes even if not methods.[3] In his *Prefatory Epistles*, because he had entered into "pious work, but a dangerous undertaking,"[4] in the translation of the Bible, Jerome had set out a number of specific interpretive problems raised by his translating activity that deserve the attention of medievalists.

The *Prefaces* must have carried a great deal of authority since they were part of the Vulgate that was included in the Wycliffite translation project, initiated in the 1370s.[5] Jerome's interpretive concerns emerged in his translation of the Bible from Greek to Latin, for most of the Christian West from a "silent" language to a "spoken" language. That Jerome's *Prefaces* appeared in the Wycliffite Bible suggests that similar concerns must have arisen in the translation from Latin to English. Many of the specific interpretive issues that the Prefaces raise also appear in Chaucer's literary presentation of the complexity of understanding in *The Canterbury Tales*.

As medievalists have argued in recent years, a well-educated reader in the fourteenth century had access to numerous approaches to literary exegesis, many aspects of which find parallels in contemporary theory.[6] Jerome's

---

[3] Whether or not all the original Latin prefaces that appear in the Vulgate Bible were in fact the work of Jerome is still very much a matter of speculation, but what matters for a discussion of their importance in the fourteenth century is that they were believed to be Jerome's work.

[4] Jerome, "Epistula ad Damasum," *Novum Testamentum Latine*, Secundum Editionem Sancti Hieronymi (London: British and Foreign Bible Society, 1985), xiv. My translation; subsequent quotations from "Epistula ad Damasum" are from Frank Sadowski, ed. and trans., "Jerome's Preface to the Four Gospels," *Church Fathers and the Bible: Selected Readings* (New York: Alba House, 1987), pp. 198–200.

[5] Dating the Wycliffite Bible is controversial, according to Anne Hudson, *The Premature Reformation: Wycliffite Texts and Lollard History* (Oxford: Clarendon Press, 1988). She argues that the earliest datable manuscript must have been made before 1397; if Wycliff was involved in the project, it would be hard to date the start of the project later than 1382. For Hudson's arguments about dating, see ibid., p. 247. Some scholars, as, for example, Lindberg, in *Middle English Bible*, p. 58, argue for the 1370s for the first translation attempt of the *Prefaces* and the 1380s for their revised form.

[6] For an overview see A. J. Minnis and A. B. Scott, eds., *Medieval Literary Theory and Criticism, c. 1100–c. 1375: The Commentary Tradition* (Oxford: Clarendon Press, 1988). For a discussion of the differences between current theories and medieval interpretive method, see Robert S. Sturges, *Medieval Interpretation: Models of Reading in Literary Narrative, 1100–1500* (Carbondale and Edwardsville: Southern Illinois University Press, 1990); see also Jesse M. Gellrich, *The Idea of the Book in the Middle Ages: Language Theory, Mythology, and Fiction* (Ithaca, N.Y., and London: Cornell University Press, 1985); Judith Ferster, *Chaucer on Interpretation* (Cambridge: Cambridge University Press, 1985). To compare Jerome's theories and contemporary hermeneutical theory, see Hans-Georg Gadamer, *Truth and Method* (New York: Crossroad, 1982).

Prefaces deserve the attention of medievalists interested in the problems of interpretation, for he discusses how to interpret the Bible and takes up issues of authority over scriptural interpretation, the preconceptions of interpreters, the intrinsic ambiguity of words, and the different impact of spoken versus written words, all interpretive concerns raised in one form or another by Chaucer in *The Canterbury Tales*. Jerome's comments on interpretive matters as announced in the *Prefaces* to the Bible also claim special attention because of their general accessibility during the late Middle Ages. They are particularly interesting for Chaucerians who have argued for decades for totalized readings of *The Canterbury Tales*[7] because Jerome, as a trained rhetorician immersed in Horacian and Ciceronian rhetorical theory, had to wrestle with the problem of ambiguous meanings, a concern which is at the center of the act of translation and which he raised in the *Prefaces*.

Jerome's *Prefaces* and the fact that they were considered important enough to be included in the Wycliffite "translations" of the Bible[8] show that in the fourteenth century different attitudes about how to understand texts, including the Bible itself, were circulating. The project of translating the Bible into the vernacular language, like Jerome's project in the late fourth and early fifth centuries, drew "violent" attention to the implications of the "polysemous" sacred text in a common or spoken language. In fact, at the time that Pope Damasus assigned the Bible translation project to Jerome, there were as many different Latin versions of the Scriptures as there were manuscript copies.[9]

---

[7] As typified by Robertson, *Preface to Chaucer*.

[8] I am indebted to the following studies of John Wycliff and the Lollard movement: Anne Hudson, *Lollards and Their Books* (London and Ronceverte: Hambledon, 1985); Hudson, *Premature Reformation*; Margaret Aston, *Lollards and Reformers: Images of Literacy in Late Medieval Religion* (London: Hambledon, 1984); Herbert D. Workman, *John Wycliff: A Study of the English Medieval Church* (Hamden, Conn.: Archon Books, 1966), particularly his chapter "Wycliff and the Bible," 2.149–200, for an overview of the climate for the creation of the fourteenth-century English Bibles.

[9] "For if we are to pin our faith on the Latin texts, it is for our opponents to tell us *which*; for there are almost as many forms of texts as there are copies. If, on the other hand we are to glean the truth from a comparison of *many*, why not go back to the original Greek and correct the mistakes introduced by inaccurate translators, and the blundering alterations of confident but ignorant critics, and, further, all that has been inserted or changed by copyists more asleep than awake?" Jerome, "Epistula ad Damasum," xiv. Also, Augustine notes: "We can enumerate those who have translated the Scriptures from Hebrew into Greek, but those who have translated them into Latin are innumerable. In the early times of the faith when anyone found a Greek codex, and he thought that he had some facility in both languages, he attempted to translate it." *De doctrina Christiana* 2.11.

In some respects the vernacularization of the Bible in the late Middle Ages parallels the circumstances of the translation of the Bible into Latin in the fourth century. Greek had become a dead language in the Latin West (Augustine, for example, probably could not even read Greek), and numerous corrupt Latin texts were in circulation. As a consequence, Pope Damasus asked Jerome to straighten out the problem of the Bible.[10] In fact, translation is the main issue in Jerome's letter to Damasus, which appears in the *Prefaces*: "For it is oon to be a profete. & an othire to be a translatour of langage / For in profecie the spirit seith bifore siche thingis that ben to come / but in translacioun: enformacioun & plentee of wordis translatith siche thingis as he undirstondith."[11] This passage shows that Jerome is fully conscious that, in contrast to "prophecy," i.e., a direct, unmediated communication between God and a prophet, translation is an act of understanding or interpreting and that the translator is a mediator. The translation project raised central hermeneutical problems, as witnessed in the testy correspondence between Jerome and Augustine,[12] although even Augustine was compelled to recognize that the meaning in sacred Scriptures was "fluid," a conclusion that the numerous translating activities forced upon him (*De doctrina Christiana* 2.11–13).

In England the late-medieval vernacularization project, combining nationalist interests and religious reform, led first to clashes in authority and finally to the rupture characterizing the Reformation. In the fourteenth century few prelates, let alone the laity, knew Latin well enough to "interpret" the Bible and in some cases even "read" it (i.e., sound out the words);[13] thus the Latin Bible was in a sense "silenced." It was also so vulgarized by copying errors that the idea of a standardized text that could

---

[10] See Jerome, "Epistula ad Damasum."

[11] *Preface of Seint Jerom* 66–71. All quotations from *Preface of Seint Jerom* are from the later Middle English version in Lindberg, *Middle English Bible*.

[12] See St. Augustine, *Letters*, vol. 1 (1–82), trans. Sr. Wilfrid Parsons, S.N.D. (New York: Fathers of the Church, 1951), particularly nos. 28, 71, 72, 73, 75, 81, and 82, which include both Augustine's and Jerome's letters. For a recent collection of their correspondence see Carolinne White, ed. and trans., *The Correspondence (394–419) Between Jerome and Augustine of Hippo* (Lewiston, N.Y.; Queenston, Ontario; and Lampeter, Dyfed, Wales: Edward Mellen, 1990).

[13] Margaret Deanesly, *The Lollard Bible and Other Medieval Biblical Versions* (Cambridge: Cambridge University Press, 1920, repr., 1966), writes, "It seems broadly true to say then, from the evidence of the registers and contemporary writers, that between the Conquest and Wycliffe's day, the average parish priest was not a graduate, and probably could not read Latin freely; sometimes, even, he could not translate it at all" (p. 161). Deanesly elaborates on this point on pp. 195–204.

undergird absolutist interpretations was also undermined. Vernacularization illuminated the question of "authority," particularly over "written
words," which, once in English, whether read or recited, would be accessible to a greater number of people, all free and capable of imposing their
own authority over their reading. As Anne Hudson shows in her work on the
Lollards and their texts, "language" was the crucial issue in the reaction to
the translation of the Bible.[14] The same vehement reaction to vernacularization occurred with the French translations.[15] Jerome's *Prefaces*,
partly a result of his awareness of the multiplicity in meanings that translation highlights, were attempts to direct and educate readers. They served a
similar purpose when they reappeared in the Wycliffite Bible. Once in
English, the Bible became of necessity open to "diverse" interpretations;
the translation is itself the most radical assault on the static interpretive
authority of Jerome's Latin text.

Despite the fact that translations of the Bible into French preceded the
Middle English versions, themselves preceded by Anglo-Saxon versions of
the Gospels,[16] a furor over the partial translations into the "mother tongue"
arose in the fourteenth century, a preface to what would continue in the
sixteenth century. These fierce controversies led to a parliamentary debate
in 1395 intended to condemn "vernacular Scriptures." Part of a clerical
program to attack the Lollards, this official effort to condemn the Bible
translated into English was countered by John of Gaunt, who argued in
Parliament:

We will not be the refuse of all men, for sithen other nations have God's law, which is
law in our belief, in their own mother language, we will have ours in English, who
that ever it begrudgeth.[17]

Nevertheless the unofficial assault against an English Bible continued until
it was settled by Archbishop of Canterbury Thomas Arundel's Constitu-

[14] Hudson, *Premature Reformation*, pp.166–67.
[15] Emmanuel Pétavel, *La Bible en France ou les traductions françaises des Saintes Écritures*
(Geneva: Slatkine Reprints, 1970; repr. of Paris ed., 1864), pp. 9–65.
[16] See F. F. Bruce, *The English Bible: A History of Translations* (New York: Oxford
University Press, 1961), pp. 5–9; Pétavel, *La Bible en France*; Samuel Berger, *La Bible
française au moyen âge: Étude sur les plus anciennes versions de la Bible écrites en prose de
langue d'oïl* (Paris: Champion, 1884); Jean Bonnard, *Les Traductions de la Bible en vers
français au moyen âge* (Geneva: Slatkine Reprints, 1967), introd., pp. 1–10.
[17] As quoted in Deanesly, *The Lollard Bible*, p. 282.

tions of Oxford (which drew attention to Jerome's remarks on translation), drafted in 1407 and formally issued in 1409:[18]

Item, It is a dangerous thing as witnesseth blessed St. Jerome, to translate the text of holy Scripture out of the tongue into another; for in the translation the same sense is not always easily kept, as the same St. Jerome confesseth, that although he were inspired, yet oftentimes in this he erred: we therefore decree and ordain, that no man, hereafter, by his own authority translate any text of the Scripture into English or any other tongue, by way of a book, libel, or treatise; and that no man read any such book, libel or treatise, now lately set forth in the time of John Wickliff, or since, or hereafter to be set forth, in part or in whole, privily or apertly, upon pain of greater excommunication, until the said translation be allowed by the ordinary of the place, or, if the case so require, by the council provincial. He that shall do contrary to this, shall likewise be punished as a favourer of error and heresy.[19]

The intrusion of the vernacular into religious territory in the biblical translations forced attention to the meaning of words, and particularly of written authoritative words, and therefore threatened normative teachings based on Scripture and the authorities who heralded them.

The controversy also coincided with the expansion of the vernacular languages into other written forms. In the links to *The Canterbury Tales*, Chaucer dramatizes this invasion of vernacular exploration, parading the exercise of personalized interpretations and how recognized or unrecognized interests direct readers' or audiences' responses to literary experiences. He shows that he was acutely aware of the problem of prejudice in the interpretive process.[20] Also, if Chaucer knew Jerome's *Prefatory Epistles* to the Vulgate — which seems likely, since they appeared in English in the Wycliffite Bible; were defended by John of Gaunt, an avid supporter of English;[21] and were commonplace in editions of the Latin Bible — he was

[18] Hudson, *Premature Reformation*, p. 15.

[19] From John Foxe, *The Acts and Monuments of John Foxe*, ed. Josiah Pratt, 8 vols. (London: George Seeley, 1870), 3.245; trans. from D. Wilkins, *Concilia magnae Britanniae et Hiberniae* (London: R. Gosling, 1737).

[20] See Ferster, *Chaucer on Interpretation*, in which she applies Gadamerian notions of "prejudice" and "preconceptions" to a number of *The Canterbury Tales*. Ferster argues for the "too-powerful powerlessness of selves, and especially of authors," in imposing their authority over literary works (p. 22).

[21] Chaucer's close connection to John of Gaunt is well known among Chaucerians. Chaucer's wife, Philippa, was in the service of John of Gaunt's second wife, Constance, and John's third wife and mistress for many previous years was Chaucer's sister-in-law. John Wyclif was John of Gaunt's protégé. See Donald R. Howard, *Chaucer: His Life, His Works, His World* (New York: Dutton, 1987), pp. 87–88, 122–23, 130–31, 219.

aware of authoritative discussions of "the ambiguities of figurative words" (*De doctrina Christiana* 3.5.9), which he indulges in the links to *The Canterbury Tales*. One of the best examples of this is *The Wife of Bath's Prologue*. Proving Jerome's point about the potential abuse of Scriptures (and, for that matter, the arguments of the anti-Lollards, who wanted to silence the Bible), the Wife of Bath interprets the Bible to suit her own intentions, showing that the Bible itself is open to contradictory interpretations: "Poul dorste not comanden, atte leeste, / A thyng of which his maister yaf noon heeste" (*WBP* 73–74).

Jerome was trained in Classical rhetoric and learning, a central feature of the education of many of the church fathers in the patristic period. Of the eight most important Latin fathers, five (Tertullian, Cyprian, Arnobius, Lactantius, and Augustine) were professional rhetoricians before they became Christians, while the other three (Ambrose, Hilary, and Jerome) received their training in the rhetorical schools.[22] Jerome was particularly learned in Ciceronian rhetoric and his unreserved admiration for Cicero ("Tullius is to be trowid to be blowen with the spirit of retorik & to have translatid..."[*Preface of Seint Jerom* 72–73]), whose influence is evident both in Jerome's style and in his literary theories, led to the nightmare Jerome recounts in Letter 22, in which he was accused of being a Ciceronian, not a Christian.[23] In his "Letter to Pammachius" (395 a.d.) he elaborated his theory of translation, differentiating his method for translating Scripture from his standard practice of translating other Christian documents:

For I myself not only admit but freely proclaim that in translating from the Greek (except in the case of the Holy Scriptures where even the order of the words is a mystery), I render sense for sense and not word for word. For this course I have the authority of Cicero, who has translated.... [Jerome, Letter 57, lines 5–11][24]

As Jerome points out, it was the Ciceronian theory to translate "sensum de sensu" ("sense from sense") rather than "verbum e verbo" ("word for

---

[22] George Kennedy, *Classical Rhetoric and Its Christian and Secular Tradition from Ancient to Modern Times* (Chapel Hill: University of North Carolina Press, 1980), p. 146.

[23] "When asked my status, I replied I was a Christian. And He who sat upon the judgment seat said: 'You lie. You are a Ciceronian, not a Christian. Where your treasure is, there lies your heart also.'" Letter 22 in St. Jérôme, *Lettres*, vol. 1 (Paris: Société d'Édition "Les Belles Lettres," 1949), pp. 110–60. My translation.

[24] Sadowski, ed., *The Church Fathers and the Bible*, p. 174; "Ad Pammachium," Letter 57 in St. Jérôme, *Lettres*, vol. 3, text and trans. Jérôme Labourt (Paris: Société d'Édition "Les Belles Lettres," 1953), p. 59.

word"), and he follows in that tradition. Moreover, despite his insistence to the contrary in this letter, he invariably translates sense from sense in the Bible too. He unfolds his literary methodology in his numerous letters, particularly his correspondence with Augustine and other colleagues about problems with translating the Bible, and in his *Prefaces* to the biblical texts in the Vulgate. His convictions reflect his Ciceronian education, a humanistic approach to rhetoric and all language-related activities, which combined philosophy, the study—that is, interpretation—of revered secular literary texts, and ethics.[25] They also reveal his profound understanding of the way words work, which he developed as he constructed his theory of translation and interpretation, based on Cicero, Horace, and, of course, Origen, whom he credits with inspiring his biblical translation activity:

The studie of Orygen stiryde me therto / the which medlide the translacioun of Theodosyon. . . whanne he made ony scripturis more clereli to shyne that weren biforre lesse cleer. [*Preface of Seint Jerom* 16–21][26]

Like Origen, a brilliant philologist, biblical commentator, and theologian,[27] Jerome advanced the respective roles of the literal, historical, and spiritual meanings in the biblical texts.[28] He insisted that readers must have an accurate text; understand the words and their sense, that is, their literal and historical meaning; and, finally, comprehend their spiritual significance. Jerome was assigned the Bible project because of his philological and linguistic erudition, and as a consequence he earned a reputation as the most intelligent commentator on the literal level of the Bible.[29]

---

[25] Rita Copeland, *Rhetoric, Hermeneutics and Translation in the Middle Ages* (Cambridge: Cambridge University Press, 1991), pp.9–62, discusses Cicero's theories of rhetoric, hermeneutics, and translation and Jerome's transformation of Latin theories for his own intellectual purposes. For a recent survey of Cicero's contribution to Western humanistic studies, see C. Jan Swearingen, "Cicero: Defining the Value of Literacy," in *Rhetoric and Irony: Western Literacy and Western Lies* (New York: Oxford University Press, 1991), pp. 132–74.

[26] For the influence of Cicero and Origen in Jerome's theories of translation, see also "Epistula ad Damasum"; "Ad Pammachium," in St. Jérôme, *Lettres*, vol. 3.

[27] Origen, *On First Principles*, trans. G. W. Butterworth, introd. Henri de Lubac (New York: Harper Torchbooks, 1966).

[28] S. Hieronymi Presbyteri, *Commentariorum in Hiezechielem, 14*, in *Corpus Christianorum series Latina*, vol. 75 (Turnholti: Typographi Brepols Editores Pontificii, 1954), pp. 615–16.

[29] For an overview of the respect accorded Jerome for his philological studies, see Eugene F. Rice, Jr., *Saint Jerome in the Renaissance* (Baltimore, Md., and London: Johns Hopkins University Press, 1985), pp. 1–83.

Jerome distinguished between the revelatory power of the spoken word and the inherent ambiguity of the inscribed word. Marking the differences between spoken and written words, he argued that the disciples Peter and John did not need the kind of "study" he recommends for both "learned" and "unlearned" because they experienced the unmediated revelation of the Holy Spirit and learned from "Our Saviour":

... the Farissees ben astonyed *or merveilen* in the doctrine of the Lord and won-dryden in Petir & Joon hou they kouden the lawe sithen thei lerneden no lettris / For the Hooly Goost telde hem al that evere exercise *in studie* & every dayes thenkyng in the lawe of God was wont to gyve to othere men as it is writun / and thei weren disciplis of God able to be taugt. [*Jerom in his Prolog* 4.34–41]

As for other words, on the other hand, in contrast to unmediated logocentric communication, Jerome realized their inherent openness to multiple interpretations, which thus causes controversy because everyone thinks that he or she can be an interpreter of Scripture. Arguing for specialists, whether grammarians, rhetoricians, philosophers, logicians, musicians, astronomers, astrologers, physicians, earth tillers, masons, smiths, or carpenters, for example (*Jerom in his Prolog* 6.1–16), he also insisted that "the crafte of hooly scriptures is that science aloone" (*Jerom in his Prolog* 6.22–23) which requires specialists for its understanding. Though he sought, like Augustine, to close down the interpretive pos-sibilities in the biblical texts, at the same time he admitted that there are many who will "shape" Scriptures to their own will and interpret them for their own service, particularly those trained in secular letters:

the which peraventure whanne thei ben come to hooly scriptures aftir seculer lettris & with a fair sermoun delyten the eeris of the puple, whatevere thei seien, they weenen it be the lawe of God / neither thei dedeynen to knowe what the profetis what the postlis feeliden: but to her owne wit thei schapen uncovenable witnessis, as thoug it were myche worth & not a vyciouse maner of seiyng: to deprave sentenses and to drawe at her wille hooly scripturis repungnynge. . . . [*Jerom in his Prolog* 6.38–47]

While arguing against these free interpretive activities, he revealed his awareness of all the contingencies that written words, even Scripture itself, evoke.

For Jerome, spontaneous insight (or revelation), as experienced by the apostles, because it is due to direct spoken contact, is rare. Therefore, the

119

mediation of a teacher or a method is essential before "intelligent" interpretation can occur; interpretation is a science, or a sophisticated method. Jerome wanted to control a potentially anarchical reading or interpreting public. He clearly realized the inherently fluid nature of the inscribed word and wanted to exercise authority over this inscription. Such a recognition empowers "written words" as "signifiers" in themselves. This status for written words of necessity invests readers with the power if not the authority to read the words with whatever freedom the words inspire. But Jerome was conscious of the role of personal prejudices in the act of interpreting and so argued for a means to assess their power. Also, these references in the *Prefatory Epistles* suggest that in valorizing the authority of tradition and continuity he restricted the authority of an interpreter and questioned the ideology of unbiased reading, noting the "immediacy" of reading. Making an analogy between working with wax and interpreting, he writes:

Neische[30] wax & ligt to fourmen. yhe thoug the hondis and the crafti man & of the fourmere ceessen. netheles withinne forth in the wax thourg vertu is al maner shap that may be maad therof. . . . [*Jerom in his Prolog* 3.8–11]

Since wax can be shaped to whatever form one chooses, he writes, "we taken not heede what thou shuldist fynde: but what thou shuldist seche"(*Jerom in his Prolog* 3.6–8), suggesting that the reader make intellectual provisions for what he or she may be looking for rather than merely responding to what he or she is able to "form" spontaneously.

Knowing the dangers in the free operation of the inquiring interpreter, Jerome, like his colleague Augustine, sought a method or means to restrict a totally free exercise in interpretation, particularly with regard to Scriptures. In discussing his own translation project, he relied on the revelations of the New Testament to translate the Old Testament, not because he did not trust the seventy translators of the Septuagint, but because they, unlike the apostles, did not experience direct revelation of the Word:

I dampne not the seventy interpretours: but tristylich I putte the apostlys tofore alle hem *in autorite* / for by the mouth of thes apostlis: Crist sownede openli to me. . . . [*Preface of Seint Jerom* 93–96]

Testifying to the difficulties of biblical interpretation as well as the need for a process for interpreting, Jerome emphasized the need for specialized guidance before entering into the meaning of these most subtle texts:

30 "Neische" means "pliable."

For thou shuldist undirstonde that thou maist not entre in holy scripturis withoute a forgoere & shewynge the weie therof. [*Jerom in his Prolog* 6.3–6]

The capacity to understand these Scriptures, Jerome wrote, is a craft requiring a teacher, just as tailors, doctors, or smiths require teachers to learn their crafts, and just as the most learned of all (Plato and Pythagoras, for example) sought greater learning (*Jerom in his Prolog* 1.15–20). Thus, in the absence of unmediated revelation, Jerome argued for intellectual mediation, which is essential for penetrating the meaning of Scriptures. He promoted the means, if not to provide closure, at least to control arbitrary misreadings of Scripture.

But, finally, Jerome knew that the learned and the unlearned understand according to their own intellectual capacities, "& that the lerned man mygte / feele in o wise in the same sentence / and the unlerned in an other maner" (*Jerom in his Prolog* 8.44–46). Such an opinion underlies Jerome's effort to emphasize the need for teachers who will, as Chaucer's Parson said, "shewe . . . the way" (*ParsP* 49).[31] Jerome's emphasis on self-consciousness in interpretation sought to recognize prejudice in the interpretive act, and he focused on the necessary mediation of teachers who approach the Bible with an interpretive method and a "universal" understanding, formed from the transforming significance conferred by the Incarnation. This "universal" outlook, Jerome's "legitimate prejudice," ruled his translation of the Old Testament, for, while he chose not to defame the work of the seventy, he argued that a radical new understanding of the Scriptures was made possible by the "coming of Christ":

What thanne: dampne we the olde: nay / but aftir the studies of othere men that weren bifore us: what that we may we traveylen in the hous of the Lord / thei han translatid scriptures bifore the comyng of Crist / they han spoken with douteful sentences that they knewen not / but we aftir the passioun and the resurreccioun of him not onely writen profecie, but open storie / For thingis seyn ben telde in o maner & thingis herd ben told in an other maner / for the bettere that we undurstonden a thing the bettere we tellen it. [*Preface of Seint Jerom* 81–92]

Both tradition and the unveiling of its doubtfulness by the Redemption are measures by which he judged his own understanding.

In expounding in the *Prefaces* on the difficulty of interpretation, Jerome

---

[31] All quotations from *The Canterbury Tales* are from Larry D. Benson, gen. ed., *The Riverside Chaucer*, 3d ed. (Boston: Houghton Mifflin, 1987).

drew attention to the subjective interests and attitudes of audiences who will advance personal interpretations, reflecting, of course, their own presuppositions, education, and interests in the act of interpretation. Such sophistication about biblical interpretation shows both his awareness of the necessity for interpretive method and his preoccupation with the openness of the texts to diverse meanings. The trained may have brought a systematic self-reflexiveness to the act of interpretation, but, as Jerome points out, not all readers and audiences have such sophistication. Jerome reveals a notable tension about the problem of the inscribed word, making efforts to "close the text" while at the same time making clear the difficulties in such a proposition. Audiences then, just as today, had a habit of imposing their personal presuppositions on the stories they read or heard, whether sacred or profane, just as tellers are redactors or recreators of their tales.

Two issues connected to Jerome's *Prefaces* and the translations of the Bible into English in the fourteenth century are particularly interesting for a discussion of Chaucer's *Canterbury Tales*. The first is the significance of vernacularization for the poetic agenda of the fourteenth century, and the second is the potential for interpretive anarchy — because once the Bible is vernacularized and made open to "speech," the question of who holds authority over biblical words, or any words, is thrown open to controversy. The various responses and spontaneous remarks of the internal audience of *The Canterbury Tales* demonstrate the interpretive anarchy made possible by a vernacular participation in literary exegesis. Chaucer's characters express various literary responses: some reflect the diversity possible in the more immediate medieval audience (Chaucer's court company); others serve as Chaucerian explanations intended to guide or control his audience's or readers' responses; still others are authorial attempts to excuse the writer for responsibility for the text and the audience's response. Whichever explanation underlies Chaucer's design, all reflect the author's recognition of the "openness" of the texts to multiple meanings and Chaucer's own lack of "authority" over the interpretations his audience might assume. In fact, for decades Chaucerians have argued unconvincingly about whether the author imposed an overall authority on the poem; all the contingencies of individual interest seem to undermine these absolutes and to abrogate authority in favor of personal agendas.[32] The kind of authority that Jerome

[32] See for example, V. A. Kolve, *Chaucer and the Imagery of Narrative: The First Five Canterbury Tales* (Stanford, Calif.: Stanford University Press, 1984); Dieter Mehl, *Geoffrey Chaucer: An Introduction to His Narrative Poetry* (Cambridge: Cambridge University Press, 1986), pp. 120–204; A. J. Minnis, *Medieval Theory of Authorship: Scholastic Literary Attitudes in the Later Middle Ages* (London and Berkeley, Calif.: Scolar, 1984); Alfred David, *The Strumpet Muse: Art and Morals in Chaucer's Poetry* (Bloomington: Indiana University Press, 1976); E. Talbot Donaldson, *Speaking of Chaucer* (London: Athlone, 1970).

would like to have imposed on the interpretation of the Bible seems to have eluded the author of *The Canterbury Tales*.

This personalization of motive that appears in the vernacular literature of the fourteenth century, some have argued, may have resulted from the spread of private reading; it may be responsible at least for Chaucer's awareness of his inability to control his audience's responses.[33] Brian Stock's *Implications of Literacy* traces the impact of reading on medieval society in the eleventh and twelfth centuries, showing the historical emergence of

the distinction between an inner linguistic model, based upon Latin's explicit grammar, and common, at least in theory, to many members of a group, and an outer, speaking-capacity, chiefly associated with the vernaculars, which demanded individual performance and flexible social allegiances.[34]

Stock's connection between the vernacular languages and the explosion into social diversity that accompanies their emergence must have partly directed this evolving consciousness. Also, literacy, many have suggested, is partly responsible for the consciousness of seeing oneself as different and separate from a group.[35] But literacy is an important cultural issue because it reflects changes in the social and economic conditions as well as in linguistic environments, all of which could contribute to a consciousness of self as distinct from others.

Chaucer's internal audience in *The Canterbury Tales*, the characters who respond diversely to the *Tales*, represents different interpreters and interpretations,[36] aesthetic and moral attitudes,[37] and medieval hierarchical views of social place and status.[38] Ostensibly content with the role of compiler,[39] Chaucer presented a spectrum of audience responses and in so

[33] Ferster, *Chaucer on Interpretation*, p. 10.

[34] Brian Stock, *The Implications of Literacy* (Princeton, N.J.: Princeton University Press, 1983), p. 528.

[35] Walter Ong, S. J., *Orality and Literacy* (London and New York: Methuen, 1982); Jack Goody, *The Domestication of the Savage Mind* (Cambridge: Cambridge University Press, 1977); Eric Havelock, *Preface to Plato* (Cambridge, Mass., and London: Harvard University Press, 1963).

[36] Mehl, *Geoffrey Chaucer*, pp. 120–204.

[37] Kolve, *Chaucer and the Imagery of Narrative*.

[38] See Paul Olson, The Canterbury Tales *and the Good Society* (Princeton, N.J.: Princeton University Press, 1986); Jill Mann, *Chaucer and Medieval Estates Satire: The Literature of Social Classes and the* General Prologue *to the* Canterbury Tales (Cambridge: Cambridge University Press, 1973).

[39] Minnis, *Medieval Theory of Authorship*, p.210.

123

doing showed his recognition of the openness of his own poetic texts to spontaneous commentary, which many current theorists suggest explains diverse interpretations, conflict in interpretation, or no meaning at all.[40] Among the characters who comprise the internal audience for the *Tales*, some treat a story as "play"; others as revenge, doctrine, or dialogue; and still others as pure art. Ahistorical responses like these clearly come to nothing when they are scrutinized with the "best" historical methodologies, but most fiction, and particularly the fiction experienced by the pilgrims within the literary boundaries of the *Tales*, is apprehended far less conscientiously than it would be by an "ideal" reader. The literary climate of the *Tales*, on the contrary, points to Chaucer's recognition that in the world of fiction there is no final or definitive interpretation. The responses show the capacity of Chaucerian narrative to be self-reflexive, as it both draws attention to itself and focuses on its own diverse modes of public presentation.[41]

Chaucer was conscious of the subjectivity of readers and of his own inability to control their interpretations.[42] He also knew that this was a problem of literary textuality, whether written or spoken. In *The Man of Law's Tale* and *The Second Nun's Tale*, Chaucer also represents the kind of spontaneous insight or unmediated knowledge through hearing and consequent conversion that Augustine attributes to St. Anthony (*De doctrina Christiana*, Prologue, 4), or Jerome to the apostles, on the grounds that "and whanne the voys is spred abroad in to the eeris of the disciple, from the mouth of the auctor: it sowneth the more strongly" (*Jerom in his Prolog* 2.19–20). In *The Man of Law's Tale*, when Constance is slandered, with the slanderer's hand on the New Testament, "A Britoun book, written with Evaungiles" (line 666, a possible reference to an Anglo-Saxon translation of the four evangelists), "A voys was herd in general audience, / And seyde,

---

[40] Paul Ricoeur, *The Conflict of Interpretations*, ed. Don Ihde (Evanston, Ill.: Northwestern University Press, 1974); Gadamer, *Truth and Method*; Jacques Derrida, *Of Grammatology*, trans. Gayatri Chakravorty Spivak (Baltimore, Md., and London: Johns Hopkins University Press, 1974); Stanley Fish, *Is There a Text in This Class?* (Cambridge, Mass.: Harvard University Press, 1980).

[41] David Aers, *Chaucer, Langland, and the Creative Imagination* (London: Routledge & Kegan Paul, 1980), pp. 81–82; Peter Elbow, *Oppositions in Chaucer* (Middletown, Conn.: Wesleyan University Press, 1975). Likewise H. Marshall Leicester, Jr., *The Disenchanted Self: Representing the Subject in the* Canterbury Tales (Berkeley: University of California Press, 1990), p. 13, argues that the *Tales* must be understood not as representing "performing selves" but as "texts" whose voices are to be analyzed.

[42] Ferster, *Chaucer on Interpretation*.

'Thou hast desclaundred, giltelees, / The doghter of hooly chirche in heigh presence'" (lines 673–75), and there is instant marvel and acceptance of this unmediated oral communication, which leads to the conversion of King Alla. Again, in *The Second Nun's Tale*, Cecile's husband is led to his conversion through a similar direct experience with the Word, for in a vision of an old man in white, holding a book with letters of gold, inscribing the omnipotence and universality of the Christian God (lines 200–10), he responds to the question, "Leevestow this thyng or no?" (line 212), immediately with, "I leeve al this thyng" (line 213). In both these instances we have conversion narratives that are outside interpretive experiences, for they occur in response to unmediated communications of the Word. But, important as these stories are for a satisfactory understanding of Chaucer's literary program in *The Canterbury Tales*, they nonetheless stand as examples of precisely what both Jerome and Augustine say of such experiences. They are rare because the Word is not present, and most of the time we must depend on interpretive activities in an effort to conjure Its presence. It is in this activity of interpreting that most of us operate.

Chaucer dramatizes the potentiality of anarchical interpretations in the links to *The Canterbury Tales*, where we experience the understanding and the various prejudices of the hearers of the *Tales* on the pilgrimage to Canterbury and at the same time are made aware of Chaucer's sense of the presuppositions of the audience, both real and imaginary, and of their diverse responses since there are no ideal readers in the audience.

The internal audience for *The Canterbury Tales*, shaping stories to its own will, however, never goes beyond these spontaneous interpretations and never, except for Chaucer the pilgrim, who changes literary style and purpose, reverses its *modi agendi*. The Host, in contrast to the narrator, who arrogates to himself total authority for the tale-telling, becoming lord of the game in which he does not participate, invariably imposes his own literal sense on the *Tales*, which he bases on his personal experience. Together these divergent commentaries on the *Tales* attest to Chaucer's awareness, like Jerome's, of the interpreter's or reader's ability to perceive various possibilities in spoken or written discourse and to create competing interpretations; they point, in contrast to Jerome's efforts to make readers' interpretive choices informed by some self-reflexive method, to Chaucer's own abdication of power or authority over the interpretations assumed by the participants in the literary drama.

Even the most cursory reading of *The Canterbury Tales* shows that the author was deeply influenced by exegetical traditions and medieval interpretive habits; thus the narrator's disclaimers about consistent meaning, or

125

"sentence," are an apparent subterfuge for the author's not-so-hidden intentions.[43] In addition, Chaucer's borrowings, imitations, reworkings, and outright theft of source texts adapted for his poetic purposes demonstrate how conscious he was of the role of rhetorical intention in creative activities. His own renderings of biblical texts highlight the exercise of authorial intention and how it rearranges the original "sentence" of a source text when rewritten, translated, or transformed in some way, whether in the sacred or secular language domains.

The narrator has recorded the pilgrimage "as it semed me" (*GP* 39) and also refuses to "telle his tale untrewe" (line 735). These consciously adopted *modi agendi* of the narrator allow him to include stories that represent the personalities of the characters on the pilgrimage, for he (lines 3173–75)

> . . . moot reherce
> Hir tales alle, be they bettre or werse,
> Or elles falsen som of my mateere.

While these remarks of the compiler express his narrative purposes, they also facilitate Chaucer the poet's guise of detachment from the literary work, revealing his awareness of the limits of his power over the stories he collects once they are made public, as well as the limitless possibilities the *Tales* provide readers.

The narrator as character and persona of the poet has his reasons for assuming the role he does, but the Host, who lacks sophistication about his role in the fiction, regularly reconstructs the pilgrims' stories according to his personal experiences and attitudes, interpreting the *Tales* and the tellers' intentions according to what he imagines are their personal experiences. He exemplifies Jerome's distinction between the reading or responding habits of the learned and the uneducated: "the lerned man mygte / feele in o wise in the same sentence / and the unlerned in an other maner" (*Jerom in his Prolog* 8.44–46).

As the organizer of the game, the Host does not tell a tale himself, but he manages nevertheless to comment on the tales according to his own precon-

---

[43] See Lawrence Besserman, "'Glosynge Is a Glorious Thyng': Chaucer's Biblical Exegesis," in David Lyle Jeffrey, comp. and ed., *Chaucer and Scriptural Tradition* (Ottawa: University of Ottawa Press, 1984), pp. 65–73; Douglas Wurtele, "Chaucer's *Canterbury Tales* and Nicholas of Lyre's *Postillae litteralis et moralis super totam Bibliam*," in ibid., pp. 89–107; David Lyle Jeffrey, "Chaucer and Wyclif: Biblical Hermeneutic and Literary Theory in the XIVth Century," in ibid., pp. 109–40. This collection of essays provides a thorough introduction to the influences of scriptural and exegetical traditions on Chaucer's poetry.

ceptions. He also projects his own "intentions" on what he imagines must be the "intentions" of his fellow pilgrims, often locating their attitudes with their social status. For example, he objects to the Reeve's preaching and his speaking of holy writ (*RvP* 3901–3903), yet he does not object to "som doctryne" from Chaucer the pilgrim (*Th–MelL* 935) or a "thrifty tale" from the Man of Law, (*MLE* 1165) or a "lerned" one from the Parson (*MLE* 1168); he expects a "noble storie" from the Knight (*MilP* 3111), but not from the Miller; a tale of love from the Squire (*SqH* 2), but not one of "gentillesse" from the Franklin (*SqT* 695). In all these instances, as in his deference to the socially elite characters, the Host reveals his literary and social prejudices, convictions, and assumptions, all of which control his responses to and expectations of the pilgrims and their stories.

In fact, in his approach to understanding the *Tales*, or perhaps "refusing" to try to understand the *Tales*, he exemplifies what Jerome suggests in his development of the "wax" analogy, "netheles withinne forth in the wax thourg vertu is al maner shap that may be maad therof" (*Jerom in his Prolog* 3.10–11), presenting, instead of a virtuous reading, a willful response, for he does not "unduryoke al unbuxumnesse" ("harness all lack of humility") (*Jerom in his Prolog* 3.21), for Jerome a necessity if one is to engage in interpretive activities with honesty. What Chaucer exposes here is the power of words to be molded like wax, saying one thing and meaning many others, depending, of course, on the speaker, reader, listener, or interpreter and the circumstances of their use. Chaucer's Host is a subversive authority figure whose function and literary responses contrast with Jerome's emphasis on the necessary authority of trained teachers to guide readers of the Bible. The Host's ambiguous managerial role dramatizes Chaucer's argument that in fiction it is difficult if not impossible to impose absolute authority.

The Host and the narrator, as important characters in the links, create the circumstances for the tale-telling and the interpretive freedom that takes over the pilgrimage. The question remains, however, whether Chaucer the poet sought to close the play in interpretation that Jerome and Chaucer himself, through the links and the imposition of personal power in the tale-telling activity itself, show is fundamental to any language-related activity. For Jerome, interpretive method is a tool to recognize the subjectivity in the act of understanding and therefore to direct its potential for an arbitrary exercise of reading and responding freedom, the kind engineered throughout *The Canterbury Tales*. Chaucer critics still disagree about whether the religious tales and the final tales of the collection are intended to express

Chaucer's desire to impose an ultimate authority on the tale-telling.[44] In the last two tales, the Manciple's[45] and the Parson's, the compiler associates the dangers of speaking the truth, for which a grim retribution follows, with the nonfictional reminder of the reality to which every medieval person must respond. The crow, like the poet, "moot reherce as ny as evere he kan" (*GP* 732) and therefore make himself vulnerable to the consequences of his truthfulness. As the *Tales* draw to their conclusion, the poet behind the Manciple forces us to see that the retribution for brute honesty may be death, just as it augurs the demise of fiction. The tone of the last fifty lines of *The Manciple's Tale* has moved us uncomfortably into the uncompromising nonfictional conclusion, the poet showing his painful awareness of what befalls those who confront us with the truth. Nevertheless, right up to the end, Chaucer emphasizes the role of individual human consciousness in the worlds we perceive or construct.

Finally, however, like Jerome, who recommends that trained teachers assist in the interpretation of the Bible, it is the teacher who takes over, who will show us the way and interpret the world according to a universal conviction that his prose rendition lays out for us. The spontaneous interpretive carnival that characterized the pilgrimage is over. The Parson, adopting a similar intellectual humility to Jerome's — ". . . it is foly to feyne thee to knowe that thou knowist not" (*Jerom in his Prolog* 6.61–62); ". . . thus I knowe oneliche this thing that I knowe no thing fully" (*Jerom in his Prolog* 7.229–30) — tells his audience, ". . . this meditacioun / I putte it ay under correccioun / Of clerkes, for I am nat textueel; / I take but the

---

[44] See, for example, Kolve's argument in *Chaucer and the Imagery of Narrative* that *The Man of Law's Tale* is the rebeginning of the collection along more authoritative religious lines (pp. 285–358). Jill Mann, in *Geoffrey Chaucer* (Atlantic Highlands, N.J.: Humanities Press International, Inc., 1991), argues on the other hand that, because the *Tale* explores "woman's subjection to man as the human subjection to God's purveiance" (p. 154), the *Tale* "deconstructs power" (p. 136). Likewise Rodney Delasanta, "And of Great Reverence: Chaucer's Man of Law," *ChauR* 5 (1971): 288–310, questions the Man of Law's authority, as also Olson, in The Canterbury Tales *and the Good Society*, probes whether the government of the *Tale* is ideal (pp. 276–99). Even *The Parson's Tale*, which appears an unproblematic, religious conclusion to the collection, has been discussed as a satire; see John Finlayson, "The Satiric Mode and the *Parson's Tale*," *ChauR* 6 (1971–72): 94–116; see also Carol V. Kaske, "Getting Around *The Parson's Tale*: An Alternative to Allegory and Irony," in Rossell Hope Robbins, ed., *Chaucer at Albany* (New York: Burt Franklin, 1975), pp. 147–77.

[45] For three recent analyses of *The Manciple's Tale*, all of which appeared in *ChauR* 25 (1991): 318–54, see Peter C. Herman, "Treason in the *Manciple's Tale*"; Michaela Paasche Grudin, "Chaucer's *Manciple's Tale* and the Poetics of Guile"; and Marc M. Pelen, "The Manciple's 'Cosyn' to the 'Dede'."

sentence..." (*ParsP* 55–58). The Parson's distinction between the "tex-tueel" and the "sentence" is already familiar to us in Cicero's and Jerome's distinction between "words" and "sense." Jerome writes of the Catholic epistles (James, Peter, John, and Jude), "...they ben bothe schorte in wordes & longe in sentences so that selden it is..." (*Jerom in his Prolog* 8.26–27). Similarly, the Parson expounds a lengthy "sentence" on penance elaborated from one short text from Jeremiah (6:16). In *The Canterbury Tales*, Chaucer has indulged the subjective interests of human beings, letting the "learned" and the "unlearned" understand according to their abilities, although in the end he lets the Parson present his "meditacioun," (*ParsP* 69) in a final gesture toward closure, which remains, because of its literary medium, nonetheless tentative.

In this article I have shown how the arguments about hermeneutics advanced by Jerome in his *Prefaces* apply to the problematics of interpretive anarchy as dramatized by the Host, the narrator, and the internal audience of *The Canterbury Tales*. In creating a fictional world in which storytellers and listeners impose their personal power over the literary experience, Chaucer, like Jerome in the *Prefatory Epistles*, showed his awareness of the potential arbitrariness of literary response, identifying both the pleasure and the danger of interpretation. Both authors show the essential openness of literary texts to diverse interpretations and the willful desires of readers, depending on their own preconceptions, to impose their authority on their reading. The availability of these fundamental rhetorical assumptions through a medium as socially and theologically respectable as Jerome's *Prefaces* is convincing evidence that notions about textual or linguistic polysemy were far more intellectually widespread in the Middle Ages than either our inherited nineteenth-century historical-critical literary meth-odologies or new criticism have permitted us to realize.

I have also suggested that the vernacularization program of the late Middle Ages encouraged consciousness of the polysemy of literary works because it drew attention to the spontaneity of spoken language as dis-tinguished from the inscribed nature of Latin, which was no longer a living language, except for the few. Jerome's effort in the *Epistles* is to guide and direct potentially capricious renderings of biblical texts, which he recog-nized, from his knowledge of Ciceronian rhetoric, resulted from the intrinsic flexibility in the meaning of words. But, while Jerome, also in the tradition of Cicero, sought to guide literary exegesis (in Jerome's case, biblical interpretation) and to avoid its potential for abuse, Chaucer's characters, in the links and the *Tales* themselves, dramatize unharnessed interpretive activity. Chaucer revels in the polyphonic chorus of attitudes and ideas expressed and in the spontaneous and carnival reversal of authoritative exegesis that invades much of the pilgrimage, as the journey becomes an opportunity for the pilgrims to mold with the wax "al maner shap that may be maad therof" (*Jerom in his Prolog* 3.8–11).

The Pardoner's Pants
(and Why They Matter)

Richard Firth Green
University of Western Ontario

W HEN, AT THE END of his *Tale*, Chaucer's Pardoner offers the Host the first chance to kiss his spurious relics, the offer produces a surprisingly violent reaction (*PardT* 946–55):

> "Nay, nay!" quod he, "thanne have I Cristes curs!
> Lat be," quod he, "it shal nat be, so theech!
> Thou woldest make me kisse thyn olde breech,
> And swere it were a relyk of a seint,
> Though it were with thy fundement depeint!
> But, by the croys which that Seint Eleyne fond,
> I wolde I hadde thy coillons in myn hond
> In stide of relikes or of seintuarie.
> Lat kutte hem of, I wol thee helpe hem carie;
> They shul be shryned in an hogges toord!"[1]

This passage has provoked considerable critical interest, but almost all of it has focused on the reference to the Pardoner's "coillons" and the question whether a threat to castrate a putative eunuch is to be seen as ludicrously improbable or wittily appropriate. My interest here, however, is not directly with those "coillons" but rather with the Pardoner's "olde breech."[2] I shall

---

[1] All citations of Chaucer's works are from Larry D. Benson, gen. ed., *The Riverside Chaucer*, 3d ed. (Boston: Houghton Mifflin, 1987).

[2] This detail has generated far less discussion, the main exception being Daniel Knapp's suggestion that it might have been prompted by the recollection of St. Thomas of Canterbury's hair breeches, which, at least in the early sixteenth century, were to be seen in the crypt of Canterbury Cathedral; "The Relyk of a Seint: A Gloss on Chaucer's Pilgrimage," *ELH* 39 (1972): 1–26. Melvin Storm, "The Pardoner's Invitation: Quaestor's Bag or Becket's Shrine," *PMLA* 97 (1982): 815, seems to regard Knapp's case as proved. Joseph Grennen, "The Pardoner, the Host, and the Depth of Chaucerian Insult," *ELN* 25 (1987): 21, sees in the "old breech" a sacrilegious parody of the vernicle that the Pardoner wears on his cap.

argue that the passage contains a previously unrecognized allusion whose exposition may, nevertheless, throw some light on the vexed question of the Pardoner's sexuality.

The allusion, I will argue, is to a tale belonging to the general folktale type "Adulteress Outwits Husband,"[3] whose best-known surviving English-language representative is probably the ballad "Our Goodman."[4] This ballad, which is widely distributed throughout Europe and North America, presents a dialogue between an incredulous husband, who has returned unannounced to find a trail of incriminating objects leading from the stable to the bedroom, and his unrepentant wife, who offers an increasingly implausible explanation for each of them in turn. In a spirit of local chauvinism I quote one of their exchanges from a version collected in southwestern Ontario in 1962:

> When I got home the other night my loving wife to see,
> I spied some pants upon the rack where my pants out to be.
> So I said to my wife, the light of my life: "Explain this thing to me.
> Whose are those pants upon the rack where my pants ought to be?"
> She said: "You're drunk, you skunk, you silly old skunk, you're drunk
> as a skunk can be.
> 'Tis only a dishrag my neighbor left with me."
> Now in all my years of travelling, a million miles or more,
> A zipper in a dishrag I never have seen before.[5]

Like most of the Child ballads, "Our Goodman" is not recorded before the eighteenth century, but the general tale type to which it belongs reaches back a long way — further back, indeed, than the Middle Ages.[6] One of its incarnations is the widespread medieval tale "The Friar's Pants," some

---

[3] Stith Thompson, *Motif Index of Folk Literature*, 6 vols. (Bloomington: Indiana University Press, 1955), K1510–40 (the specific tales we shall be concerned with are indexed as K1526).

[4] F. J. Child, ed., *The English and Scottish Popular Ballads*, 5 vols. (Boston: Houghton Mifflin, 1882–1898), 5.88–95 (no. 274).

[5] Edith Fowke, "A Sampling of Bawdy Ballads from Ontario," in Bruce Jackson, ed., *Folklore and Society: Essays in Honor of Benj. A. Botkin* (Hatboro, Pa.: Folklore Associates, 1966), p. 56.

[6] In Apuleius's *Metamorphoses* 9.17–21, the interrupted lover leaves a pair of sandals to be discovered by the returning husband, though here it is the lover, not the wife, who explains away their presence (as having earlier been stolen from him by the slave set by the husband to guard his wife); Apulée, *Les Métamorphoses*, ed. D. S. Robertson, 3 vols. (Paris: Budé, 1956), 3.77–81.

variant of which I believe to lie behind the detail of the "olde breech" that Chaucer included in the Host's diatribe against the Pardoner.

This story may best be represented by a version given by Poggio Bracciolini in his *Facetiae*, written in the middle of the fifteenth century. Here, in a particularly concise and witty form, are most of the main elements of the tale; its only eccentricity is that Poggio's husband is not himself duped but actually connives in passing off a pair of all-too-secular pants as a sacred relic to be kissed by devout onlookers:

Something funny, and worth telling in company, once happened in Amelia. A married woman, moved I believe by a genuine conscience, was confessing her sins to a Franciscan friar. As they were speaking, he was consumed with lust, and when the woman had finally been won over by his many speeches, they sought an opportunity and place for doing the deed. It was decided that the woman should pretend to be ill and call for the friar to confess her, for it is usual for men of this type to be left alone, that, with no witnesses present, there might be freedom to speak of those things that pertain to the soul. She, having feigned physical illness, took to her bed, pretended she was in great pain, and summoned her confessor, who, as he came to her when the others were out of the way, "knew" her several times in private. Since they lingered a long while, the others came back, and the friar left, as if with the confession still incomplete, intending to return the next day. He returns and, leaving his pants on the woman's bed, "examines her sins" as before. The husband, somewhat suspicious of so lengthy a confession, enters the bedroom, and the friar, disturbed by this sudden interruption, flees without his pants. On seeing the pants, the husband cries out that he is an adulterer not a friar, and on the evidence of the pants the whole household denounces the shameful crime. Hotfoot, he goes shouting to the superior of the friars' convent, complains of the shameless act, and threatens death to the perpetrator. The other, who was an old man, restrains his anger, suggesting that he is publicizing the disgrace of his own household and of himself, and that the affair requires them to act quietly and with decency in order for the outrage to be covered up. The husband says that with the discovery of the pants the thing is such public knowledge that it cannot be hushed up. The old man suggests a remedy for that: he will say that they are the pants of St. Francis which the friar had taken to heal the woman, and he offers to go there with a splendid procession and publicly bring back the pants. The plan having been agreed on, the superior called the friars together, *and with a crucifix and sacred vestments went to the man's house, reverently collected the pants and, holding them in his hands like holy relics upon a silk napkin, offered them first to the husband, then the wife, then to the remaining onlookers to kiss* [ac cum cruce uestibusque sacris domum illius accedit, brachasque deuote capiens, & tamquam reliquias religiosas super peplum sericium suspensis manibus ferens, tum viro, tum matri, tum reliquis obuiis exosculandas porrexit], and when they had been carried back to the convent with great ceremonial and chanting, he placed them in the sacristy with the other relics. When the trick was later discovered, representatives of the city came to inquire into the misdeed.[7]

This mid-fifteenth-century version is the earliest I am aware of that contains both key motifs (the relic and the kiss), but a slightly later version by Masuccio Salernitano (ca. 1475) improves upon it somewhat by making the wife herself devise the plan to explain away the pants as a sacred relic (in this case, of the improbably named San Griffone).[8] She conveys the plan to her lover by means of her maid, and Masuccio's convent superior becomes merely a reluctant accomplice, co-opted into organizing a triumphal procession to retrieve the pants. In this version the cuckolded husband, "having placed unhesitating faith in the fraudulent claims of the superior,"[9] is completely taken in by the ruse. Poggio and Masuccio differ from one another in a number of other small details, and thus it is impossible to be sure whether we are dealing here with two independent versions or whether the second is merely a clever reworking of the first. There are, however, enough other medieval examples of this tale type to prove that it had been in circulation for some time,[10] and there are good reasons for thinking that a similar story could easily have been known to Chaucer.

The earliest example seems to be a fabliau called *Les Braies au cordelier*, dated by Richard O'Gorman to the mid-thirteenth century.[11] Here the lover is a clerk, not a friar, and the cuckolded husband, rather than simply stumbling across the telltale pants, actually puts them on by mistake. The husband, a merchant, asks his wife to wake him before dawn so that he can

[7] Poggio Bracciolini, *Facetiae*, in *Opera omnia*, ed. Riccardo Fubini, 4 vols. (Turin: Bottega d'Erasmo, 1964–69) 1:480. Facs. ed., originally printed Basle, 1583 (italics added). Unless otherwise noted, all translations are mine.

[8] Masuccio Salernitano, *Il Novellino*, ed. Alfredo Mauro (Bari: Laterza, 1940), pp. 30–41 ("Novella 3").

[9] Ibid., p. 39.

[10] For an exhaustive catalogue of examples (mostly from the sixteenth and seventeenth centuries), see Johannes Bolte's notes to his edition of *Jakob Freys Gartengesellschaft*, Litteranischen Vereins in Stuttgart, vol. 209 (Tübingen, 1896), pp. 248–51.

[11] Richard O'Gorman, ed., *Les Braies au cordelier: Anonymous Fabliau of the Thirteenth Century* (Birmingham, Ala.: Summa Publications, 1983), pp. 3–5. O'Gorman's edition has a useful appendix containing several French analogues, including the fabliau *Les Braies le prestre*, a story from the *Livre du Chevalier de La Tour Landry*, and the farce *Frère Guillebert*.

134

make an early start for market. She, in order to enjoy her lover the longer, bundles him out of the house well before the appointed hour, only to have him return inconveniently for some extra sleep when he discovers the real time. Rising once more, he dresses in the dark and, mistaking them for his own, picks up the pants and purse of the clerk, who has been concealed in the bedroom the whole time. The next morning the wife and her lover discover the error and realize that the irate husband will soon be returning to demand an explanation. The wife's solution — to pass off the clerk's pants as those of a friar which she had borrowed after dreaming that they would act as a charm to cure her infertility — involves a quick trip to the local convent to establish her cover; she soon finds a friar willing to help her out, though his motive for doing so is unclear. All the main features of the later tale are present here. True, the friar is not himself the lover, merely an accomplice, and the pants are represented not as a holy relic, merely a superstitious folk remedy,[12] but it is not difficult to see how the later story could have developed from such a plot. One might even go so far as to argue that the motif of the holy relic could have been present in the source of *Les Braies au cordelier* and was deliberately recast in an effort to avoid appearing overly antifraternal; we shall see that other versions show some discomfort with the racier form of the ending.

Two fourteenth-century French versions might also be argued to be suppressing the sacrilegious motif of the relic. The earlier, *Les Braies le prestre*,[13] a fabliau by Jean de Condé, follows *Les Braies au cordelier* with only minor variations (the husband, for instance, is a butcher rather than a merchant) up to the point where the husband discovers that he is wearing the priest's pants and purse; then the story is brought to an abrupt conclusion, with the husband simply mocked by his companions in the market square while the priest steals the money from the purse that had been left at home. One would feel more confident in claiming this to be a truncated form of the same tale type were there not other, clearly independent, examples of a similar story. The late-seventeenth-century broadside ballad "The Debtford Frollick," for instance, ends not with any clever excuses on the part of the wife but merely with the cuckolded husband "mad and monstrous sad" to find himself wearing his rival's "shag-

---

[12] Fertility cults hardly less bizarre (particularly those surrounding a rather intimate relic of St. Foutin) seem actually to have existed at the margins of the medieval church; Niall Rudd, *The Satires of Horace* (Cambridge: Cambridge University Press, 1966), pp. 69–70. I am grateful to A. R. Littlewood for this reference.

[13] O'Gorman, ed., *Les Braies au cordelier*, pp. 76–82.

breeches."[14] Nevertheless, the fact that *Les Braies le prestre* and *Les Braies au cordelier* match one another so closely to this point makes the suggestion that Jean de Condé deliberately suppressed the whole episode of the quick-witted wife and her ingenious solution somewhat more plausible.

The second French version, one of the stories in the *Livre du Chevalier de la Tour Landry* (ca. 1371),[15] shows clearer signs of bowdlerization. Here the husband is a ropemaker (*cordier*), and his wife's lover a prior, and, rather than putting on his rival's pants in the dark, the cuckold, mistaking them for his purse, picks them up and sets off to market with them slung over his shoulder. The ending preserves the wife's table turning, but, as befits a tale told by a knight for the instruction of his daughters, all traces of scurrility have disappeared. The wife's gossip (*commère*) manages to calm the husband by convincing him that, like other local women, his spouse wears men's pants as a way of preserving her chastity.[16]

About a hundred years later another version of the same story is told by Sabadino Degli Arienti, but this one is very much less decorous.[17] The wife of a peasant grants her favors to a lecherous priest in return for the promise of a pair of red slippers but demands that he deposit his purse with her as security for the debt. Unable to detach his purse from his pants in the dark, he leaves the whole ensemble behind, and the next morning the husband, who had been sleeping in the same room, sets off for market wearing it. Anticipating trouble, the wife turns, as in *Livre du Chevalier*, to her gossip for help, but this *comatre* has a fat purse as well as a pair of pants to explain away. For the pants she uses the same explanation as her French counter-part, but she accounts for the money by saying that it had been left with the wife for safekeeping by a woman who wished to commission a portrait of St. Pancracio for the local church. Although a church image is not the same as a holy relic, the resemblance is sufficiently close to suggest that both these stories derive from the same general tradition.

The final fourteenth-century version, "Novella 207" in Franco Sacchetti's

---

[14] W. Chappell and J. W. Ebsworth, eds., *The Roxburghe Ballads*, 9 vols. (London and Hertford: Ballad Society, 1871–97), 4.30–32.

[15] O'Gorman, ed., *Les Braies au cordelier*, pp. 83–84. Cf. Thomas Wright, ed., *The Book of the Knight of La Tour-Landry*, EETS, vol. 33 (London: Kegan Paul, 1868), pp. 80–81 (a fifteenth-century English translation).

[16] O'Gorman, ed., *Les Braies au cordelier*, p. 84; the English version has, "For in good sothe she and y weren breches for because of the harlotis that handelithe women, and takithe hem hastely by thaire priuite" (p. 81).

[17] Sabadino Deglia Arienti, *Le Porretane*, ed., Giovanni Gambarin (Bari: Laterza, 1914), pp. 231–35 ("Novella 39").

collection *Il Trecentonovelle* (written in the mid-1380s),[18] brings us close to the story as Chaucer might have known it. Sacchetti, a Florentine, was Chaucer's near contemporary (ca. 1332–1400), and the two writers could easily have met when the Englishman visited Florence in 1373. Be that as it may, Sacchetti is the first explicitly to make the pants the relic of a saint, though he does betray a certain squeamishness in his treatment of this motif. He tells of "a gullible husband," Buccio Malpanno of Amelia (a small town near Todi), who was "shown the moon in a puddle" by a lecherous Franciscan called Brother Antonio (lines 2–3). Antonio, surprised in bed with Buccio's wife, Caterina, by her husband's unexpectedly early return from a stint of guard duty with the town watch, leaps into the street from a low window, leaving his pants behind him (lines 25–26). The next morning, while his wife is still asleep, Buccio comes upon the pants under the pillow, realizes that they are not his, and hides them in a chest. Caterina and Antonio guess from Buccio's brooding expression that he has found the damning evidence but are at a loss to know what to do. Finally, Antonio confides in an older companion, Brother Domenico, who is far from pleased but decides he must preserve the honor of the convent. The two friars meet Buccio in the street, and Domenico tells him that his wife has borrowed from their sacristy a holy relic which has the most valuable property of curing infertility, namely, the "nether garments" of the blessed St. Francis (lines 73–75). Since, he says, another woman is now in need of the relic, he asks Buccio for it back, and they set off for the house. When he is shown the pants jumbled with other household linen in the chest, Domenico reproves the husband for his terrible sacrilege (line 103). To make the deception more convincing, Domenico holds the sacred pants on a silk napkin, chants "De profundis" and other Psalms over them, hears Buccio's confession, and scourges him on the shoulders with a rod (lines 104–109). The one detail not explicitly included in this ceremonious veneration of the pants is the actual kiss.

There are, however, reasons for thinking that other forms of this story were circulating at the time, some of which may well have contained the motif of the kiss. Though Poggio may have known Sacchetti's version (both, for instance, set the story in Amelia), he seems to be drawing on other, probably oral, sources for his tale.[19] Poggio's husband is not "uno semplice

---

[18] Franco Sacchetti, *Il Trecentonovelle*, ed., Emilio Faccioli (Turin: Giulio Einaudi, 1970), pp. 628–36.

[19] The differences between the versions of Poggio and Sacchetti, for instance, are far more marked than those between Poggio and Masuccio.

marito," absent with the town watch, nor is the story of the relic intended to deceive him; moreover, Poggio says nothing of the pants' being a cure for infertility (a motif, as we have seen, at least as old as *Les Braies au cordelier*). Franco Sacchetti's friar, on the other hand, though he often visits Caterina "as her chaplain" (lines 7–8), does not use the privacy of confession as a cover for his lechery, nor do his brothers carry the pants back to the convent in a grand procession.

If Sacchetti had indeed heard other versions of "The Friar's Pants," it is quite likely that some were more risqué than the one he gives us, for, as I have said, he shows at times a certain squeamishness. We have already noticed the euphemistic reference to St. Francis's "nether garments" ("panni di gamba"), but there is another curious detail that plays no function in the plot. Before setting out for his assignation with Caterina, Brother Antonio, who is described as reeking like a goat, is specifically said to exchange his filthy underclothes for "lini sottili e bianchissimi" ("fine and spotless linen"; lines 15–17). Could Sacchetti have heard a version in which Antonio's pants were, as Chaucer puts it, with his "fundement depeint," and was he then carefully drawing our attention to the cleanliness of this new pair out of respect for St. Francis? Masuccio's version certainly implies that the sacrilege was the worse for having been perpetrated with "a pair of stinking pants, harboring lice and filled with all kinds of dirt" (lines 40–41). The somewhat disingenuous moral ending of Sacchetti's story provides support for such a reading: the lecherous Brother Antonio, we are told, was punished for defaming the blessed St. Francis with so disgraceful a falsehood by dying horribly of leprosy (though Brother Domenico, since his object was to save the honor of his convent, was spared). If Sacchetti did indeed suppress the detail of the dirty linen, might he not, from a similar motive, have omitted the devout kiss that first appears in the version of his fellow Florentine some sixty years later?

One final version of the story is worth mentioning, for, although it is late, it is in many ways the most Chaucerian of all: the French farce *Frère Guillebert*.[20] This farce, written in the Norman dialect, was printed in the mid-sixteenth century but could well have been composed somewhat earlier.[21] In any case, it combines elements found in both the Italian and

[20] In André Tissier, ed., *Recueil de farces (1450–1550)*, 7 vols. (Geneva: Droz, 1986–), 6.185–261.

[21] On the assumption that it is post-Reformation, most commentators have agreed that it was written for performance within a seminary (despite the fact that its prologue is addressed to both men and women), apparently on the grounds that its sacrilegious tone would hardly have been suitable for general consumption (ibid., pp. 189–91). An alternative explanation might be that it was written somewhat earlier and that its anticlericalism is what recommended it to its first printer, Jehan le Prest, of Rouen, a town known to have had Protestant sympathies.

the French traditions, as well as adding a number of its own. As in the versions of Sacchetti, Poggio, and Masuccio, the lover here is a Franciscan, Brother Gilbert, but the events that lead to the pants' being taken to market by the husband in mistake for his purse are closer to those in the *Livre du Chevalier*. The reason for the husband's unexpected return is simply that he has forgotten his purse, and the long scene in which he searches for it in the dark, while the bare-arsed friar gibbers with fear at the possibility of discovery (lines 258–362), is classic bedroom-farce comedy. The next morning, as in the *Livre du Chevalier* and Sabadino, the wife turns for help to her *commère* (Dame Agnes), and this gossip has little difficulty convincing the husband that the pants are really (as in Sacchetti and Poggio) a holy relic: ". . . ce sont les brays sainct François, / Ung si precieux reliquère" ("these are St. Francis's pants—a most precious reliquary"; lines 459–60). Her explanation of their presence in the bedroom is the same as the one given in *Les Braies au cordelier* and Sacchetti, that they will promote conception (lines 464–66):

> Et pensez-vous bien, Dieux avant,
> Que vous eussiez faict un enfant
> Sans l'aide du sainct reliquaire?

[Do you really believe, before God, that you could have fathered a child without the help of this holy reliquary?]

Finally, Brother Gilbert, returning to collect his pants, invites the husband, the wife, and the gossip to kneel and kiss the relic (lines 510–13):

> Mais boutez-vous tous à genoulx,
> Affin que le sainct prie pour nous;
> Et si vous fault baiser tous trois
> Les brayes de monsieur sainct Françoys.

[But fall to your knees, all of you, that the saint may pray for us; also you should all three kiss St. Francis's pants.]

There is even a hint in the closing scene that, as in Poggio and Masuccio, the pants are to be returned to the convent in procession: "Allons les reporter, beau père," says the husband, as the characters begin to exit, "que chascun voyse à son degré" ("Let us carry them back, good father, and let each go according to rank"; lines 519–20).

Frère Guillebert, by far the coarsest surviving version of the story,

139

contains at least three elements that have a bearing on the Host's remarks about the Pardoner's "olde breech" (*PardT* 948). First, Brother Gilbert's pants, unlike Brother Antonio's, are far from being "sottili e bianchissimi," as a pun on *l'haleine* ("breath")/*la laine* ("wool") in the line following the passage quoted above suggests: "You should all three kiss St. Francis's pants," says Brother Gilbert, and "Vous aurez l'alaine plus doulce" ("You will find *l'alaine* most delicate"; line 514). The same point is made just before the husband discovers that his purse is not what he had assumed: "Mais je suis quasi estouffé, / Tant se bissac sent l'eschauffé" ("I feel as if I'm choking, this purse smells so stale"; lines 422–23). Second, the play makes a clear association between Brother Gilbert's pants and his "coillons." When he first discovers that the pants are missing, for instance, he refers to them as his "sac à coilles" (line 375), and when the husband finds out what he has really been carrying to market he bursts out (lines 425–27):

> Bissac! Bissac, par Dieu, non est,
> C'est l'abit d'un cul guères net,
> Car y voycy l'estuy à couilles.

[Purse! By God, it's not a purse; it's the covering for a none-too-clean bum, for here's the pouch for the balls.]

The use of the word *bissac*, which denotes "a bag, stitched down the middle to form two pockets," is obviously intended to reinforce this association.[22] Finally, there is the curious use of the word *reliquère/reliquaire*, rather than *relique*, to refer to the holy pants (lines 460, 466, and 518), for we might recall that Chaucer's Host says, "I wolde I hadde thy coillons in myn hond / In stide of relikes or of *seintuarie*" (lines 952–53). In both instances the comic effect is the same: the pants are precious not in themselves but for what they contain.[23] The cluster of sacrilegious, bawdy, and scatological imagery that attaches itself to the Pardoner's "olde breech" seems to have occurred quite independently to the author of *Frère Guillebert*.

Before leaving the French farce for good, we should consider one more pair of pants which, though they belong to a different story, are significant because they associate the motif of the spurious relic not with a friar but

---

[22] See ibid., p. 211, n. on line 14. Tissier says that the word *bissac* "pouvait désigner les parties sexuelles de la femme," but that can hardly be its connotation here. Cf. the earlier Fr. *esboursser*, "to castrate."

[23] But see Benson, ed., *The Riverside Chaucer*, p. 910, n. on line 953.

with a pardoner. In the early-sixteenth-century farce *Le Pardonneur, le triacleur et la tavernière*,[24] two rival mountebanks, a pardoner and a snake-oil salesman, join forces to defraud a tavern hostess. After eating and drinking their fill at her establishment, the two rogues arrange to decamp without paying their bill. To allay her suspicions, they entrust to her care a parcel containing one of the pardoner's most precious relics (lines 283–86):

> C'est, ainsi comme je l'entens,
> Le beguin d'un des Innocens.
> Gardés le nous bien apoint;
> Mais ne le desveloppez point.

[It is, as I understand, a bonnet of one of the Holy Innocents. Keep it in good condition for us, but be sure not to unwrap it.]

After they have left, the innkeeper is of course unable to restrain her curiosity; there are no prizes for guessing what she finds inside (lines 311–14):

> Vierge Marie, et qu'esse sique?
> Se sont brayes, par ma conscience,
> De quelqu'un. Mon Dieu, pascience!
> Vierge Marie, qu'ilz sont breneuses!

[Holy Mother, what have we here then? Upon my soul, it's somebody's pants. God give me patience! Holy Mother, how shitty they are!]

It seems hardly necessary to point out that by the early sixteenth century the passing off of a pair of filthy pants as a holy relic had evidently become a stock comic routine in French farce.

I have spent so long on the various versions of "The Friar's Pants" to show that, though there seem to be no examples of it from fourteenth-century England,[25] it was widely disseminated throughout the later Middle Ages. When the main elements of the plot are set out in tabular form (see table 1), it becomes obvious that we are dealing here with variant forms of a popular tale that circulated freely in both oral and written versions over a

---

[24] Tissier, ed., *Recueil des farces*, 5.231–73.

[25] The earliest English version I have found (an adaptation of Poggio) is in *Tales and Quicke Answeres, Very Mery, and Pleasant to Rede*, printed by Berthelet ca. 1535 (*STC* 23, 665); P. M. Zall, ed., *A Hundred Merry Tales and Other English Jestbooks of the Fifteenth and Sixteenth Centuries* (Lincoln: University of Nebraska Press, 1963), pp. 313–14.

Table 1. Plot Elements in Eight Medieval "Friar's Pants" Stories

Story or Author	Setting	Cuckold's Occupation	Lover's Occupation	Opportunity
Les Braies au cordelier (mid-13th C.)	Orleans	Merchant	Clerk	Husband sent off to market before dawn
Les Braies le prestre (early 14th C.)	Not specified	Butcher	Priest	Husband sent off to market before dawn
Franco Sacchetti (late 14th C.)	Amelia (near Todi)	Trade not specified	Franciscan	Husband on duty with town watch
Le Chevalier de la Tour Landry (late 14th C.)	Not specified	Ropemaker	Prior	Husband goes to market
Poggio Bracciolini (mid-15th C.)	Amelia	Trade not specified	Franciscan	Friar acts as wife's confessor
Masuccio Salernitano (ca. 1475)	Catania (Sicily)	Doctor	Franciscan	Husband goes to visit patients
Sabadino Degli Arienti (ca. 1480)	Corechio (near Imola)	Laborer	Priest	Husband asleep in same room
Frère Guillebert (early 16th C.?)	Meulers (?) (near Dieppe)	Merchant	Franciscan	Husband goes to market

considerable period of time. I cannot of course prove that Chaucer knew such a tale, but to my ear the echoes of it in the Host's speech are unmistakable (lines 948–50):

> Thou woldest make me kisse thyn olde breech,
> And swere it were a relyk of a seint,
> Though it were with thy fundement depeint!

Once we allow that Chaucer might be alluding to "The Friar's Pants" in these lines, other details in the passage appear in a new light: the trouble-

Crisis	Ally	Resolution	Reason
Husband takes clerk's purse and pants in dark	Franciscan	Wife pretends clerk's pants belong to friar	Friar's pants a charm for infertility
Husband takes priest's purse and pants in dark	None	Husband mocked; priest steals money in purse	
Husband finds friar's pants under pillow	An older friar	*Pants a relic of St. Francis* (husband shriven)	A cure for infertility
Husband takes prior's pants instead of purse	Gossip (*commère*)	Gossip tells husband all women wear pants	To protect chastity
Fleeing friar leaves pants on bed	Convent superior	*Pants a relic of St. Francis* (kissed by husband)	Saves face for husband and convent
Fleeing friar leaves pants on bed	Wife's maid and superior	*Pants a relic of St. Griffone* (kissed by husband)	A cure for wife's sickness
Husband takes priest's purse and pants in dark	Gossip (*comatre*)	Gossip says women wear pants, money belongs to friend	Saved to pay for image of St. Pancracio
Husband takes friar's pants instead of purse	Gossip	*Pants a relic of St. Francis* (kissed by husband)	A cure for infertility

some "Lat kutte hem of" (line 954), for instance, may remind us that castration was a recognized form of summary punishment for an adulterer caught in the act—it is, indeed, a fate the terrified friar expects at any moment in the bedroom scene in *Frère Guillebert* (line 298).[26] We may

[26] In three fabliaux, *Le Prestre crucefié* (no. 18), Anatole de Montaiglon and G. Raynaud, eds., *Recueil général et complet des fabliaux des XIIIe et XIVe siècles*, 6 vols. (Paris, 1872–90), 1.194–97; *Connebert* (no. 138), ibid., 5.160–70; and *Le Prestre et le leu* (no. 145), ibid., 6.51–52, the lover is actually castrated by the husband; in a fourth, *Le Fabel d'Aloul* (no. 24), ibid., 1.155–88, he escapes this fate at the very last moment; and in a fifth, *Le Dit des perdriz*

even be tempted to hear in the second half of this line, "I wol thee help hem carie," and in the "hogges toord" shrine proposed for the unholy relics, a sardonic echo of the processional motif that occurs in Poggio, Masuccio, and *Frère Guillebert*. If the possibility of these echoes is granted, it remains only to ask what might follow from this identification.

A few years ago, C. David Benson and I argued that the various interpretations of the Pardoner's sexual identity that have been offered (a eunuch, a hermaphrodite, a homosexual) were founded on very slender, and far from unambiguous, textual evidence.[27] We pointed out that, in fact, effeminacy in the Middle Ages might imply something very different, "too great a concern with women,"[28] for, as Thomas Laqueur has recently confirmed, this was a world where "bodies actually seem to slip from their sexual anchorage in the face of heterosexual sociability; being with women too much or being too devoted to them seems to lead to the blurring of what we would call sex."[29] In such a world, then, the Pardoner's sexual life might just as easily be construed as "ordinary in everything... but its debilitating excesses."[30] For both Benson and me, the portrait of the Pardoner drawn by the author of *The Tale of Beryn*, an early and careful reader of Chaucer, "suggests a very different... sexual figure from the one created by modern critics."[31]

(no. 17), ibid., 1.188–93, a potential lover is frightened off by the threat of such a punishment. Interestingly, in every case the lover is a cleric. The castration of adulterers was not confined to the fabliaux, however: a letter of remission, dated Paris, November, 1400, seeks pardon for a squire named Robert de Sales for an assault on his servant Mérigot de Maigne; having earlier caught Mérigot in bed with his wife, Robert hunted him down, and eight days later "with a little knife the said suppliant cut off and removed the said Mérigot's testicles [fendit audit Mérigot la couille et lui osta les couillons], saying that he would do him no harm except in the members with which he had shamed his wife." L. Douët d'Arcq, ed., *Choix de pièces inédites relatives au règne de Charles VI*, 2 vols., SHF (Paris: Renouard, 1863–64), 2.73–76. Léonce Celier notes a similar case from Poitou in "Les Moeurs rurales au XVe siècle d'après les lettres de rémission," *Bulletin philologique et historique jusqu'à 1715* (Paris, 1958), p. 418. For three English cases from the thirteenth century, see Frederick Pollock and F. W. Maitland, *History of English Law Before the Time of Edward I*, 2d ed., 2 vols. (1898; Cambridge: Cambridge University Press, 1968), 2.484–85 n. 6.

[27] C. David Benson, "Chaucer's Pardoner: His Sexuality and Modern Critics," *Mediaevalia* 8 (1985, for 1982): 337–49; Richard Firth Green, "The Sexual Normality of Chaucer's Pardoner," ibid., pp. 351–59.

[28] Benson, "Chaucer's Pardoner," p. 342.

[29] Thomas Laqueur, *Making Sex: Body and Gender from the Greeks to Freud* (Cambridge, Mass.: Harvard University Press, 1990), p. 124.

[30] Green, "Sexual Normality," p. 357.

[31] Benson, "Chaucer's Pardoner," p. 345. Our arguments have received welcome support from Helen Cooper in *Oxford Guides to Chaucer: The Canterbury Tales* (Oxford: Clarendon Press, 1989), p. 59.

The evidence presented in this article is offered as further support for our position. If Chaucer, consciously or otherwise, is making the Host echo an incident from the story of "The Friar's Pants" when he launches into his diatribe against the Pardoner, it is difficult to avoid the conclusion that the Pardoner is here being cast mentally in the role of philanderer: "You are the kind of man," the Host is in effect saying, "who would not only cuckold me but add insult to injury by trying to get me to kiss your filthy pants." In thus conflating one order of sanctimonious lechers (friars) with another (pardoners), Harry Bailly is hardly making any great leap: both, in the popular imagination at any rate, divided their time between relic pushing and womanizing.[32] On the other hand, it might be thought, at the very least, an odd association for someone confronted with a eunuch, a hermaphrodite, or a homosexual to make. Is it not, then, simpler to believe that the Host recognizes in this man who boasts of having a "joly wenche in every toun" (line 453) the kind of randy troublemaker any hardworking innkeeper could well do without? On the evidence of *The Tale of Beryn*, such a view would certainly have been endorsed by his counterpart at the Checker-of-the-Hope in Canterbury.[33]

[32] For pardoners as relic pushers see Siegfried Wenzel, "Chaucer's Pardoner and His Relics," *SAC* 11 (1989): 37–41 (also the farce *Le Pardonneur, le triacleur, et la tavernière*, discussed above). For pardoners as womanizers see William Langland, *Piers Plowman: The B Version*, ed. George Kane and E. T. Donaldson: "Thus [ye] gyuen [youre] gold glutons to [helpe] / And leneþ it Losels [þat] leccherie haunten" (*Prologue* 76–77); and G. R. Owst, *Literature and Pulpit in Medieval England* (Oxford: Blackwell, 1966), p. 373 n. 3: "ȝyf they may gete here dowter or here mayde, [they] wol lyȝtely stele hem a-wey and defowle hem wyth synne." The association between pardoners and friars is made by John Heywood in his interlude *The Pardoner and the Frere* (1533).

[33] I should like to thank Monica McAlpine for taking the time to read a draft of this article and for the generous encouragement she has given me; I fear we must still agree to disagree, however, over the question of the Pardoner's sexuality (see her "The Pardoner's Homosexuality and How It Matters"; *PMLA* 95 [1980]: 8–22). I wish also to thank my colleagues Sharon L. Collingwood, Madeline Lennon, and Antony R. Littlewood for looking over my French, Italian, and Latin translations; needless to add, any errors that remain are entirely my own. To Sharon Collingwood I owe a greater debt for having introduced me to *Frère Guillebert* in the first place.

REVIEWS

PETER F. AINSWORTH. *Jean Froissart and the Fabric of History: Truth, Myth, and Fiction in the* Chroniques. Oxford: Clarendon Press, 1990. Pp. xvi, 329. $79.00.

One reads and rereads Peter Ainsworth's densely textured volume on Froissart's *Chroniques* with a growing sense of gratitude for the riches it contains. The fruit of more than twenty years of study, this book offers a fresh conceptualization of the "literariness" of the *Chroniques* and identifies evolutionary stages in both Froissart's discursive practices and his attitudes toward chivalry. The volume concludes with a climactic reading of the Rome manuscript of book 1 of the *Chroniques*, probably Froissart's last work, as a layered text in which Edward III's nostalgically memorialized reign becomes a mirror for princes of the late-fourteenth and fifteenth centuries. The first full-length study in English of Froissart's literary achievement in the *Chroniques* since F. S. Shears's monograph of 1930, Ainsworth's volume offers a relatively broad audience access to the problems and achievements of recent scholarship while making its own distinguished contribution.

No study of this kind could succeed without a reconsideration of how to define what makes the *Chroniques* a part of the canon of literature as well as historiography. The limitations of the nineteenth-century emphasis on character and description are only more obvious than the relative inflexibility of the modern distinction between medieval historical discourse and medieval romance manner, or the inadequacy of stylistic analyses alone, however brilliant. Drawing on the work of such contemporary theorists as Genette, Todorov, Iser, and Lodge, Ainsworth classifies the *Chroniques* as a "*potentially* literary" text ("Introduction," p. 16), one that in different degrees at different times invites a *régime de lecture* appropriate to one or another literary genre, procedure, or device. The fundamental characteristics of fully literary texts provide the criteria for this classification and for the discrimination of degrees of literariness. Such texts, defined by "the presence of a high quotient of (patterned) indeterminacy, inevitably accompanied by a proportionate increase in the range of potential connotations" (pp. 15–16), invite the reader to engage in "hypothesis-building" and the tracing of "theme constellations" by reading "in all directions" for recurrences, contrasts, preoccupations, etc.

147

Noting the coincidence of these concepts, most of them intended to elucidate modern texts, with the concerns of medievalists such as Vinaver (typology of texts) and Jauss (horizon of expectations), Ainsworth asserts that we are now in the fortunate position of having acquired tools for the study of qualities that were always there in Froissart's text. To the extent that the value of a theory can be established by the practice it makes possible, Ainsworth's readings of the *Chroniques* richly justify his recourse to this understanding of the literariness of Froissart's text.

After tracing briefly the different paths taken by chronicle, history, and romance in the two hundred years before Froissart, Ainsworth proceeds (in chapter 1) to reconstruct the evolution of Froissart's own concept of *histoire* by explicating his *autocritique* in the much-debated Prologue to the A manuscript of book 1 (as designated by Siméon Luce in the edition of the Société de l'Histoire de France). Ainsworth believes that the "lost" chronicle referred to in this Prologue, which Froissart presented to Queen Phillippa in 1362, was in verse and that Froissart abandoned that work because he was converted to Jean Le Bel's preference for prose as the vehicle for historical narrative and to Le Bel's model of extensive inquiry to establish the truth of event. Froissart did not adopt Le Bel's ideal of concision, however, but over time became ever more committed to the idea that *histoire*, as contrasted with chronicle, required "writing things out—at length" (p. 49). This practice, uniquely Froissartian among fourteenth-century chroniclers, produced the "proto-literary" text: one in which, at certain points, "an optional 'bifurcation' becomes possible:... certain textual developments allow themselves to be read according to the *régime* of narrative history, or according to other [more literary] *régimes*" (p. 49).

Emphasizing the range of kinds of narrative, of varying degrees of sophistication, to be found at such points of bifurcation, Ainsworth analyzes (in chapter 4) a number of stories dealing with freebooters, the capture of castles or defense of besieged positions, the use of ruses or disguises, and the motif of the biter bitten. He deftly explicates several anecdotes, in which every detail is motivated but there is little that could be called plot or theme; a more elaborate tale in which ironies of action are developed and themes surface and acquire some moral coloring; and lastly, a virtual *nouvelle*, a relatively short, dramatically structured, and highly unified narrative that develops a degree of psychological interest in a limited number of protagonists placed in a realistic setting. Ainsworth's example of the *nouvelle* is the story of the fall of Merigot Marches (*Oeuvres*, ed. Lettenhove, 14.159–212), the amoral, cheerfully cynical captain of a notorious Free Company, at the hands of a traitorous cousin and the coolly cruel Duke de Berry. The story exhibits varieties of hypocrisy, loyalty, self-interest, and treachery which invite the reader into moral reflection rather than confident judgment. Their literariness makes such narratives essentially self-contained:

Meaning here is essentially intra-textual: the reader knows there is an extra-textual referent at the source of the tale (and indeed potentially throughout its duration...), but finds pleasure in the relations obtaining between protagonists and situations within the emergent structure of the text itself. [Pp. 112–13]

Froissart's fullest (though, Ainsworth suggests, possibly unconscious) realization of the mythopoetic possibilities of narrative occurs in the account (in book 3) of his *voyage en Béarn* and sojourn with Gaston Fébus, Count of Foix. Through the analysis of two kinds of "textual phenomena" (in chapter 5), Ainsworth extends what are ordinarily thought to be the boundaries of the Béarn material into book 4 of the *Chroniques*. The first of these phenomena is the association of contiguous or near-contiguous narratives — specifically, the stories of Fébus's imprisonment of his cousin Pierre-Arnaut de Béarn; of his son and original heir, Gaston; and of his subsequent heir, the Vicomte de Castelbon — in such a way as to suggest the reaches, the limitations, and the reasons for Fébus's cruelty. These three narratives are then linked to three others — the story of the somnambulist Pierre de Béarn, Fébus's brother, and the accounts (in book 4) of the deaths of Fébus himself and of his bastard son, Yvain — through a second textual phenomenon, the repeated synecdochic use of a limited number of objects and animals, e.g., bear, knife, key, ring. Fébus's death while hunting bear is prefigured, for example, by catastrophes that befall the other bear hunters here, Pierre de Béarn and his father-in-law, and poetic justice is suggested when Yvain is unable to claim his inheritance through the possession of his dead father's knife, a knife that recalls the instrument with which the count inadvertently slew his legitimate heir, Gaston. This associatively linked collection of tales thus invites a reading as a family tragedy and develops a richly ambiguous portrait of the Count of Foix as both noble and cruel.

In this same sequence concerning the *voyage en Béarn*, Ainsworth finds a key place where the literariness of the *Chroniques* comes together with Froissart's treatment of the chivalric life. The *translatio militi*, or transmission of the ethic of prowess, presented didactically as a *topos* in the prologues of the various books, becomes here a true theme whose am-

149

bivalent handling invites reflection by the reader. Fébus's history becomes a synecdoche for such transmission, Ainsworth suggests, and raises questions about the inevitability of the replication of the chivalric life. The theme is doubled, so to speak, by the unique attention Froissart pays here to his own roles as reporter, narrator, chronicler, and "Secretary of Chivalry" and to the memorializing function of his chronicle. This sequence, whose boundaries Ainsworth has redefined, he also links in an original way to the *Chroniques* as a whole by seeing it as the "introit" (p. 170) to Froissart's more probing analysis of good and bad governance in book 4 and finally in the Rome manuscript.

In a preliminary survey of the ideology of the *Chroniques* (chapters 2 and 3), Ainsworth characterizes Froissart's basic outlook as "profoundly conservative" (p. 76) and his voice as "on the whole... reassuring" (p. 85) as he satisfies the aspirations of his aristocratic audience for the memorialization of their feats of prowess. Froissart's concept of chivalry embraces not only its most abstract ideals but also those pragmatic laws of war meant to reconcile ideals with self-interest; thus his depiction is, from the first, neither the most idealistic nor the most critical of contemporary treatments of chivalry. Yet, toward the end of book 3 and in book 4, Ainsworth argues (chapter 6), Froissart begins to question the adequacy of traditional values to the crises of his time, such as the vulnerability of boykings, the madness of Charles VI, and the power struggles of Richard II's reign.

The recurrent theme of the young and promising prince suggests potential conflicts between prowess and the wisdom needed to govern; the theme of good counsel exposes the probability that magnates, favorites, and advisers around the king are as likely to undermine the throne or become sources of oppression as they are to support legitimate authority or resist tyranny. Froissart focuses his consequent concern for the transmission of chivalric values, Ainsworth suggests, on the relationship of father and son (as anticipated in his stories of Gaston Fébus). Froissart deals with his unease over the deposition of Richard II by weaving all these themes together: his Thomas of Gloucester is an evil counselor whose willingness to countenance regicide justifies his death and draws criticism away from Henry Bolingbroke; at the same time, Henry is depicted as the son of John of Gaunt, sharing his father's concern for the stability of the realm and thus identifying himself, and not Richard II, as the true heir of Edward the Confessor and Edward III.

Edward III is the focus of Ainsworth's climactic study (chapters 7 and 8) of the Rome manuscript, which he approaches as Froissart's "fresh *reading*" of his other versions of book 1, motivated, perhaps, by his trip to England in 1395 and by his recent or concurrent treatment of the last years of Richard's reign in book 4 of his *Chroniques*. In what was probably his last composition Froissart seems more consciously aware of the gap between chivalric ideal and practice. Thus the Rome manuscript becomes the premier example of Ainsworth's belief that amplification, moral glossing, and rewriting most frequently appear in Froissart's text when the chronicler "hesitates" between "fascination" and "aversion" toward his chivalric subject matter (e.g., p. 109). Ainsworth agrees with George Diller, editor of the Rome manuscript (*Chroniques: Dernière rédaction du premier livre...*, 1972) that Froissart attempts to re-create in this late text the golden age of Edward III, but with the qualification that it is "recollected as an already precariously distant ideal" (p. 241).

Ainsworth describes his study of Rome as a "macrolecture" intended to demonstrate that this extensive text is unified by a consistent thematic focus on good and evil royal government:

The principal textual feature ensuring that we never lose sight of the theme is the central position occupied by Edward III. . . . For the fundamental originality of the Rome manuscript. . . is that it offers us an account of the sometimes arduous, but finally triumphant apprenticeship and chivalrous education of a great king. [P. 257]

After a detailed treatment of Edward's landing at Orwell on his return to England in 1325 with his mother, Isabella, a scene associated with the return of *prowess* to England, Ainsworth traces the king's development into "Edward the Wise," stressing his interactions with counselors and commenting briefly on critical moments such as the surrender of Calais when he learns how to rule. While Diller sees Froissart as probing into the causes of the Hundred Years' War and seeking a realism and exactitude more typical of the true (modern) historian than of the mere chronicler, Ainsworth convincingly presents him as essentially a (medieval) moralist, exploring the ironic gap between ideality and reality (pp. 284, 301–302). Having contrasted Froissart's earlier outlook with Phillippe de Mézières's (e.g., p. 85), Ainsworth sees the chronicler's later perspective as comparable in some respects with Mézières's (p. 279). The Rome manuscript becomes a mirror for princes in which a historical personage is presented as a figure of the ideal, even as other mirror literature at the turn of the century was making new attempts to translate the ideal into practical terms (p. 279). The moral quality of the work, along with other features, such as the use of ex post facto prophecy, creates the layered text: focused on Edward III, it looks backward to Edward II, comments on Richard II, and advises Henry IV as well as other kings to come.

This important literary study of Froissart's treatment of Edward III will make the volume of special interest to Chaucerians. As Sumner Ferris remarked in these pages (*SAC* 5 [1983]: 186), J. J. N. Palmer's landmark collection of essays by several hands, *Froissart: Historian* (1981), unfortunately did not contain any historical study of Froissart's Edward. Ainsworth stresses the incomplete nature of his study, and indeed it tends both to open new lines of inquiry and to create new appetites. Although Ainsworth gives good reasons for presenting a "macrolecture" on the Rome manuscript, I wish the author had favored us with "microlectures" on more scenes from Edward's reign of the same high quality as his detailed studies of other episodes in the *Chroniques*. Also, Ainsworth's original suggestions concerning the relationship of the Rome manuscript to the mirror-for-princes tradition (as well as his glance at Edward as an Arthurian figure [p. 307]) raise in my mind the question whether it might be possible to prepare a collection of edited excerpts in translation for use in the classroom. Whether this could be done without grossly distorting the multifariousness of this long manuscript I do not know, but the wish may be taken as testimony to the interest and excitement Ainsworth's study can arouse.

In the last chapter Ainsworth's respectful differences with George Diller are relatively prominent; in the rest of the volume his departures from earlier scholarly opinion are lightly touched upon, and, indeed, his own original contributions are sometimes so modestly announced in mid-argument that a reader might not fully register them. Although some of his quotations from earlier studies may seem superfluous, on the whole readers are likely to be grateful for his extensive citations and summaries of French scholarship, as of Marie Thérèse de Medeiros's study of how fourteenth-century chroniclers treated the Jacquerie (chapter 2). The volume also contains a useful fourteen-page bibliography.

Finally, although Ainsworth's focus is consistently literary throughout, he does occasionally engage the issue of historical interpretation of the *Chroniques*. He acknowledges, for example, that the historian may find in Froissart's glossing of Gaston Fébus's actions a suspicious deference to men of high station which must be demystified (pp. 161–62). Ainsworth argues against pursuing such demystification as the sole way to establish the truth, a single truth, about the text, however. Rather, a valuable aspect of Froissart's text would be lost if we could not surrender to its poetic suggestiveness, and, indeed, Froissartian glossing has historical value as a window on medieval perceptions and beliefs, providing an instance where the tools and interests of literary and historical interpretation intersect (pp. 170–71). Moreover, the chief interest of the *Chroniques* for the historian may lie in its revelation of how one late-medieval writer conceived of history and history writing. Although these views of the historical value of the *Chroniques* are not new, they acquire a new clarity and salience when set in the context of Ainsworth's literary reading.

That reading, it must be said in conclusion, is extraordinarily tactful. Ainsworth not only refuses to identify the category of the literary in the *Chroniques* with a collection of purple passages only but also warns against insisting on exhaustive exegesis of even the most fully literary segments (pp. 5–6). He testifies to the importance of experiencing the whole of the work, its contrasts, surprises, and rhythms (p. 12) and, while advancing our knowledge of the *evolution* of Froissart's discursive practices and ideological perspectives, allows the text, as he says (p. 19), to breathe, to retain its mysteries.

MONICA MCALPINE
University of Massachusetts, Boston

JOHN A. ALFORD. Piers Plowman: *A Guide to the Quotations.* Medieval and Renaissance Texts and Studies, vol. 77. Binghamton, N.Y.: Center for Medieval and Early Renaissance Studies at the State University of New York at Binghamton, 1992. Pp. xiii, 153. $9.00.

With this volume John A. Alford continues to educate and inform the growing readership of William Langland's extraordinary poem. Like one of the poet's own personifications — Study and Clergy come first to mind — Alford keeps appearing with outstretched hand to help us, even as they help Long Will, in our search for deeper, if never-to-be-completely-satisfied-in-this-world, understanding of a lifetime's work. In his editing of *A Companion to* Piers Plowman (Berkeley: University of California Press, 1988) and his coediting with M. Teresa Tavormina of the first six volumes of *The Yearbook of Langland Studies*, in his numerous learned articles, and in this and his earlier reference work, *Piers Plowman: A Glossary of Legal Diction* (Cambridge: D. S. Brewer, 1988), Alford has made an indispensable contribution to the field of *Piers Plowman* studies.

A Guide to the Quotations is based on the Athlone editions of the three versions of *Piers Plowman: The A Version*, ed. George Kane (London: Athlone, 1960); *The B Version*, ed. George Kane and E. Talbot Donaldson (London: Athlone, 1975); and *The C Version*, ed. George Russell (in press). Permission to use a computer printout of the Athlone edition of the C version along with the two published versions has enabled Alford to compile his guide with the benefits of a full account of variants and a consistent handling of the quotations in all three versions. The three versions of the poem contain some 600 individual quotations from Latin and French (1,200 counting repetitions). Alford has organized these quotations in three separate indexes: in the first index the quotations are recorded and listed in the order of their appearance in the texts; in the second index the biblical quotations are listed according to their order in the Bible by citation of book, chapter, and verse followed by letter reference to version of the poem, passus, and line, e.g., Genesis 2:18 C.18.227; and in the third index the quotations have been arranged in alphabetical order. Users may thus pursue intelligence about the quotations in *Piers Plowman* from three different perspectives, but they will undoubtedly find the first index, with its rich information about sources and analogues and secondary works comprising eighty-five pages of the volume, the most valuable.

It would be a mistake, however, for almost all its users, especially those who are relatively new students of the poem, to consult this guide without first reading the thirty-page introduction. In it Alford is concerned not so much with preparing his readers to make hands-on use of the guide as with educating them about the significance of the numerous editorial and interpretive questions that the quotations raise. In the first part of the essay Alford writes about the concerns of modern readers of *Piers Plowman* that have been revealed by the editorial treatment of the quotations in terms of the numbering of lines, the use of italics, and the establishment of the text. It is important for students of the poem to understand that, even though almost all editorial approaches to line numbering accept the threefold division of quotations into those that are extraneous to the text, those that articulate syntactically with the text, and those that are macaronic, disagreements among the poem's editors about which quotations will be assigned line numbers with the English text and which will be treated as detachable from that text are both inevitable and subject to individual interpretation. Such decisions have a way of implying values placed on the quotations, and, along with the question of their authorial or scribal status, particularly of the scriptural quotations, the practice and conventions of numbering them not only reflect our modern conception of the text but also play a role in our critical arguments over serious issues concerning the poem's allegorical meaning and its complex intertextuality.

154

Similarly, in his treatment of all italicized words in the Athlone editions, Alford explains their significance in reference to such diverse matters as alliteration, the assimilation of loan words into fourteenth-century Middle English from Latin and French, and manuscript rubrication. In his brief but important consideration of the text, he reminds us of two important facts, namely, that, while the poet's own words survive in the fifty-two extant manuscripts of his poem, "the quotations can be checked against a vast body of external evidence" and that Langland "was capable of misquoting as well as deliberately modifying his borrowings to fit new contexts" (p. 14).

The second part of the introduction, "The Question of Sources," provides a summary of the provenance of Langland's scriptural and nonscriptural quotations. Stressing that many of Langland's quotations, including those from the Bible, came from secondary sources, Alford introduces the possibility that much of the poet's learning came from florilegia, encyclopedias, and commentaries and gives some specific examples of how many of the poem's quotations, especially the ones from Scripture, come from the Apocrypha, the liturgy, canon law, grammatical miscellanies, and theological works. For the poem's readers perhaps the most important point concerning biblical quotations is one that Alford makes with great care: what appear to us to be inexact or inaccurate quotations are actually reflections of the instability of the medieval Latin text of the Bible in Langland's day.

This is a book that will serve students of *Piers Plowman* for years to come, especially those who seek to understand better its compelling nature and the genius of its maker. To quote Alford's closing words to his introduction: "That *Piers Plowman* is more than the sum of its borrowings hardly needs stating. But no study of the poem — whether of its author, its audience, or its art — can afford to ignore them" (p. 30).

GEORGE D. ECONOMOU
University of Oklahoma

PRISCILLA BAWCUTT. *Dunbar the Makar.* Oxford: Clarendon Press, 1992. Pp. xiii, 396. $95.00.

Seventeen years ago Priscilla Bawcutt's *Gavin Douglas: A Critical Study* appeared, an impressive work of scholarship that at once summarized much of what was known at that time about Douglas, put forth fresh and compelling arguments about one of the great Middle Scots *makaris*, and served (albeit for a relatively small number of enthusiastic scholars) as a necessary foundation for further study. *Dunbar the Makar*, impressive in its own right despite a few disappointing limitations, does and will do much the same thing for readers of William Dunbar.

Dunbar the Makar opens with a long introduction in which the author remarks on the poet's "many voices" and the immense variety of his poems, rightly admitting from the outset the difficulty of viewing his work as a coherent whole. This discontinuity, however, is too much replicated throughout Bawcutt's book itself, which is wide-ranging and compendious, sometimes frustratingly so. In the introduction alone the author moves from a summary of common approaches to Dunbar, to a consideration of biographical facts related to the *makar*, to a discussion of the Dunbar canon; she includes interesting remarks on the terms *maker* and *ballat* in Scots and English, dismisses firmly but tactfully portraits of Dunbar as either a "Scottish Chaucerian" or a "Scottish Lydgatian," and examines how Dunbar appears to have viewed his own poetry. The treatment of these subjects, each touched on only briefly, is bolstered by Bawcutt's scholarly authority, but the concluding observation of this first chapter, "Again and again Dunbar defeats easy, simple formulations" (p. 38), while true, is unsatisfying.

Chapter 2 focuses on "Dunbar's World," by which Bawcutt means "Dunbar's use of place, people, and time" (p. 39). Bawcutt examines representations of Edinburgh and Aberdeen in the poems, figures of Dunbar's "fellow-servitours," and time references in some of the poems, especially those related to holy days. After this chapter the book unexpectedly begins to be organized around the poems' various genres and modes. Chapter 3, "Court Poems: Praise and Petition," includes interesting comments about James IV and his court, as well as a very solid section on Dunbar's "begging-poems." Chapter 4, "'Moralitee and Hoolynesse,'" presents a successful defense of Dunbar's moral poems, suggesting the disparity between current critical estimation of these works and their popularity in Dunbar's day. This organizational pattern, however, tends to be recursive and sometimes a bit baffling. Why, for instance, should the poem *Blyth Aberdeane thow beriall of all tounis*, though mentioned twice in the chapter on Dunbar's world, be discussed at length only in the chapter on court poetry? It is not that in the latter chapter such a discussion is inappropriate but that the method of organization seems to admit too much overlap. Consequently, one finds it difficult to discern a fully developed argument on any one text and often has to consult several different chapters to gather all that Bawcutt has to say about a particular poem. A more effective way might have been found to arrange the book's somewhat overwhelming mass of information and analysis.

Chapters 5 through 7 discuss Dunbar's use of what Bawcutt terms the literary "modes" of parody, irony, flyting, and fantasy, and here the limitations of Bawcutt's fairly conservative critical stance are occasionally evident. In her chapter on "'Sportis and Jocositeis,'" for example, Bawcutt rejects the too-ready application of the Bakhtinian term "carnivalesque" to Dunbar's comic poems and suggests rather that such poems participate in "the temporary lifting of taboos [that] reaffirms hierarchical principles" (p. 191). This is an intriguing observation, but one relegated to a footnote and never explored at any length. Similarly, Bawcutt concludes this fifth chapter by observing that Dunbar "seems to delight as much in the exploitation of equivocal and ambiguous language as in the exposure of human frailty and self-deception" (p. 219), a comment that again seems rich yet remains largely unexamined. "Flyting" (chapter 6) and "'Elrich Fantasyis'" (chapter 7) are stronger. No scholar can speak more authoritatively on flyting than Bawcutt, and her long discussion of *The Flyting of Dunbar and Kennedie* is one of the most interesting sections of the book. Bawcutt's exploration of Dunbar's "blackly comic dream-visions" (257) in chapter 7 is equally engaging.

Chapter 8, "'Ladeis Bewtie . . . Luiffis Blys,'" deals with Dunbar's poems about love, including primarily a long discussion of *The Tua Mariit Wemen and the Wedo*; the chapter serves as a touchstone for the organizational problems and methodological limitations that emerge at points throughout the book. Bawcutt comments that *The Tua Mariit Wemen and the Wedo* "exposes not only women's desires but men's fears — concerning sexual satisfaction, material possessions, and, above all, power" (p. 328). A thought-provoking assertion, but the author's impressive command of contextual materials, both social and historical, is not brought to bear on how this poem might operate within the matrix of gender and power relationships in early-sixteenth-century Scotland; instead, Bawcutt immediately turns her attention to the poem's eavesdropping narrator, who is explained away as merely conventional. At the chapter's end Bawcutt returns to the question of how *The Tua Mariit Wemen and the Wedo* "reflects social reality" (p. 344) but devotes only a paragraph to the subject. The author readily admits here that she has been "chiefly concerned with [the poem's] literary artifice and use of comic stereotypes" (p. 344); however, even this focus, which does allow for a useful close reading of the text, is marred by the fact that the reader must turn to the subsequent final chapter for a discussion of Dunbar's unusual metrical choice (for a Scots writer) of the unrhymed alliterative line in this poem, a choice that seems important for an analysis of the poem's "literary artifice" as well as suggestive if considered simultaneously with the poem's subject matter and dialogic techniques.

This last chapter, "Language at Large," strikes one as the heart of the book. The title indicates the subject that seems to interest Bawcutt most and that she is most masterfully able to analyze: the breadth and diversity of Dunbar's linguistic resources and this *makar's* incomparable ability to move "with freedom and immense confidence" among various generic and linguistic domains (p. 382). Along with discussing Dunbar's macaronic verse, Bawcutt perceptively remarks on the drawbacks of employing overly rigid stylistic categorizations when assessing Dunbar's poetry, showing his flexibility with diverse levels of style. Although its very presence contributes to the book's organizational problems—as suggested above, there are comments here that could have been better placed elsewhere—the chapter is one of the most illuminating sections of the book.

Despite its somewhat haphazard organization, *Dunbar the Makar* should become a much-consulted resource for anyone doing work on Dunbar or Middle Scots literature in general, although readers will likely first refer to the book's index and mine its wealth of material from that direction. In collecting between two covers so much of what is now known about Dunbar and his poems, *Dunbar the Makar* is indispensable, and Bawcutt's consistently sensible and thoroughly informed readings are always valuable. They are not at all, however, definitive (and I do not mean to suggest that Bawcutt claims them to be): this book is at once a testament to how much work has been done on Dunbar and Middle Scots as well as an indicator of how much still needs to be done, not the least being readings of the poetry that address medievalists for whom representations of, say, gender relations and social power in literature are anything but peripheral. (Recent books by Louise Fradenburg and by R. James Goldstein, of course, are now beginning to chart such territories.) *Dunbar the Makar* is impressive in the breadth and force of its scholarship and sound in its readings—as far as they go. Middle Scots studies can go farther.

DANIEL J. PINTI
New Mexico State University

JULIA BOFFEY and JANET COWEN, eds. *Chaucer and Fifteenth-Century Poetry*. Medieval Studies, vol. 5. London: King's College London Centre for Late Antique and Medieval Studies, 1991. Pp. x, 174. £8.75 paper.

The genealogy of this volume accounts for most of its disappointments. With their genesis in a series of intercollegiate lectures at the University of London in 1989, the pieces often descend into the chattiness, excessive quotation, and long summaries of contents that typify lectures aimed at British undergraduates. As a final product of the King's College London Computing Centre, the book displays some of the infelicities common to desk-top publishing, such as uneven copyediting, unjustified right-hand margins, and no index. Since the two editors have provided no general introduction, the reader is left to search independently for the book's unifying strands, which generally trace lines of indebtedness and claims for originality on behalf of various Chaucerian poets from Clanvowe to Skelton, in no particular order.

Pamela M. King's opening piece, "Chaucer, Chaucerians and the Theme of Poetry," proposes that metafictions of aesthetic introspection, particularly *The House of Fame*, thematize the creative process by questioning the reliability of the analogous mode, the dream, while *Troilus and Criseyde* systematically dismantles the authority of books themselves as sources of reliable knowledge. These strategies of self-reflection and intertextuality are viewed as Chaucer's enduring legacies in *The Kingis Quair*, that vexing mix of autobiography and poetic echo-chamber in which life and art are rendered indissoluble. The historical James I of Scotland represents himself congruent with a protagonist who is constructed from the materials of his literary culture.

As a complement to this piece, Julia Boffey's fine study "Chaucerian Prisoners: The Context of *The Kingis Quair*" approaches the poem by looking at imprisonment as a narrative feature in *The Knight's Tale* and as a metaphorical image for love in *Troilus*, then examining patterns of emulation under the added influence of Boethius in the works of Thomas Usk, George Ashby, and Charles d'Orléans. Chaucerian models helped these actual prisoners to formulate their emotional experiences and to represent these interpreted selves as social identities. The striking overlap between powerful textual models and actual lives is probably more than a literary-historical curiosity, as Boffey concludes (p. 99), but prompts questions

159

concerning the social role of Chaucerian poetry at a very deep level in the courtly tradition. Who provided James I with such a mass of Chaucerian reading material that his mind became saturated with the language? Did the motives of his captors figure in some larger strategy for conditioning the future king of Scotland to Lancastrian cultural values? Revealing evidence probably lies in the identity of the ladylove celebrated in the poem. She was Joan Beaufort, cousin of Thomas Chaucer and ward of her uncle Bishop Henry Beaufort, the noblewoman wedded to James on the eve of his return to Scotland to take the throne in 1424.

In "Madness and Texts: Hoccleve's *Series*," James Simpson acknowledges various theoretical initiatives, mainly deconstruction's move to dislodge texts from their historical contexts, in a stimulating study of an authorially linked group of texts that steadily resists such antihistorical readings. As a work whose unifying plot is the account of its own composition, it also resists the destabilization of subject often achieved by Chaucer, since Hoccleve wanted to impress his audience that he himself was stable, that is, he had recovered from his bout with insanity. While the series is convincingly explicated as a text of "social rehabilitation" in which the poet's identity is intrinsically a "social phenomenon," perhaps Simpson should have made much more of the fact that we know precisely the intended audience of the work: Hoccleve himself copied out a presentation manuscript, now Durham Cosin manuscript V.III.9, with a concluding envoy addressed to the Countess of Westmoreland, the first Joan Beaufort, sister of Henry Beaufort and only daughter of Katherine Swynford by John of Gaunt, hence Chaucer's niece. As with *The Kingis Quair*, probably much more needs to be said about the congruence of the Chaucerian poetic tradition with the patterns of Chaucerian kinship.

W. A. Davenport's "Bird Poems" starts with the observation that *The Parliament of Fowls* was one of Chaucer's most imitated poems and then surveys the imitations from Clanvowe's *The Cuckoo and the Nightingale* to Skelton's *Phyllyp Sparowe* to reach (at considerable length) the unremarkable conclusions that "birds are useful to writers as mirrors of human activity" and that these writers "could use bird poems to be sophisticated and funny" (p. 82).

Janet Cowen's "Women as Exempla in Fifteenth-Century Verse of the Chaucerian Tradition" also indulges in a considerable amount of plot summary in tracing the clerkly tradition of writings about women, especially the collections of examples by Jerome and Boccaccio, making the point that these assemblages were by nature "double-edged," bringing together the stories of some good women, some bad. Chaucer exploited

160

this inherent tension in *The Legend of Good Women*, increasing the sense of paradox by appropriating the generic properties of hagiography turned from Christianity to the religion of Cupid, a renegade religion whose authority figure accuses the Chaucerian narrator of "heresy" (an accusation fraught with significance in the late 1380s, when Courteney's visitations were scouring the countryside for followers of Wyclif). The figure of Medea is traced along the anterior tradition of Ovid, Seneca, Benoit, and Guido delle Colonne to show the cumulative ambivalence that Chaucer increased, then into the next century to illustrate the erasure of moral ambiguities by Hoccleve and Lydgate.

Against allegation of Lydgatian banality, Jane Roberts's "Rereading Henryson's *Orpheus and Eurydice*" reasserts a Chaucerian ingenuity on behalf of the poem and its organic linkage with the *moralitas*. Henrietta Twycross-Martin's "Moral Pattern in *The Testament of Cresseid*" shows how Henryson's continuation of a Chaucerian narrative and imitation of Chaucerian techniques mask an attitude toward human love radically different from his master's. Whereas the Boethian perspective in *Troilus* insisted on viewing the tragedy from inside and outside simultaneously, with the limitations of the hero's pre-Christian vision bestowing a paradoxical nobility and pathos, the Scottish poem (before 1492) treats love as an earthly experience not always already measured by an Augustinian yardstick. The comparison is not between earthly love and heavenly charity but between fickle human emotion and stable human devotion, the latter defended as something of real value.

The more substantial pieces come at the end of the volume. Rosamund S. Allen's "*The Siege of Thebes*: Lydgate's Canterbury Tale" considers the poem as a continuation of Chaucer's tale-telling narrative and as a "prequel" to *The Knight's Tale*, but also as a companion piece to *Troilus* with its significant inclusion of episodes from Theban history pertinent to Diomede. Replacing Chaucer as the pilgrim-narrator, Lydgate "quytes" the Knight for interrupting the Monk's series of tragedies by offering his own vast account, almost twice as long as *The Knight's Tale*, of a great national tragedy. Indeed, a national audience was probably intended by Lydgate: "If the *Siege* is a mirror for princes, it is a mirror for dowager queens, princesses and royal nannies as well" (p. 129). His persistent themes are the responsibility of one individual to another and the disastrous consequences for the state if these ethical links are disrupted. Very much "a poem of endings," the *Siege*'s vision of a great city that went down to absolute destruction is interpreted as Lydgate's attempt to give an absolute sense of closure to *The Canterbury Tales*.

161

Peter Brown's "Journey's End: The Prologue to *The Tale of Beryn*" brings the volume to an end with a magisterial investigation of what is perhaps the most fascinating Chaucerian inspiration from the early fifteenth century. A fine discussion of editorial history gives way to a wide-ranging analysis of contents to reveal the anonymous writer's persistent, detailed familiarity with the operation of the "pilgrimage trade" in Canterbury. The conclusion, prompted by the manuscript colophon designating the *nomen autoris* as a *filius ecclesie Thome*, is that the author was a monk whose duties included custodial care for the shrine of St. Thomas. This identification would explain, for example, his fierce hostility toward the Pardoner set up as the butt of the fabliau misadventure: "The Pardoner as a traveling shrine, a purveyor of false relics and cash absolutions, is a threat to those who might consider themselves to be the guardians of true relics and the means of obtaining legitimate forgiveness of sin" (p. 159). The slippery question of dating is resolved in favor of 1420, or thereabout, as the jubilee occurring every fifty years to commemorate Becket's martyrdom, an occasion for intense pilgrimage activity that may also have inspired Lydgate's Prologue to *The Siege of Thebes* datable to 1420–22.

Although Brown suggests that the *Beryn* Prologue may have figured as a response to Wycliffite critics of pilgrimage, and specifically the shrine at Canterbury, we are left with the nagging sense that the narrative functions equally well as a critique, that is, as a warning to visitors perhaps more than a promotional advertisement. The Pardoner's being swindled by Kit at the Checker-of-the-Hoop Inn seems uncannily to correspond with the complaint of the Lollard William Thorpe before Archbishop Arundel in 1407: "...siche madde peple wasten blamfulli Goddis goodis in her veyne pilgrymageyng, spendynge these goodis upon vicious hosteleris whiche ben ofte unclene wymmen of her bodies." Thorough as this study is, Brown does little to extend his discussion beyond the Prologue to account for *The Tale of Beryn* itself as a monastic production. It may therefore be a revealing omission that his otherwise superb bibliography seems to have missed only Richard Firth Green's "Legal Satire in *The Tale of Beryn*" (*SAC* 11 [1989]: 43–62) with its own candidate for author, Thomas Astell, a lawyer and not a monk.

JOHN M. BOWERS
University of Nevada, Las Vegas

PIERO BOITANI and ANNA TORTI, eds. *Religion in the Poetry and Drama of the Late Middle Ages in England.* J. A. W. Bennett Memorial Lectures, Perugia, 1988. Cambridge and Wolfeboro, N.H.: D. S. Brewer, 1990. Pp. viii, 239. $70.00.

The papers in this collection were read in their original form at Perugia in 1988, for the sixth symposium commemorating J. A. W. Bennett. Two excellent essays on the mystics introduce the series. Douglas Gray prefaces his study of the *Book of Margery Kempe* with a discerning analysis of the strands of popular religion and its connections with official teachings. He finds Margery's *Book* "full of energetic and unruly life." Appropriately, his essay, also surging with life, does justice to her vitality. Contrary to those who underestimate Margery, he judges her to be "an extraordinary example of 'homeliness' combined with intense visionary qualities, of mysticism rooted in everyday experience."

Similarly vital is Domenico Pezzini's study of the theme of the passion in Richard Rolle and Julian of Norwich. Pezzini's overview of the medieval theology of redemption, as well as his definitions of spirituality and mysticism, are useful for the study of other medieval treatises on spirituality.

Margaret Bridges wrestles with the topic of "Narrative-engendering and Narrative-inhibiting Functions of Prayer in Late Middle English." She includes in her concept of prayer in literature any expression of a wish, whether or not it is addressed to God or the saints. Even when analyzing the legend of St. Margaret of Antioch, she bypasses the theological underpinnings of her subject. Thus her approach throws only minimal light on the specifically religious character of the works she examines.

Four essays on Chaucer address the problem of faith and literature from creative perspectives. Przemyslaw Mroczkowski, in "Faith and the Critical Spirit in Chaucer's Life and Times," presents Chaucer as neutral on the subject of religion. Writing, not doctrine, he holds, was Chaucer's principal vocation: while accepting Christian teachings, Chaucer presented what lay outside creed and acceptable conduct without combating either. Unfortunately, Mroczkowski's analysis is flawed by references to "the adoration of Mary" and "the accepted medieval worship of Christ's mother." Whatever may have been the stance of popular piety, official church teaching did not sanction Marian adoration or worship.

By contrast, in "The Aesthetic of Chaucer's Religious Tales in Rhyme Royal," C. David Benson sees Chaucer's faith commitment not as marginal

163

but as central to his concerns. Benson argues that Chaucer is not "a moral relativist, with no fixed principles or deep beliefs." Rather, he celebrates transcendent faith, and in his attitude toward secular affairs he is far from reassuring to the established political powers. In fact, according to Benson, the "female heroines who dominate these works create what might be called a Christian feminism, in which Chaucer uses the historical marginality of women (and a child) to criticize the operation of the secular world, which is run entirely by men."

In the third Chaucer piece, "*The Pardoner's Tale*: An Early Moral Play?" Paula Neuss presents new arguments for reading the tale as a drama. She shows how Chaucer's text anticipates and draws on the techniques and devices of the English moral plays. She believes that the moral play is an offshoot of the moral sense of Scripture, as developed in traditional four-part biblical exegesis.

Focusing on characters in *Troilus and Criseyde* and *The Nun's Priest's Tale*, Saul N. Brody shows how these works present conflicts in the area of making moral choices, even when moral principles are clear. He shows in the Chaucerian narratives he examines how animal passions can subvert reason and how reason, in any case, can barely make sense of the confusions that assault the human subject. Therefore Chaucer's moral tales implicitly caution against making final judgments.

The first of two papers on *Piers Plowman* also deals with the complexity of human morality. In "A Will with a Reason: Theological Developments in the C-Revision of *Piers Plowman*," Bruce Harbert traces Langland's growth from a narrow didactic perspective to a mature moral vision manifested in the later form of the work. In the C text the poet achieves a greater balance between reason and will, similar in part to that of Walter Hilton, as comparative passages illustrate. The mature Langland is less individualistic and more compassionate. The moral vision embedded in the C text includes a "sense of the solidarity and interdependence of all members of society."

In a similar vein Derek Pearsall traces the role of the lunatic lollers in *Piers Plowman*. They appear first as beggars and as an answer to the question of who is worthy to receive alms. They later become exemplars of wise spiritual poverty. These fools, utterly dependent on God's providence and stripped of pomp and ceremony, stand for the true nature of the spiritual life.

Richard Axton makes a convincing case for taking seriously the bizarre legends about Judas, the betrayer. Underlying these legends, Axton shows, is a strong curiosity among medieval readers about the place of destiny in the theology of salvation.

Two studies of the mystery plays bring out neglected aspects of the cycles. Hans-Jürgen Diller claims that the didactic function of the mystery plays has been overstated. Instead, they aim at developing the emotional side of Christian faith and at times indulge in peripheral matters. In the Creation to Doom cycles N. Town is virtually alone in seeking to dramatize essential church dogma. It differs from the other cycles in its strategy of transforming the intangible aspects of Christian faith into tangible stage events.

Going against the grain of modern critical practice, Richard Beadle analyzes the exact verbal texture of the York Barkers' pageant of the *Creation and Fall of Lucifer*. He argues for and demonstrates a high degree of integration in the play's language, dramatic structure, and theological substance.

These papers as a whole help break down the resistance of contemporary audiences to perceiving the integration of religion and artistry in Middle English literature. Individually the essays exemplify fruitful approaches for studying religion as a component of medieval poetry and drama. These approaches include analyzing the author's principal stance toward religion or the author's growth in moral or faith outlook from early to later compositions; studying what themes the medieval populace took an interest in, especially when these themes raised issues not dealt with to their satisfaction by the church fathers; classifying religious themes found in several genres and individual texts and showing their relation to orthodox or popular beliefs; reexamining the underlying beliefs and religious focus implicit in tales of a biblical character and associated legends; examining interrelations of medieval writings with other works of literature across the ages; and describing the spirituality taught through the text and disentangling strands of popular belief and official dogma. All these approaches enable the critic to assess a work for its degree of integration of language, structure, imagery, and theological substance. They invite the scholar and the general reader to take a new look at author, audience, and text under the perspectives of spirituality, morality, and belief.

Many of these essays fill in blind spots that cause some contemporary critics to overlook such matters as Christian feminism. The authors offer patterns for finding the artistry of overtly religious pieces, which are sometimes dismissed as merely didactic or simplistic.

The vitality of the essays is rooted in part in their being first designed for oral delivery. They are free of befuddling jargon. Though the price is daunting, the volume has lasting value and should have wide appeal. It offers a wealth of ideas for the ongoing in-depth study of medieval texts.

RITAMARY BRADLEY
St. Ambrose University

BETSY BOWDEN. *Eighteenth-Century Modernizations from* The Canterbury Tales. Chaucer Studies, vol. 16. Cambridge: D. S. Brewer, 1991. Pp. xx, 263. $90.00.

Recent scholarly interest in the literary uses of the historical and poetic past has called attention to translation as a commercial exchange between distinct sets of cultural and aesthetic forces. Eighteenth-century scholars and Chaucer scholars alike will thus be interested in Betsy Bowden's *Eighteenth-Century Modernizations from* The Canterbury Tales as a document revealing the commerce between Chaucer and his eighteenth-century modernizers. The use of "modernizations," rather than "translations," in the title of this volume calls attention both to the continuity between Chaucer's England and eighteenth-century England and to the inevitable failure facing Chaucer's modernizers. None of the forty-five modernizations in this volume has seen print for two centuries, and each characterizes the eighteenth century as much as it characterizes Chaucer.

The eighteenth-century character of these modernizations is most clearly evident in the bent toward moralization and in the fascination with Chaucer's *fabliaux*: in this volume there are four versions of *The Shipman's Tale*, three of *The Miller's Tale*, and three of *The Reeve's Tale*. The need to instruct and even control the reader's interpretation of Chaucer's ribald tales is especially evident in the three versions of *The Miller's Tale*, each of which closes with a moral not provided by Chaucer's less anxious original. When John Smith (1662–1717) modernized *The Miller's Tale*, for instance, he replaced Chaucer's concluding laugh with a sour triplet (lines 825–28):

> As for the Clerk I leave him to resent,
> The injur'd Husband to his Discontent,
> The Philomath and Wife for ever to repent.

Where Chaucer's intertextual jokes are lost in the translation of single tales, moralization again takes over. The version of *The Reeve's Tale* attributed to Thomas Betterton replaces the concluding attack launched by Chaucer's Reeve on the Miller with a jab at women's libido: "And Thus the Miller of his Fear is eas'd, / The Mother and the Daughter both well pleas'd." The imposed moralization and the care with which the moral is explicated for the reader in many of these modernizations reflect an anxiety that the reader interpret these works correctly, an anxiety not seen in Chaucer's original.

Each author's struggle with Chaucer's misunderstood metrics and rhyme scheme is also evident; thus this volume provides a rich resource for scholars of eighteenth-century prosody. The revision of end rhymes predictably leads to substantive changes in diction, even when an effort is made to keep the line-by-line sense the same. All but three of the modernizations are in iambic pentameter, but the frequent use of elision reveals the eighteenth-century's struggle to smooth Chaucer's pentameter line: "'Twas when the Fields imbibe the Vernal Show'rs, / And Venus paints her Month with early Flow'rs."

Overall, the authors vary widely in their latitude of poetic license. Samuel Cobb (1675–1713) provides a fairly accurate adaptation of *The Miller's Tale*, revising the meter and rhyme and elaborating the hint of moralization provided by Chaucer but straying from Chaucer's original line count by only a handful of lines. An anonymous 1715 tetrameter version of *The Reeve's Tale*, on the other hand, adds more than 500 lines to Chaucer's original by inserting a scholarly argument over the respective merits of blank verse and rhymed couplets. The debate over rhyme is referred to in a clever brushstroke as "the Clink and Blank of Poetry" (p. 847). The volume provides a record of the eighteenth-century's effort to correct Chaucer's prosody, and this may be its chief richness.

Additionally, the volume presents us with a problem of attribution. Bowden argues here, as she has in *Chaucer Aloud* (1987), for Alexander Pope's authorship of the versions of *The General Prologue* and *The Reeve's Tale* attributed to Thomas Betterton and first printed in Pope's *Miscellaneous Poems and Translations* (1712). The problem of attribution arises because Betterton died two years before these two modernizations were published, and Pope never claimed them as his. In attributing these works to Pope, Bowden agrees with Betterton's 1891 biographer, Robert Lowe, who claims in a footnote that Pope "published a modernization of some of Chaucer's poems in Betterton's name, though they were, no doubt, the poet's own productions" (Lowe, p. 186). Maynard Mack is more cau-

167

tious, claiming only that Pope probably revised these works, perhaps extensively (Mack, *Alexander Pope*, p. 92). The reasoned rhymes of the opening of *The General Prologue* may, in fact, bring Pope to mind, and while the syntax is more halting than what we expect, even from a young Pope, it is surprisingly fluid for the aging Betterton. The possibility of some sort of collaboration seems likely, but firmer internal or external evidence is necessary to attribute these works solely to Pope.

Bowden's two-part introduction touches on both theoretical and practical uses of the volume, though it does not adequately address the difference between the theory and the practice of eighteenth-century modernization and translation. Bowden opens by applauding unspecified twentieth-century literary theorists who argue that "different readers may have different *but equally valid* responses to the same text" (p. ix; italics added). This claim does not explain the striking similarities shared by these modernizations; far from exhibiting "different but equally valid responses," these works reflect shared cultural interpretive strategies requiring a more sophisticated theoretical introduction. Furthermore, the moralization imposed on these texts reflects a concern that the reader interpret correctly rather than independently. Similarly, Bowden compares modernization, too literally, with oral performance, claiming that modernization "conveys [the modernizer's] sense of a passage by elaborating or adding audiovisual effects . . . thereby show[ing] his audience the performance that he has seen and heard inside his head while silently reading Chaucer's text" (p. xvi). The consistent failure of the thirteen authors in this volume to escape specific interpretive strategies suggests that modernization is more complex than Bowden's analogy acknowledges.

In theory, the chief translation theorists of this period were more demanding of their interpretive task than Bowden suggests by her interest in the multiplicity of responses available to any given text. John Dryden, who in 1680 codified the art of translation for his century and the next, carefully placed the stopping points of metaphrase, paraphrase, and imitation on a trajectory of increasing poetic license. Two years later, in *Religio Laici*, he again touched on translation and poetic license, this time focusing on the threat that translation posed to the integrity of sacred text. Alexander Pope proved no less anxious about the relationship between translation and interpretation: his learned translation of Homer inspired repeated nightmares of being lost on an endless journey. In practice, however, Dryden's and Pope's various translations today appear time-bound despite their authors' toil at producing something like an authoritative text. Similarly, the shared cultural markers evident throughout Bowden's edition—the

168

concern for moralization, the anxiety toward literary interpretation, the interest in correcting Chaucer's prosody — need to be taken into account to explain eighteenth-century modernization in theory and in practice. Such a theory might also explain why Chaucer's original finally seems more modern than do any of these more recent adaptations.

This double-column edition is readable, though at sixty-three lines per column the type is admittedly small. Line numbers have been added, and parallel lines are noted parenthetically, though "parallel" is defined broadly. Footnotes appear sporadically. A brief biographical introduction precedes and textual information follows each modernization.

ANNA BATTIGELLI
State University of New York at Plattsburgh

RACHEL BROMWICH, A. O. H. JARMAN, and BRYNLEY F. ROBERTS, eds. *The Arthur of the Welsh: The Arthurian Legend in Medieval Welsh Literature.* Cardiff: University of Wales Press, 1991. Pp. xiv, 310. $55.00.

In 1959 Oxford University Press published *Arthurian Literature in the Middle Ages: A Collaborative History*, which soon became an essential book for all students of Arthurian literature. Comprising forty-one essays by thirty eminent scholars, it surveys the facts, documents, and speculations concerning Arthurian material across Europe from its first appearance in written sources through the work of Malory. It is an immensely useful project, and references to *ALMA* have steadily appeared in the footnotes of Arthurian studies ever since. An especially valuable dimension of *ALMA*'s contribution is the inclusion of a substantial group of essays on Arthurian material in Welsh. This undoubtedly reflects the interest of the editor, Roger Sherman Loomis, who had long sought to establish the origins of Arthurian themes and characters in the literary, historical, and mythological traditions of the Celtic peoples, particularly the Welsh.

It cannot be said that the essays by Welsh scholars in *ALMA* give strong support to Loomis's theories, but they do open a window onto the isolated field of Celtic studies and transmit to a wider world a large fund of specific information regarding the figure of Arthur in Welsh tradition. Here are, in early historical writings, glimpses of Arthur and his men in battle against the Saxons centuries earlier, enigmatic references to lost stories about them in early Welsh poems and bardic lists, and complete Arthurian narratives in polished Welsh prose.

In 1985 the Vinaver Memorial Trust of the British Branch of the International Arthurian Society decided to commission a series of volumes that would "supplement and revise" *ALMA* in the light of recent scholarship and thinking. *The Arthur of the Welsh: The Arthurian Legend in Medieval Welsh Literature* (henceforth *AOW*) is the first volume of that projected series.

Going well beyond simply reconsidering the Welsh essays in *ALMA* (chapters 1–8, 12, and 16), most of the essays in *AOW* are completely new work by different hands. Two of the original contributors to *ALMA* appear again: A. O. H. Jarman has greatly expanded his earlier discussion of the legends and poems associated with the Welsh figure of Myrddin (Merlin), and Rachel Bromwich, whose earlier essay on the Welsh Triads unfortunately has been dropped, has two new essays, one on the surviving Welsh fragments (disappointingly few and late) of the Tristan story and another on "First Transmission to England and France," especially valuable for its discussion of the personal names of Welsh, Cornish, and Breton origin that appear in the Latin and French Arthurian works of the twelfth century. In a field where hard evidence is difficult to find, that substantial body of names, she points out, "constitutes the most important and incontrovertible evidence for the Celtic contribution to Arthurian romance."

Two works of the Latin chronicle tradition that have always been important to studies of Arthur are the ninth-century *Historia Brittonum* (long attributed to "Nennius"), which lists twelve victorious battles fought by Arthur against the Saxons, and the twelfth-century *Historia Regum Britanniae*, by Geoffrey of Monmouth, which presents a picture of the whole reign of Arthur so compelling that very little Arthurian material, Welsh included, was afterward untouched by its influence. Both works receive in *AOW* careful discussion that reflects an interesting shift of attention away from gleaning historical evidence about a legendary king active around the year 500 and toward examining the processes and forms of historical writing itself, how the authors thought about national history.

Thomas Charles-Edwards's "The Arthur of History" is really an essay on the *Historia Brittonum*, most interesting when he discusses that work as a ninth-century fusion of two genres of early-medieval historical writing, the "history of a people" and the "ecclesiastical history." From that perspective, it is a work looking forward not to military victory but to the role of the Britons in Christian providential history.

170

Brynley F. Roberts's essay on the *Historia Regum Britanniae* and the subsequent Welsh translations of that work is a good guide to the structural artistry and resonant themes of Geoffrey's book. The large space given to the advent and reign of Arthur, he writes, suggests that, for Geoffrey, Arthur was "a personification of British history" and the book a history not of kings but of a nation. Because that history is pervaded by the theme of loss, and by "the moral principle that a nation reaps what is sown in past ages," it is a cautionary tale as well: "In Welsh eyes," Roberts comments, "it is a rather somber book in its final effect." Translations of Geoffrey into Welsh began to appear in the thirteenth century; it would be difficult to say whether it was despite that somber effect or because of it that the *Brut y Brenhinedd* (*Chronicle of the Kings*) came to be one of the most frequently copied texts in Welsh manuscript literature.

Several early Welsh poems involve Arthur in an allusive and sometimes enigmatic way. Texts of the poems survive only in manuscripts of the thirteenth and fourteenth centuries and cannot be precisely dated at all, but they seem to show no influence from Geoffrey of Monmouth and to draw on a native body of stories, long since lost, about marvelous exploits by Arthur and his men. The poems themselves are not narratives but belong to the venerable Celtic genres of boast, panegyric, prophecy, and lament. In one poem, Arthur catalogues for a recalcitrant gatekeeper his various warriors and their deeds; in another the legendary poet Taliesin speaks of a bold but disastrous raid on the Otherworld by Arthur and three shiploads of warriors, from which only seven returned; yet another refers in passing to the site of Arthur's final defeat at Camlan and seems also to hint at the legend of his survival. Those poems and others are discussed with characteristic thoroughness in a splendid essay by Patrick Sims-Williams (the documentation packed into the 158 footnotes is worth the price of the book), who also keeps in mind the wider audience for whom this book is intended. The poetry is quoted at length (in close translation) with detailed commentary, so that there is a good look at its generic characteristics, its textual difficulties, and its sense of someone obliquely referring to a complicated story told much earlier by someone else.

Literary history is the primary purpose of *AOW*, as it was of *ALMA*, but some medieval Welsh Arthurian works bring into the book the interests of literary criticism as well. Two such are complete prose narratives in Welsh, each unique and very different from the other: *Culhwch and Olwen*, composed in its present form sometime around 1100, and *The Dream of Rhonabwy*, written approximately two centuries later. The extensive and irregular narrative of *Culhwch and Olwen* is marked by swift movement

171

and comic energy, and also by two extremely long catalogues—one naming Arthur's warriors and courtiers, the other naming a large number of tasks they must perform in the great quest they undertake. Our first picture in European literature of an Arthurian court is in this tale, though it is clear that it is based on a strong medieval tradition of oral or written story in Welsh. Brynley F. Roberts's short essay on *Culhwch and Olwen* is a fine analysis of the structural and stylistic dimensions of the tale, which reveal the unknown author's careful literary manipulation of the traditional material. Someone wishing to incorporate this early and distinctive tale into an Arthurian course, but puzzled over what to say about it, would find the essay very helpful. The problem of *Culhwch and Olwen* is that it is a wonderful tale of no apparent significance—no codes of chivalry to live by or to fail, no conflicts of loyalties or of love and honor, only the exhilaration of what Gwyn Jones called "the buoyantly heartless tone" of its narrative. But precisely in that lies its interest, Roberts suggests, in its double nature as a work rooted in the oral tradition of performance and entertainment but also a literary creation with an unconsummated desire for some thematic purpose.

The Dream of Rhonabwy gives a much later picture of the Welsh Arthur, a curiously static picture. He sits on an island in the middle of a river while the important Battle of Badon awaits him, then sits and plays the Welsh board game *gwyddbwyll* while his men lose a different battle against a troop of ravens. Ceridwen Lloyd-Morgan marshals the evidence which argues that this strange dream vision, full of ambiguities, ironies, and inversions of traditional material, is a full-blown Arthurian parody. But who or what is being parodied? Her answer, "the whole fabric of Arthurian literary conventions," is uncomfortably broad and yet plausible, for it does appear that by the time of this late work Welsh literature had accumulated centuries of Arthurian themes and conventions, indigenous and imported, of which one talented author perhaps had become somewhat weary.

Three Arthurian romances in Welsh from roughly the late twelfth or the first half of the thirteenth century correspond in a manner not quite clear to three romances of Chrétien de Troyes. *Geraint*, *Owain*, and *Peredur* may derive directly or indirectly from Chrétien's *Erec*, *Yvain*, and *Perceval*, or Chrétien and the Welsh authors (a different one for each work is assumed) may have used common sources, perhaps Breton stories that passed into both French and Welsh. The question has been a scholarly controversy, "die Mabinogionfrage," for more than a century, but recent discussion has tended instead to consider them as essentially Welsh works that adapt alien narrative subjects and techniques to the styles and traditions of medieval

Welsh narrative and refract through the chivalric and courtly material the interests and patterns of medieval Welsh society.

These three romances are covered in one chapter in *ALMA*, but *AOW* has a chapter for each—a big improvement, though they are short chapters. Once the authors have covered the external business of manuscripts, dates, sources, and influences, little space is left to suggest what is interesting in the works themselves, why we read them (disappointed readers can look to published and forthcoming essays by Brynley Roberts, Helen Fulton, and Susan Aronstein for innovative critical studies of these works). Nevertheless, each author does find the space to take up a topic of critical interest. Roger Middleton shows that the large proportion of formulaic phrases and passages in *Geraint* implies not "translation" from a Breton or French story but a much more thoroughgoing "transformation" of the text by a developed system of oral storytelling in Welsh. R. L. Thomson, writing on *Owain*, looks at interesting differences from *Yvain* in the "Arthurian" characters, the narrative structure, and the represented world, all of which again point up signs of Welsh transformation of the work. Ian Lovecy effectively dismantles attempts to demonstrate a structural and thematic unity in *Peredur*, arguing that it is less a coherent "romance" than an amalgamation of stories connected by little else than the identity of the hero, not unlike a television series.

Three remaining essays, which bring the total to thirteen (plus an introduction), are an interesting "archaeological" group of studies. Rachel Bromwich's survey of the poetic fragments and allusions involving the Tristan story shows that only shards remain from the early period, though there is a late *Ystorya Trystan*. In "Brittany and the Arthurian Legend," J. E. Caerwyn Williams reconsiders the "Breton bridge" of Loomis's theory (the idea that bilingual Breton *conteurs* first transmitted Welsh and Cornish tales of Arthur into French) from a more historically based perspective; clear and measured, it is an ample review of all the evidence. O. J. Padel's essay is literally archaeological, telling us what excavations have revealed of four southwestern sites with Arthurian associations—Tintagel, "Kelli wic," and Castle Dore, all in Cornwall, and South Cadbury ("Camelot"), in Somerset. His discussion is precise and economical—and fascinating, in part because he knows just the right questions to ask, such as "what visible remains the story-tellers might have had in mind" when they spoke of Tintagel in the twelfth century, when Geoffrey of Monmouth first associated the site with Arthur's birth tale.

AOW is wholly a British production, its dozen contributors all from Wales or England. Inevitably there are the occasional descents into minutiae and donnish mutterings. There is little theorizing, old or new. We hear next to nothing of the old speculations about lost Celtic myths hidden in Arthurian literature (the Grail, the Fisher King, and the Waste Land are mentioned only in passing, as motifs in one group of romances), and oracles of contemporary theory such as Barthes, Derrida, and Foucault — the triad most likely to be invoked in a *PMLA* essay, according to a recent survey by the editor — are here entirely absent without presence (for that matter, *PMLA* itself does not appear once in the 900 footnotes, a significant change from *ALMA*). The contributors, all seasoned scholars who know their fields thoroughly, are primarily concerned to inform, and that is what they do. This will be a valuable book to medievalists for many years.

ANDREW WELSH
Rutgers University

MARINA S. BROWNLEE, KEVIN BROWNLEE, and STEPHEN G. NICHOLS, eds. *The New Medievalism*. Parallax: Re-Visions of Culture and Society Series. Baltimore, Md., and London: Johns Hopkins University Press, 1991. Pp. vi, 330. $42.50 cloth; $14.95 paper.

How new is the "new medievalism"? For some years now, a growing contingent of American medievalists has been following the lead of such Continental counterparts as Jauss and Eco, in attempting to situate the traditional model of medieval studies, which roots the discipline in history and philology, within a larger theoretical framework. While medieval studies inevitably retain a certain marginal status among the academic disciplines, this attempt has finally brought medievalists into closer contact with methodological trends long established in other fields: the insights of various poststructuralist methods and ideologies have caused medievalists not to abandon their traditional interests but to reformulate the ways in which we think about them. Strictly speaking, then, little about the general nature of this movement is actually new; the past fifteen years have witnessed the publication of many books, collections of essays, and special issues of journals illustrating these theoretical and methodological developments. When even *Speculum*, that least trendy of journals, has seen fit to publish a special issue on "The New Philology" (January, 1990), the advocates of these approaches to medieval studies may be regarded less as pioneers than as an alternative medieval-studies establishment, or even as the predominant establishment.

"New," then, in the title of this collection of essays (most of which first appeared in a special issue of *Romanic Review* in 1988) should not be taken to mean either that most of the essays included are themselves new or that much truly new ground is to be broken here, at least in the readings offered of specific texts. One of its "newest" features, instead, is precisely its attempt to redefine and to theorize this notion of "newness" with regard to medieval studies as a discipline; indeed, the present volume is the first of the many books mentioned above to devote as much space to theorizing this movement as to illustrating it. In the introductory essay, by Stephen G. Nichols ("The New Medievalism: Tradition and Discontinuity in Medieval Culture"), the term "new medievalism" is recognized as cognate with "New Historicism," but, unlike that term, it does not predicate a specific methodology, "designating instead a predisposition to interrogate and reformulate assumptions about the discipline of medieval studies broadly conceived" (p. 1). "New," then, can be taken to refer to an intellectual project that seeks continuously to renew itself, although the attempt at constant renewal may not, paradoxically, be itself a new idea. This rigorous definition and theorization of the "new medievalist" project is the volume's first avowed aim and produces its most interesting essays; its second goal, to present a "coherent illustration, representative rather than exhaustive, of the work being done by new medievalists" (p. 1), duplicating as it does the goal of many similar books, will perhaps be of less interest to those not working in the specific fields addressed by the individual essays.

Most of the scholars represented in *The New Medievalism* are, in fact, part of the current medieval-studies establishment mentioned above, and their names, which, aside from the editors' (Marina S. Brownlee, "Language and Incest in *Grisel y Mirabella*"; Kevin Brownlee, "The Problem of Faux Semblant: Language, History, and Truth in the *Roman de la Rose*"; and Stephen G. Nichols, "An Intellectual Anthropology of Marriage in the Middle Ages"), include Giuseppe Mazzotta ("Antiquity and the New Arts in Petrarch"), R. Howard Bloch ("The Medieval Text — 'Guigemar' — as a Provocation to the Discipline of Medieval Studies"), David F. Hult ("Reading It Right: The Ideology of Text Editing"), Alexandre Leupin ("Raoul de Cambrai: The Illegitimacy of Writing"), Rachel Jacoff ("Transgression and Transcendence: Figures of Female Desire in Dante's *Commedia*"), Jeffrey T. Schnapp ("Dante's Sexual Solecisms: Gender and Genre in the *Commedia*"), Eugene Vance ("Semiotics and Power: Relics, Icons, and the *Voyage de Charlemagne à Jérusalem et à Constantinople*"), Maureen

175

Quilligan ("Allegory and the Textual Body: Female Authority in Christine de Pizan's *Livre de la Cité des Dames*"), and Hans Ulrich Gumbrecht ("Intertextuality and Autumn/Autumn and the Modern Reception of the Middle Ages"), will be familiar to most medievalists. Many of those essays that seem to have been chosen for their illustrative, rather than their theoretical, value, will present few surprises to readers who have followed current developments in the field. At least one contributor seems aware of the problem, common to several of them, that the "new medievalism" can, in practical application, yield rather old-hat results: Alexandre Leupin, after three pages demonstrating the reflexive nature of *Raoul de Cambrai*, goes to some pains to defend his essay against the charge that we have heard it all before, claiming that "the tautology 'literature does nothing but speak itself' may be true, but it is always written in a different way" (p. 134). Yet the conclusion, in support of which epigraphs from Lacan and Rousseau as well as diagrams are mustered, is banal: "Readers must be silent when they come to the realization that their task is endless" (p. 151).

The need for another collection illustrating the kinds of work in which "new medievalists" are engaged may, then, be questioned; of the illustrative essays, only Schnapp's is on the "cutting edge," informed as it is by current theoretical work on homosexuality and gender, an area that has only recently received serious scholarly attention. While a number of the other illustrative essays will be of considerable interest to scholars working in their particular areas, few will compel the attention of those coming to this volume for a coherent sense of the current state of medieval studies as a discipline.

Those readers will find considerably more to think about in the theoretical articles. Aside from the introductory essay mentioned above, this category includes the articles by Mazzotta, Bloch, Hult, and Gumbrecht, as well as the second piece by Nichols. Most intriguing is the inclusion of an essay by one literary theorist who is not usually identified with medieval studies, Michael Riffaterre, whose "The Mind's Eye: Memory and Textuality" considers the intersections between orality and textuality, a topic of considerable current interest to medievalists—though the essay does not refer to any medieval texts. This inclusion under the rubric "new medievalism" of a purely theoretical, nonmedieval article by a prominent nonmedievalist scholar suggests what is perhaps the field's newest development of all: the use of medieval literary concerns as a basis for theorizing all literature, and indeed "literariness" itself. Along these lines, Hult's essay is especially interesting in its attempt to bring the old controversy over how best to edit medieval texts (Lachmann versus Bédier) into line with current debates on the nature of the literary object itself. Here as elsewhere in this volume, medieval literature is seen not as marginal to but as epitomizing current literary-theoretical concerns.

The editors' division of this collection into four sections, "Theoretical Dimensions," "The New Philology," "Literary Anthropology," and "Authority and History," may thus be less useful to the reader than it would have been to signal which articles are primarily theoretical and which primarily illustrative. The former, at least, are an important contribution to the field of medieval studies and should be of considerable interest to all medievalists.

ROBERT S. STURGES
University of New Orleans

J. A. BURROW and THORLAC TURVILLE-PETRE. *A Book of Middle English.* Oxford and Cambridge, Mass.: Blackwell, 1992. Pp. vii, 303. $20.65 paper.

Given the distinguished scholarly stature of the compilers, John Burrow and Thorlac Turville-Petre's anthology of Middle English texts and extracts deserves careful consideration by teachers of Middle English language and literature.

The book consists of two major parts, each distinctive in its own way. The first part is an extended description (some sixty pages) of Middle English, covering general history, dialectal varieties and diachronic change, pronunciation, vocabulary, inflections, syntax, and meter, with a short section on the process of editing the manuscript and a concluding bibliography. Most of this part is a solid and lucid exposition of traditional grammar, characterized rather modestly in the preface as "inevitably selective and somewhat simplified." The presentation is a skillful blend of paradigms and narrative explanations, liberally illustrated by quotations from the texts. Possibly the compilers assume too great a familiarity with Old English (especially among students in the United States), but the account is generally clear, and any opaque spots could be explained by a philologically competent teacher — an increasingly *rara avis*, however.

The first part reflects well certain aspects of current scholarship. Besides the traditional account of Middle English dialects (Northern, West Midland, East Midland, etc.), Burrow and Turville-Petre have included up-to-date references to the methodology of the *Linguistic Atlas of Late Mediaeval English* and to recent studies on the importance of Chancery English. The account (pp. 62–64) of the steps by which an edited text (a passage from *St. Erkenwald*) is generated is a good idea. It is, of course, too brief to act as a paleographical training guide for students, and the plate is rather small, but it serves to show the problems often encountered by a modern editor and the decisions that have to be made in the preparation of a printed text. The short discussion of how different choices of editorial punctuation affect the sense of the opening lines of *Sir Gawain and the Green Knight* (and the remark that Burrow and Turville-Petre disagree thereover) should be salutary for students who think that medieval texts are — and have always been — fixed on the printed page. Most of the books in the select bibliography belong to the last twenty years; the date of the latest citations is 1990.

The second part of the book is a reader of fourteen verse and prose texts (counting the lyrics as one text), chosen, the compilers say, for literary merit rather than simply as illustrations of the language. They range in date of composition from about 1150 to about 1400. The selection is fairly standard, from the "Anarchy" annal from the *Peterborough Chronicle* (1137) to the York *Play of the Crucifixion* (composed before 1400, though the manuscript dates from between 1463 and 1477). Several of the intervening texts are given in their entirety — *Sir Orfeo, Patience, St. Erkenwald*, Trevisa's *Dialogue Between a Lord and a Clerk*. The remainder are represented by extracts — *The Owl and the Nightingale*, Laȝamon's *Brut*, *The Cloud of Unknowing, Piers Plowman, Sir Gawain and the Green Knight*, and Gower's *Confessio Amantis*. Chaucer is deliberately omitted, since "the book is designed to be read in conjunction with an edition of Chaucer" (preface).

I think the texts will prove reasonably easy of student access. The headnote to each selection typically places the work in context, notes the manuscript(s) used, and comments on the language. The typographical presentation is handsome and easy to read, a feature that is particularly important in a teaching text. Explanatory footnotes provide good glosses to difficult words and phrases as well as judicious background information and learned commentary. The student has to supplement such lexical information by reference to the glossary at the back of the book, which is inevitably slower than being spoon-fed a series of marginal glosses. It also imposes a fair amount of wear and tear on a paperback book — my review copy is dog-eared from the reading process and subsequent reference for this writing, though the spine is standing up well.

Burrow and Turville-Petre have reedited their texts from the manuscripts, inserting editorial word division, capitalization, and punctuation and regularizing to a minimal extent (for example, *i*/*j*, *u*, *v*). While I am all in favor of a fresh look at the original manuscripts in editions for advanced scholars, I wonder whether that enjoyable travail was necessary for the present volume, given its primary audience and the availability of reliable editions of these standard works that could have been used as base texts. A short section of textual notes (pp. 260–64) records manuscript readings that have been emended in the body of the book; these could be used as an effective teaching tool in conjunction with the notes on textual transition from manuscript to printed text. However, a list of any new or more accurate readings that have resulted from the reediting process would have been welcome to advanced scholars.

A number of new collections of Middle English works have appeared recently, and one must consider how Burrow and Turville-Petre's compares with these and with older tried-and-true teaching texts that are still available. *A Book of Middle English* aims at a different audience than, say, the compendious Oxford or St. Martin's anthologies, which are designed for core literature courses. It is more scholarly in compilation and contains better headnotes than Garbáty's *Medieval English Literature* or Dunn and Byrnes's *Middle English Literature*, but it does not contain the much wider range of texts found in them. The part on language, though, is by far the best on the current market, superseding the cumbersome and old-fashioned account in Mossé's *Handbook of Middle English* (though again the range of texts is wider in Mossé).

Burrow and Turville-Petre's *Book of Middle English* belongs, I think, to a line of textbooks that is essentially German and British, with some French and American clones. The tradition is characterized by a strong philological element linked to the study of Old English grammar. Representative works include Kaiser's *Medieval English*, Mossé (the first part of whose *Handbook* is devoted to Old English), Emerson's *Middle English Reader* (American, but "following the best practice in reading Old English, or Anglo-Saxon" [p. v]), Sisam's *Fourteenth-Century Verse and Prose*, Dickins and Wilson's *Early Middle English Texts*, Bennett and Smithers's *Early Middle English Verse and Prose*, and so on — the kinds of books that used to be assigned in departments of English language rather than English literature in British universities, once laboriously read, never forgotten. It is not surprising, then, that *A Book of Middle English* is intended as a companion to Mitchell and Robinson's *Guide to Old English*, and it succeeds worthily in this purpose.

Teachers will no doubt find ingenious ways to use this book or to incorporate it into courses, probably at the graduate level in the States. Using recent publications or reprints as assigned textbooks, I can envisage one possible incarnation of a year-long Middle English "super-course" that would not break a tight graduate student budget: Kolve and Olson's *Canterbury Tales* and Shoaf's *Troilus* for Chaucer, Schmidt's *B-Text* for Langland, Dunn and Byrnes for the traditional also-rans, Barratt's *Women's Writing in Middle English* and Speed's *Medieval English Romances* for less familiar works, and Burrow and Turville-Petre's *Book of Middle English* for pronunciation and language.

LISTER M. MATHESON
Michigan State University

NORMAN F. CANTOR. *Inventing the Middle Ages: The Lives, Works, and Ideas of the Great Medievalists of the Twentieth Century.* New York: William Morrow and Co., 1991. Pp. 477. $28.00.

If the title of this book evokes Renaissance humanists coining the term *medium aevum* to evade the interval from the classical period to their own time, the subtitle asserts its true subject: the relation between the lives and works of some twenty medievalists of the last one hundred years, or, in Cantor's biographical style, from William Maitland as the legal historian created by late Victorian England to Richard William Southern as the ruler of a withered Camelot that was once medieval studies in England. There are also full portraits of such Continental and American figures as Ernst Kantorowicz, Erwin Panofsky, Ernst Robert Curtius, Marc Bloch, Étienne Gilson, Charles Homer Haskins, and Joseph Strayer. Cantor portrays each exemplary figure by summarizing his (or, in the single instance of Eileen Power, her) writings and sketching major moments in his life.

This approach has its dangers: it assumes some coherent relation between the circumstances of the life and the nature of the work, and it relies on anecdotal evidence not always verifiable from other sources. At moments this book reads like a tabloid in its tales of illicit sex, hidden pasts, and personal betrayals. Cantor can use this material both appositely, as with Dom David Knowles, and also scurrilously, as with Marc Bloch. *Inventing the Middle Ages* is not a sober account of the field, a companion to Gerald Graff's *Professing Literature: An Institutional History* (Chicago:

180

University of Chicago Press, 1987) but rather a vivid, sometimes reckless essay on those who shaped their discipline through the force of personality.

In fact, Cantor is after something more than the history of a discipline. For him, the life of each medievalist should be understood as a response to the intellectual and political history of the twentieth century: "Creating a medieval world picture and projecting themselves into it were one thera-peutic recourse by which sensitive and benign twentieth-century people sought to regain their sanity and get control of their feelings in the evil times of slaughter and madness" (p. 43). For some, this "therapeutic recourse" meant rewriting medieval tales into moralized, cozy fantasies of a world that never was in order to evade the harshness of both the medieval and the modern periods. Cantor praises J. R. R. Tolkien and C. S. Lewis at length in a chapter entitled "The Oxford Fantasists," a term I would extend beyond Cantor's sense of their literary genre to describe their provincial and deluded vision of politics.

Much of *Inventing the Middle Ages* is an implicit defense of those for whom the Middle Ages are, in Brian Stock's sharp phrase, "a refuge for religious archaism and political reaction."[1] Thus Tolkien and Lewis receive uncritically gentle treatment, as do scholars with whom Cantor feels com-fortable. But all this is prelude to Cantor's concluding peroration evoking a "retromedieval world": "one that has consciously turned back the welfare and regulatory state from impinging drastically upon, or even in total-itarian fashion swallowing up, society in the corrosive belly of the brackish public whale represented by its self-serving bureaucrats" (p. 416).

Cantor's vision of the medieval world is not simply a rejection of the contemporary world; it is also a never-never land of harmony and grace: "Retromedievalism means personal sentiment shaped and controlled by formal traditions as well as institutions and structures that recognize the privilege of private feeling and personal love" (p. 416). It is astonishing that anyone who knows as much as Cantor does about the Middle Ages should conclude that they were just like the medieval fairs currently popular on college campuses, unmarred by serfs, violence, rape, malnutri-tion, plague, and religious intolerance. What drives Cantor's "retro-medievalism," as well as these fairs, is not historical accuracy but the desire to escape from our time and place.

Cantor may indulge his fantasies of "retromedievalism," but the reader

---

[1] Brian Stock, *Listening for the Text: On the Uses of the Past* (Baltimore, Md.: Johns Hopkins University Press, 1990), p. 73.

must ask how they affect his portrayal of the chosen medievalists. Those he can fit, whether convincingly or not, into this vision are depicted very charitably, especially if they are English (Knowles, Lewis, Southern, Tolkien). But those whom Cantor suspects of holding a grimmer view of the medieval world are dismissed, especially if they are French and might by a very long stretch be termed Marxists. As a contributor to the neoconservative *New Criterion*, Cantor can spot contaminations of Marxism even in those who never thought themselves Marxists. He wildly misrepresents Marc Bloch by calling him a Marxist and likening him to Theodore Adorno (p. 143). Bloch's writing, particularly after 1939, suggests that his politics were classically liberal, even somewhat old-fashioned for the time. That he learned from Marx about economic and agrarian history hardly makes him a Marxist, only a product of his time. Nor does it make those who followed him in the *Annales* school into Marxists, as if the father's politics were a mutant gene passed on to his intellectual children, most especially to Fernand Braudel.

Marc Bloch must be at the heart of *Inventing the Middle Ages* if Cantor is to sustain his theses about the relation between a medievalist's life and work. For Bloch is the exemplary figure as scholar and human being: he founded, with Lucien Febvre, the *Annales* and with it a new historiography; he led the resistance in Lyons until shot by the Gestapo. Who could be more relevant to Cantor's project than Bloch, the bourgeois professor who rose to his moment unambiguously as an anti-fascist, unlike Martin Heidegger or Paul de Man?

What one finds in Cantor's chapter on Bloch, whom he joins rather unconvincingly to Louis Halphen, is a routine summary of such major works as *French Rural History* and *Feudal Society* and an error-filled account of the life. Readers who compare his chapter with Carole Fink's *Marc Bloch: A Life in History* (Cambridge: Cambridge University Press, 1989), a work that Cantor dismisses as adulation (p. 124) but that gets its facts straight, can spot mistakes for themselves. One error, however, does require discussion. Cantor says that Bloch was arrested in Paris and then executed by the Gestapo "in a field outside Paris" (p. 120), when in fact he was arrested in Lyons and shot in a field outside that city (for details, see Fink, *Marc Bloch*, pp. 312–24). A minor inaccuracy, a mere slip of the map, though troubling in a book about historians? No. The mistake is major. In 1944, Lyons was the center of the underground; the Gestapo there was commanded by Klaus Barbie; it was a very dangerous place for someone to go voluntarily, as did Bloch, and join the resistance. Curiously, Cantor makes this error about Bloch one paragraph after attacking Simone de

Beauvoir and other Parisians for claiming to have been active in the resistance but in fact doing little (p. 120). Placing Bloch in Paris rather than in Lyons has the effect, in the flow of Cantor's account, of casting him as a boulevardier, a dabbler in the resistance, rather than an active partisan in Lyons. In the end, it hardly matters that Cantor admits Bloch "was very perilously involved in the resistance" (p. 120).

In a strikingly parallel error, Cantor dismisses Fernand Braudel by saying that he "spent the war in Algeria writing his enormous dissertation" (p. 150) later published as *The Mediterranean*. Cantor gives no evidence to place Braudel in Algeria and thus out of harm's way. According to Peter Burke, however, Braudel spent the war years writing his dissertation in a Nazi prisoner-of-war camp near Lübeck, on the coast of the Baltic, that northern Mediterranean sea.[2] Whether or not Braudel's war experience made his book better can be debated. What cannot be debated, however, is that Cantor owes his readers a basic accuracy about matters as important as how and where Bloch and Braudel spent the war years.

In writing about the historians of the *Annales* school, Cantor flirts with innuendo in ways that have no place in a serious work. After attacking Braudel for empire building in his creation of the Sixth Section of the École Pratique des Hautes Études, Cantor speculates without any hard evidence that "perhaps the CIA was also the disguised source for the Sixth Section's grants from America" (p. 149). The only support he offers for this smear is to preface it by noting that the British journal *Encounter* was bankrolled with CIA money. If a British magazine, why not a French institute?

In a parallel instance Cantor notes that the first biography of Bloch was published by Fink in 1989. He then strings together the following assertions: "One can only speculate on why Bloch's biography did not appear in Paris in the late forties or early fifties. One explanation may be that there was a much more complicated and controversial story involved in Bloch's betrayal to the Gestapo than his landlady's alleged perfidy. Many dark and ugly betrayals and deals happened in the resistance." No evidence for these claims is supplied. Cantor proceeds: "Bloch's death could possibly have been traced back to one or more big names of postwar France if an industrious biographer had started to work on it shortly after the war." No evidence for this claim is supplied. Cantor then suggests that Bloch's family would not have wanted a biography written that "affected unfavorably

[2] Peter Burke, "Fernand Braudel," in John Cannon, ed., *The Historian at Work* (London: Allen and Unwin, 1980), p. 193.

the buildup of the postwar Marc Bloch myth of martyrdom and sanctity" (p. 123). No evidence for this claim is supplied. Cantor finally says that Bloch was not a good father, and this he does support—with a statement from Bloch's son Étienne (pp. 123–24). In this long chain of nasty innuendoes designed to tarnish Bloch's character and thus his achievement, only one claim is substantiated and that from a less than neutral source. The point is simple: Cantor cannot support his claims and thus strings together a series of speculations from which the hasty reader might conclude that Bloch was no hero as historian or partisan. I am sure that Cantor expects more of his own students in the way of evidence and argument.

After Cantor's sour chapter on Bloch and the *Annales* group, it is a relief to turn to his chapters on Dom David Knowles and Sir R. W. Southern. About Knowles, at least, Cantor has only personal gossip to report: this Benedictine monk who turned renegade from Downside Abbey and wrote the great books *The Monastic Order in England* and *The Religious Orders in England* spent many years of his life in a deeply romantic, perhaps sexual, relationship with a Swedish psychiatrist whom he considered to be a saint (pp. 316–17). It may well be, as Cantor suggests, that Knowles's insight into the monastic temperament owed not a little to his own complicated life.

It is, in much the same way, good to know that Southern was "the most beautiful Englishman" Cantor had ever seen "in the flesh" (p. 343). His portrait of the reserved and complex Southern helps one better appreciate his masterpiece, *The Making of the Middle Ages*. Given Cantor's adulation of Southern, much of it deserved, one does wonder why he attacks him for not creating a center for medieval studies in England (pp. 350–51). The charge seems unfair, especially since he attacks Braudel for doing just that.

There are moments in *Inventing the Middle Ages* that will stay with the reader for a long time: Cantor's eerie portrait of his mentor Joseph Strayer and Strayer's CIA connections (the source of the slur against Braudel, perhaps?); his evocation of the Stefan George circle of the 1920s as it explains Ernst Kantorowicz's *Frederick the Second*; his chivalrous portrait of Eileen Power and similarly generous, if brief, references to other female medievalists. On balance, however, one takes away from *Inventing the Middle Ages* a very different impression: too much of it is general summary about the Middle Ages and the works of the chosen medievalists; too many errors undermine its accuracy; too many innuendoes mar its claim to authority. That is lamentable because it seems unlikely that anyone will rewrite this book in the future and thus correct its errors, misstatements, and omissions.

184

Of these omissions the most troubling is that of Erich Auerbach, who stands as a powerful rebuttal to Cantor's "retromedievalism." As author of the great essay "Figura" and the encyclopedic *Literary Language and Its Public in Late Latin Antiquity and in the Middle Ages*, Auerbach deserves a place beside Curtius and Southern, Panofsky and Huizinga. But it is Auerbach, as he wrote *Mimesis* in Istanbul while a refugee from Nazi Germany, who best demonstrates whatever relevance medieval studies might still have for the current moment. Cantor would have us believe that "the wise university president will invest in medieval studies as the focus of a seminal cultural renaissance and retroheuristic movement of the coming century" (p. 412). I am far from certain that I know what Cantor means by this, but if pressed to argue the worth of medievalism in a world that sees the Holocaust as ancient history, I would begin with Auerbach's great pages in *Mimesis* concerning Augustine's portrait of his friend Alypius, who is corrupted by the violence of the Roman games. When Auerbach writes of this portrait that "the forces of the time are at work: sadism, frenetic bloodlust, and the triumph of magic and sense over reason and ethics," we hear him speaking as well about the horrors of his own time and the need to bear witness against them.[3] From such encounters between past and present we can invent a Middle Ages that are not "retro" and thus can help us do something better with our training than evade our time and place.

NICHOLAS HOWE
Ohio State University

F. R. H. DU BOULAY. *The England of* Piers Plowman: *William Langland and His Vision of the Fourteenth Century.* Cambridge: D. S. Brewer, 1991. Pp. 147. $59.00.

It is with a feeling of dismay rather than censure that, having like so many fellow students read and enjoyed his *Age of Ambition*, I must comment on Du Boulay's *The England of* Piers Plowman. It would at first glance appear to be a historical contextualizing of the poem for undergraduates. The ten-page summary of the poem in the introductory chapter does not seem to

[3] Erich Auerbach, "The Arrest of Peter Valvomeres," in *Mimesis: The Representation of Reality in Western Literature*, trans. Willard R. Trask (Princeton, N.J.: Princeton University Press, 1953), p. 68.

lead in that direction, however, and the following chapter is even more puzzling. After nodding to George Kane's *Autobiographical Fallacy*, the author proceeds to give a full biography of Langland, written, for the most part, out of the poem itself. Though admitting that it is his duty under the circumstances to be tentative about the poet's life, he nevertheless contends that the "form of *Piers Plowman* and the additions to the C-text do not just permit speculation but demand it about this story-teller who dodged in and out of the first person":

> In a curious way the lack of "historical" evidence about Langland is an advantage. We have no option but to approach him through what he wrote. We cannot be side-tracked from the imaginative but real highroad of his life into paths littered with the concrete irrelevancies of mortgages or little fees paid for odd jobs. With all his reticence Langland responds well to this mode of enquiry precisely because he was introspective. [P. 17]

Throughout his analysis Du Boulay assumes that Langland is identical with the narrator and that he wanted his audience to assume the same. Among other things, Du Boulay discovers in the poem that Langland made his living in part by going around to people's homes and reading out pieces (passus) of his poem in return for money (pp. 36–37, 57, 102). He also assumes that Langland was a family man: "For all that, it is hard after reading *Piers Plowman* to think of the poet as a lifelong celibate or even... as a single man.... What gives the sense of Langland as a married man is a kind of friendliness to the idea of happy marriage" (pp. 25–26). He seems to know when the author is bewildered or uncertain and when he is writing out of his own experience (i.e., usually). In short, he repeatedly speculates, draws back from the speculation and partly disowns it, and then assumes the truth of the speculation in what follows.

The task the author seems to have taken upon himself is to clear away all the complications and uncertainties of literary scholars and replace them with a historian's reading of what is clearly (for him) a strongly historical work. Why the sheep in the opening passage? Well, what with Malvern being sheep country and all the wealth wool generated, it makes sense. Just as the author seems to give short shrift to the literary scholars and their work on the poem, so he seems to have limited patience with linguists and philologists. Langland lived before the meaning of the word *truth* "became loaded." *Gentil* generally means "gentle," and *kind*, "kind." The history of ideas plays no part in this work either. He sees in the lines "Thow shalt see in thiselve Truthe sitte in thyn herte / In a cheyne of charite" an image of "a locket dangling heart-shaped on a chain" (p. 104). Two pages farther on, he seems not to know of (at least he certainly does not explain) the twofold purpose of literature ("sentence" and "solas," in Chaucer's terms). His handling of biblical material is imprecise at times, too. He chooses the second of the two great commandments (love of neighbor, the "new" law of Christ, which "superseded the detailed prescriptions of Judaism") and says, "On this hung all the Law and the Prophets" (p. 124). But *both* are Old Testament laws (Deut. 5:6; Lev. 19:18), and "On these two commandments hang all the law and the prophets" (Matt. 22:40).

Chapters 2 through 6 provide historical context for the poem, under the headings "Landscapes and People," "The Religious Scene," "Being True and Doing Well," "Piers," and "The Last Vision." The author provides useful information on pardons and pardoners, on marriage laws and customs (though the anecdote on p. 100 is confusing), on what it meant to be free or unfree, on law and the clergy. The historical background is not always tied closely to the poem, and I found myself wondering at times why some material was included: "The student of literature may not feel a need for such explanations, but Langland cannot help being a historical source, and the historian may understand and enjoy what he wrote the better for a little history without forfeiting the poetry" (p. 39). The "poetry" seems to consist of a literal reading of the poem based on something like common sense ("difficult" or "wordy" material being any material that deals with theological concepts, as on p. 124). Du Boulay's is an "amateur" reading of the poem, not very wrong, not very right, and not very informed. His presentation of Piers himself is the one bright spot in the book; it is brief but clear and, yes, sensible.

What might an undergraduate or general reader take away from a reading of this book? First of all, an old-fashioned "biographical reading" of the poem. The assumptions it contains about the writing and dissemination of poetry are outdated. The alternation in it between "reading" and "background" is erratic and disturbing. The "warm sympathy and informed charity" that one reviewer found in *The Age of Ambition* is not to be found here. The student will learn that Langland was a frustrated malcontent, peeved at not getting his due in life and full of self-pity—a man unfairly prejudiced against the friars ("a smear across his own face") because of his own feelings of guilt, inferiority, and envy of their success.

Finally, students will almost certainly have difficulty with the style in which the book is written. One wonders what they will make of the Good Samaritan "riding barefoot along the street" (p. 13); of "your underlings whom you might quite well see one day at a heavenly top-table" (p. 49); of a checkered cloth described as "striped" (p. 56); of the term "law-keeping" to parallel "belief" (p. 124); of a pardoner referred to as a "fraudster" (p. 86); or of a (not untypical) sentence like "Langland did not live there [Westminster], and he reels off the passers-by as they pop up like snap-shot targets, suitably alliterated: assizers, summoners, sheriffs, [etc.]" (p. 64). The map of London on the endpapers is handy but would have been even more useful if it had included Westminster (discussed on pp. 59–61). Minimally punctuated, the text is marred by illogical shifts of tense, problems of pronoun reference and parallelism, misplaced modifiers, and strings of one-sentence paragraphs.

MARY-JO ARN
Bloomsburg University

HOYT N. DUGGAN and THORLAC TURVILLE-PETRE, eds. *The Wars of Alexander*. EETS, s.s., vol. 10. Oxford: Early English Text Society/ Oxford University Press, 1989. Pp. lviii, 397. $64.00.

In the beginning lines of the Middle English *Wars of Alexander*, the anonymous poet describes the types of obviously oral compositions that fourteenth- or fifteenth-century courtly audiences enjoyed hearing, after (of course) they were "festid & fed." Some of the nobility enjoyed hearing of ancient stories, which contain events and deeds "or þai ware fourmed on fold or þaire fadirs oþir." Others enjoyed hearing saints' lives, still others "lufe lay[e]s" or exemplary tales of "curtaissy, of knyȝthede, of craftis of armys." And some enjoyed the fabliaux, tales of "wanton werkis, þa þat ere wildhedid." The poet then moves to the subject of his present work: the wondrous birth and deeds of "athill Alexsandire." The poet will "rehers" these deeds in a 5,803-line poem (divided into passus, or "fitts"), provided that his listeners hold their tongues. The poet concludes this little prologue by indicating that his performance will be so divided that every listener may rest at various intervals which correspond to passus divisions in the poetic text. In fact, at the end of passus 14 the poet indicates arriving at a stop to allow himself to "tary for a time" and "tempire" his "wittes."

As many Middle English scholars know, this late-medieval description of a courtly audience may be only a conventional fiction. Whether or not actually designed for oral performance, *The Wars of Alexander* is, in narrative structure, one of the more bookishly derivative of the Middle English alliterative romances, its author a cleric, its narrative closely adapted from the third interpolated recension of the Latin *Historia de preliis Alexandri Magni*, its lines sprinkled with such narrative attributions as "þe buke tellis." In this new edition of the *Wars*, Duggan and Turville-Petre emphasize the bookish, clerical origins of the poem. By annotating citations of pertinent source passages from the *Historia* (some of which the *Wars* poet translated almost verbatim into Middle English), they have produced an edition superior to the earlier editions of Stevenson (1849) and Skeat (1886). Still other editorial achievements ensure that this edition is the authoritative, edited text of the poem.

The edition contains the standard editorial apparatuses, including facsimile plates of a folio page each from the two fifteenth-century manuscripts of the *Wars*: the Bodleian Library, Oxford, manuscript Ashmole 44 (= A) and the Trinity College, Dublin, manuscript 213 (= D). Of primary interest to the Middle English textual scholar is the introduction, which can serve as a model of editorial explanation for any budding textual editor. It is divided under six headings: "Manuscripts and Editions," "The Sources," "Metrical Criteria for Establishing the Text," "Language," "Authorship and Date," and "Treatment of the Text." Throughout these sections the editors repeatedly defend the various choices or interpretations that any editor must make in the preparation of a text.

One of these choices concerns the use of alliterative technique to determine authorial intention and consequent emendation. The editors, widely known as experts on the Middle English alliterative long line, demonstrate this expertise by deducing principles concerning alliterating sounds, alliterative patterns, syllable stress, the stress patterns of both *a* verses and *b* verses, and larger organizing units (whether or not based on consecutive alliteration) within the poem. On the basis of such principles the editors follow a moderate practice of emendation *metri causa*, utilizing such principles in particular when readings from A or from D or from both manuscripts are in dispute. Many of these emendations are justifiable, for example, line 1960, emended to regularize alliterative pattern. Other emendations involve the addition of letters and syllables to regularize what the editors consider defectively patterned *b* verses. Other emendations may not be as justifiable. It is to the editors' credit that I could not find any instances that are totally unjustified. Still, some scholars would be uneasy over even the cautious assumptions that authorial intention and scribal practice can be distinguished on the basis of alliterative technique or that alliterative technique must be primarily the poet's while any departure from such technique must be due to scribal corruption. At any rate, metrical cruces and the editorial decisions concerning them are explained in the annotations. The editors' methodology at least provides a logical system of clarifying not only problems of prosody but also those of dialect.

More defensible is the assertion that the authorial text or the archetype was a West Midlands text. Accordingly, the editors view both A and D as "linguistically composite texts" containing "two regionally distinct strata" of scribal dialect.[1] The A scribe consistently translated his exemplar into a Northern dialect yet retained a few West Midland relict spellings. The D scribe translated less consistently, producing more *mischesprachen* composed of Northern and West Midland dialect items. As evidence the editors cite such instances as the alliteration of the reflexes of OE *hw* and OE, ON, and OF *cw* (alliterating together as /xw/) to indicate a Northern provenance for the manuscripts. Other dialect usages indicate a more Southerly provenance, while the possible alliteration of such words as *answer* with words beginning with *o* may indicate the West Midlands usage of rounding the reflex of OE /a:/ before nasals. From this confluence of variant scribal dialect usages the editors theorize that the author may have lived in "an area within Lancashire, perhaps as far north as the Ribble Valley where the Midland and Northern isoglosses meet" (p. xlii). Such an identification can be only tentative; the editors caution that they do not "know how many distinct copyings separate either A or D from the poet's original" and that "the thoroughness of A's dialect translations shows how easily the distinctive features of the original dialect might well have been erased in a short series of copyings" (p. xxxi).

Equally defensible (but, alas, more unfortunate) was the editors' decision to record spelling variants that affect meter or lexical meaning but not "purely orthographic variants" or such "dialectal variants" as *agayne/ ayayns*, *at/þat*, *fra/from*, and so on (p. xlv). The edition occupied ten years of the editors' lives; recording every single variant could have possibly added an extra five years to the work and another 500 pages to the edition. However, the absence of such records will hinder the scholar who wishes to conduct a dialect investigation independent of the conclusions either reached by the editors or summarized in "Linguistic Profiles" from *A Linguistic Atlas of Late Medieval English* for either A or D. The dialect

---

[1] Margaret Laing, "Dialectal Analysis and Linguistically Composite Texts in Middle English," *Speculum* 63 (1988): 83–84.

investigation that the *Wars* editors conducted utilized the *Atlas*'s dot maps for analyses of select phonological and morphological items. A third investigating party might wish to compare other orthographic occurrences in A or D with the forms plotted on the dot maps or on the item maps of the *Atlas*, or listed in the *Atlas*'s "County Dictionary." Such an investigation must now be performed only by consulting the original manuscripts or electronically produced copies.

The more literary-minded scholar might fault the edition for its lack of critical analysis, which could have been written much like the introductory materials of the various York Medieval Texts. Duggan and Turville-Petre do some analysis of this kind in a discussion concerning the similar descriptions of the Sun God in the *Wars*, lines 5049–50 and 5057–58, and the Green Knight/Bercilak in *Sir Gawain*, lines 143–44, 303–304, 308, and 847. This discussion only supports editorial comments on common authorship of the two poems or on shared alliterative styles. Critical analysis is not part of the aim of this edition. The editors have fulfilled their stated aim — the establishment of text, textual and linguistic backgrounds, and sources for a little-edited Middle English alliterative romance. It is now up to literary theorists to assign *The Wars of Alexander* its place within the list of canonical medieval English literary works.

JAMES R. SPROUSE
North Georgia College

RICHARD EMMERSON, ed. *Approaches to Teaching Medieval Drama*. New York: Modern Language Association of America, 1990. Pp. xi, 182. $17.50 paper.

This volume is a welcome addition to the field of early drama studies. To some extent its appearance in this important MLA series marks the final acceptance of early drama into the teaching canon of American universities. The editor, Richard Emmerson, has done an admirable job bringing together a fine group of contributors varying from the acknowledged leaders in the field to lesser-known scholars and teachers who are bringing the material alive for their students.

The format, dictated by the format of the series, works well. Emmerson himself has undertaken the first section, "Materials." Basing his comments both on the results of a survey of teachers of early drama and on his own common sense, he has produced a forthright, useful essay that does not avoid the problems inherent in teaching the material—particularly those surrounding the availability of texts. Emmerson points out the strengths and weaknesses of the available anthologies and also describes the situation with the editions of the full cycles. Three additions can now be made to Emmerson's information. Since this volume appeared, a new teaching anthology, edited by John Coldewey, has been published, as has Stephen Spector's long-awaited new edition of the N-Town Cycle from the Early English Text Society and a teaching version of the full Chester Cycle edited by David Mills.

The other subsections in this first part of the book tackle such issues as "Recommended Readings for Students," "The Instructor's Library," and "Aids to Teaching." I was struck by the thoroughness of his survey. I have only two books to add, again books that have been published since this one appeared. These are Gail McMurray Gibson's *Theater of Devotion* and the *The Theatre of Medieval Europe*, edited by Eckehard Simon in the Cambridge Studies in Medieval Literature series. Gibson's book is a rich example of the kind of contextual work that can help a teacher bring the material alive for students, and the Simon collection, besides five essays on English drama, has extensive new information on research being done on French, German, Italian, Hispanic, and Dutch drama.

The second major section of the book is divided into two parts. The first part is devoted to essays that "provide extensive scholarly introductions to ways of presenting these plays from certain theoretical perspectives," and the second part to essays that "are more focused and describe specific strategies that their authors have successfully used in the classroom" (p. 33). There are six articles in the first section. The first one, by Martin Stevens, though somewhat uneven in tone, clearly sets the study of early drama in its new context, emphasizing the changes in our understanding of such essential underpinnings of our field as the nature and dating of the manuscripts and the nature of the canon itself.

Stevens's essay is followed by a contribution by Clifford Flanigan, who discusses the need to understand the religious and cultural phenomena—such as the liturgy—in which the Latin drama of the church was embedded. It is Flanigan who first emphasizes that this material is "alien to modern culture."

Despite the efforts of Kathleen Ashley, in the next dense and satisfying essay on the context of vernacular drama, to dispel the sense of the alien, it returns with Peter Travis's opening statement in "The Semiotics of Christ's

Body": "Medieval plays are not easy to teach" (p. 67). Travis's contribution is, for me, the least satisfying of the series. It ends with the lament that graduate students are not choosing to enter the field of early drama because they have dismissed it "as being unworthy of sustained theoretical attention" (p.78). It is perhaps not the drama but the nature of the theory being applied that is at fault.

Teresa Coletti's article on feminist approaches follows and makes the ground for such an application perhaps more stony than is necessary by not giving sufficient attention to the mature Mary of the Passion sequences and the plays devoted to her death and Assumption. This section ends with Pamela Sheingorn's very fine essay of the "typological" method that is a model for this kind of essay—learned yet extremely helpful to a non–art historian in preparing materials to supplement the reading of the texts with the reading of the visual art.

The Sheingorn essay provides a good bridge to the next section of the book, which contains five contributions on methods of teaching early drama within the context of a literature course and four within the context of a theater course. These essays are widely divergent in their approaches and provide helpful hints and pointers for the teaching of the material in different contexts. Some address the problem of having two weeks to introduce the subject within a larger survey course. Others outline successful in-depth studies over a ten-week semester or a sustained period of preparation for a class performance. I was struck by how the sense of the alterity of the material is reflected in these essays as well as in the longer ones. I was equally struck, however, by the number of well-thought-out methods of facing this sense of otherness and finding ways to bring modern American undergraduates to an understanding of early drama.

The entire collection is framed by an introduction by V. A. Kolve and an "Envoi" by David Bevington. These two essays with the essay by Martin Stevens should be read by all teachers of English literature of the late-medieval and early-modern period. These three acknowledged leaders in the field provide an overview of the fundamental changes that have taken place in our understanding of this material since many of us who are still teaching were undergraduates. I know of no other field where the ground has shifted more fundamentally. Yet only as books like this one appear will people outside the field itself begin to understand what has happened. Too many colleagues still choose to teach *Everyman* and the *Second Shepherd's Play* in medieval survey courses because those are the plays that they were taught without realizing how unrepresentative they are of their genres. Too many colleagues still believe in and teach the idea of the evolution of drama from its primitive form in the church and in the marketplace to the glory that was Shakespeare. Richard Emmerson and his contributors are to be congratulated not only for their practical advice but for the way in which they have conveyed how the changes in our understanding have come about.

ALEXANDRA F. JOHNSTON
Victoria College, University of Toronto

JOHN H. FISHER. *The Importance of Chaucer.* Carbondale and Edwardsville: Southern Illinois University Press, 1992. Pp. xi, 198. $22.50.

John Fisher's presence in Chaucer studies has been a distinguished one, as editor of a fine text of *The Complete Poetry and Prose of Geoffrey Chaucer*, as a founding father of the New Chaucer Society (and hence of *Studies in the Age of Chaucer*), and for many years as Executive Secretary of the Modern Language Association. His first published book, however, was on John Gower's place in fourteenth-century English literature as *Moral Philosopher and Friend of Chaucer*. In this new book Fisher returns to many of the concerns of that early study, this time focusing on Geoffrey Chaucer himself, although his friends certainly are given their due as part of the social milieu in which Chaucer moved and which in specific ways produced his literary *importance*.

Fisher's audience is the same in this book as in the commentary of his Chaucer edition: American undergraduates and beginning graduate students and their instructors. He has not produced a new reading of Chaucer, nor has he engaged the theoretical debates current in sessions both at the MLA and the NCS, though he is not hostile to either set of projects. His concern is to show to undergraduates why Chaucer is "important" by way of describing how and by whom he came to be regarded as "important." And Fisher is too much a student of critical fashions himself (perhaps after all those years spent guiding professional organizations) not to be keenly aware of how fashions are shaped and changed over time. This concern is emphasized in several chapters in this book and is, to my mind, its best feature. No undergraduate could come away from this study without a lively (if summary) sense of how Chaucer's position and the role he has played in English literature has changed over 600 years, and how an "Important Poet" is the creation as much of social forces and even political agendas as of talent (let alone genius).

Not that Fisher belittles Chaucer's poetic gifts. But in this book they are taken as givens, and relatively little effort is made to reevaluate them from the standard Companion to English Literature judgments: "The Chaucerian voice has since the inception of literature in Modern English provided a touchstone for urbane, sophisticated expression" (p. 105). Later:

The ironic voice, the humanistic world view, awareness of the individual, awareness of the audience, awareness of a world outside the court and church, a sense of the power of the English language to express "the best that has been thought and said" — these are the qualities that account for the importance of Chaucer. [P. 139]

Chaucer's aesthetic values, in this accounting, are "natural," "spontaneous," "serious" (opposed to "contrived"), "limpid," "ironic," "psychological," "colloquial." Little in this literary character of Chaucer has changed, as Fisher says, since Dryden: here is Chaucer the democrat, chronicler of God's plenty; Chaucer the optimistic skeptic (or skeptical optimist, depending on your emphasis); Chaucer the secularizer; and, above all, Chaucer the *English* poet.

Fisher begins with an elegant description of the state of English in the fourteenth century as "the disdained patois of an occupied island" (p. 1), destined for greatness, a process that began when "Chaucer and his contemporaries began the transmutation of the profundity and eloquence of Latin into English" (p. 5). It is the credit of this book to situate Chaucer's importance firmly in the fortunes of the English *language*, an emphasis that Chaucer studies used to have but that has been so long out of fashion as to seem fresh, and indeed to *be* fresh to many American undergraduates. Fisher emphasizes the role of patronage and state craft in the "Englishing" of England and the consequent establishing of Chaucer.

In the second chapter Fisher develops some current themes of Chaucerian biography. He evidently dislikes the emphasis on Chaucer as a courtier and so balances such accounts by contending that Chaucer was educated in the Inns of Court, in preparation for his bureaucratic career. Experience in the Inns (with their "rowdy fraternity life") and in the City, plus his own mercantile background and the years he spent in the "locker room world" of "soldiers and campgrounds" (p. 43), gave Chaucer "range" and "breadth" (p. 37) and "concern with the psychology of behavior"

(p. 43). The Englishing of courtly literature may be the "least important" part of Chaucer's importance: "His introduction of satire and realism and his experiments with philosophical and scientific prose [about which Fisher says disappointingly little, given this buildup] . . . demonstrated the capacity of the [English] language" (p. 37).

These first two chapters should be of considerable interest to students. Though the material in them is well known, Fisher writes clearly and cogently. The axes he wants to grind are so candidly delineated that I think most students will find his style of argument refreshingly — well, "limpid." Fisher argues that the formulary book, used in chancery education to teach stylistic variety, was at least subliminally important to Chaucer's poetic achievement: "The *Canterbury Tales* can be regarded simply as a dramatized formulary" (p. 65). Not many instructors (or students) will want to leave their judgment of Chaucer at that (nor does Fisher), but this kind of remark has an argumentative virtue that might stir a torpid student.

Fisher's chief axe is articulated in his last chapter, "Chaucer Since 1400." This is his argument, developed in a number of earlier publications, that

in the period from 1399 to 1417, the royal establishment appears to have undertaken a program to elevate the prestige of English. This took the form of encouraging the production of a body of sophisticated writing in the national language. . . . The public relations agent for the program appears to have been the poet John Lydgate and the writer chosen to exemplify the new culture, Geoffrey Chaucer. [P. 144]

The problem I have with the pride of place Fisher gives this idea is that, as he states it here, it tends to put Chaucer in the position of a poetaster, without major cultural ambitions for his own making, plucked from obscurity mostly because of the fortunate marriage of a bastard son. This characterization begins to take on the trappings of yet another "modernizing" of Chaucer, giving him the compromised biography now required of a cultural "hero." But it does not quite square, to my mind, with the poet who placed his English epic on the steps with Virgil, Ovid, Homer, Lucan, and Statius. It would seem to me that, whatever the reasons for Chaucer's failure to commission presentation copies of his poems (unlike Gower), lack of poetic ambition was not among them.

In his last pages Fisher summarizes the changing character of Chaucer over the centuries, from the courtly "cynosure" of Spenser and the Tudors, to the Restoration genius of human manners, to the Victorian protonovelist of the human heart, to the contemporary "Chaucer the social critic." This material should be particularly valuable to casual or novice students still caught in banal notions of "relevance" and "timelessness." Its presentation alone is worth the price of the book; it will certainly find its way to my undergraduate reserve list and into my course.

MARY CARRUTHERS
New York University

ROBERT FOSSIER, ed. *The Cambridge Illustrated History of the Middle Ages*. Vol. 1, *350-950*. Trans. Janet Sondheimer. Cambridge: Cambridge University Press, 1989. Pp. xxiii, 556. $49.50.

Perhaps the best way to approach this large and comprehensive volume is simply to explain to the hypothetical readers — the students or scholars of the "Age of Chaucer" — what they are getting. This volume surveys in eleven chapters of roughly the same length the early Middle Ages, beginning with the end of the fourth century and ending with the middle of the tenth. Less obvious but more telling than this chronological sweep, there is what might be called a geographic sweep. The work begins in the Latin West, then after two chapters moves to the Byzantine East, then to the Arab East, then back to Byzantium, finally ending in the West again with the Carolingian renewal and its aftermath. The virtue of this cyclical organization is that greater coverage is given to Byzantium and to Islam than is usually the case in one-volume histories, and that is surely to the good.

Other aspects of the work are less easy to summarize. Although the sweep of chronology and geography suggests an overarching sense of unity to the work, it is in fact somewhat less unified than might appear at first glance. For one thing, each of the three areas is written by a different author (or, in the chapters on Islam, coauthors). If one adds the introduction, written by the editor, there are five authors. It is as accurate to describe the work as a series of separate essays as to describe it as a continuous narrative. Sometimes, as, for example, in the switch from Islam back to Byzantium in chapter 7, more of a transition is clearly needed. The chapter begins as though none of the previous discussion of Islam had taken place, as though its author were not even aware of the intervening chapters. Even more than such an obvious kind of disjunction, the separate authorship inevitably points to larger questions about unity that go to the heart of the work: not a unified narrative on the one hand, but clearly something other than a reference work on the other; not a coffee table book, despite its lavish illustrations — many of them full-page color plates — but not a textbook either, at least in my reading. Is it a book that one might profitably read from beginning to end, or is it a book that one would go to to find out about a specific movement, battle, figure, or event? I find no easy or even satisfactory answer to this question.

That is not to say that there is not an enormous amount of important information packed into the volume. As someone whose scholarly roots are almost entirely in the West, I found the material on Islam the most interesting part of the volume, but there were many suggestive interpretive forays throughout the volume, especially with respect to the end of the Empire in the West, in what is usually called the transition from ancient to medieval. And if the work tends to emphasize social, economic, and military history, there is also an attempt to include intellectual, religious, and artistic history as well. Even when all due praise is given to the enterprise, however, it seems to me to be a work in search of an identity. The fact that the title includes the word "Illustrated" is yet another signal of this identity crisis: the full-color plates are almost entirely 'decorative; that is, they are not integrated into the text in any serious way. The black-and-white illustrations are more integral, containing as they do some descriptive material in the legends and placed so that they can be used as a gloss to the text (although the maps could also have been more closely correlated to the text). Which is once again to raise the question, Whom is this work for?

One way in which such a question is often answered is through the prefatory matter. In this volume there is none, an absence that is especially puzzling. Such explanatory material as a preface usually contains would seem to be more than a luxury in a work with multiple authors, and a work that is also a translation from a French original. Literally nothing is said about the French version. When was it published? Was it also illustrated? Whom was *it* designed for? For the scholar of the age of Chaucer who wishes to have a handy reference tool on the early Middle Ages, this is a volume of real but circumscribed usefulness. There is a lot here. It is not always easy to get hold of.

RONALD B. HERZMAN
SUNY Geneseo

LOUISE OLGA FRADENBURG. *City, Marriage, Tournament: Arts of Rule in Late Medieval Scotland.* Madison and London: University of Wisconsin Press, 1991. Pp. xv, 390. $49.75 cloth; $19.95 paper.

After a chapter or two, impatient readers might be provoked to question the premises of this book. If one is interested in arts of rule, why write about Scotland? If one is interested in Scottish literature, why concentrate whole chapters on such out-of-the-way texts as the Latin poems ascribed to one James Foullis, or the 1482 charters to Edinburgh of James III? Why look to the wedding (in 1503) of Margaret Tudor and James IV to demonstrate the "transformation of inequality into equality" in a royal wedding (p. xiv)? As it stands, there would appear to be operating throughout the book the expectation that the reader will, unpersuaded, accept the same value and emphasis the author has initially placed on the subject, as well as the assumption that this rather out-of-the-way material will serve as peculiarly, self-evidently rich ground for the unfolding of modern theories of power and identity. Because it does not come to terms in a full introduction with either the perceived marginality of its subject or (more important) with those particular qualities that differentiate Scottish literature and history from, say, English literature and history, this book may seem more disjointed and less innovative than it actually is.

Large ideas are sought in out-of-the-way places here. That is not a bad thing in itself, but there are dangers. Not least among these is that the reader probably lacks familiarity with the material and, without clear signposts and explanations, may simply get lost. The landmarks referred to may seem arbitrarily chosen and not adequately reveal all the corners and turns along the way. The reader is likely to experience disorientation, most obviously during Fradenburg's discussion of theories about the late-medieval development of Edinburgh as a capital (pp. 31–34): this section cries out for a map. For the book as a whole, the other much-needed missing map would be a full, clear introduction that sets forth the context of its author's leading ideas and the relations among them.

Granted, there is some brief introductory justification of the emphasis of the book: "Late medieval Scotland is of particular interest to a study of the arts of rule both because of its comparative 'decentralization' and because of the comparative flexibility which that decentralization gave to monarchical imaginings" (p. xv). These brief references to complex issues are left undeveloped, however. The reader (especially the nonspecialist) must allow the author much from the outset, notably that the three topics named in the title (lacking obvious integration, especially in the case of the first section, "City") will turn out to be connected in interesting and revelatory ways. Perhaps such things ought not to be assumed, but, after all, neither as history nor as literature is this material considered by many scholars and readers (outside Scotland, at any rate) as a Subject, possessing broad interest or central importance.

There are advantages to Fradenburg's approach. The author takes risks and challenges the reader. She writes to demonstrate the real strengths and richness of this material, but she does so without special pleading or resorting expediently to a pantheon of great national events and works. Leading ideas are presented and then subside, to be alluded to chapters later. Still, this approach has its problems. At first look the sequence of chapters seems arbitrary, notably in the first section, in which the reader is expected to leap rapidly from the early history of Edinburgh to two poems by William Dunbar, to the Trinity Altarpiece (Edinburgh, attributed to Hugo van der Goes), to the uneasy relations between James III and his capital, to the remaking of the identity of the city in the early sixteenth century, as revealed in contemporary Latin poems.

Given the perception that introductory and connective exposition is lacking, criticism of the larger contexts that the author does provide for her analyses may hardly seem fair. Nevertheless, the book may be seen thus to move from potentially bewildering lack of articulation to distracting over-articulation. Does recent discussion of Edinburgh as a royal creation provide a notable and especially telling example of "the discourse of origins exemplified by Henri Pirenne's work" (p. 3)? Is Fradenburg's interesting and valuable relation between inner and outer in capital and court usefully signaled by reference to Augustine's depiction of memory as both *sinus* and *aula* (pp. 9–11, 44, 187)? Must one go to Lacan to discover that physical self-awareness "is constructed by the way in which one is seen" (p. 205)? Does the movement from the Song of Songs to Jonson's *Masque of Blacknesse* help to illuminate the relation between sovereign and blackness at the court of James IV (pp. 70–72)? Is a brief chapter (drawing on Julia Kristeva) on the Annunciation of the Virgin as a paradigm of marriage (pp. 84–90) a necessary stage toward interpreting the wedding of Margaret Tudor and James IV? Is it helpful or bewildering to learn that the "god armypotent" in Gavin Douglas's *Palice of Honour* "risks the 'formal stagnation' of image that Mulvey associates with the 'to-be-looked-at-ness' of the woman in film" (p. 190)? Fradenburg tends to rely on recurrent allusions and comparisons such as these to flesh out the leading ideas of her book. For lack of clear and full explanation, the reader may assume that such references are in fact attempts to bestow larger relevance upon otherwise marginal findings. That would be a shame, given the great value of much that is found.

The author reaches into twentieth-century discourse on culture, politics, and the individual, sometimes with great insight. Still, the reader may take this reaching outwards as a sign of lack of confidence in the late-medieval Scottish material: one Latin poem under discussion, for instance, is "an attempt to give voice to the tortured body of whose isolation, exposure, and voicelessness Elaine Scarry so movingly writes" (p. 49). At such moments the less patient reader may wonder which text is in fact under discussion.

Opportunities to broaden discussion of Scottish writings are not, mystifyingly, always taken. Both in her discussion of plague in Edinburgh and again in her perceptive account of the part played by the black lady in the 1508 Tournament of the Wild Knight and the Black Lady, Fradenburg could well have moved with great effect to discussion of Henryson's *Testament of Cresseid*. The opportunities are passed over: nowhere in the book is Henryson even mentioned; attention to Gavin Douglas's translation of Virgil's *Aeneid* is limited to a brilliant discussion (pp. 91–93) of "imagining and making the future" in the pendant thirteenth book (from the Latin of Maphaeus Vegius). There would thus seem to be a reluctance to broaden the area of discussion to consider relevant and fruitful areas of late-medieval Scottish writing. Fradenburg severely limits her extremely perceptive and controversial discussion of Dunbar to a very few poems (notably "Ane Blak Moir," "The Thrissill and the Rois," "The Dregy of Dunbar," and "To the Merchandis of Edinburgh"), so that her concluding survey of this poet's achievement (pp. 148–49) seems breathlessly hasty, and her insight into his thematic and stylistic preoccupations ("Variance is the heart of Dunbar's attempt to bear, with honor, his need of a world to which he was not essential" [p. 149]) merely romantic. As a consequence of this restraint, the writings of late-medieval Scotland may seem, frustratingly, thin and impoverished.

Still, it is manifestly not the author's intention to write a history of late-medieval Scottish literature. This book is instead a compressed, highly suggestive study of the devising and presentation of identity and purpose by three kings of Scotland, James III, IV, and V. One need not always be persuaded by assertions (for instance, that the Tournament of the Wild Knight and the Black Lady celebrates James IV's campaign in the Gaelic West of Scotland [pp. 97, 156, 170, 239]) to find particular strengths to the approach. There is trenchant discussion, for instance, of the historical legends out of which the character of James IV has been memorialized (pp.

69–70, 153–64). The pages on Gavin Douglas's *Palice of Honour* offer what is most characteristically stimulating and challenging about this book: here Fradenburg writes about the narrator's presumptuous "desire to see" (p. 186) and the crises that arise from it; although one need not agree that the final part of the poem shows the narrator achieving "heroic shape and language," Fradenburg's emphasis on the "fear of the evanescence of worldly honor" (p. 190) opens up avenues between Douglas's dream poem and earlier works, notably Henryson's *Fables* and *Testament of Cresseid* and Lydgate's *Fall of Princes*. And although Fradenburg's analysis of the pageants for the entry of Margaret Tudor into Edinburgh (1503) might have been more securely related to her earlier speculations on pageantry and policy in the Edinburgh of the late 1520s (pp. 56–64), here the author is especially attentive to the nuances and affiliations of a complex occasional text, the *Fyancells of Margaret*.

What is perhaps most challenging in this regard is Fradenburg's attention to the liminal figure of the queen and her counterparts in Scottish pageantry (pp. 75–80, 244–64). Whether or not one accepts her argument that the Black Lady of James IV's tournament "serves also as a displaced, feminized version of the king" (p. 263), what she has to say about femaleness, foreignness, and masquerade must be taken into account in future study of royal identity. Fradenburg's approach may turn out to be especially productive in relation to later Scottish queens, notably Marie de Guise and Mary Stewart.

A leitmotif of *City, Marriage, Tournament* is the recurrent emphasis in late-medieval Scottish literature and history on the opposition between inward and outward movement, entry and expulsion. Fradenburg's references to this relation (e.g., pp. 14–15, 60–61, 73–74, 187) are at the core of this book's substantial contribution to late-medieval Scottish studies. Particularly revealing and valuable are the author's comments about the gendering of space by this opposition. Fradenburg has much to offer here, but one must be alert and willing to do without straightforward exposition.

From the perspective of this stimulating, thoughtful, often difficult book, poetry is consistently a secondary manifestation of the "arts of rule." As a consequence, matters that deserve and require detailed attention seem far too often to be referred to in passing. Still, Fradenburg's emphasis on the occasion will enable, indeed provoke, the writing of literary history in an area rich in opportunity.

DAVID PARKINSON
University of Saskatchewan

FAYE MARIE GETZ, ed. *Healing and Society in Medieval England: A Middle English Translation of the Pharmaceutical Writings of Gilbertus Anglicus*. Wisconsin Publications in the History of Science and Medicine, vol. 8. Madison: University of Wisconsin Press, 1991. Pp. lxxiii, 378. $37.50.

Faye Marie Getz identified the Middle English text at folios 48–310v in Wellcome manuscript 537 as translated from Gilbertus Anglicus's thirteenth-century *Compendium medicine*. Her edition provides an introduction, the Middle English text with manuscript notes and a commentary, "a rough guide" to the folio numbers of source passages in the 1510 printing of Gilbertus's Latin *Compendium*, a glossary of Middle English, a list of plants by genus, and a bibliography.

To acquire some sense of what sort of book the Middle English translation might be, we must look to the manuscript in which it occurs. Section 6 of Getz's introduction describes Wellcome 537 as a codex comprising a collection of six booklets, written on paper and bound together. If we set aside for the moment the question of intended utility raised by the presence of the gold-leaf initials in the Middle English translation, the implied reader or user of Wellcome 537 appears to have been a practicing *medicus*, knowledgeable about making sizable quantities of the medicines he prescribed and capable of consulting a book containing both Latin and English texts. The editor's descriptive enumeration of the contents shows that Latin items alternate with Middle English in the book. The first seven items (fols. 6–10v, line 12), mostly calendrical or astrological, appear in Latin, followed by two folios of short English recipes (fols. 10v–12v, line 16) after which follow Latin astrological texts (fols. 12v–14v) to complete one booklet of the manuscript. Another booklet (fols. 15–46v), entirely in English, consists primarily of materials translated from four uroscopies, followed by recipes. The largest booklet (fols. 48–310v, pt. 4 of the manuscript) contains the Middle English Gilbertus translation of diagnoses and treatments of ailments from headache to hemorrhoids, followed by a medicine for the stone in English. The next booklet (fols. 311–22v) includes mathematics for calculating dates of the moon and the first Sunday in a year and short Latin items on the course of the moon in the signs of the zodiac, information useful, as our editor points out, for astrological medicine. The last booklet (fols. 323–36), which has "cover" pages of its own, contains the changes of the moon and lunar tables in English. Given these contents, we can conclude that, *if* Wellcome 537 was used by a practitioner, he was one whose praxis encompassed astrological prognostications and calculations, humoral and uroscopic diagnostics, and the therapeutics of mostly herbal recipes. Dietary and behavioral regimens, phlebotomy, and surgery also regularly play roles in the Middle English Gilbertus text.

Comparing this book to recipe collections, whether late antique like Marcellus's or medieval like the *Liber de diversis medicinis* in the Thornton manuscript, we are immediately struck by how much more there is to this Middle English text than just herbal or animal recipes. For here we find many of Gilbertus's descriptions of symptoms, Middle English "tokens," accompanied by his complex humoral etiologies, as well as a range of treatments that extend well beyond medieval pharmacopoeia. Each chapter opens with a definition of the organ discussed ("A man-is tonge haþ two seruicis. Oon is to taast with a mannes metis and drinkis; anoþir is to speke"). The "greuancis" (Latin *dolores*) from which the organ suffers are enumerated in the order they are taken up by each chapter's subdivisions. The various humoral causes call for various remedies. When first remedies fail, other treatments are available.

At the level of the individual recipe we observe differences between the Gilbertian recipes for earache and the early-fifth-century recipes, which Getz brings forth for comparison. The recipes for earache in Marcellus can be translated as follows:

Bruise the tenderest leaves of the ash and squeeze out their juice and pour it warmed into the painful ears. Put a young ash branch, that is already flowing with its own sap, partly in the fire-place. When the juice flows along the other part, catch it carefully and drip it, with oil added, lukewarm, into the ears. The seed of cardus silvaticus [a thistle] cook in oil so slowly that it does not burn up. Afterwards tend that through a linen cloth and pour it warmed into the painful ear and then stop it up with dark wool.

The Gilbertus *Compendium* recipe, in contrast, designates quantities rather precisely: a full eggshell of the ash distillation with two spoons of butter or oil, one spoonful of juice of *barbarum porrorum* (leek), two of the juice of *sempervive* (ME synegrene, "houseleek"), one of clear honey, and one of the milk of a woman nursing a male child. The ingredients are enhanced by the leeks and woman's milk. Marcellus's thistle-seed recipe has no correspondent; instead we find *sagimen anguille* (eel fat) mixed with leek juice. The ash sap recipe has become, in the medieval manuscripts, a compound. The milk of the woman nursing a male child, the leeks, and the eel fat do not derive from the early-fifth-century *medicus*; Marcellus's recipes here remain stubbornly herbal and simple. On the basis of these recipe texts alone we have little reason to assume that Marcellus's text served as a source for Gilbertus. Warm ash sap may have become a traditional remedy for earache; the means of extracting it, well known. The "commonality of shared material" that Getz claims the earache and "red snail" recipes demonstrate might arise either from wide copying of late-medieval medical manuscripts or from wide circulation of traditional cures.

Of the Middle English translation Getz correctly predicts that "new MSS of the Middle English Gilbertus are sure to be identified as the nature and scope of Middle English medical literature are increasingly realized" (p. lxv). She lists fifteen manuscripts; however, Wellcome 537 now represents one of eighteen Middle English Gilbertus texts located by Voigts and Kurtz's "Catalogue of Incipits of Scientific and Medical Writings in Old and Middle English," which is about 91 percent completed.

An attempt was made to verify the transcription of folio 275v, the book's clearly reproduced facsimile page. The first eleven lines of folio 275v appear in the edition on pages 214 and 215, following folio 275. These lines end the chapter on "falling oute of a man-is ers." The last eleven lines of folio 275v, the beginning of the manuscript's chapter on "reynes," were found following folio 221 on page 244 of the edition. The order of the chapters in the edition incorporates the rearrangement directed by a scribal note in the margin of folio 221. Notification of this reordering of the manuscript material occurs in the editor's footnote to line 12 on page 153, the occasion of the first chapter shift, and on page xiii of the preface. A more conspicuously placed list of reordered folios would prevent difficulties for the reader looking for references using the folio numbers in the footnotes to the introduction and in the glossary.

The transcription of folio 275v proved accurate, barring a quibble about the expansion of what appears to be *chapitr* plus curl, transcribed "chapitir," a spelling not exemplified in the glossary. There we find the spellings *chaptir* and *chapt(i)re*, but not the spelling *chaptre* (Getz's readings on fols. 138v and 146v). A note on how the editor derived *him* after *a-forsen* would be useful. No notice of the boxed title "the reynes" at the top of the folio appears in the manuscript notes or in the commentary.

Faye Getz's edition places in our hands a medical book that looks two ways: toward the massive Latin compilation of Gilbertus, whose rhetoric of medicine comes through surprisingly unfiltered, and toward the "practises" of medicine mediated in English during the fifteenth century for, perhaps, a community of men. This is a valuable and welcome book.

LEA OLSAN
Northeast Louisiana University

KATHARINE S. GITTES. *Framing* The Canterbury Tales: *Chaucer and the Medieval Frame Narrative Tradition.* Contributions to the Study of World Literature, no. 41. New York, Westport, Conn., and London: Greenwood, 1991. Pp. ix, 170. $39.95.

Styled throughout as a useful digest rather than a comprehensive discussion of those frame narrative traditions that themselves circumscribe Chaucer's last great work, Katharine Gittes's compact book introduces some new titles and topics into the ongoing critical conversation concerning sources, analogues, and questions of textual influence on *The Canterbury Tales*. These welcome additions include an early chapter devoted to the *Panchatantra*, an eighth-century prosemetric compilation with certain portions arguably originating in India and other parts coming from the Middle East, all of it intricately contained in a series of "framed" or "boxed" narrative structures of nearly infinite recession. There is also a final chapter that considers Christine de Pizan's *Book of the City of Ladies* as a kind of postscriptum to the medieval textual tradition of framed stories that should enter any informed discussion of Chaucer's narrative praxis in *The Canterbury Tales*.

In between these early and late exemplars, and following upon a brief introduction that lays out the terms of her discussion to follow, Gittes considers Petrus Alfonsi's twelfth-century *Disciplina clericalis*, Boccaccio's fourteenth-century *Ameto* and *Decameron*, Gower's *Confessio Amantis*, Don Juan Manuel's *El Conde Lucanor*, and Sercambi's *Novelle*. She also touches briefly on *The Book of Sinbad* and *The Thousand Nights and a Night* to fortify her central idea that Chaucer, in *The Canterbury Tales*, has ingeniously blended two frame narrative traditions, one "Eastern," the other "Western."

For Gittes, "Western" aesthetics involve principles of organic unity, harmonious balance, stylistic subordination of parts to whole, and the predominating presence of a preconceived central idea toward which all the component parts can be perceived as tending in a triumph of teleology and proportionate decorum. "Eastern" aesthetics, by contrast, feature open-ended, episodic, additive forms that express the concept of "boundlessness," are designed to accommodate any number of fictional accretions in the course of their narrative nomadics, and consequently display a resultant sense of arbitrary rather than necessary order and number for the component parts of the deliberately flexible structure. While "Western" aesthetics are thus relational, theoretically ideal, and bound by formalism and a sense of appropriate enclosure, "Eastern" aesthetics allow for the discontinuous, are seemingly indifferent to sudden thematic or stylistic shifts, rely on first-person, eyewitness accounts rather than on theoretical principles for their authority, and rest ultimately upon a commitment to practical accommodation of the exigent and the circumstantial.

The dangers of essentializing that attend Gittes's above-described paradigmatic approach to the problem of "Greek and Arabic Outlooks" (chapter 3) are real dangers that she does not always successfully avoid or overcome. Particularly in light of Said's revisionist *Orientalism* (1978), which never enters her discussion, and Menocal's critique of "The Myth of Westernness" in *The Arabic Role in Medieval Literary History* (1987), which Gittes does acknowledge and draw upon, it is particularly discomfiting to find essentialistic footprints everywhere along the path of her discussion of the cultural matrix from which Chaucer derives so many textual features of articulation and design in *The Canterbury Tales*. The intellectual over-determination that results, however, should not be allowed to obscure Gittes's real and often very shrewd analogical insights that spring from her consideration of nonliterary disciplines like architecture, mathematics, natural history, and geography.

Particularly provocative, and a useful supplement to Jordan's now-standard *Chaucer and the Shape of Creation* (1967), are her discussions of the medieval mosque as a diffuse and directionless architectural concept based on social needs of shifting populations, contrasted with the medieval cathedral whose central focus on the altar and whose dedication to principles of organization according to ratio and proportion were essentially geometric expressions of a theological concept of Divine Presence, accompanied by a systematic attempt to regularize human access to its numinous reality. The translation of these conceptual notions into observable narrative strategies based on natural chronology and artistic arrangement of material (the rhetorical *ordo naturalis* and *ordo artificialis*) empower many of Gittes's discriminating comments on the gradual fixations into allegorical abstraction that attend Gower's structuring of *Confessio Amantis* according to the Seven Deadly Sins and the three orders of medieval society, all in need of reform.

In this discussion of the *Confessio*, however, with its overt inclusion of *Amans* and Genius as fictional figures, Gittes never even mentions the *Roman de la Rose* whence they derive. This is the more surprising as de Meun's textual "rosary" is itself such an important medieval frame narrative and one whose omnium-gatherum dedication to both Eastern and Western textual traditions forms its encyclopaedic meaning as a work, translated by Chaucer and enormous in its influence on his own subsequent imaginative fusions of varying narrative frame traditions, Gittes's announced topic of examination.

Equally tantalizing are her discussions of the Arabic science of number, which avoided Western "rounding"; considered every number, large and small, as significant; invented the zero as a computational placeholder; and accommodated the idea of limitless series and chains. Nevertheless, while Gittes is particularly astute in her application of these mathematical concepts to the essentially atomistic organization of the Arabic *qasida*, or pre-Islamic ode, and the later framed diffusions that are the *Panchatantra*, she brings no equivalent agility to the analysis of number as a textual trope in the Italian *Decameron* (100 stories, 10 narrators, 10 days) or the Spanish *El Conde Lucanor* (5 parts, as in *Panchatantra*, devoted to morality, statesmanship, tales, proverbs, and religion, framed in a conversational asking of advice by Count Lucanor and receiving of it from Patronio, his advisor), nor does she probe the Gowerian numerical schematics, noted above, for any further possibilities, settling instead on conventional observations. Noting that there is an "ostensibly rigid structure" implied in such numerical surfaces and citing occasional deviations from it as instances of "openness" and "boundlessness" associated with Arabic aesthetics do not advance the critical discussion.

In fact, in Gittes's own noting that Arabic computation was a particularly refined science whose parameters were designed to "find the correct position of Mecca" and to "determine the exact moments of sunrise and moonrise so that they could observe their fasts," one might discover the basis for arguing (as I have recently done in *Ars Legendi*, 1991) that Chaucer's own pilgrimage poem makes refined imaginative use of just such numerical systematics as he brings into harmonic balance the 24 *Tales*, representing solar computation, told by a company of narrators with a necessarily flexible number that may be calculated, by turn, as 29, 30, or 31, a figure representing lunar computation. Gittes's discussion of *The Canterbury Tales* (chapter 6) offers a major menu of standard observations on open-ended groupings, loose narrative connections, and categorical overlaps, including generic mergers; it fails, however, to find the way to the many fresh and productive insights that her own considerable learning and study have positioned her to investigate with particular result. In her salutary impulse to compact and digest a great deal of information and idea into a readable and focused format of commentary on the medieval frame narrative from which Chaucer drew and to which he contributed, Gittes too often flattens the incredibly convolute terrain that she has clearly discerned but has inadequately described for her readers. The book consequently seems more a relief map than a genuine critical itinerary, well conducted.

It is the same with her discussion of the *Panchatantra*, a cultural compendium whose weaving of prose and verse incorporates a comprehensive data base on topics of Oriental geography, history, myth, poetry, folklore, astronomy, arithmetic, music, religion, government, and cuisine, both vegetarian and carnivorous. In this fictively whimsical wonder we can also discern a constant crimson thread of semiotic fable that describes poetic performance and textual tradition as these oral-and-written performances are shown to be constantly adapting to shifting cultural conditions. The semiotic fabulae are explicitly conducted under the narrative aegis of debates between crows and owls; tales of snares and nets and of skins and hides, greed for money and for manuscript wrappers, constant challenges to relocate, carpenters rebuilding, weavers making *textus*, and snakes shedding their skins for new and more beautiful forms, as well as — in a daring burst of brilliance — a seminal fiction involving the male members of a bull named Hang-Ball. Hang-Ball's seminal members, "plainly on the point of falling," are watched for a period of fifteen years by a greedy jackal, whose wife, tired of mere mouse meat, hankers for something more toothsome, but the desired downfall of these reproductively potent organs never comes about: "Loose they are, yet tight. . . ."

Though one might never guess from Gittes's description of the *Panchatantra* that such involucral refinements have been regularly concealed therein, no reader introduced to this Chaucerian avatar could be anything but grateful to the work that had accomplished such an introduction. *Framing the Canterbury Tales* strikes this grateful reader as a careful, if somewhat oversimplified, account whose mainline items will offer no surprises but whose familiarity with, and attention to, less-discussed exemplars will prove rewarding. Despite its lack of critical stylishness — of nearly 150 bibliography items fewer than 30 are dated later than the 1970s, suggesting a work undertaken at some distance in time and never fully brought up to date—this book possesses a straightforward clarity and a lack of pretense that lends its own kind of luster and authority to a useful study.

DOLORES WARWICK FRESE
University of Notre Dame

BARBARA HANAWALT, ed. *Chaucer's England: Literature in Historical Context*. Medieval Studies at Minnesota, vol. 4. Minneapolis: University of Minnesota Press, 1992. Pp. xxii, 240. $39.95 cloth; $16.95 paper.

In this entertaining and valuable volume Barbara Hanawalt gathers essays by five distinguished scholars whose work clearly belongs to the most traditional side of the discipline we know as "history," with essays by five distinguished scholars whose concerns are those conventionally classified as "literature and culture" or "cultural studies." After the editor's introduction, the book is organized in three parts: "The Political Context," "London as a Literary Setting," and "Literature of the Countryside."

Part 1 opens with an essay by Michael Bennett, "The Court of Richard II and the Promotion of Literature." Bennett wants to persuade his readers that Richard II and his court should be considered as a major cause, perhaps the first cause, in "the sudden scaling of the heights of vernacular eloquence." In pursuing this ambition, Bennett adds no new empirical evidence. He seems driven by an assumption that something called "assurance" in the poetry of Chaucer, Gower, and the *Gawain*-poet "could only come from the highest sponsorship," by which he means not the one whom Milton recorded as visiting his slumbers nightly to govern his song but Richard II and his court. The evidence for such "sponsorship" is lacking, however. Bennett himself acknowledges the "lack of documentation of the king's patronage to Chaucer in his capacity as a poet," while he also notes that any "evidence for a connection between the court of Richard II and the *Gawain*-poet is highly circumstantial," but this "problem" does not deter him from his quest.

The next essay is Paul Strohm's "Saving the Appearances: Chaucer's *Purse* and the Fabrication of the Lancastrian Claim." This is a fascinating study of the "Lancastrian propaganda machine" at work. It examines the processes through which Henry's claims to the throne were forged in 1399–1400.

210

Strohm brings out "the eccentric and contradictory nature" of Henry's claims, showing how these contradictions emerged and how they were handled in image and narrative. He sets *The Complaint of Chaucer to His Purse* in this "generative matrix," demonstrating how the poet's "fresh and conceptually energetic fabrication" produces a thoroughly distinctive defense of Henry. In this perspective we come to see the "exchange-value of Chaucer's poem" and understand why Henry sought "to enlist litterateurs in his dynastic cause."

After this comes Nigel Saul's essay on "Chaucer and Gentility." A substantial part of the essay is on the concept of gentility in the Middle Ages. It maintains contradictory arguments. On the one hand, Saul claims that for "over half a millennium" gentility was universally defined in the "qualitative" way found in the passages he extracts from three poems by Chaucer. There is, therefore, no question of significant cultural change. On the other hand, Saul claims that "the character of the old aristocratic ethic was being re-defined" in the later Middle Ages in ways that made lineage and pedigree "no longer so important" and led to the legitimization of "rank and social position" by "possession of 'virtue'." Furthermore, Saul asserts that such cultural changes were "not entirely divorced" from changes in "contemporary reality." Saul appears not to notice the contradictions here. Saul's essay also includes a discussion of "gentility" in Chaucer's *Gentilesse*, *The Wife of Bath's Tale* and *The Franklin's Prologue* and *Tale*. Saul finds that Chaucer's work "evinces little interest in the world of the market" (texts such as *The Shipman's Tale*, *The Cook's Tale*, *The Wife of Bath's Prologue*, and *The Canon's Yeoman's Prologue* and *Tale* are not mentioned), while his ethical discourse, "derived largely from classical antique and Christian sources," assesses gentility "in qualitative terms" — those that had informed Europe for "over half a millennium" before Chaucer. Nevertheless, in a reproduction of the contradiction remarked above, Chaucer is also said to reflect changes in the royal court and an allegedly "general trend toward the interiorization of values that affected all areas of belief," including "hostility towards images, the rejection of transubstantiation, and the skepticism towards outward ceremony." This is a confused and strange story.

The part of the book on "London as a Literary Setting" begins with David Wallace's "Chaucer and the Absent City." Wallace is struck by the absence of the City of London in Chaucer's fiction and his essay offers an intriguing account of the significance and causes of this absence. He argues that Chaucer had models of urban narratives, knew these, and rejected them. It seems that he rejected such narratives because they carried ideological

211

frameworks he found inappropriate to his experience of London, just as Wallace finds them inappropriate to his own experience of reading the city's *Letter Books* edited by H. T. Riley. Instead of either Dante's "pretensions to omniscience" or Boccaccio's "ideology of associational form," produced for an allegedly "self-sufficient, self-regulating city" (*Decameron* 6.2), Chaucer produced an "antisassociational rhetoric" in a London where "the conditions for the possibility of a credible ideology of the city do not yet exist" (it never did, as a host of witnesses from Dekker to Blake to Mayhew to the present dispossessed of Thatcher's and Major's London can testify). The writing of Chaucer that shows this "rhetoric" is *The Cook's Tale*, the Cook of fragment IX(H), and *The Canon's Yeoman's Tale*. Here Wallace presents a brilliant reading of the minute particulars of Chaucer's astonishing inventiveness, a reading informed by an always disciplined use of the social and political experience Chaucer's language both takes for granted and explores.

The second essay in this part of the book is by Caroline Barron, "William Langland: A London Poet." Instead of the neoscholastic theologian one meets in so many studies of Langland, here we find "the literate spokesman for a largely illiterate society," an immigrant poet in "a city full of immigrants," full of people "endlessly on the move." Langland is "much more a London poet" than Chaucer (Barron's London is not identical with Wallace's), and *Piers Plowman* "is rooted in the streets of London in the 1370s," its trades, its poor, its merchants, its government. Indeed, she argues that any serious political thought in the poem is grounded in specifically urban forms of government, dismissing his wider reflections as "naïve" and "simplistic." Barron puts her immense knowledge of medieval London to a welcome consideration of Langland's first audiences and to providing further information about John But.

The final essay in this part is Lawrence Clopper's "Need Men and Women Labor? Langland's Wanderer and the Labor Ordinances." Clopper searches "the historical record" in Shropshire, Hereford, Oxfordshire, and London to establish "a close relationship between persona and poet" in *Piers Plowman*. The "obsessive" quest, as he calls it, "largely fails," but it took Clopper to the labor legislation of the period and an understanding of its relevance to the poet's interrogation by Reason and Conscience in passus 5 of the C version. This is certainly a persuasive link, especially given the poet's partisan defense of the Statute of Laborers in B 6 (C 6, ed. Derek Pearsall). Less felicitous is the detailed discussion of the failed quest. It is never clear to me what would be the consequences for any reading of *Piers Plowman*, or late-medieval culture, had Clopper's quest been successful—

for example, had Clopper been able to establish that the 1328 acolyte called William le Longe in a register of the Bishop of Hereford was the "London poet" writing after the great plague, what would have been achieved?

The third part of the book is on "Literature of the Countryside." It begins with Nicholas Orme's study of hunting in "fact" and hunting in "fancy." This very traditional juxtaposition of "history" and "literature" is perhaps most interesting for its documentation of the clergy's extremely wide involvement in hunting and for the way the "sport bridged the divisions. . . between noblemen and merchants." Literature is used in this essay as positivist historians have always used it.

The next chapter is Barbara Hanawalt's "Ballads and Bandits: Fourteenth-Century Outlaws and the Robin Hood Poems." This essay, by a historian who has made outstanding contributions to our knowledge of medieval communities, compares "real bandits" with "ballad bandits," compares "real" victims (peasants and, disproportionately, women) with "imagined" victims, and examines the appeal of the myth of Robin Hood in contrast to the "general fear and distaste felt for people engaging in criminal activities." This essay has plenty of material that should be of interest to cultural historians, such as the prominent role of the clergy in leadership of bands in criminal court and the reproduction of hierarchic relations in the bandits' world, both in ballads and in the organization of actual gangs.

After bandits we come to "John Ball's Letters: Literary History and Historical Literature," an essay by Richard Green. From some rather bland reflections on the current practices of "literary critics" and "historians" Green moves to Knighton's and Walsingham's version of letters attributed to John Ball. Green provides a context for these writings in "popular" preaching, an "explication de texte," an account of "Ball's individual contribution," the letters' relations to 1381, and their contribution to an "interpretation of the Peasants' Revolt." He concludes that those who took part in the English rising of 1381 were "conservatives" who were "trying to prevent a new age," "Luddites," "firmly to the right" of the "political spectrum." To me these judgments, insofar as they are intelligible, are groundless. Green even seems to forget specific grievances over taxes, services, bond status, and the statute of laborers, none of which can possibly be classified as "conservative" or "firmly to the right," as contemporaries correctly understood.

The final essay in the book is Susan Crane's "The Writing Lesson of 1381." Her concern is "with how writers imagine rebels and interpret the actions they impute to rebels," offering what she calls a "literary perspective" in which she is "not primarily concerned with the accuracy of the record to the events." She sees literacy as, unequivocally, a force for oppression: "the essence of writing," it is claimed, is the "control of others." This, she argues, was also the view of those involved in the rising of 1381. So John Ball's letters are said to have "meant more to the rebels as documents per se than as meaningful messages." In my view Crane fails to notice that the rebels, like Lollards, were perfectly capable of making discriminations concerning the *different uses* of writing, although some of her own examples actually exemplify just that. Ironically, the essentialist approach to writing comes from the modern scholar who invokes Lévi-Strauss and Derrida, *not* from the women and men of 1381. Crane then turns to two passages from Langland and Chaucer to "illustrate briefly how we might look to literary works for reactions to the rising of 1381" within the framework she has elaborated. The passages chosen are from the Prologue to *Piers Plowman* and the closing encounter of *The Wife of Bath's Prologue*. The latter leads into an extremely interesting dialogue with Lee Patterson's reading of *The Miller's Tale* and the role of the Wife of Bath, an engaging conclusion to the book.

DAVID AERS
University of East Anglia

ELAINE TUTTLE HANSEN. *Chaucer and the Fictions of Gender.* Berkeley, Los Angeles, and Oxford: University of California Press, 1992. Pp. ix, 301. $42.50 cloth; $15.95 paper.

Elaine Tuttle Hansen in this new book on Chaucer seems to appropriate the role of Christine de Pizan in the fifteenth-century *Querelle des femmes* as critic of the (male-dominated) canon. As Hansen's title suggests, she wishes to deconstruct certain gender fictions in Chaucer's poetry and Chaucer criticism, chief among them that humanist Chaucer was an androgynous poet whose greatness depends on his sympathetic presentation of female characters. She argues that Chaucer (as poet, pilgrim, man) is misogynistic both in his representation of the Female (*sic*)—more fictions, or images— and in his own authorial identification with the feminine — "women characters and the feminine are deployed as the battleground over which author-

214

ity, selfhood, and unity can be established" (p. 291). In positing female sexuality as a threat to male authority, Hansen reads the women characters and speakers in Chaucer as projections of their male speakers' (or author's) anxiety. These characters are essentialized as Women situated on a continuum ranging from the meretricious, irrational, and carnal to the ideal, virtuous, silent, perceived as powerless, silenced or silencing, monstrous, unreal, marginalized. The problem is, Chaucer is not Meun, who was criticized not only for the *Roman's* denigration of women but also for its lack of truthfulness, its idleness, and its shameful and sinful teachings.

Arguing for thematic continuity between Chaucer's early and late fictions, Hansen breaks up the conventional chronological sequencing of Chaucer works in her ten chapters. She begins by attacking the Evelike Wife of Bath (chapter 2) for being deceptive, self-absorbed, and "self-descriptive" — that is, she talks about herself — as opposed to the "good silent women" Constance and Griselda. Alcyone and White (chapter 3) reflect crucial fictive ideals of Woman for the male lover or poet, termed "essential to the healing of the polymorphous, disordered condition of historically gendered subjectivity and discourse" (p.74). Dido of *The House of Fame* (chapter 4) likewise becomes Everywoman opposed to the ideal of White (or the Virgin Mary), a role also occupied by the formel eagle of *The Parlement of Fowls* in chapter 5. According to Hansen's retro-feminism, because desire marks a male as manly, for the formel to become empowered she must therefore "speak silence and figure absence" (p. 127). Criseyde (chapter 6), a "realistic female character," threatens Troilus's "problematic and unstable" male sexuality (p. 146): this *"archetype* of *wommanhede"* figures forth "all moral and linguistic error and instability" (p. 155; italics added). What mediates for Criseyde between "crossing the fine but fatal line between a Mary and an Eve, a White and a Dido, an otherworldly ideal and 'any of the frape'" is Troilus in the gendered role of male protector (p. 167). Identifying Criseyde as an *"archetypal* interpreter" who cannot decipher or control, Chaucer finally "feminizes" the reader by having his narrator at the end criticize men who love women too much (p. 186; italics added).

This Eva/Ave dichotomy stitched together with some gender and deconstruction terminology (such as homosociality) renders the poet in *The Canterbury Tales* as a divided self unsure of his gender. Griselda (chapter 7) is read as a strong female within a context of masculine authoritarianism who must suffer because she is virtuous. Ideal because she abstracts "certain gender-specific characteristics into the ideal state of 'wommanhede,'" Griselda thus reveals that the Clerk fears women and being a woman

(p. 199). Emily as Woman in *The Knight's Tale* appears to be the antithesis of Alison in *The Miller's Tale* (chapter 8) but in reality reveals the confusion between the anal and the genital in the focus on the dirtiness of female sexuality in *The Miller's Tale*. Nicholas is feminized through the threat of castration or homosexuality, what Hansen calls preempting the female body; the Knight and the Miller come together through feminization so that class divisions do not wholly separate them in their concern for male bonding. In chapter 9, Evelike May, who shares with Adam the same (male) body, is thus "made in the image of both January and her maker" to enable men both to see themselves more truly and to understand their own feminization (p. 249). In the discussion of Dorigen (chapter 10) the "feminized narrator" is identified with male interests and characters to affirm the possibility of male bonding and of masculine virtue because of "proper gender difference" (p. 269), primarily because of Dorigen's "bodiless, nonthreatening power and subjectivity" (p. 277), with the black rocks symbolizing "the monstrosity of female sexuality." Omitted without explanation are the Prioress and Second Nun, Constance, Virginia, and Apollo's wife.

Chaucer, who identifies in part with the creatures of his masculine imagination, is equally powerless and marginalized. For example, *The Book of the Duchess* (chapter 3) is about the loss of masculine identity as projected through the death of Blanche, or White—the loss, in short, of the Ideal Woman (*sic*). Both the Black Knight and Chaucer are "consoled" by understanding that a good woman has died and therefore extricated from a "negative, *feminized* state—apathetic, mournful, solitary, irrational, and unnatural" (p. 72; italics added).

By positing a binary dualism in differentiating "male" from "female," Hansen herself essentializes, and therefore stereotypes, certain characters, situations, and ideas very much in the manner of the misogynistic male poet(s) and critics she claims to be deconstructing. In discussing "unmanly" or feminized men, Hansen assumes that we understand what Woman is, or what female difference entails, for she defines "feminized men" as those who act as women are said to act or are treated as women are often treated (p. 3). Hansen uses "feminization" not in the modern feminist sense as "subversive position in culture" to attack and deconstruct phallocentrism (p. 18 n.19) but as equivocal with "emasculation" (p. 16)—the not-male otherness of the female contagious to the male, and, in an extension of the culpability of Eve, in a sense *caused* by her very female difference. In discussing May in *The Merchant's Tale*, Hansen makes this astounding statement: "The condemnation of men for the feminine part of their

nature and behavior—a condemnation that is also part of orthodox discourse—cannot logically and does not in the tale's unfolding either redeem
human corruptibility or subvert the asymmetrical and internally contradictory alignment of Woman and women with blindness, sensuality, fleshly
corruption, and absence" (p. 265). In essentializing traits associated with
the female, Hansen details passivity, coyness, vulnerability, and dependence (p.7) without foregrounding whose traits these are (Chaucer's? hers?
fourteenth-century culture? twentieth-century culture, as reflected in male
critics?). When Hansen resorts to history as a rationalization for this
approach, she is least successful, for she seldom strays from the Chaucerian
poem, even though she may skip here and there over the Chaucerian text to
make the points she desires. What she omits in her theoretical assumptions
is an understanding of postmodern subjectivities.

Following in the footsteps of recent gender and postmodernist studies of
Chaucer by Carolyn Dinshaw and Marshall Leicester, *Chaucer and the
Fictions of Gender* moves away from the misogynistic image of female
textuality and sexuality and focuses more narrowly on issues of homosociality and homosexuality linked to class aspirations predicated upon
male (sexual) rivalry and competition for female characters. For this reason
I would describe *Chaucer and the Fictions of Gender* not as a feminist book
but as a book about men and masculine identity and authority (p. 207),
even though Hansen envisages her project as feminist because "feminist
criticism of the canonical male author offers a place in which to examine the
risks and benefits of critiquing hegemonic discourses and masterworks from
a position of exclusion and to analyze the limits and powers of being
constructed, as feminisms are constructed, in opposition to (rather than
outside or beyond) the structures they seek to modify" (pp. 291–92). That
is, because androgynous Chaucer identifies his character as female or with
female characters, he creates a subjectivity appropriate to feminist discourse—a form of literary female impersonation. In a brilliant twist
Hansen adds that "the primal fear of feminization in Chaucerian fictions... is the fear that men may be women. Akin to this is the fear that
literary critics occupy a feminine position in modern culture" (p. 288).
Finally, Hansen suggests the current direction in literary criticism as equally
feminizing: "In the wake of efforts to deprivilege and decenter this curriculum, literary studies may well worry that all criticism will have to become
feminist criticism"(p. 289).

But if women characters represent the projection of masculine imagina-
tions, then to study them is to study male subjectivity, gender relations, not
feminisms. If her argument is reversed, only women writers could project

217

female difference into their masculine characters—but then the study of their male characters would be phallogocentrist. Hansen assumes that no writer can construct heterosexual characters with any authority and that monosexual characters are ipso facto legitimately constructed—that all women writers are 100 percent female, all male writers 100 percent male. Performance, in Judith Butler's terms, becomes a negligible factor in any discussion.

Hansen in her opening argument fears that Lee Patterson's (and Marshall Leicester's) reading of Chaucer's Wife of Bath (the Wife is a creature of male imagination; there is no Wife of Bath) is postfeminist and will now return the field to a prefeminist phase where there is no woman in criticism (pp. 44ff.). At the end she presents her study as a means of feminizing Chaucer criticism: "It may also offer a way in which to make masterworks more available and interesting, open them to interested, partial, situated interpretative acts of those for whom, as interested, partial, situated texts, they were not written, those whom they have hitherto helped to silence and exclude from the game" (p. 292).

As one silenced and excluded from the game, I share her fear but believe that her own book inadvertently moves us farther down that track by repeating those threats to female autonomy, her very reiteration a means of valorization and privileging similarly erasing the woman reader. If the modern critical consciousness is male, then her invocation of Lee Patterson in its re-creation of their arguments merely renames and therefore validates the patriarchy. To use her logic, if *criticism* by men projects onto the female masculine anxiety, then their interpretations of the Wife reflect their desire for her monstrosity to be absent and therefore nonthreatening—and Hansen's appropriation of their supposedly postmodern fantasy suspect because it "sleeps with the enemy." By collapsing the distinctions among author's voice, narrative strategy, characterization, and reader, Hansen reduces artistry to a kind of verbal masturbation and displaces the possibility of irony as a resident technique. She also, most unfortunately, displaces women as readers and feminism as a method of reading. In that sense, there are no women in Hansen's book—they are as absent from her text, as silent, as they are in what she perceives as Chaucer's text.

Granted that the book's framing theoretical assumption may be itself a fiction, nevertheless Hansen asks some important if disturbing questions that we will need to answer, whether in agreement or disagreement. The study is provocative and controversial and, like the fifteenth-century *Querelle des femmes*, will stir up reactions in part because it reflects so many of the larger controversies aswirl in the profession. There are, along the way, wonderful insights about Chaucerian characters and passages of brilliance. In accord with what seems to have become a trend, there is an index but no bibliography; notes are fashionably skimpy and basically post-1980s.

JANE CHANCE
Rice University

ERIK HERTOG. *Chaucer's Fabliaux as Analogues.* Mediaevalia Lovaniensia, 1st ser., vol. 19. Leuven [Belgium]: Leuven University Press, 1991. Pp. viii, 290. Bel Francs 1490.

Hertog's monograph is an innovative study of the traditions in which Chaucer worked. He focuses on the tales of the Summoner, the Reeve, the Miller, the Merchant, and, to a lesser extent, the Shipman. The argument is that an acquaintance with the analogues heightens our response to Chaucer's complex variations.

It is like stag-party jokes: if you know the tradition, you will understand the clever variations. If the jokester opens with "Hey, waiter, what's this fly doing in my soup?" or "This guy comes into this bar, see, with this parrot (or this mouse and this tiny piano)," you are prepared for variations on familiar themes, characters, and situations. A gifted storyteller can startle and amuse.

If these jokes had been part of Chaucer's (and his audience's) repertoire, he would have made such trifles into supremely successful anecdotes. Hertog maintains that one can better appreciate the poet's sophisticated complexities (in *The Merchant's Tale* especially) if one knows the analogue tradition.

There is a problem: as we all know, before Chaucer there were no fabliaux in English, as Hertog admits several times. There was *Dame Sirith*, of course, but it is a feeble "piece of entertainment" (p. 4) that does not really qualify as a fabliau.

Hertog wisely resists the temptation to reconstruct hypothetical Middle English fabliaux. Instead, he focuses on extant Continental versions that Chaucer probably knew. He does not fall into the *Ur-Hamlet* trap, familiar to Shakespeare scholars (some of whom have acceded to the temptation of guessing what the nonexistent play was like).

219

Hertog establishes, in minute detail, the nature of the fabliaux that Chaucer and his listeners and readers probably knew. It is a laborious process that calls upon many of the fashionable modern and postmodern techniques, including those of Barthes, Greimas, and Eco.

To demonstrate his points (not *pointes*, as the publisher misprints it several times), Hertog uses some two dozen charts, with arrows and other, more arcane, symbols. He is careful to distinguish his methodology from old-fashioned source study, but he is a little embarrassed by his own ponderous reconstruction: "The following enumerative survey describing these analogous semantic fields. . . is inevitably a bit dry, but I hope it has its moments" (p. 158); "To bring this conclusion — and study — to an end long overdue, a few final thoughts on Analogy" (p. 246); "We began this study with a rather elephantine definition of the fabliau. I am afraid we shall have to conclude it in a similar fashion in an attempt to define the second term of our title, viz. the phenomenon of those very similar stories, called 'analogues'" (p. 251).

Hippopotoman though his study may sometimes be, Hertog succeeds in persuading us that Chaucer was familiar with the Continental tradition. He does not concede that the poet used some lost version (in English or whatever) that included all, or most, of the modifications that have delighted readers for 600 years. No, the artistry is Chaucer's own.

The study includes chapters on plot, character, thematics, and genre, all persuasively argued. Hertog does not treat style, which many readers would call the glory of the fabliaux included in *The Canterbury Tales*, but imaginative reconstruction can do only so much. At its best the analysis is a genial and enthusiastic (and refreshingly old-fashioned) close reading of Chaucer's clever retellings. The poet's great achievement is obvious, and Hertog does not neglect it: all the tales in the collection, and perhaps especially the fabliaux, are enriched by the intertextuality created by their inclusion in the framework narrative, with its devilishly cunning links of tale to tale, tale to narrator, and tale to *General Prologue* portraits. Hertog also includes a brief appreciation of *The Canterbury Tales* as compared with Chaucer's earlier works.

There are two valuable byproducts: first, a gracious appreciation of the artistry of Boccaccio (and an appropriate insistence on Chaucer's indebtedness, often unacknowledged), and, second, an encouragement to other scholars to investigate the analogue tradition of other Chaucerian genres, notably the beast fable.

The study is marred by some misreadings, two examples of which occur on page 203: "The semiotic form of these deceptive messages can be aural, e.g., the deafening fart in *MilT*, mistaken by the carpenter for a thunder-clap accompanying the Second Flood," and "Absalon kissing Alysoun's pudendum." No, John the carpenter sleeps blissfully through the "thonder dent" and is not awakened until the later cry for water. And it is not Alison's pudendum: granted there is some ambiguity (see the note to my edition of the *Tale* in the *Variorum Chaucer*), but Chaucer's "naked ers" is pretty unequivocal.

There are some unfamiliar terms (at least to me): (*accaperated*, pp. 13, 15) and abbreviations (c.g., a.o., resp., i.o.w., o.c., i.o.), and there are many typographical errors (*occassionally*, *alright*, *copiist's*, *defeath*, *prex-pdilection*, *contemtuous*, *John Welsh* [*Webster*] *Spargo*, *vilain*, *phi-losphical*, *Parson'Tale*, *Karry* [*Larry*] *D. Benson*).

Hertog includes some tangentially relevant excursus—e.g., on meta-phor (pp. 144ff.) and on *Romeo and Juliet* (pp. 148ff.)—that could be abbreviated or omitted in a revised edition of this valuable study.

THOMAS W. ROSS
Colorado Springs, Colorado

MILO KEARNEY. *The Role of Swine Symbolism in Medieval Culture.* Lewiston, Queenston, and Lampeter: Edwin Mellen, 1991. Pp. xiv, 385. $79.95.

This is an odd book, a sprawling anthology of pig allusions organized according to a vaguely evolutionary chronology, with much retelling of folktales in a very arch and circumlocutory style ("Winding down the path of porcine personification..." p. 6) and many curious drawings by the author loosely based on badges, illuminated letters, misericords, and other sources. It most resembles those early Victorian collections of tidbits of folklore, such as William Hone's *Every-day Book* (1830) or Robert Cham-bers's *Book of Days* (1863), that were published to cater for the newly reawakened interest in folktales and their symbolism.

The historical scheme is of a two-stage development from "The Mar-velous Magical Pig" (where the pig symbolizes strength and fertility) to "The Despicable Unethical Pig" (where the pig, under the influence of Christianity, comes to symbolize greed, filth, excessive sexuality, and lowlife), with a special space reserved for the fifteenth century as a time of

221

rampant eclecticism, when "a crescendo of confusion regarding the pig symbol" led to a revival of "the entire spectrum of its contradictory meanings" (p. 305). A scheme so vague is difficult to argue with, and the attempts to refine it, by introducing notions of "resurgence of interest," contradictory tendencies, and temporary "blows to pig prestige" are perfunctory. The significance of pig symbolism generally is explained as having to do with the way in which the pig, more than any other beast, stands for mankind, "with its difficult antinomy of positive and negative characteristics" (p. 322).

Though it is difficult to take the book seriously, or explain how one comes to be reviewing it, it is a serious book, and a work of loving dedication, care, and assiduity. The vast trawl through classical, Germanic, Celtic, and other sources ensures that everyone's favorite pigs are here somewhere, from the winged pig of Gullinbursti to Richard III's "Blanc Sanglier." Some of them appear in unexpected contexts. The boar hunt in *Sir Gawain and the Green Knight*, for instance, is apparently an allusion to transmigration initiation rites, in which the boar in some sense represents Gawain himself: such initiates are enabled to "touch base with their piggish lower nature and emerge the wiser" (p. 55). Elsewhere we learn something new about Troilus's dream of the boar embracing Criseyde: "This scene puts the final seal on the failed experiment of the winged pig" (p. 41). Chaucerians will want to buy the book to find out why.

The book resembles nothing so much as a gigantic pigsty, and the experience of reading it that of having great barrow loads of information tipped out promiscuously on top of one. Everything one would want in the way of raw material on the subject is here somewhere (I particularly profited from the pages of factual information about domestic pigs, pp. 95–104), and there is an excellent index and a probably exhaustive bibliography of pig literature. It comes as a slight surprise to find that there are already many books of this kind in existence.

DEREK PEARSALL
Harvard University

ALBERT C. LABRIOLA and JOHN W. SMELTZ, eds. and trans. *The Bible of the Poor [Biblia Pauperum]: A Facsimile and Edition of the British Library Blockbook C.9.d.2.* Pittsburgh, Pa.: Duquesne University Press, 1991. Pp. ix, 190. $38.00 cloth; $20.00 paper.

As Labriola and Smeltz explain in their preface to this very useful book, the idea of producing a facsimile edition of the *Biblia Pauperum* grew out of their experience using the work in teaching various courses in medieval and Renaissance Christian literature, art, and theology (p. vii). This edition does not replace the recent scholarly (and much more expensive) one by Avril Henry (Ithaca, New York: Cornell University Press, 1987), as the authors themselves make clear (pp. vii–viii), but Chaucerians and other teachers of medieval and Renaissance literature and art will indeed find this book to be a valuable, and affordable, pedagogical resource for themselves and their students.

Having said this, however, there are several problems with the volume that need to be addressed. On the question of audience, the authors write: "As a work intended for the common folk, accessible to their understanding and useful for their religious instruction, the *Biblia Pauperum* was not a repository of erudition but a compendium of commonplace interpretations" (p. viii). Yet how "common" could the "folk" who constituted the putative intended audience of the *Biblia Pauperum* have been if they were expected to read and correlate its sometimes recherché biblical Latin texts and corresponding images? Indeed, as Labriola and Smeltz themselves point out:

...the *Biblia Pauperum* is a brief compendium of harmonies and concordances among biblical texts and a guide to interpretations thereof. By its citation, juxtaposition, and interpretation of biblical passages, the blockbook epitomizes the technique of medieval commentary compiled in monumental works such as the *Glossa Ordinaria* of the twelfth and thirteenth centuries and the *Catena Aurea* by St. Thomas Aquinas. Despite its relative brevity, the blockbook provides a frame of reference for understanding biblical allusions in religious writing, including sermons, hymns, penitential literature, and devotional poetry as late as the seventeenth century. [Pp. 7–8]

This would hardly be fare for the "common folk" ("...clearly it was not for the simple poor, who did not buy books, let alone read Latin—especially heavily abbreviated Latin printed in black letter of peculiar illegibility" [Henry, *Biblia Pauperum*, p. 3]). The authors seem to me to be nearer the mark when they suggest that "the clergy whose preaching was aided by the *Biblia Pauperum* were often mendicants or 'poor men'" (p. 5).

Leaving aside the question of its audience, the value of the *Biblia Pauperum* as a key to medieval Christian poetics in general and to the stylistic and thematic vocabulary of medieval Christian art in particular, is hard to overstate. As Labriola and Smeltz point out, the illustrations in the *Biblia Pauperum* show us typology in action in a way that sheds light on the functioning of typology in other media as well (p. 8). As the authors also assert, the *Biblia Pauperum* aimed to inspire "an emotional response of devotion and gratitude for Christ's ministry of Redemption, emphasized in scenes of the Passion and Crucifixion" (p. 9). This observation—true with reference to the *Biblia Pauperum*—might helpfully be placed in the context of a wider late-medieval turn to lay piety, featuring highly emotive meditations on the Passion in several media in various European countries (see Richard Kieckhefer, *Unquiet Souls: Fourteenth-Century Saints and Their Religious Milieu* [Chicago and London: University of Chicago Press, 1984], esp. chap. 4, pp. 89–121).

The plates reproducing the blockbook appear next (pp. 11–54). The quality of the reproductions is reasonably good. Following the plates (pp. 57–96) are transcriptions of the Latin texts that accompany the illustrations, and these are in turn followed by English translations (pp. 99–139); spotchecking, I found no errors. Then, in a section entitled "Iconography and Typology in the *Biblia Pauperum*: A Brief Commentary" (pp. 141–79), the editors describe and explicate the plates and their accompanying biblical texts one by one. This "ekphrastic" section is the most interesting and important in the book (after the plates themselves, of course), especially for students unfamiliar with the Bible. There is no end to what one might have said about details of the scenes portrayed in the forty plates; everything Labriola and Smeltz do say in this section is of value, and if the book had been more detailed, it would have been less likely to engage its anticipated student audience. Nevertheless, important points seem to have occasionally been overlooked.

For example, in the discussion of plate *a* ("Annunciation," reproduced on p. 15 and discussed on pp. 143–45), the editors speak (on p. 144) about "the utterance of Gabriel ('Ave Gratia Plena')" in the central panel—but this leaves out the rest of the angel's words: "Dominus tecum" (correctly transcribed and translated, however, on pp. 57 and 99, respectively). They also neglect to mention that the words "Ecce ancilla Domini fiat mihi" ("Behold the Handmaiden of the Lord; may it be done to me")—once again, correctly transcribed and translated (pp. 57 and 99, respectively)—are Mary's reply to Gabriel. These words appear on the right-hand scroll in the central panel—there are actually two separate scrolls, the left-hand one recording the angel's words, the right-hand one the Virgin's reply, not just one "scroll center" as the notations (pp. 57 and 99) state; nor is the identification of these texts as quotations of parts of Luke 1:28 and 38, respectively, anywhere to be found. Similarly, for the inscription on the scroll held by an angel "Dominus tecum virorum fortissime" ("The Lord is with you, the bravest of men") (noted on pp. 144–45), the reader should be referred to Judges 6:12. The latter three verses are not included in the appendix of biblical verses (pp. 183–90), which otherwise lists all the biblical verses transcribed and translated earlier in the book in the order in which they appeared, referred to both the Douay-Reims and New English Bible chapter and verse numberings, but it would have been more convenient, for student users especially, if the authors had cited the King James for comparison rather than the New English Bible translation, with apocryphal (or deuterocanonical) verses not found in the KJ version supplemented by the RSV or the NEB version. Indeed, instead of, or in addition to, the latter appendix one would have liked to have an index, in alphabetical order or by biblical book, of all the biblical personages and quotations in the *Biblia Pauperum*. This would have eliminated some of the problems caused by the lack of detailed identification of verses in the "Brief Commentary" and would also have added to the general usefulness of the edition.

In the commentary on plate *a*, Labriola and Smeltz also note that Gedeon (Douay spelling of the King James Gideon) appears with a woolen fleece "moistened by dew while the area nearby remains dry" (p. 145), but it is impossible to discern that the fleece is moist and the ground dry in the panel as it is reproduced; moreover, the authors neglect to point out that only on the first night was Gideon's fleece wet and the ground around it dry — the next night the fleece was dry and the ground wet. A reference to Judges 6 would help clarify the matter. It would also explain what the very prominent tree growing out of a rock in this scene represents. Similarly, in their commentary on the central panel of plate *r* ("The Chief Priests Pay Judas," pp. 161–62), the authors fail to note the presence of a woman in the scene depicted, in addition to Judas and another man (not the high priest, who appears in plate *q* and is dressed very differently from the man in plate *r*). Once again, apocryphal traditions may hold the key to a scene which the Bible alone does not explain (see the Middle English Judas ballad, discussed by Schueler, *PMLA* 91 [1976]: 840–45).

In the discussion of plate *b* ("Nativity," pp. 145–47), the description of the triptych becomes very confusing, for scenes from the Old Testament not portrayed in the panel are mentioned along with, but not distinguished from, the scenes that are portrayed. Further on in the discussion of this plate (p. 147), how is the student expected to locate the relevant passages in the noncanonical Gospel of Pseudo-Matthew and Gospel of the Nativity of Mary, the former invoked to explain the motif of the emergence of a dove from St. Joseph's staff, the latter invoked to explain the motif of St. Joseph's flowering rod — neither of which, as far as I can make out, appears in the

225

picture? For the Gospel of Pseudo-Matthew and the Gospel of the Nativity of Mary, students should have been referred to the texts in Edgar Hennecke and Wilhelm Schneemelcher, eds., *New Testament Apocrypha*, trans. and ed. R. McL. Wilson, 2 vols., (Philadelphia: Westminster, 1963–65). In general, the absence of a bibliography is a drawback. For example, references to the encyclopedic works on Christian iconography of Réau and Schiller would help students compare scenes in the *Biblia Pauperum* with relevant representations of the same and related biblical and apocryphal scenes in medieval art, sculpture, and manuscript illustration. And even if "Typology" is succinctly and accurately enough explained (pp. 3–4), it would surely not have been out of place to refer to one or two of the classic treatments of this mode of reading the Bible (e.g., Auerbach, Smalley, or De Lubac).

A few typical cross-referencing omissions and slipups should be noted. The usefulness of the reference to Christ's "exit from Egypt" (p. 150) would be enhanced if it were immediately followed by something on the order of "(See plate *h*, reproduced on p. 22 and discussed on p. 153)." In another place (p. 151, bottom of par. 2), the editors comment on the "twenty-third triptych (.c.)," but on the same page (five lines from top) they also speak of the "twentieth triptych" without parenthetically identifying it as *v*—because the plates are not numbered seriatim, this usage is inconvenient, and the editors give no page references for either of the latter plates (pp. 37 and 34, respectively), or for the discussion thereof (pp. 122 and 119, respectively), which increases the inconvenience.

Without the plates to look at, a reader of this review may have found it difficult to follow my brief remarks on the layout and commentary in this new edition. With the book in hand, however, and with Avril Henry's edition nearby for reference, the reader will find that the minor problems encountered in using it are far outweighed by the major importance of the visual and textual material it includes. The authors, and Duquesne University Press, are to be warmly commended for making available this edition of the *Biblia Pauperum*.

LAWRENCE BESSERMAN
Hebrew University of Jerusalem

LAUREN LEPOW. *Enacting the Sacrament: Counter-Lollardy in the Towneley Cycle*. Rutherford, Madison, Teaneck, N.J.: Fairleigh Dickinson University Press, 1991. Pp. 167. $28.50.

As she admits in her introduction, Lepow cannot hope to prove that the Towneley Cycle is a deliberate attempt to "counter Lollardy." What she tries to do in this book is show that the cycle could be conceived in that sense and that nothing in the text would confute such an interpretation. This much she accomplishes in admirable fashion. She clearly points out the Lollards' chief objections to the established church. Since the plays are a Corpus Christi cycle, it is easy enough to show that they reaffirm the value of holy communion. And since they are in English, they respond to the Lollard objection that the word of God was being withheld from the common man. Her response to the Lollard objection to drama, however, I found somewhat misguided. Most of Lepow's quotations from Lollard tracts are not against plays on the life of Christ but oppose those on the lives of men and women — that is, the miracle plays, not the mystery cycles. As we know, the much more numerous saint's life plays focused on miracles performed by people, not by Christ, and this is what the Lollards seem to be objecting to.

Finally, the most prevalent concern is in showing that the cycle is an answer to the Lollards' objections to the priesthood, and these are the portions of the book that seem the least convincing. Lepow is constantly trying to find good characters in the play who are "proto-priests" or "priest-like" as opposed to the evil characters who are like Lollards, and this gets into some curious interpretations of the plays. For instance, in *The Killing of Abel*, while Cain might possibly be seen as a Lollard by someone looking for that trait, to a Yorkshire peasant audience he would more likely be seen as a familiar greedy landlord, ill-treating his tenants and, like Oliver in *As You Like It*, an older brother who could not stand to see his younger brother more approved of than he was. The possibilities for an anti-Lollard interpretation are indeed in the play, as Lepow argues, but it is hard to see that this is what the playwright had in mind or what the audience would perceive. And while one can easily see Abel as a proper Christian, it is difficult to see him as "a familiar type of the priest at Mass." He strikes one more as a devout fifteenth-century Christian who wants his brother to do the right thing in his tithing.

A more difficult problem is in *Noah*. Seeing Noah in "a priest's role" may be possible, but never in the many productions of the play that I have seen does that interpretation come through. He may be a devout Christian husband with an obedient trio of sons and a recalcitrant wife who fulfills his duty to guide his family to do what God has ordered. In production, however, he invariably comes across as comic, not "priestly." I have seen this play performed, for instance, before English audiences at Wakefield Cathedral and before American audiences in Toronto, and the comic effect was always the same. In fact, in the Toronto performance Noah was so inept that God sent an angel down to help him build the ark when he pleaded, "Bot if God help amang, I may sit downe daw / To ken." Even so, Noah's wife still "cannot find / Which is before, which is behind." Again in *Abraham and Isaac*, one sees a distraught father who wishes to be obedient to God and who reluctantly obeys God's order even though he does not understand why his son should be slain — not a "priestlike character," who ought to understand God's will.

Perhaps the most convincing analysis in the entire book is that of *Magnus Herodes*, where Herod anachronistically tells his counselors to look in Virgil and Homer but not in saints' lives, Epistles, graduals, the Mass, or matins — exactly the sort of church writings the Lollards were suspicious of. But the analysis of this play is curiously limited to a single paragraph. Lepow does a much more thorough job in showing the *John the Baptist* play as stressing not only baptism but the Eucharist as important to Christianity, the two sacraments most heavily attacked by the Lollards.

The analysis of the entire Passion sequence does not reveal very much anti-Lollard intent. Of course, the Eucharist itself is based on this Passion sequence, but the Towneley Cycle's version of the sequence seems no more anti-Lollard than any of the other extant cycles. Lepow does admit that "it must be conceded that these plays show less emphasis than their predecessors on the portrayal of Lollard-like characters" (p. 102). And she also concedes that *The Last Supper* hardly emphasizes the significance of the Eucharist. The argument that in the trial, flagellation, and Crucifixion Jesus' reluctance to speak demonstrates that "the Word present in the sacrament is a silent one" might be made by a critic, but it is hard to see how this would be obvious to a play audience. And it is not at all clear to me how in the *Processus Talentorum* Christ's seamless coat can be equated with "Christ's body in its sacramental manifestation" (p. 113). On the other hand, Lepow might have made more of *The Harrowing of Hell* as the first evidence of the efficacy of the Redemption. Perhaps the Lollards would not have objected to this, and she saw no need to stress its significance in her analysis.

The final plays in the cycle, the appearances to the disciples, *The Ascension*, and *The Last Judgment*, do indeed support Lepow's position that they consistently stress the importance of the Eucharist as the expression of true belief in Christ and hence as the way to heaven — as well a Corpus Christi cycle should do. This stress may well have been less clear if the plays before *The Last Judgment*, now missing from the Towneley manuscript, were still there, but as the text now stands, Lepow's point is valid. Except for Tutivillus's boast that "now am I master Lollar" and his inclusion of all sorts of misusers of language in his list of those going to hell, I do not see much that is explicitly anti-Lollard in these final plays. The general effect is more a positive support of the established church than a negative attack on Lollards.

As for attention to secondary sources, although Lepow does consistently in her text refer to the cycle as Towneley rather than Wakefield, her footnotes make clear that the term is "not intended to cast doubt on this probability" that the cycle was from Wakefield. While she frequently cites Martin Stevens's *Four Middle English Mystery Cycles* (1987), she seems not to have read from the same year Barbara D. Palmer, "Towneley Plays or Wakefield Cycle Revisited" (*Comparative Drama* 21:318–48; repr., *Drama in the Middle Ages*, 2d ser., New York: AMS Press, 1991), or A. C. Cawley, Jean Forrester, and John Goodchild, "References to the Corpus Christi Play in the Wakefield Burgess Court Rolls: the Originals Rediscovered" (*LSSE*), which prove that most of the evidence for Wakefield as the source of the plays was forged in the 1920s by the Wakefield historian J. W. Walker. Possibly the manuscript was sent to the publishers between the publications of Stevens's book and the two articles, but one would think that this error could have been caught in reading the page proofs later. Other than these two unfortunate late omissions, Lepow's research into secondary sources is admirable and provides an excellent bibliography of materials on both the Towneley Cycle and the controversy between orthodoxy and Lollardy in the Middle Ages.

JOHN WASSON
Emeritus, Washington State University

MONICA E. MCALPINE. *Chaucer's* Knight's Tale: *An Annotated Bibliography, 1900–1985.* Chaucer Bibliographies, vol. 4. Toronto; Buffalo, N.Y.; and London: University of Toronto Press, 1991. Pp. lii, 432. $85.00.

Several years ago I thought it inevitable that the Toronto Chaucer Bibliographies would cover much of the same ground surveyed in the *Variorum*

Chaucer and that one project would make the other at least in part redundant. With the appearance of Monica McAlpine's annotated bibliography of *The Knight's Tale*, the fourth volume in the Toronto series, the extent of the overlap is starting to become clear, and I find that the two projects do not so much compete with as complement one another, largely owing to differences in structure. Whereas the Variorum fascicles anatomize commentary and reassemble its pieces under the rubrics of various classifications (and thus keep the focus chiefly on features of Chaucer's work that attract commentary), the Toronto bibliographies tend rather to preserve the integrity of critical work and to signal its relationship to topics and other criticism by different means. To illustrate these means it will be convenient simply to describe the features of McAlpine's admirable bibliography.

The book begins with a 27-page introduction that provides a general history of the commentary on *The Knight's Tale*. Its categories begin as follows: "Composition and Revision," "Early Appreciation," and "Modern Criticism." The last category — the real matter of the bibliography — traces various critical concerns. Its headings three times disclose the principle of chronology — "Modern Criticism (Continued)"; five other headings indicate the focus of critical interest along the time line — Boethius's *Consolation of Philosophy*; Boccaccio's *Teseida*; the Knight's Portrait; Statius's *Thebaid*; and relation to *Miller's Tale*, *Fragment I*, and the *Canterbury Tales*. McAlpine's procedure within this structure is a sensible one: she identifies seminal scholarship and then follows out responses to it. For younger scholars especially this presentation will be useful as a guide to critical debate; it offers too an implicit recommendation of what is essential reading. Furthermore, McAlpine offers brief assessments that effectively challenge the reader to attempt further work on a critical problem; see, for example, her comments on Emelye (p. xxxix).

The bibliography proper begins with a 20-page section listing editions and translations that include *The Knight's Tale*. It is full of interesting information, such as the names of illustrators or the fact that the Kelmscott Chaucer "includes additional corrections [to its copy text, Skeat's edition of 1894] approved by Skeat." This portion of the bibliography is followed by a nearly 60-page section entitled "Backgrounds and General Studies." Its subheadings are "Chaucer and Italy," "Romance and Romances," "Courtliness and Courtly Love," "Chaucer and Women," "Paganism and the Gods," "Chaucer and Science, Especially Astrology," "Estates and Social Status," "Chivalry, Including Tournaments," and "Miscellaneous." For the most part entries in these categories do not address *The Knight's Tale* but

230

provide useful perspectives from which one might approach the *Tale*. Relatively recent work is favored in this section; indeed, on the subject of chivalry McAlpine identifies "essential reading" that has appeared after the cutoff date for her bibliography (for which, many thanks).

The next section, "Studies of Sources," treats separately the *Teseida*, the *Thebaid*, and the *Roman de Thebes*, providing for each the following classes of information: "Editions and Translations," "Backgrounds and General Studies," and "Criticism." The information compiled here, up to date and convenient, is valuable to teacher and researcher alike. Again, it does not necessarily make explicit connections with *The Knight's Tale*, but it provides the reader with a firm foundation for further intertextual investigation.

The final two sections of the bibliography—the Knight in *The General Prologue* and in the *Links* and *The Knight's Tale*—are alike in structure: scholarship is divided into five periods of time, with works listed alphabetically by scholar in each period. This structure represents a compromise, McAlpine says (p. xvi), that, without atomizing the scholarship, allows one to see generally how information and commentary evolve over time. The artifice of this arrangement highlights the difficulties of organizing nearly intractable material. It presupposes that one might read the entries seriatim and happily pass, as happens in one instance, from *God's Plenty* to "Chaucer and the Trots." Even allowing that some people will read these bibliographical entries in sequence, the alphabet seems less useful than simple chronology as a principle of organization, especially given that the authors are listed alphabetically in the index and are recoverable there.

The index is where the book's "real" organization is to be found. It is 50 pages long, elaborate in its cross-indexing and in its categories. Here one sees how dense and various are the materials to be analyzed and how Herculean was the compiler's task. Like all other classification of myriad details, this one has some intriguing inconsistencies and some inevitable errors of omission and commission. For example, why do the entries for Arcite (compared to Palamon) and Palamon (compared to Arcite) have 22 items in common and 23 items that appear in only one of the two entries? And why does one entry not cross-index to the other? Similarly, "Humor" (p. 402) is separate from "*Knight's Tale*, comedy" (p. 406), without cross reference, and each entry has independent as well as shared references. (One notes also that "comedy" and "colloquial elements" have switched alphabetical positions.) Among omitted references one might include, under "*Knight's Tale*, lines" (p. 407), "I.2895:922"; under "*Knight's Tale*, realism" (p. 408), "551"; under "Portrait of the Knight (I.43–78), lines,

I.70–71" (p. 419), "340." A more noteworthy omission is failure to include the AMS reprint (1972) of Tyrwhitt's landmark edition of *The Canterbury Tales* (originally published 1775–78). McAlpine does cite (item 640) the Folcroft reprint (1973) of Tyrwhitt's "Introductory Discourse" to that edition. But this item provides insufficient information, and a cross reference to it in item 345 is misleading since the "Discourse" does not itself address the issue raised in item 345.

Errors that are certainly typographical include the date of Morell's edition (p. xxviii), which is 1737, not 1727; in item 345, "I.601" should read "I.60"; in item 1122, something has gone awry with the sentence fragment that begins "Given the weight of the astrological machinery." These shortcomings do not, however, undermine McAlpine's achievement. Her annotated bibliography of *The Knight's Tale* is a monument of scholarship and will be an indispensable tool in the study of one of Chaucer's most important tales.

DANIEL J. RANSOM
University of Oklahoma

TIM WILLIAM MACHAN, ed. *Medieval Literature: Texts and Interpretation.* Medieval and Renaissance Texts and Studies, vol. 79. Binghamton, N.Y.: Medieval and Renaissance Texts and Studies, 1991. Pp. vii, 198. $20.00.

Tim Machan's useful anthology of essays is devoted to theoretical and practical issues in editing and interpreting Middle English texts. The issues are, to a degree, the old ones, those that scholars have debated for the past century and more. First, and perhaps most important, is the often-ignored truism that both editors and literary critics ought to work in full knowledge of all the available evidence, codicological, metrical, and historical, what Richard Beadle felicitously calls "the careful cultivation of acquaintance with the primary materials on which a text may be based and its apparatus assembled." Only slightly less central is the discussion of the extent to which editorial intervention can be justified and whether modern editors, like modern museum restoration curators, can or ought to restore ancient works. The analogy between manuscript texts and old paintings is imprecise, primarily because each painting is a work, while each manuscript only attests, with greater and lesser fidelity, to a work. The poem *Pearl* is not to be confused with the graphies in British Library manuscript Cotton Nero A.x. in which it survives, though if the manuscript had not survived into the print era, we would not have the poem. What are responsible editors to do when they are certain that witnesses only imperfectly represent what the author wrote and aware that an indeterminate number of scribes have intervened in the process of copying, each introducing new readings, both inadvertent and intentional?

A. S. G. Edwards argues persuasively in "Editing English Romance: The Limits of Editing, the Limits of Criticism" that no single theory or methodology is adequate to address the multitude of textual traditions we encounter in Middle English texts. Addressing the large and extremely diverse corpus of fictional narratives we have lumped together under the term "verse romance," Edwards describes the material conditions of the production and dissemination of both the poems themselves and the manuscripts in which they survive. Though noting that a mindless editorial conservatism has made many a modern editor "the preserver of the aberrations of transmission," Edwards delineates the historical elements that make genuinely critical editing virtually impossible — the effects of oral transmission, our ignorance of audience and milieu, and (not least) "the untranscendable banality of such texts."

Charlotte Brewer, Ralph Hanna III, and Derek Pearsall address very different literary corpora in the works of Chaucer and Langland. Pearsall addresses emendation *metri causa* in modern editions of Chaucer in an elegant essay full of wit, charity, and good sense, avoiding the *odium philologicum* that tends to mar the work of metrists, whose passions often appear to flare in inverse proportion to the available evidence. However, not everyone will grant the "special claim" for textual authority claimed for the Hengwrt manuscript of *The Canterbury Tales*. Pearsall sometimes appears to have confused the productions of the Hengwrt scribe with the work of the poet, for he steadily characterizes the choice among variants of a metrically regular reading from the Ellesmere (or other) manuscript over a metrically rough reading in Hengwrt as an "emendation." Though retreating gracefully from his condemnation of the editorializing Ellesmere scribe in his edition of *The Nun's Priest's Tale*, Pearsall nevertheless renews his claim for the same editorial propensity. If Chaucer is the first English poet to write iambic pentameter in English, where and how did the Ellesmere scribe develop an ear for iambic pentameter verse superior to the poet's? Pearsall addresses that question neither here nor in his useful edition. Because he does not, I remain unconvinced that editors have misled metrists (or the

233

reverse) because "both seem to have an interest in devising systems that obscure the freedom, variety, and flexibility of Chaucer's meter."

Fully cognizant of the contradictory impulses motivating a modern editor pressed to provide a single authoritative text, "a clean single column inescapably connected with authorial remains and including a minimum patina of visible editorial activity" (p.21), Ralph Hanna in "Presenting Chaucer as Author" shows how such a text is necessarily untrue to the "textual exuberance which comprises Chaucer's fifteenth-century reception." Hanna surveys modern editorial practice regarding the order of tales, the treatment of the birds' roundel in *The Parliament of Fowls* 680–92, and attitudes toward emendation *metri causa*. His sophisticated treatment of metrical fillers shows Hanna's awareness that editors can now perform searches on large data bases to distinguish the *usus scribendi* of individual scribes from that of the poet. He provides examples of his methodology in relation to *ful* and *eek*, suggesting that computerized editors can make choices among manuscript readings on grounds other than intuition or metrical prejudice.

Charlotte Brewer in "Authorial vs. Scribal Writing in *Piers Plowman*" continues a line of argument begun in *The Yearbook of Langland Studies* (1989), where she argued that George Kane's editorial method in producing his *Piers Plowman: the A Version* (1960) is fundamentally flawed by (1) an unrealized circularity owing to Kane's willingness to generalize to difficult cases from the nature of scribal variants when originality is not in doubt and (2) Kane's conviction that none of the A text's variants were authorial. Her description of Kane's method in that essay is crudely parodic, and Kane will perhaps find occasion to point to the inadequacies of Brewer's characterization. The present article, continuing much the same line of argument with respect to the Kane-Donaldson edition of *Piers Plowman* B, includes Brewer's charge that the B editors tended to err often by emending the B archetype in defense of decisions made in editing A. That charge in fact appears to have much to recommend it, as Robert Adams has demonstrated in his clearheaded essay "Editing *Piers Plowman* B: The Imperative of an Intermittently Critical Edition," *SB* 45 (1992): 31–68.

Her second claim, that some of the "better" variants in the B tradition represent authorial revision, is less convincingly argued. Even were all of Brewer's criticisms of Kane and Kane-Donaldson valid, she offers no theory of textual editing to replace the interventionist theory she rejects. I suspect, though it is nowhere clearly stated, that Brewer would wish to produce a "best text" edition of each version, probably with all variants recorded in an apparatus. Would Brewer's editorial principles permit creation of a truly critical edition, one that attempts to separate authorial readings from scribal error? By demanding a standard of absolute certainty for choosing among manuscript variants and for making conjectural emendations, Brewer would appear to make critical editing impossible.

Richard Beadle offers the fruits of his analysis of British Library manuscript Additional 35390, the "Register" of the York Corpus Christi cycle, compiled between 1463 and 1477, citing several instances of faulty critical generalization based only on printed editions. In common with all contributors to this collection, Beadle maintains that both editors and literary critics need to work as directly as possible with the manuscripts and other basic sources. Textual critics need to know codicology and study historical archives as well as understand *recensio, examinatio,* and *emendatio.* Literary critics, for their part, have "a duty to be possessed of all the codicological, philological, and external documentary evidence that might at any point bear upon the interpretative enterprise, which otherwise runs the risk of being inherently flawed."

After deftly summarizing recent scholarship on Middle English lyrics, Julia Boffey, with equal deftness, demonstrates how essential codicological analysis is both to potential editors and to interpreters who approach the "unanchored mysteriousness" of the short poems. Using two short courtly poems, numbers 139 and 140 in Rossell Hope Robbins's *Secular Lyrics of the XIVth and XVth Centuries,* Boffey speculates about their relation to Lydgate's *Temple of Glass,* from which they appear to have been abstracted, about the diverse intentions that may have prompted their copying, and about their original audience and social functions for that audience. Much that we would like to know in order either to interpret or to edit such lyrics, not entirely unexpectedly, turns out to be irrecoverable. Nevertheless, Boffey's arguments open exciting new possibilities for investigators of lyric tradition.

Because devotional works such as Lydgate's *Lyf of Our Lady* or the non-Chaucerian versions of the legend of St. Cecilia have tended to fall outside the mainstream of literary and cultural studies, the essays of George R. Keiser and Sherry L. Reames are welcome for their substantial contributions to our knowledge. Reames demonstrates the existence and nature of textual *mouvance* in the text of the legend in British breviaries, a widely disseminated "quasi-official Latin text." She shows clearly that there was considerable editing by copyists or compilers. Countering the expectations of some scholars that such nonvernacular documents would be resistant to scribal revision, Reames shows that "the need to abbreviate the lessons seems to have been widely perceived as an imperative to convey the gist of each saint's legend in as few words as possible — and the compilers and scribes responded... with considerable independence and ingenuity." In general, the scribes tended to displace allegorical readings with literal ones and to bring the content of each saint's exemplary life into closer accord with the reviser's own cultural values.

Ordinatio in late-medieval vernacular manuscripts is George Keiser's concern in "*Ordinatio* in the Manuscripts of John Lydgate's *Lyf of Our Lady*: Its Value for the Reader, Its Challenge for the Modern Editor," but in passing he has sensible things to say about the works of Chaucer, Gower, Nicholas Love, and Malory. Until recently, modern editors of Lydgate (and most other English medieval works) have tended to ignore the layout of the manuscript page, attributing such physical features to scribes rather than authors and thus throwing away valuable evidence about authorial meanings. Keiser points to critical misconceptions that have resulted from such editorial fecklessness.

Tim Machan's "Late Middle English Texts and the Higher and Lower Criticism" is in many ways at odds with the achievement of the volume it introduces. Under the dual influences of Jerome J. McGann's critique of the Bowers-Tanselle school of textual scholarship and of recent critical theories that prompt his observation that "valorization" of the authorial text is "necessarily an interpretive imposition on the manuscript evidence," Machan argues that critical editing "is only one of the things, and perhaps the most historically problematic, which one can do with a medieval work." Postmodernist critics will find much to admire in Machan's essay, but textual scholars of a more traditional stripe will be glad that the other contributors work from more empirically based epistemologies.

HOYT N. DUGGAN
University of Virginia

C. WILLIAM MARX and JEANNE F. DRENNAN, eds. *The Middle English Prose* Complaint of Our Lady *and* Gospel of Nicodemus. Middle English Texts, vol. 19. Heidelberg: Carl Winter, 1987. Pp. 232. DM 112 paper.

The Complaint of Our Lady (*Planctus Mariae*) and *The Gospel of Nicodemus* in their various forms were common, if not popular in the modern sense, in the late Middle Ages and are well known to medieval scholars, who, if they differ on some of the specific lines of influence, agree that such influence was very great indeed. There is virtually no medieval literary genre that is not profoundly affected by these "eyewitness" accounts of Christ's trial, passion, death, descent into Hell, and resurrection. It is only natural that two such works would fall together and even be combined in medieval collections of religious and devotional works. The form represented in the volume here reviewed is an extended *planctus*, or "complaint," of the Virgin, to which is attached a greatly abbreviated *Gospel of Nicodemus*.

Editors C. William Marx and Jeanne F. Drennan present in this volume the two texts that often appeared together in both French and English versions, the French being the original of the one which was translated into Middle English, instead of the Latin versions, especially of *The Gospel of Nicodemus*, which were current all over Europe in the late Middle Ages. The principal text reproduced and edited here is Cambridge, Magdalene College, manuscript Pepys 2498 (hereafter P). This version is frequently emended from two other English texts, and beneath the English one is supplied a parallel Anglo-Norman text of the same material, which, although not the actual source of the Middle English versions, is the closest known to survive, according to the editors. As well, there is appended a complete edition of another fairly close Middle English version, edited from Henry Huntington Library manuscript HM 144 (hereafter called Hh). To these is added a complete critical apparatus — an extensive critical and editorial introduction, commentary on the English texts, a brief glossary, and a bibliography — which together accounts for nearly two-thirds of the volume. Indeed, the featured text takes up only 63 pages.

The editors emend their text of P freely, especially from Leeds University Library manuscript Brotherton 501 (hereafter Br), and provide a full array of variants both beneath the texts and in the following commentaries. I have not had the opportunity to compare the manuscripts with the edited texts, but the editors are meticulous and so generous with variants that one could hardly wish for more. Though their emendations sometimes seem unnecessary, they rarely seem forced or unreasonable. The editors are not so ambitious as to attempt a reconstruction of the original, like Kane-Donaldson with *Piers Plowman*, but the emendations are so frequent that the result is an edition of no existing version, though with some labor one can reconstruct P from the variants. The editorial procedure is described in the following passage:

. . . the text in P is the best representative of the early ME version of the sequence in that it is overall closest to the ME translation. It is not identical with it but preserves better than do the other ME manuscripts the form and substance of the ME translation. Emendations [from Br and Hh] to P correct obvious scribal errors. . . . Occasionally conjectural emendation has been used for this purpose. Also Br and Hh contain some readings which . . . are clearly closer to those in the original ME translation than their counterparts in P, and here readings from Br or Hh have been adopted in the edited text. In these instances the rejected readings make sense in context, but have been treated as errors because they reflect scribal misreading or substitution. A more rigorous policy would see such rejected readings as genuine features of the recension of the text represented by P and would allow them to stand, but emended readings have been adopted here in order to give the reader a better sense of how the translator handled the AN text. [Pp.70–71]

What this amounts to is that, after the admission that the definitive versions of the Anglo-Norman original and its Middle English translation no longer exist, the editors still feel free to emend as though they knew fairly precisely the exact contents of these documents. However, the editors have been so generous with the listing of these rejected readings and other variants that more conservative researchers like me can reconstruct P, though with considerable effort. This, however, is mere difference in editorial ideology, and Marx and Drennan seem to have kept close to their stated principles, which is all one can reasonably ask.

The apparatus is another matter and, with its many tables, lists, charts, and commentary, seems frequently liable to the charge of overkill. Also, the philosophy that led to the listing of certain variants at the foot of the text and of others in the commentary is not clear at all. The introduction contains some rather naïve statements, like the observation that in *The Complaint of Our Lady* the "largest element in the narrative is drawn from the Bible [!]" (p. 26) and that about the "reviser's preference for the Vulgate" (p. 58) — preference over what at this time — the English Wycliffite version, which was a translation of the Vulgate?

The editors also seem misled by fondness for the text, over which they have spent so much time that they fall into the error of claiming too much for it. No one familiar with medieval manuscripts is likely to be surprised by the yoking together of two even remotely (and in some instances apparently unrelated) texts, and one can only wonder about statements that the redactor "recognized the integrity of each but also had a sense of the larger narrative possibilities of the sequence" (p.8). The fact is that in this version the *Complaint* and the *Gospel* do not merge or complement each other very well. Their unity comes only from their common concern about events before, during, and after the passion. *The Gospel of Nicodemus* is especially likely to be drawn into collections of passion materials and outright romance cycles as well. The editors' point would be greatly strengthened if Mary were made the narrator of the *Gospel* as well, and medieval adaptors were certainly not above such modifications, but that is not what has happened here. As well, the attempt to pull in the *Revelaciones* of St. Bridget of Sweden as a source for the *Complaint* is rather forced. Also, after pages of argument held together with words like "if," "might," "could," and "problematic" (a favorite of the editors), one finds it difficult to accept absolute statements like "there is no possibility that Hh is derived independently from the AN text" (p. 23).

I could quibble on about such matters, but I do not wish to detract too much from the genuine service Marx and Drennan have rendered medieval scholarship. This certainly is a good buy—three full texts in two languages—and either a serviceable or excellent edition, depending on how closely one agrees with the editors' editorial philosophy.

Actually, my main problem with this book is one of aesthetics, and one that I share with many others, especially now, when books like this are so expensive and camera-ready copy can look very professional indeed. In a paperback priced at DM 112, one has a right to expect something that looks like a real book—not just like a reduced typescript, which in fact this actually is. The overstamped *p* and *b* for *þ* is especially hard on the eye. This, however, should more properly be laid at the feet of the publishers and printers than at those of the editors, who have made available to us manuscript texts that most of us up to now have known only through scant references in books often difficult to find.

JERRY L. BALL
Arkansas State University

MALDWYN MILLS, JENNIFER FELLOWS, and CAROL M. MEALE, eds. *Romance in Medieval England*. Cambridge: D. S. Brewer, 1991. Pp. viii, 228. $70.00.

This collection of essays grew out of a conference on "Medieval Romance in England," held at the University of Wales Conference Centre, in Gregynog,

Newtown, on August 23–26, 1988, which also served as the initial meeting of the Society for the Study of Medieval Romance. The society and its conference, like the collection itself, exclude Arthurian romances and the Arthurian sections of chronicles as well as all vernacular romances of Continental origin.

Like many of the romance collections it studies, *Medieval Romance in England* is a fine miscellany that makes little effort toward unity. The book aims "to exemplify some of the most significant recent trends in literary studies in general. Notable among these are an interest in women's history and female points of view; in the application of Marxist theory to literary texts; and in the reception of texts." Yet the volume remains firmly rooted in codicological and literary-historical approaches, and it is these far from recent methodologies that make for the more important contributions here to romance studies.

In the opening essay, "Editing Middle English Romances," Jennifer Fellows offers a sensible overview of editorial methodologies: recension, "an editorial method devised by classical scholars for the treatments of classical texts"; the single-text edition; the "eclectic," or "direct-method," edition; and the parallel-text edition. Using *Sir Bevis of Hampton* as her focus for an analysis of the effectiveness of these four, she shows the illogic of recension: "The editor must go some way towards editing the text in order to identify what may be termed 'error' and to formulate the stemma which will be used to justify editorial choices. So the recensional method is also a circular one." The eclectic and the single-text methodologies are also found wanting, for one text is "implicitly exalted to a position of authority." Fellows favors, therefore, the parallel-text method, despite its expense, concluding that the ideal editor has the duty "to edit and, as far as possible, to present his/her readers with a readable text or texts. The ideal to be aimed at here, I think, is to correct but not to try to improve—to account for and, where appropriate, eliminate obvious error, to clarify obvious nonsense, to establish the 'right' reading *for that* text—but not to attempt to get at the ultimate source of that reading."

Fellows's essay is a fitting prelude to four important essays on medieval and postmedieval manuscripts and manuscript collections. John J. Thompson draws attention to the diversity of fifteenth-century English book-production procedures in the period before printing by isolating and studying three manuscript miscellanies: Lincoln, Dean and Chapter Library, manuscript 91, one of two manuscripts copied by Robert Thornton; Edinburgh, National Library of Scotland, manuscript Advocates' 19.3.1, the northeast Midlands collection associated with a scribe called Hegge;

and Cambridge, University Library, manuscript Ff.1.6, a manuscript copied by more than forty scribes and usually associated with the Findern family. Gillian Rogers describes in detail the Percy Folio: its compiler was "a collector, an antiquarian, an addict of popular, sensational literature," who, "wittingly or not, performed a valuable service to posterity in preserving, in however imperfect a form, a microcosm of seventeenth-century popular taste." The scribe of Oxford, Bodleian Library, manuscript Ashmole 61, according to Lynne S. Blanchfield, altered the versification and reshaped his many texts toward a religious and family bias: the devotional content of the manuscript "has a greater priority than the entertainment value. The patterns of adaptation show the scribal editing to be purposeful and slanted towards a family preaching context." And Carol M. Meale examines New York, Pierpont Morgan Library, manuscript M 876, containing *Generides*, "to investigate how the romance may have been perceived by some, at least, of its earliest readers, and to suggest ways in which the text was presented to meet the specific requirements of a fifteenth-century audience": the romance appears in an up-to-date, luxury book where illustrations and rubrics work together to produce a text more accessible to the reader.

These four essays testify to the importance of understanding the manuscript collection in its historical context to appreciate the individual romance. The implicit — and sometimes explicit — intentions of the scribe reveal new dimensions of the romance and attest to the wisdom of Fellows's own concluding advocacy of "a movement *away from* traditional editorial assumptions as to the desirability of pursuing archetypes and *towards* a greater respect for scribal intention and the individuality of variant texts."

Two equally important contributions focus on "women's history and female points of view." In the unfortunately — and vaguely — mistitled study "Female Perspectives in Romance and History," Rosamund Allen offers an incisive account of Layamon's portraits of women: he focuses on "the woman as a member of a family group, not as an individual making an impact on another individual and voicing her own impressions," and depicts "the violence of medieval society conventionally veiled by chivalry, but then offers a critique of that violence through the women and their private values of family stability, which reactivates the sense of public duty." And Judith Weiss contrasts twelfth-century Anglo-Norman romances with those of France of the same period to show that the Anglo-Norman writings are unique in their presentation of wooing women, both attractive and formidable figures, who are capable of making their own choices and decisions; such figures seem ominously absent from the French romances.

Other interesting essays include a careful reexamination by S. H. A. Shepherd of *The Sege of Malayne*, David Burnley's interesting analysis of the epic moment of "comforting the troops" as it reappears in popular romance, and Elizabeth Williams's detailed account of the motif of "hunting the deer" in the Middle English romance and the saint's life.

Many miscellanies contain only a few interesting essays. *Romance in Medieval England* contains a larger-than-average number of fine essays, and a few of them, I suspect, will come to be regarded as seminal essays in their field.

DAVID STAINES
University of Ottawa

RICHARD NEUSE. *Chaucer's Dante: Allegory and Epic Theater in* The Canterbury Tales. Berkeley, Los Angeles, and Oxford: University of California Press, 1991. Pp. xi, 295. $42.00.

From the early nineteenth century, when the Reverend Cary made his first few simple notes on the correspondences between Dante's *Divine Comedy* and Chaucer's *Canterbury Tales*, to the late twentieth century (when Howard Schless made a gathering of their verbal and thematic correspondence), scholarship has generally approached the subject of the influence of Dante upon Chaucer on largely philological grounds. Under the influence of the great scholars of the early part of our century, it has been accepted that the influence of Dante upon Chaucer has been profound; and the idea has been pressed that Chaucer may have known Dante's work in minute detail, that, far more than in verbal correspondences alone, *The Divine Comedy* underlies much of Chaucer's poetry as a referent, as I have said elsewhere, "even as a touchstone, for much in Chaucer that is merely glancing or oblique." Now, in the last decade or so, scholarship has re-addressed itself to the more purely thematic and ideational relationships between the two poets, with an underlying assumption that Dante was everywhere present in Chaucer's mind. The methods used are for the most part the wide-ranging techniques of the meta-criticisms of our time, which, in their newness, have the capacity to challenge and to expand what may be assumed to be true. Neuse now invites us into an ongoing debate on the ways in which Chaucer may be deemed to have appropriated Dante to his use; he presents his case in eight chapters centered around a variety of theses: *The Canterbury Tales* is closely modeled on *The Divine Comedy*; the *Tales* has an overarching plot (much like that of the *Comedy*), part of which is to be read as an attack upon the deleterious aspect of allegory; both poems are quest journeys in which either an individual or a group searches for a lost image of itself; Chaucer's pilgrims are, like Dante's blessed in the Empyrean, engaged in a symposium; the context in which the poems are presented is that of epic theater, i.e., long narratives, often of a political nature, employing the multivoiced method of drama. The first four chapters lay out his theoretical assumptions; the remaining chapters attempt several demonstrations.

In each poem the pilgrim-narrator is the catalyst and primary character who has his alter ego in each character he creates and who in a sense speaks for him in a dramatic mode. As all actors do, they create their characters, "bodying" themselves forth entire as human beings compounded of body and soul, recognizable by the audience as truly human selves freed from the suffocating grip of any idealization or allegory that tends to separate body from soul. In this formulation Dante's experience as a pilgrim interacting with the persons he encounters is recapitulated piece by piece in the experiences of Chaucer's several pilgrims. Both poets are striving, Neuse suggests, for a depiction of a true original self, seen not necessarily as a child of God but as a part of an entire fallen creation in search of its identity.

Common to both poets, Neuse believes, is the recognition of the erotic in nature as the means by which the human being gives recognition to his human-ness, his body-ness. It is this thesis that comes to dominate the second half of the book. Like *The Divine Comedy, The Canterbury Tales* is an account of a personal spiritual experience; thus the *Tales* becomes Chaucer's spiritual autobiography imagined in and through the individual pilgrims, in which he leaves behind Boccaccio's antique world and emerges as the creator of a popular epic, a secular scripture.

For Neuse the Geryon episode in *Inferno* 16–17 becomes an epiphanous moment in which the poet discovers the possibility of an epic poem "in which the past may be rewritten or rewrite itself in such a way as to recuperate a lost authenticity." In short, Dante's fears (p. 68) suggest that the poem has taken on a beastlike life of its own for both Virgil and Dante, being symbolic of the treacherous and fraudulent medium of poetic language, Geryon's decorated hide being a metaphor of sorts for an alluring purely ornamental art. Only by recognition of the duplicity and instability of poetic language can Dante continue his search for "the authentic human image in this life" (p. 70). Neuse imputes to Dante a desire to escape from

243

his task, directing anger and sullenness at the authoritarian Virgil. None-theless, he has learned a great lesson, namely, that he is "no (longer) Geryon" (p. 83), i.e., a deceiver. While the pilgrim Dante experiences a moment of personal illumination, it is not Chaucer but we who as readers of *The Canterbury Tales* are encouraged in our common pursuit of "nostra effige" (p. 87).

In Neuse's chapter dealing with epic theater, the Knight is seen as coldly aristocratic, a distanced ironist, while the Miller is viewed as representing the forces of rampant life and creativity; the one coldly remote from his subject, the other fully involved with his subject, but pagan and potentially diabolical; the story yields for the audience some interesting conclusions: the hot coultour may be seen as signifying the hostility and repressed anger men feel toward women, while Alison's posture at the shot window is an affront aimed ultimately at all men and their unceasing quest for "taille." Nicholas, taking delight in having tricked the carpenter and Absolon, is like Dante's demon Barbariccia. Thus, what is feared and abhorred in an uncontrolled eros is rather to be interpreted as the acting out of the "unaccountable plenitude of creation." More has been learned: the Miller's cynical words to the Reeve about his refusal to inquire too closely into his wife's sexual wanderings are seen here as praise of a union in which free persons respect "the otherness of the other" (p. 135).

The second half of the book has to do mainly with specific applications of the similarities between the Italian and English poets. More interesting than the discussion of the Friar and the Summoner (which lacks something of Neuse's usual enthusiasm) is the essay dealing with *The Monk's Tale* as a response to *The Divine Comedy*. Though much smaller in scale, it still constitutes "a meditation on history as a record of mankind's struggle for autonomy and freedom." This lesson is to be perceived throughout the human condition, whether in exalted or degraded persons. The Monk, Neuse thinks, provides a critique of providential theories of history and challenges any assumptions of justice as the operative force in the world. Here, he maintains, Chaucer and Dante are aligned in their refusal to accept any notion of theodicy (though one needs to ask whether the examples of Nebuchadnezzar and Balthasar do not imply the opposite). Neuse sees the Monk as a figure of considerable intellectual acumen, whose tales offer a view of humanity working not with divine assistance but with will and strength of character. This humanistic view of a radical indi-viduality has its element of optimism: in the midst of the most catastrophic failures, whether due to sin, error, or simply "misfortune," "there is a vision of hope for humanity" (p. 150). The Ugolino episode, by its full-scale demolishment of any notion of justice, says Neuse, becomes a "grotesque parody of Christianity," with the suggestion that hell implies a vengeful God "who is, in a manner of speaking, a cannibal to his own creation" (p. 155). With the further example of Croesus, who by dying on a tree becomes a Christus and whose dream becomes a parodic version of the Crucifixion, Neuse concludes that the church's view of the Crucifixion as "a definitive cosmic and historic event is a subtle form of paganism." We must not conclude, Neuse suggests, that the tragedies are an expression of pessimism or despair. On the contrary, for the audience in the theater, they provide beneficial insights into the conduct of life. The deaths of Samson, Hercules, and the nefarious Nero have something of the heroic about them, the working out of autonomy and freedom. Even Lucifer, the monster with three heads and their ghastly preys, represents the urge for freedom and independence (p. 195), and his tears should cause the audience to recognize their interdependence and their responsibility toward and for each other (p. 195).

For Neuse, *The Clerk's Tale* provides a point of conversion for the Clerk, as he comes to develop doubts, in the process of composing his *Tale*, about the truth of the Petrarchan idealization of women. In short, he becomes less interested in the spiritual truths Petrarch's version seeks to express than in a critiquing of the narrative itself. The idealization of women is interpreted as a form of masculine tyranny, an effort to disguise the fear of death and of change. Moving between allegorical and literal levels of the tale, Neuse's Clerk sees Walter as apprehensive about marriage to a social inferior and the prospect of an heir who will replace him. Griselda is indicted for offering her child up to death as a way of saving her own life. When Griselda cries out, "Deth may noght make no comparisoun unto youre love," the words produce in Neuse the explanation: "The world we consider home is in fact ruled by a dark and arbitrary power that turns it into a battleground and earthly life into a brief holding action that ends with a violent defeat for everyone" (p. 233). For the Clerk, this oppression of woman becomes, tropologically, "repression of the instincts, a hatred for life in the flesh, and a theology in which God and Satan become interchangeable" (p. 234). The envoy, however, saves the Clerk. By invoking the Wife of Bath, he finds an answer to the fear of death; her robustness becomes a battle cry for women. For the moment, says Neuse, the Wife of Bath is his Beatrice (p. 240).

In his final chapter Neuse sums up some of his views by means of *The Merchant's Tale*. For both Dante and Chaucer marriage is the mirror of society and civilization. January's conventional views of marriage as a benign sacrament, even of youth and age, becomes an "indirect critique of

Christendom's fixation on the penitential and its opposition to eroticism" (p. 251). By way of parody, January becomes a type of Dante entering into his Solomonic union with Beatrice, and the symbols of garden, well, and fountain are clearly expressions escaping from a dammed-up psyche. Nonetheless, the Merchant is openly at work censoring his *Tale*, setting aside the allegorical implications of the Song of Songs, which are for him part of the repressive allegory of clerics. By way of Claudian's *De raptu Proserpinae*, May's marriage is seen as a form of "otherworldly" bondage from which the gallant adulterer Damyan is unable to rescue her. As the Wife of Bath has reminded us, Pluto, his wife, and the fairies "point to an age before an ascetically inspired exegesis had read or written the erotic out of the sacred text," and the fate of women in the time of Christianity is to become objects of fear or desire. In the curing of January's blindness we have "a perfect instance of the mystery of conception, birth, and death "in the unintelligible and unknowable continuity which is the secret of eroticism" (p. 262). Neuse closes with the assertion that the admission into literary discourse of the obscene, the repulsive, the grotesque, the blasphemous "constitutes part of Chaucer's redefinition in the *Canterbury Tales* of epic decorum" (p. 264).

Neuse displays a sportive irony in asking us to believe in the Miller as a kind of Socrates, the Wife of Bath as Beatrice, *Sir Thopas* as an inverted model of the whole *Canterbury Tales*. When he attaches special importance to Dante's use of the word *nuovo*, he generalizes from too few instances (Dante uses the word more than 100 times). His thesis about epic theater neglects the implications of Plato's discussion of the three radicals of presentation, and the metaphor does not get us much farther along than the earlier view of it as, in its middle, a kind of satura. Most difficult to deal with is the rejection of allegory as the suppressor of one aspect of man's nature, while substituting for it a variety of modern allegorical approaches, with echoes of Freud and Jung, of which his own is the most provocative and elaborate to date. Though one wishes to quarrel with it at virtually every juncture, it is a stimulating read. It is wide-ranging, though much too selective in its bibliographical support, and it is unfortunate that in its earnest desire to see *The Divine Comedy* as Chaucer's ever-present vade mecum, it neglects to pay proper respect to the *Roman de la Rose*, to Boccaccio (dismissed largely as a creator of antique inventions), and to Ovid, among others, in whom there is a strong affinity with the erotic as a component of human nature, and who also employ the modes of address that Neuse associates with epic theater.

PAUL G. RUGGIERS
University of Oklahoma

CHARLES A. OWEN, JR. *The Manuscripts of* The Canterbury Tales. Chaucer Studies, vol. 17. Cambridge: D. S. Brewer, 1991. Pp. xii, 132. $70.00.

I find Charles Owen's book a necessary prolegomenon to a major and desired study — a full narrative history of the transmission of Chaucer's *Canterbury Tales*. Such a study would rest upon extensive hands-on examination of all the manuscripts, regardless of what may have been said in the past about their textual centrality. And Owen's volume, predicated on just such studies (and, importantly, on a chronologically ordered narrative history), offers some substantial and important rethinkings of basic facts about the transmission. Yet, like all other prolegomena, the volume will lend itself to protracted expansion — and expansion which avoids the debilities of Owen's scholarship — underreliance on modern codicology and illogical argumentation.

Owen makes very clear at the outset the goals and emphases of his study. Past reconsiderations of the problem, he says,

fail to meet what I have come to see as the two crucial tests for theories about *Canterbury Tales* manuscripts. They do not account successfully for the Hengwrt manuscript; they do not explain the wide difference in the number of independent textual traditions for different parts of the *Canterbury Tales*. [P. 2]

Although rather different claims, these two goals often interface productively in Owen's account of *Canterbury Tales* manuscripts. On the one hand, Owen staunchly and wisely opposes Norman Blake's theories of the origins of the Hengwrt manuscript. Blake argues that Hengwrt came directly from Chaucer's papers, that it comprised a full single set of exemplars, and that those exemplars remained intact for use by all other

247

early *Canterbury Tales* compilers;[1] in contrast, Owen adopts the more probable view that Hg is but one product of several early efforts at collecting *membra disiecta* and that its archetypes, although they apparently remained collected and could very occasionally be accessed by much later scribes (notably the one who copied Christ Church [Oxford] manuscript 152), in fact had no universal availability.

Yet more productively, Owen generalizes the situation faced by the Hengwrt production team and in doing so essentially inverts the broad textual history usually constructed for the *Tales*. This, in spite of a salutary article by Daniel S. Silvia,[2] has usually privileged Manly-Rickert's[3] "constant groups" — i.e., those where full *Tales* exemplars remained intact for several generations of copyists — and has found these the central (and typifying) mode by which *The Canterbury Tales* was transmitted. Against this view Owen vigorously and largely successfully contends. He demonstrates, especially in a variety of post-1450 instances, the palpable unavailability to many scribes of any single full archetype for the *Tales* and those scribes' necessary involvement in collection procedures precisely like those engaged in by the Hengwrt team and other early copyists. Owen thus resituates our sense of the transmission by arguing that the *Tales* as such did not commonly exist but that separate bundles of small groups of *Tales* were widely available. This demonstration, for him, fulfills his second stated argumentative goal.

But does it? Owen shows in a generally logical way how multiple traditions for individual tales might develop. In the context of many individual loose tales one should discover substantial scribal dissimilation of the text. But such a view does not logically address the more important question Owen has posed — why the multiple traditions are differently multiple for different tales or why, given the manuscript survival, they should have the exact distribution (two lines of descent for *The Parson's Tale*, twelve for *The*

---

[1] See, most extensively, N. F. Blake, *The Textual Tradition of the* Canterbury Tales (Baltimore, Md.: Edward Arnold, 1985). I have offered one form of rebuttal to Blake's project, which is in most ways in conformity with Owen's views, in "The Hengwrt Manuscript and the Canon of *The Canterbury Tales,*" *English Manuscript Studies, 1100–1700* 1 (1989): 64–84.

[2] Daniel S. Silvia, "Some Fifteenth-Century Manuscripts of the *Canterbury Tales,*" in Beryl Rowland, ed., *Chaucer and Middle English Studies in Honour of Rossell Hope Robbins* (London: Allen and Unwin, 1974), pp. 153–63.

[3] The indispensable John M. Manly and Edith Rickert, eds., *The Text of the* Canterbury Tales, 8 vols. (Chicago: University of Chicago Press, 1940); hereafter, in the notes, MR. In the notes I also adopt, without signal, the traditional abbreviations for Chaucer's works and the conventional sigla of manuscripts.

Franklin's Tale; p. 3) they do. Owen broaches an extremely important question; answering it adequately will have to be left to others.

Those who take up this challenge will need to avoid another logical difficulty inherent in Owen's argumentation. If transmission occurs by the individual tale or the small group, then study of "the manuscripts of *CT*" as integers (Owen's general method) cannot ever contact the vicissitudes to which individual tales have been subjected. Only isolated histories of the individual texts—a history which necessarily must utilize Owen's discussion of full manuscript contexts—can perform that job.[4]

Yet, although Owen studies manuscripts as wholes and often tells us a great deal about their external appearances, fundamentally the weakest parts of his arguments are codicological. Indeed, Owen's volume might more accurately be titled *The Manuscript Transmission of The Canterbury Tales*. Any variety of misleading codicological assessments, many integral to or slanted to support Owen's argument, might be singled out here. For example, the inferred change of affiliation of Cambridge University manuscript D.4.24 at A 1880 from an Ellesmere to Hengwrt version of *The Knight's Tale* (see pp. 12–13, 17) is unlikely to have been the result of damage to the archetype: this scribe Wytton, who routinely consulted multiple exemplars (cf. the nearly infamous correction procedures at D 44a–44f) initially acquired *The Knight's Tale* through two eight-leaf quires of roughly 32 lines per page.[5] For whatever reason, he had no access to additional quires from this copy and completed the *Tale* from a different source.

Frequently Owen's arguments fail to command respect because of his apparent unawareness of total codicological context. He overdefers to Manly-Rickert and ignores, sometimes willfully, more recent relevant developments. Simply consider a few comments about Cambridge University manuscript Gg.4.27: why does he retain (pp. 4–5 n. 11, 23) Manly-Rickert's relatively late dating (and defer discussion of the manuscript for

---

[4] And such a study should especially address the construction of the early benchmark manuscripts (Cp Dd El Gg Ha⁴ Hg La) in exactly the way Owen does, for example, Ht and Ra², pp. 61–64. Owen's silence on this point seems to imply that these are uninterrogable, but Dan Mosser's fine unpublished work on Dd would suggest otherwise.

[5] The Dd shift can only be inferred from its *Dd* cogeners, especially En¹: Owen follows uncritically such loci as MR 1:102, not his own inspection of Dd, where the relevant leaf (quire 2, fol. 1) is lost. The exemplar quires included A 859–1880 = 1,022 lines = 32 (the number of pages in 1–2⁸) × 31.94 (the number of lines per page), two lines short of 32 × 32. Dd belongs to a line of descent completely unrelated to El and Hg in *GP*, and affiliation with either manuscript would presuppose a break in exemplar supply at A 858.

two chapters), in the light of Parkes and Beadle's discussion? Why does he quote (p. 23) Manly-Rickert's statement that the texts are "comparatively unedited," in the light of Kane's discussion of the scribe's handling of *The Legend of Good Women*? Why does he second (p. 23) Manly-Rickert's claim of "access to special sources," in the light of the scribe's *Troilus and Criseyde* (which came to him in quires from two separate manuscripts, each of differing inferior textual traditions, although both pretty certainly from the London book trade)?[6] In following outdated views in these instances and others, Owen manages to present issues of lively intellectual debate as if finally adjudicated half a century ago.

Problems like these become pandemic in even the strongest parts of Owen's survey, the discussion of loose texts. Frequently, seeing these productions in the full context of a scribal oeuvre would reveal Owen's claims as nothing more than special pleading. Consider, for example, Owen's discussion of Huntington manuscript HM 144 (pp. 117–18), a manuscript in eight booklets, one (fols. 81–112) containing *The Tale of Melibee* and *The Monk's Tale*. This professional scribe — he also copied Oxford, Trinity College manuscript 29, another collection of excerpts from Caxton's *Polychronicon* (as fols. 54v–64 here) — presumptively was producing cheap small collections, a quire or two, for selection by patrons of a London shop about 1500;[7] to argue that this production demonstrates lack of access to a full *Canterbury Tales* thoroughly ignores the piecemeal construction of the entire book, likely simply a representation of a single buyer's taste. Or again, consider Longleat manuscript 29 (see pp. 105–106), which, in a large booklet (fols. 19–130) contains an important Rolle collection, Hilton's *Medled Life*, and *The Parson's Tale* (from the same exemplar as Ellesmere).[8] I fail to see how this survival testifies to any form of *Canterbury*

---

[6] See, respectively, *The Poetical Works of Geoffrey Chaucer: A Facsimile of Cambridge University Library Ms Gg.4.27*, 3 vols. (Norman: Pilgrim, 1979–80), 3:6ff.; "The Text of *The Legend of Good Women* in CUL Ms Gg.4.27," in Douglas Gray and E. G. Stanley, eds., *Middle English Studies Presented to Norman Davis* (Oxford: Clarendon Press, 1983), pp. 39–58; and my "The Manuscripts and the Transmission of Chaucer's *Troilus*," in James Dean and Christian K. Zacher, eds., *The Idea of Medieval Literature* (Newark: University of Delaware Press, 1992), the results communicated orally to Owen before publication.

[7] Cf. his versions (fols. 21–54v) of two connected "early London" texts (first copied in Cambridge, Magdalene College, MS Pepys 2498).

[8] Most recently described by S. J. Ogilvie-Thomson, *Richard Rolle: Prose and Verse* (EETS, vol. 293), pp. xvii–xxxi, with substantial revisions (see esp. pp. xxx–xxxi) of MR 1:343–48, which Owen follows dutifully. Owen's claim for El editing, p. 106 (and thus that there was a twin exemplar used by Ll²), is a further example of overreliance on MR. See George Kane, "John M. Manly and Edith Rickert," in Paul G. Ruggiers, ed., *Editing Chaucer: The Great Tradition* (Norman: Pilgrim, 1984), pp. 220–23: El's variations from other manuscripts are entirely consonant with a simple scribal copying, rather than a text rigorously preedited, and the need to postulate any second archetype is thus obviated.

Tales circulation. In an anthology devoted to the love of God (and including a form of confession, fols. 24v–29v, 31), I cannot imagine any other appropriate Canterbury tales, but I can imagine a production team that knew Chaucer's whole collection simply ignoring most of it in favor of a brief yet precise and comprehensive sacramental tract that they tailored to fit the manuscript. In the analysis of these and other copies Owen frequently raises telling and provocative points. But, as in various other instances, scholars of greater codicological acumen will need to test these points thoroughly. They will then bring Owen's useful first assay at a full transmission history toward completion.

RALPH HANNA III
University of California, Riverside

LEE PATTERSON. *Chaucer and the Subject of History*. Madison: University of Wisconsin Press, 1991. Pp. xiv, 489. $45.00 cloth, $14.95 paper.

Chaucer and the Subject of History has been much anticipated as a major contribution to the "historicizing" reinterpretation of Chaucer's poetry. In fact, this impressive, ambitious study manifests resistance as well as adherence to the New Historicism.

In his editorial introduction to *Literary Practice and Social Change in England, 1380–1530* (1990), Patterson subscribes wholeheartedly to Fredric Jameson's motto "Always historicize!" (p. 1). By contrast, the afterword to the present work offers a more nuanced credo:

"Think socially" is one of the mottos that has been in my mind as I tried to understand the shape of Chaucer's career and the claims of his writing. . . . In this book I have tried to think socially about Chaucer. In terms of scholarly practice, this has meant locating each of his texts in relation to a discourse — a specific set of texts and practices — that can make explicit the social meaning of his poetry. . . . Nonetheless this program has been tempered, at times even countered, by a different concern. For surely it is a mistake to think that the only meaning worth explicating is social meaning. . . . However much they may have served to mystify the concrete relations of social power, neither liberalism nor individualism can be simply banished into the outer darkness of the politically incorrect. [Pp. 423–24]

Hence Patterson renounces "absolutizing, totalizing schemes" in favor of "the specific, the particular, the local, and the contingent," because it is "here that the *relationship* between the individual and the social, in all its irreducible complexity, becomes visible. It is finally this relationship, as it is worked out in both Chaucer's poetic career and in his writing, that I have tried to understand" (p. 425; author's italics).

In the introduction to *Chaucer and the Subject of History*, Patterson defines this relationship in terms of two impulses battling for primacy in Chaucer's poetry. One is a "modernist" impulse to deny historical process a role in the construction of subjectivity. (Patterson relates this impulse to Chaucer's socially "anomalous situation. . . . Not bourgeois, not noble, not clerical, he nonetheless participates in all these communities. Surely this sense of marginality. . . is related to the sense of subjectivity, the sense of a selfhood that stands apart from *all* community" [p. 39; author's italics].) The other is a vivid perception of history as inescapable, language as inherently equivocal, and character as contingent, changeable, and thus subject to temporality. Hence "the Chaucerian imagination is at once caught within the middling world of history and haunted by the dream of origins" (p. 20), and as a result the poetry "everywhere records the attraction of modernity but is finally unwilling to annul its own historicity" (p. 21). In short, Chaucer's famous, almost universally applauded fascination with "character" functions "as one term in an oppositional dialectic constituted on the other side by history, . . . the persistent presence of the past and the pressure of social realities" (p. 11).

Chaucer and the Subject of History traces this dialectic through two main phases in Chaucer's poetry, each occupying four of the book's eight chapters. In the first phase, under the influence of court culture, Chaucer avoids contemporary history by "staging the problematic of historical action in terms of antiquity" (p. 25), in *Anelida and Arcite, Troilus and Criseyde, The Knight's Tale*, and *The Legend of Good Women*. In the second, i.e., in *The Canterbury Tales*, he investigates "not just the idea of history. . . but the historical world itself" (p. 26).

Chapter 1, " 'Thirled with the Poynt of Remembraunce': The Theban Writing of *Anelida and Arcite*," analyzes this little-read poem as "an exploration of the Theban condition refracted through the tropes of Ovidian eroticism" (p. 201)—an exploration that calls into question any attempt to ground history or subjectivity in a hypothetical point of original, empowering stability.

Chapter 2, "*Troilus and Criseyde* and the Subject of History," traces the same pattern of frustration inscribed in Chaucer's greatest narrative poem, which retells Boccaccio's story of love in Troy only to discover that "the modernist desire for originality, for a new beginning founded on an antique moment of true beginning, was impossible of fulfillment; and that the notion of the self as an analogously ahistorical entity, self-identical and socially autonomous, was equally illusory" (p. 169). Patterson offers analyses of medieval views of history (religious and secular-aristocratic) and of Trojan historiography (Latin and vernacular), in support of his argument that the story of Troy's fall, "the originary moment of secular history," is both "an overwhelming catastrophe" and "a catastrophe whose causes are obscure, whose events stand in a painfully enigmatic relationship to the individual, and whose ultimate meaning resists decipherment," thus making "the Trojan story a continual anxiety for the medieval historical consciousness."

No less unsettling is *Troilus and Criseyde*'s presentation of subjectivity "as a site where not one but many intentions — in effect, many selves — are in a ceaseless process of constitution" (p. 142). Reflecting the inability of medieval historians of Troy to make sense of the relationship between individual effort or culpability and Troy's fall, *Troilus* invites and foils our desire to see a stable relationship between this "equivocal subjectivity" and the "doubled history" in which the poem encloses it. "We can establish clear causal lines in neither direction; the poem will not allow us to say that the failed love of Troilus and Criseyde causes the fall of Troy nor that the fall of Troy causes the failure of the love affair" (p. 152).

Hence, baffled in its attempt to arrive at "the cause whi" of events or subjectivity, "Chaucer's essay in the philosophy of history must end as inconclusively as both Criseyde's career and Troilus's life" (p. 154). Seeking to place *Troilus* in its time, Patterson ends the chapter with analogous inconclusiveness: "the poem's deepest message is not about the failure of any particular historical moment but about the failure of history, and of historical understanding, per se" (p. 163).

Chapter 3, "The *Knight's Tale* and the Crisis of Chivalric Identity," argues that "if we are to understand KnT, both as a text in its own right and as the initiating movement of CT, we must recognize it as the fictive expression of an aristocratic self-understanding typical of the late fourteenth century" (pp. 197–98). By attributing to a particular knight the tale's meditations on life and death, love and honor, order and chaos — by presenting these concerns as "the substance of chivalric identity" (p. 168) — Chaucer distances himself from attitudes that underlie the self-canceling representations of history and subjectivity in *Anelida and Arcite* and *Troilus* and prepares for their replacement by the more historicized attitudes of later Canterbury narrators and narratives.

Patterson ingeniously deploys phenomena such as the Scrope-Grosvenor dispute over a coat of arms both claimed (1385–91) and the late-medieval aristocratic obsession with astrology to explicate how the Knight, in attempting to "construct an allegory of the progress of chivalry" (p. 201), unwittingly incorporates into his *Tale* all the tensions, uncertainties, and mystifications of the chivalric order in late-fourteenth-century England. The strain, and finally the self-subverting quality, of his enterprise is reflected both in the narratorial voice of the *Tale* and in its story of insecurity and powerlessness concealed beneath an ideology of honor and control.

Following 4, a brief consideration of *The Legend of Good Women* (wittily characterized as "the road not taken after the *Troilus*"), chapters 5 and 6 expound a theory of *The Canterbury Tales* as a work incorporating Chaucer's mature approach to "the subject of history" in both senses of the locution. In chapter 5, "The *Miller's Tale* and the Politics of Laughter," Patterson argues that *The Miller's Tale* inhabits a realm of class analysis and protest aimed squarely at the aristocracy and its allies; its comic climax suggests that the elaborate structure of governance that undergirds the exploitation of the peasantry is unnecessary (since nature contains its own principle of retributive justice), while its denouement, in which the clerks of Oxford conspire to portray John as a madman, alludes to the clergy's characterization of peasant protest (such as the rising of 1381, in which millers participated) as the deranged activity of an irrational, barely human mob.

But Chaucer, whose own class origins would surely, Patterson argues, have endowed his attitudes toward the peasantry with "a powerful ambivalence" (p. 254), cannot maintain this level of class-based, overtly political criticism. The remainder of fragment 1 involves a withdrawal: *The Reeve's Tale* shows the peasantry divided against itself and substitutes a sour, self-subverting moralism for the naturalism of *The Miller's Tale*, while the Cook's depiction of urban criminality threatens the whole social order and is thus abandoned.

As chapter 6, "The Wife of Bath and the Triumph of the Subject," argues, however, fragments 2 and 3 of *The Canterbury Tales* reenact the dynamic of fragment 1, and this time Chaucer finds a solution to the problem of political and social engagement that allows the tale-telling to continue until the Parson, with the consent of the pilgrim *compaignye*, abandons the scheme. That solution, according to Patterson, involves a crucial recourse to the idea of the autonomous subject, located in and affected, but not determined, by the flow of history.

In contrast to *The Man of Law's Tale*, in which "feminine virtue is brought into existence by male authority" (p. 284), the achievement of the Wife is to construct a viable subjectivity for herself out of, and against, male stereotypes of female garrulity and carnality, as exemplified in the stock figure of the old widow. Chaucer—imitating, but going beyond, Jean de Meun's *La Vieille*—exploits precisely this figure's age and experience to shape her subjectivity as a function of her temporality. The Wife of Bath thus becomes the "subject of history," albeit a personal, gender-determined (as opposed to a political, class-determined) history.

The Wife of Bath also functions as a figure of the poet through her assumption and embodiment of the rhetorical trope of *dilatio*. Traditionally, *dilatio* in (male-composed) feminine discourse simultaneously heightens and frustrates the desire of its (male) audience by postponing their gratification. But the Wife's discourse invites instead "a dilatory postponement of meaning that yields a recuperative and inclusive understanding [of female subjectivity] rather than the dismisssive judgments rendered by a hermeneutic committed to the maintenance of hierarchy" (p. 368).

Chapter 7, "Chaucerian Commerce: Bourgeois Ideology and Poetic Exchange in the *Merchant's* and *Shipman's Tales*," explores the ways in which these two tales reproduce the identity of the urban merchant class in Chaucer's day. Patterson defines this class in terms precisely of its lack of a sense of itself as a class—a lack for which it compensates by its invention of the autonomous self, created from within by its unconditioned responses to experience. Accordingly, Patterson posits an "*absence* of representability—of, that is, a social identity derived from a confidently articulated class ideology" (p. 338) as an explanation for the intense personal feelings—of self-disgust, of hatred for women—animating the *Merchant's Tale*: "Denied a secure prospect upon the world, the Merchant's gaze instead focuses with obsessive attention upon the inner landscape of unsatisfied desire that is staged in his own failed marriage" (p. 338). Balancing this animus, however, is the nonideological, domestic negotiation between Pluto and Proserpina that "opens the narrative as a whole to the situational, individualistic, market-based ethic that accords with the Merchant's historical condition" (p. 344).

A similar atmosphere of domestic negotiation shapes *The Shipman's Tale*, which shows friendship and marriage thoroughly invaded and commodified by commercial monetary notions but does not thereby function as an indictment of mercantile life and ethics; rather, "the Tale refuses to ascribe responsibility for the process it dramatizes to any particular historical class or social condition" (p. 356). Concurrently, "the unobtrusive mastery with which Chaucer destabilizes the verbal surface of his Tale" (p. 361) suggests that language is as unfixed a medium of exchange as is money and thus forestalls a reading of the *Tale* as an allegory or parable of mercantile sinfulness, to be implicitly contrasted to a norm of rectitude available to the reader-interpreter.

Chapter 8, "The Subject of Confession: the Pardoner and the Rhetoric of Penance," constitutes a major rethinking and expansion of an essay of 1976 on the Pardoner. Combining insights gleaned from both late-medieval penitential literature and Lacanian theories of subjectivity and language, Patterson contends that "the Pardoner's discourse is offered as an effort to satisfy paternal justice, that it is an act of penance that seeks to atone for the transgression that has resulted in his 'castration,' whether it be real or only presumed" (p. 372). Trapped in despair, convinced that the penitential message of his sermons is fraudulent, the Pardoner plays out his plight and his resentment in the melodramatically evil self-presentation of his *Prologue* and the symbolic displacements of his *Tale*, while through him Chaucer constructs a subjectivity out of late-medieval exemplary and didactic poems in which contrition and despair present dangerously similar linguistic profiles. Ultimately, the Old Man of *The Pardoner's Tale*, who beats on the ground with his staff while crying, "Leeve mooder, let me in!" (line 731), embodies his creator's desire for reincorporation into his mother's womb — a desire that runs directly counter to the aim of Christian penance (i.e., forgiveness by the angry, almighty Father), thereby constituting "an oppositional political statement" in mockery of the "ossified and empty formalism" (p. 420) of the established Church, also, attacked by the age's religious reformers.

Space does not permit the full commentary that this provocative, magisterial book demands. Especially noteworthy is its *aggiornamento* of the Kittredgian "dramatic theory" of *The Canterbury Tales* by redefining subjectivity (which Patterson, in continuity with the Kittredge-Donaldson tradition, sees as absolutely central to Chaucer's mature poetic achievement) in accord with the current, social-scientific, linguistic, and psychoanalytic model of the subject position as the site where varied, historically conditioned discourses and experiences intersect. In this way Patterson can save Chaucer's most ambitious poetic project — and specifically the implications of its framing fiction, which refracts the *Tales* through the pilgrim subjectivities (or some of them) limned in *The General Prologue* — from overly prompt dismissal on textual (N. F. Blake) or critical (C. David Benson, Derek Pearsall) grounds. The first four chapters of *Chaucer and the Subject of History* are, perhaps, best understood as a preparation for this salvage operation; in them Patterson reinterprets pre-Canterbury poems, and the "gateway" *Knight's Tale*, exploring the various impasses to which they are led by the desire to locate the wellsprings of both history and subjectivity outside the play of actual social and political forces.

Patterson's mini-essays on social, political, institutional, and intellectual history bespeak an unusually broad scholarly formation and are, with one exception, well integrated into their respective chapters (the movement back and forth between poem and context in the *Troilus* chapter makes it the book's most difficult argument to follow). Less successful is the prolegomenal definition of Chaucer's poetry in terms of "modernism" and Renaissance transhistorical classicism in the introduction (attempts to clarify this argument lead to rare passages of incoherent writing on pp. 41 and 61; by and large Patterson writes with a clarity that is all the more admirable given the complexity of his agenda).

Although impracticable in this review, a comparison of *Chaucer and the Subject of History* with *The Disenchanted Self* by H. Marshall Leicester, Jr. (1990), would yield important conclusions and hypotheses about the current state of Chaucer criticism. Between them they represent a massive, highly intelligent attempt to recuperate the "humanist" (as opposed to the Robertsonian "exegetic") version of Chaucer for the 1990s. What most separates the two approaches is Leicester's commitment to the unity and sufficiency of the voice of each *Tale* vis à vis Patterson's equally strong commitment to the faulty self-understanding embedded in the subjectivity of some pilgrims (the Knight, the Pardoner), which requires for its elucidation an implied Chaucerian presence in the text, but "outside" (or behind) its teller. Thus for Patterson some aspects of the Knight's description of the temple of Mars "witness to his repressed knowledge of military chivalry's darker, more malevolent valence" (p. 226), while for Leicester "the whole of the temple of Mars testifies to the Knight's awareness of the human potential for terrible, mad violence . . . and to his determination to reveal it behind the chivalric veil it usually wears" (*The Disenchanted Self*, p. 276).

All of which is to suggest that Chaucer continues to be a site for creative disagreement among his readers. And there can be no doubt that *Chaucer and the Subject of History* represents an impressively intelligent, learned, and thoughtful contribution to that debate, one that will stand Chaucerians in excellent stead for at least the remainder of this century.

ROBERT W. HANNING
Columbia University

257

DEREK PEARSALL, ed. *The Floure and the Leafe, The Assembly of Ladies, The Isle of Ladies*. Middle English Texts Series. Kalamazoo, Mich.: Medieval Institute Publications, 1990. Pp. 146. $6.95.

ALAN LUPACK, ed. *Three Middle English Charlemagne Romances*. Middle English Texts Series. Kalamazoo, Mich.: Medieval Institute Publications, 1990. Pp. 207. $6.95.

JAMES DEAN, ed. *Six Ecclesiastical Satires*. Middle English Texts Series. Kalamazoo, Mich.: Medieval Institute Publications, 1991. Pp. 250. $8.95.

RUSSELL A. PECK, ed. *Heroic Women from the Old Testament in Middle English Verse*. Middle English Texts Series. Kalamazoo, Mich.: Medieval Institute Publications, 1991. Pp. x, 157. $8.95.

These are the first four volumes of the ambitious and timely Middle English Texts Series published by TEAMS (the Consortium for the Teaching of the Middle Ages), designed to make available for classroom use, in paperback and at a very low cost, works other than those by Chaucer, Gower, Langland, the *Gawain* poet, and Malory. Such texts are usually too expensive for students or are out of print, and several newly edited here are in fact the first scholarly editions published in this century.

The general editor of the series, Russell Peck, of the University of Rochester, has long felt the lack of good student editions of works that can be taught in conjunction with the major authors or that are otherwise important in the period. The availability of these and future volumes in the series should stimulate teachers to create courses that bring familiar and unfamiliar texts into new configurations. Their design and reasonable prices permit assigning only one or two works from a volume, mixing and matching from several volumes to create new groups of primary texts for different course units.

Within each volume every text is self-contained: it has its own introduction, bibliography, marginal glosses (or full translations of knotty lines at the bottom of the page), and explanatory notes following. Words common to all the texts in a volume appear in a short glossary in the back. The volumes are handsomely printed in modern orthography in a 7-by-10-inch format that leaves a good amount of white space for student note-taking. The level of glossing, both on the page and in the back, assumes that the reader already has some knowledge of Middle English gained by prior or concurrent undergraduate study of Chaucer.

The first two poems in Derek Pearsall's volume (respectively 595 and 756 lines, both in rhyme royal) are reprinted with corrections from his 1962 edition, now out of print. Their explanatory notes are sharply reduced or rewritten versions of that edition's notes. Both are allegorical dream visions that have female narrators, and, while the sex of their authors is unknown, they are clearly not by the same person, as Skeat thought (*Chaucerian and Other Pieces* [1897]). The first writer has "radiant and eccentric gifts" (p. 29) and often echoes Chaucer, while the second is capable only of "skillful hack-work" and is chiefly interested in the mechanics of running a noble household. *The Isle of Ladies* runs 2,235 lines, mainly in octosyllabic couplets, and thus takes up two-thirds of the volume. Its copy text is Anthony Jenkins's Garland edition (1980). Pearsall charitably characterizes this third dream vision as vapid and diffuse, with "almost no power of visualization." He sees its sentences operating to "pump out clouds of verbiage that, it is hoped, will precipitate here and there as sense" (p. 67). It was included not for its literary worth but as "an excellent complement" to the first two poems "in discussions of the fate of late medieval allegory" and its representation of relations between men and women. Its narrator's "dream of male desire" is "perfectly transparent as an allegory of sexual repression and fulfillment" (p. 65). Pearsall also finds it interesting that the "I" of the dreamer is presented on the one hand with "a stumbling earnestness" and "a desire that the audience should re-live with him his experiences," and on the other with "a carelessly sophisticated mock-naïveté" and self-conscious play with conventions that "makes us wonder, as we wonder with Chaucer, whether we have been taken in" (p. 66). Although such a formulation may seem to an unsympathetic reader like complimenting Lydgate on his irony, late-medieval literary subjectivity is a fascinating topic in its own right, and one to which *The Isle of Ladies* makes a contribution. All three of these poems, read together, would make an interesting unit in a course in medieval women's studies. *The Floure and the Leafe* is the most immediately appealing to students, I think, and the one most obviously related to Chaucer.

The first half of Alan Lupack's volume is taken up by his welcome new edition of *The Sowdone of Babylone*, 3,274 octosyllabics that are almost sinewy in their expatiation when compared to *The Isle of Ladies*. Last edited in complete form in 1881, it belongs to the Firumbras group of Charlemagne romances and contains echoes of *The Canterbury Tales*. Next comes *The Siege of Melayne*, 1,599 lines "in a twelve-line stanza rhyming *aabccbddbeeb*, though there are places where the rhyme scheme is not perfectly maintained" (p. 105). Incomplete, with no known source, it belongs to the Otinel group and "borders on being a character study" of

Turpin. Its Northern dialect will probably be initially difficult for students, despite Lupack's useful sketch in the introduction, but it will certainly be easier than the fifteenth-century Scots of *Rauf Coilyear* (972 lines in the *Awntyrs of Arthure* stanza). Lupack gives only one paragraph of linguistic information about this vigorous and entertaining poem, which is not enough. More marginal glosses are needed for students' close appreciation, and the glossary in the back could be improved as well. To take just two false friends not glossed marginally, there are no entries for "hole" (whole) or Scots "raid" (rode). I hope the next printing of this volume will contain more help for students coming to the Northern dialects after studying Chaucer, because *Rauf Coilyear* is delightful, as Lupack's introduction makes clear. The three romances in this volume should find ready use in Arthurian courses of virtually any design.

The six satires edited by James Dean consist of five antifraternal Lollard pieces and a dream vision with a female narrator that criticizes nunneries. The volume might have benefited from a brief general introduction about its contents and their possible uses. *Piers the Plowman's Crede*, last edited in 1867 by Skeat, can be connected in the classroom with *Piers Plowman* or *The Summoner's Tale*. Its 855 alliterative lines offer the student frequent difficulties, but Dean gives many full-line glosses, as he does for all the Lollard texts. *The Plowman's Tale* (1,350 lines in *The Monk's Tale* stanza) has easier language for students, since it first appeared as an apocryphal tale in Thynne's 1532 edition of Chaucer. For the following three pieces Dean relies heavily on P. L. Heyworth's excellent 1968 edition: they are *Jack Upland*, a prose address to friars; *Friar Daw's Reply*, 932 alliterative lines that answer Upland's attack point by point; and *Upland's Rejoinder* (393 lines), written by someone other than the author of *Jack Upland*. Although all three are unrelenting monologues addressed to the opposition, Friar Daw Tobias, as the invented speaker of the second work calls himself, undercuts his own arguments in the most weird and pleasant ways, creating an interesting ironic effect. He characterizes himself as "lewid as a leke" (line 45), damns his own order with faint praise, and is generally "a master of the ineffective *tu quoque*" (p. 146). His very name alludes to the noisy jackdaw. Dean suggests that the ironic undercutting that results in pairing either the first two or second two works in this sequence may be modeled on Chaucer's pairing of *The Friar's Tale* and *The Summoner's Tale*.

The final work in the volume is quite different in tone and purpose from the antifraternal satires. *Why I Can't Be a Nun*, a 393-line fragment last edited in 1862, has the liveliness and charm of a Chaucerian dream vision. The sweet-tempered voice of young "Katerine" reports that her father, having surveyed the parlous state of nunneries in England, has discouraged her from a religious vocation. Disappointed but obedient, she falls asleep on a May morning after praying to God in a garden. Lady Experience wakes her and takes her into a typically corrupt convent to show her why she cannot be a nun if she wishes to be a true handmaiden of God. Dean thinks that the unknown author who created this well-bred "domestic world remarkable for its thoughtful concerns" might be a woman. The poem could be taught in conjunction with the Pearsall or Peck volumes, as well as with Chaucer's dream visions or the other satires here. Throughout this volume Dean's editing is scrupulous, and his introductions are scholarly, straightforward, and well written. The glossing and explanatory notes are consistently full, although annotation is a bit lighter for the last text. The notes are particularly good for students, in that they do not assume that readers will know what the Credo is or who the Friars Minor were but instead give good elementary explanations of the religious references in the texts.

The chef d'oeuvre of the series so far is Peck's volume, which contains *The Storie of Asneth*, *The Pistel of Swete Susan*, and the stories of Jephthah's daughter and Judith from *The Middle English Metrical Paraphrase of the Old Testament*. His short preface locates the texts for student readers: they are "poems of considerable literary merit" that reflect how "the culture looked upon female integrity and aspiration. They also provide an unusually sympathetic look at Judaism in a time more noted for its hostility toward Jews than kindness. . . . The issues surrounding these poems will be of interest to historians, students of iconography, and students of medieval culture in general, as well as students of literature and the history of women" (p. ix). That is a pretty wide net to cast for one's audience, and I personally do not think that the four plates of the *Biblia Pauperum*, whose typology *Asneth* shares, will be of more than passing interest to most readers.

The volume is distinguished by a great deal of original scholarly work, especially on *Asneth*, an extraordinarily fine poem that deserves to be better known, having been edited only once before (in *JEGP* for 1910). All of Peck's introductions and bibliographies are more extensive than those in the previous three volumes and not only provide historical information and excellent literary judgment but also set the poems in relevant and meaningful contexts for today's students. Asneth (also Asenath, Asenath) is the Egyptian wife of Joseph in Genesis 41. Her conversion story develops first in Midrashic commentaries and then appears in a second-century Alexandrian Greek romance, whose twelfth-century Latin version is the basis for the Middle English poem. In his twenty-page introduction Peck traces this development with great skill and learning and also explores the prominence of women in the history of the unique manuscript's ownership. He sees the poem both as a manual for young women's Christian conduct and as a handbook for their aristocratic behavior, and he gives a sprightly critical reading of it using a feminist focus. The poem itself is in early-fifteenth-century West Midlands dialect, 933 lines of loosely alliterating rhyme royal, and takes up the first half of the volume. Asneth is another obedient daughter like Katerine but is strongly independent in her piety and "offers a magnificent study of a young woman coming into responsible adulthood, fully cognizant that her choices matter" (p. 11). "Magnificent" may seem strong praise, but not only is the poem rich in symbolism (a laughing angel, a honeycomb), but both the modest narrator and the characters have a sincere simplicity of speech that is genuinely moving. One can see why Peck has spent so much energy in making this work finally accessible, and accessible is the word: his annotated bibliography for this poem alone runs four and a half pages.

The other works in the volume are treated with comparable care. The retelling of the Susanna story in the *Pistel* runs to 365 lines in a difficult dialect, a mixture of Yorkshire and the Midlands, using an alliterative tailed stanza. Peck gives a number of whole-line translations in his glosses to aid student comprehension. The poem has some lovely touches of pathos and a fine purple patch in the description of Susanna's garden. The Middle English version of Jephthah's daughter is so brief, on the other hand, that one might as well read it in Modern English. It is followed by no less than 792 lines on Judith. This retelling of that triumphant story, again in a tough Northern dialect, is somewhat elongated by Judith's long-winded dissimulation to Holofernes. This last text is much more lightly annotated than the other two major pieces in the volume. These three heroic Biblical women — Asneth, Susanna, and Judith — can be studied as a group in a variety of ways. One might focus on how medieval writers saw aristocratic religious women expressing their strength and piety within the framework of patriarchy. Or they might be studied in conjunction with Chaucer's religious heroines, with whom they have many points of similarity and difference.

With the inauguration of this series of student editions not only have we gained access to some little regarded or long forgotten poems of real literary value but also we now have an exciting new teaching tool. The publisher reports that the projected titles in the series will not overlap with MART, the Focus Library of Medieval Women, or the Leeds Medieval Studies series. Among the twenty-five more titles planned, mostly from the four-teenth and fifteenth centuries, of special interest are *The Canterbury Tales: Fifteenth-Century Continuations and Additions*, edited by John Bowers, which appeared in late 1992, and *King Arthur's Death*, long out of print and much regretted by many teachers, edited by Larry D. Benson and Edward Foster, scheduled for 1993.

These volumes and those reviewed here are being printed in runs of 500 copies each, so that errors can be corrected (though I found all four typographically very clean), glosses can be augmented as needed, and introductions and notes can be updated frequently. Teachers are invited to send the general editor reports on how the texts work in the classroom as well as suggestions for improvement.

HOWELL CHICKERING
Amherst College

MAUREEN QUILLIGAN. *The Allegory of Female Authority: Christine de Pizan's* Cité des Dames. Ithaca, N.Y. and London: Cornell University Press, 1991. Pp. xv, 290. $45.00 cloth, $14.95 paper.

Women artists have sometimes been thought to work small, but Christine de Pizan (or Pisan) wrote large, in long prose and verse treatises about the big topics: history, gender, morals, politics, and literary tradition. Christine has been neither a forgotten nor a neglected author since her death about 1430; her fortunes compare favorably with those of many another late-medieval author. However, the works once most in vogue — *L'Epistre Othea*, the *Livre des fais d'armes et de chevalerie*, the *Livre des Trois Vertus*, and other courtly-chivalric works — have been, for many modern readers, decisively displaced by the *Livre de la cité des dames* (1405). That work is now well served by Maureen Quilligan's book, the first full-length study of the *Cité*.

Many of Christine's ideas were conventional enough, her style often pedestrian, and her politics distinctly conservative. What was remarkable and innovative about Christine was that she ambitiously constructed herself as author, indeed distinctively as woman author, and as public figure at a time when women — though actively engaged in productive labor of all kinds — did not often occupy those particular positions, excluded as they

263

were from the major sites of cultural production in university, priesthood, and high public office. It is Quilligan's purpose to investigate the techniques of this self-construction—"the creation of female subjectivity" (p. 237)—as they are revealed in the *Cité*.

The format—"page-by-page commentary" (p. 2) on the text—makes it somewhat difficult to follow the coherent development of an argument, but is justified as necessary to clarify "all the details of [Christine's] canonical maneuvering as she creates for herself a place in the list of texts by constructing the list through her own deft revisions" (p. 4). The idea of maternity is central to these revisions as a major source of female authority, both in the frame story (where the narrator's mother enters the text) and in many of the stories narrated. Indeed, Quilligan concludes, "the author's relationship to her mother was a foundational one for the writing of the *Cité*" (p. 237). By tracing the web of mother-daughter and father-daughter relations in the book, Quilligan is able to illuminate the inner structures of Christine's textual city.

Chapter 1, "The Name of the Author," defines some basic concepts and practices that arise early on in the text. Quilligan uses Dante as model with respect to self-naming, Chaucer and Boccaccio as foils on other issues, such as the misogynist tradition or voicing through a female character. I would have liked a quotation or page reference in support of Quilligan's assertion (p. 39) about the masculinist intention of Boccaccio's *De mulieribus claris* (Christine's main source), for her interpretation does not square with Boccaccio's dedicatory letter or preface. I saw this as a minor instance of the Boccaccio bashing that seems to inform much Christine scholarship as a prerequisite to celebrating her revisionary art (Boccaccio too was revising, of course, and, he said, in the interest of women).

This opening chapter accounts for two attitudes that modern readers might question in Christine's work: essentialism and the exclusion of women from the legal profession (hence public life). These attitudes Quilligan is at pains to interpret into something more palatable to current liberal academic taste. Thus she quotes Gayatri Spivak on the disruptive power of essentialism "when put into practice by the dispossessed themselves" (p. 37) and reads the "regressive-sounding prescription against women in law" as a statement of women's true abilities in areas of endeavor superior to the merely written, "which is here associated with masculine enterprises" (p. 67). This implied invitation to see the courtly Christine as among the "dispossessed" is scarcely convincing, and if Christine approaches "the problematic issue of writing" (p. 67) by agreeing to female exclusion from it, then surely this strategy deserves fuller discussion than it gets. If Christine encourages women to exert a special "female knowledge more powerful than . . . mere written rules" (p. 67), what does this say "to us in the late twentieth century" (p. 192)?

When we read, in the same chapter, that Christine's apparently "very conservative defense of the division of labor" is really "a defense of difference, one that authorizes a peculiarly female set of potencies" (p. 66), we recognize familiar and disputed terrain. This is the arena explored, for instance, by Carolyn Bynum, who, at the end of *Holy Feast, Holy Fast*, transforms female suffering into a special female power of transcendence, a conclusion rejected by many admirers of that book, including many feminist medievalists. I do not insist that Quilligan's interpretation of Christine is wrong; I do believe that it stages an ideological position that is not fully acknowledged in this book.

Chapter 2, "Rewriting Tradition," homes in on another paradox: while Christine's authority in the *Cité* is "markedly textual," nonetheless her aim is to "privilege the preliterate" so as to bring into textuality "previously unscripted sciences — essentializing, aural, experiential" (p. 80). This explains the incestuous, city-building ruler Semiramis, who acts "unscripted and unbound by law"; her story comes first in the collection because it so spectacularly "unmoors motherhood, and the power of procreation, from its engagement in the traffic in women" (p. 84). Other readings throughout the book are equally perceptive and provocative, constituting the main strength of Quilligan's study. Nothing is said, unfortunately, about the social meaning of exalting the preliterate at a time when some writers (including Boccaccio) recommended more education for women.

Chapter 3, "Rewriting the City," continues with "the relationship between a scripted and an unlettered female authority" (p. 104) and with the motherhood theme. The sibyls are key figures here: instances of divinely inspired female authority participating in a critique of masculinist Rome and "a means of recuperating the authority denied the language of the mother" (p. 134). Here Quilligan writes of Christine's "bitter conflict . . . , conflictual relations with the mother" (pp. 155–56) in the *Cité*, and, in chapter 4, she discusses Christine's effacement of the mother from her version of St. Christine (after whom the author was named). This ambivalence turns out, we eventually discover, to be crucial to Christine's project.

Chapter 4, "Rewriting the Body," confronts another fact about the *Cité* that some readers might find "shocking and distasteful" (p. 192): the last section of the *Cité* tells of martyr saints, hence sadistic cruelty toward women. How, therefore, can we hope to retain the *Cité* "as a text that

265

may continue to speak to us in the late twentieth century" (p. 192)? Without problematizing the question itself as it warrants, Quilligan answers that, while Boccaccio (writing only of pagan women) stages "the voyeuristic dismemberment of the female body," Christine's martyrology transforms this into "the sacred empowerment of Christian witness" (p. 196). Both the voyeurism and the dismemberment enter Quilligan's analysis by way of Laura Mulvey's theorizing of the cinematic controlling male gaze, which incorporates two possible avenues of escape from castration anxiety: "a voyeuristic pleasure in assigning guilt. . . , and a 'fetishistic scopophilia,' the display of the beauty of the female body in objectified fragments" (p. 160). This is why it does not matter that Lucretia and Dido, Quilligan's examples here, are not actually dismembered or killed, or that Lucretia's suicide in front of her family is a sociopolitical act that inspires a revolt against tyrannic monarchy—a result, Quilligan concedes, that Christine "with her pro-monarchist tendencies, would not have applauded anyhow" (p. 160). Yet if Christine "repoliticizes" (p. 159) Boccaccio's exempla to specifically gender concerns, if she "rewrites Boccaccio to insert an active female subjectivity into each story" (p. 160), surely this does not make Boccaccio an advocate of sadistic voyeurism and misogynistic violence nor prove that "Boccaccio intends his text. . . to be titillating" (p. 161).

The question of martyrology also proves central to that of maternity. Quilligan argues that Christine's excision of St. Christine's mother exculpates the mother from involvement in the torture of her daughter (p. 225), but that maternal presence is restored in the next set of stories, celebrating mothers whose faith is great enough "to allow their own children to be sacrificed" (p. 228). The immediately following set of father-daughter stories (which involve cross-dressing but no violence) prompts Quilligan to suggest that the key to masochism may lie not in relations with the father but in those with the absented mother (p. 233). Kristeva's theory of the abject, which centers on the subject's efforts to separate from the archaic mother into selfhood, language, and law, is offered (pp. 234ff.) as key to Christine's problematic of maternity and to her representation of martyred saints: because the vocabulary for a female subjectivity did not yet exist, Christine found in martyrology a genre "that can begin to speak the creation of the 'self'. . . at the site—the family—where the individual is shaped into a particular social being" (p. 237). This is a bold and intriguing account, albeit not without its own further questions: applicability to male authors, for instance, and to male saints, or the role of an archaic-maternal Jesus in pious literature.

If subtle and audacious literary and psychological readings are the strength of this book, its weakness is a pervasive insensitivity to social history. For instance, Quilligan portrays Christine as champion of companionate marriage at a time when "the prime function of marriage was not mutual comfort... but the bearing of dynastically legitimate children" (p. 140). There are two blind spots here. One is that the diagnosis is contested by some social historians who think that companionate marriage was not unusual during the Middle Ages.[1] The other is that, while dynastic considerations would be important for the nobility, they could scarcely mean much to the nondynastic majority of the population.[2] The tendency to submerge class issues becomes a problem elsewhere, for instance in this oxymoronic formulation: "Although a hierarchy is established by the articulation of the architectural metaphor, [Christine's] city is classless, the uniform class being upper" (p. 195). While it is true enough that Christine theoretically allows any virtuous woman to enter the city, she does not show it. I would argue that she cannot fully imagine it because her imagination is that of the courtier.

Quilligan's account of the Cabochian revolt of 1413, which Christine witnessed and deplored, plays fast and loose with social terms. To exculpate her author from the now unfashionable position of opposing a popular and justified bourgeois rebellion, Quilligan must misrepresent the uprising, in the traditional vocabulary of reaction, as antidemocratic "mob rule" (p. 266). Most egregious is Quilligan's mistaken identification of Christine's "own class" as "the haute bourgeoisie" (p. 269). Christine had no class link with the merchants, financiers, and businesspeople who constituted the upper bourgeoisie; she was a parasite upon the royal nobility, to whose interests she straightforwardly committed herself.

The last chapter, "The Practice of History," discusses Christine's work after the *Cité*: the *Trésor de la cité des dames* and her last piece, the *Ditié de Jehanne d'Arc* of 1429. The former, Quilligan maintains, is no "Collapse into conventionality" or "recourse to Machiavellian modes of deception" but rather a demonstration for women of "how to maximize power when given limited room for manoeuvre" (p. 245); the latter "was written because Christine believed a woman could save — and was at that moment, saving — France" (p. 245). Much of this chapter polemicizes — as does the

---

[1] E.g., Alan Macfarlane, *Marriage and Love in England, 1300–1840* (Oxford and New York: Blackwell, 1986), pt. 3.

[2] As Zvi Razi shows, even illegitimacy was not necessarily an obstacle everywhere; *Life, Marriage and Death in a Medieval Parish, Halesowen, 1270–1400* (London, 1980), p. 65. Duby, whom Quilligan cites twice here, writes exclusively of the nobility in both places.

introduction—against an essay of mine that proposes that Christine was too conservative in her own time to be characterized as proto-feminist, proto-revolutionary, or role model (as some scholars have recently done). Yet the polemical tone is misleading because Quilligan does wind up confirming my factual points, though fine-tuning them to her own perspective. In so doing she provides a far more detailed and sophisticated literary and psychological reading than could be done in an explicitly historicist essay. Despite our differences—centering on the specific contemporary meaning of Christine's work—I do not hesitate to recommend this book as a valuable contribution to medieval literary criticism.

A bibliography would have been helpful in tracking down inadequately documented references, such as that to Fredric Jameson on page 210, which is evidently different from the source noted on page 203, or for the omitted title of my essay and the main title of the book in which it occurs, referred to extensively on pages 135–38.[3] A bibliography might also usefully have listed the location of manuscripts of the *Cité* or of other works important to Christine, such as the *Speculum historiale* of Vincent of Beauvais.

SHEILA DELANY
Simon Fraser University

ANNA HUBERTINE REUTERS. *Friendship and Love in the Middle English Metrical Romances.* European University Studies, ser. 14, vol. 226. Frankfort am Main and New York: Peter Lang, 1991. Pp. 245. $46.80 paper.

To my knowledge this dissertation is the first book-length study of love and friendship in the Middle English metrical romances. There have been many articles and studies of individual romances, and themes of love and friendship have been used as ways to group and classify romances, but there has been no attempt to systematically describe the genre by analyzing the corpus in terms of these relationships. In her study Reuters surveys nearly forty narratives to develop a model of the love and friendship they depict, and of the genre itself.

---

[3] "A City, a Room: the Scene of Writing in Christine de Pisan and Virginia Woolf," in *Writing Woman: Women Writers and Women in Literature, Medieval to Modern* (New York: Schocken, 1983).

It has become almost conventional to begin a study of the Middle English metrical romances by remarking on their diversity and the difficulty of defining the genre. Reuters approaches the problem in terms of the narratives' content: relationships of love and friendship. She rather cursorily rejects attempts to find principles for analyzing the romances according to their formal characteristics (Dieter Mehl) or structures of discourse (Susan Wittig, Carol Fewster), asserting that love and friendship are "primary narrative material" whose advantages for purposes of categorization are obvious. She then suggests a typology of romance based on how the love or friendship is initiated. A love relationship may be "forward," either the heroine or the hero taking the initiative; or it may be "mutual," both lovers acting equally. Romances may also be categorized according to the social status of the partners: some tell of bonds between people of equal rank (restorative-concordant), while in others one of the partners must rise to attain the status of the other (innovative-discordant). Regardless of the dynamics of the relationships, they all pass through three stages: establishment, separation, reunion; and all have significance in three spheres: personal, social-political, and religious. Different variants develop these elements in distinctive ways, but in the reunion stage, friendship or marital harmony, social order, and religious orthodoxy always coincide. Other aspects of the model include the association of "principles" with the variants. The "*trouthe-rewthe* principle" underlies the fairy-mistress variant, the "conquest principle" underlies the forward-hero variant, etc. There are also "leitmotifs" associated with the variants, for example: "work" and "word," "will" and "deed" in the friendship romances.

The chapters are organized according to the dynamic of the relationship: first romances of "forward" heroines and "reluctant" heroes in general (for example, *King Horn*), then "forward" heroines who are fairy mistresses (Triamour in *Sir Launfal*), next romances of "forward" heroes and "reluctant" heroines (like *Eglamour of Artois*), followed by poems on relationships of mutual love (like *Floris and Blanchefleur*) and its variant, married love (*Sir Isumbrace*). Next come romances of friendship; these concern bonds between men, including lords and retainers (*Amis and Amiloun*). The final chapter surveys romances of courtly love and shows its persistence in Caxton's prose narratives. There are charts summarizing the study's findings.

Reuters's model is useful. She is able systematically to analyze and group a large number of the romances in ways that have bearing on both meaning and narrative structure. The categories, based on the dynamics of the relationships between lovers, allow her effectively to address matters of

269

gender and genre. The three spheres permit her to avoid the vexed distinction between religious and secular romances while accounting for their homiletic elements. The schema also accommodates early and late romances and allows for patterns of modification over time. Other romances not analyzed in the study follow the patterns as well.

Because she is more interested in elucidating patterns of relationships between characters than in categorizing individual romances, the author is able to point out affiliations between romances that do not conform exactly to type or do so only in certain episodes. However, despite its inclusiveness, this study (like many others devoted to the Middle English romances) defines its subject so as to largely exclude the Charlemagne poems. One would like to know how the friendships depicted in those narratives compare to those of her model. At times the schema seems too pat, with its three spheres in the vertical dimension and three stages in the horizontal, but, fortunately, one need not be committed to the whole plan to appreciate the discussions of individual romances.

Reuters insists that the romances' content and meaning be understood dynamically in terms of the authors' and audiences' expectations of such works; thus she goes beyond the analysis and grouping of narratives "to find the historical precedents of the ideas and processes found in the romances." She sees precedents in the class system and such practices as patrilineage and arranged marriage; in the social diversity of the audience, which included gentry, nobility, and members of their households; and in that audience's concern for social advancement and employment of clerics who composed romances. Other precedents are found in Classical and ecclesiastical ideals of love and friendship that would have been familiar to these clerics, and in the devotional practices they fostered among their patrons.

Acknowledging her debt to Susan Crane's and W. R. J. Barron's discussions of insular romance, the author identifies an insular aesthetic characterized by a blend of entertainment and instruction, orthodoxy and innovation. The authors guide the audience, evoking a response of immediate experience by using heightening and repetition to convey their meaning with simplicity and precision. In discussions of particular romances Reuters attempts to analyze the mechanisms of the audiences' responses (especially identification with characters and wish fulfillment) in terms of the historical precedents. She also describes an insular form of courtly love, "honeste love," which is based on such conservative values as sincerity of intention and propriety of behavior yet is innovative in that it encourages individual choice of a partner. These conclusions are not new, but Reuters's observations do provide further support for them.

Throughout the study one would like to see more detailed documentation of historical precedents, more subtle analysis of the dynamics of audience response, and less attention to old arguments like the case against Jean Bodel's *Matieres* or the usefulness of evaluating fourteenth-century English narrative by the standards of twelfth-century France. The writing occasionally lacks lucidity, and, while it is a publishing matter, the book's format requires some comment, for the double-spaced typeface and lack of paragraph indentations are distracting. Despite these drawbacks, Reuters's study gives new insight into the forms of love and friendship depicted in the romances; it also contributes to the larger scholarly task of elucidating the dynamics and contexts of literary forms.

HARRIET E. HUDSON
Indiana State University

FELICITY RIDDY, ed. *Regionalism in Late Mediaeval Manuscripts and Texts: Essays Celebrating the Publication of* A Linguistic Atlas of Late Mediaeval English. York Manuscripts Conferences, proceedings, ser. 2. Cambridge: D. S. Brewer, 1991. Pp. xiii, 214. $70.00.

The papers collected here are the fourth volume of proceedings from the biennial University of York manuscripts conference. The first of these conferences, in 1981, organized by Derek Pearsall, effectively charted the course of Middle English manuscript study for the rest of the decade and had implications that are still being felt. Subsequent conferences and the volumes that have followed them have been of no less importance in their examinations of particular aspects of manuscript study.

That is equally true of this volume, edited by Felicity Riddy. It takes as its occasion the publication of the *Linguistic Atlas of Late Mediaeval English (LALME)*, by Angus McIntosh, Michael Samuels, and Michael Benskin, an occasion that provides the opportunity for papers on aspects of regionalism as it is reflected in various manuscripts and texts. The relationship of the individual papers to this occasion varies. Most distant from it is Colin Richmond's paper on John Wyndham, of Felbrigg, Norfolk, which sits oddly in the context of the volume as a whole since it is not concerned directly with either manuscript or dialect analysis but is an

271

excellent examination of the social and political contexts of fifteenth-century local history.

Some of the earlier papers also tend rather to eschew the opportunity to demonstrate the potentialities of *LALME* in favor of more general methodological reflections. The most provocative of these is a brief paper by Samuels, who suggests some of the areas in which *LALME* might be of assistance to scholars. He reiterates some earlier observations that seem unlikely to gain universal approval; for example, he suggests that "an editor's best evidence for the B-text [of *Piers Plowman*] would be the Laud and Rawlinson manuscripts plus a reconstruction of final *-e*" (p. 6). Equally controversial is the view that *The Equatorie of the Planets* is in Chaucer's own spelling, a view that has recently been challenged in articles by Larry D. Benson and Stephen Partridge in *English Manuscript Studies III* (1992).

Others of these early articles are broadly methodological. Michael Benskin explains the "fit" technique for localizing texts, while both Margaret Laing and Jeremy Smith discuss the plans to extend *LALME* backward to cover the early Middle English period and some of the problems and procedures that this project will entail. Ronald Waldron offers the only detailed application of the resources of *LALME* in the entire volume in his study of dialect aspects of the manuscripts of Trevisa's *Polychronicon*.

The most absorbing of these early essays is Richard Beadle's "Prolegomena to a Literary Geography of Later Medieval Norfolk." It is a wide-ranging examination of the dialect evidence for literary activity in this region. Its methodological core is an appendix "A Handlist of Later Middle English Manuscripts Copied by Norfolk Scribes" (pp. 102–108) listing nearly 150 manuscripts of various kinds. Anyone concerned with understanding English vernacular culture during this period will want to study this appendix very carefully. It provides a model that could be profitably replicated for other counties and regions and provides the most compelling employment of the potentialities of *LALME* contained in this volume.

It is something of a paradox that, while the subsequent essays are notable demonstrations of various techniques of manuscript analysis, these demonstrations have little to do with regionalism or dialect analysis. The essays by Julia Boffey and Carol Meale and John Scattergood are concerned with London manuscripts. Priscilla Bawcutt's is outside the confines of *LALME* in its examination of the earliest texts of Dunbar, and Peter Meredith is concerned with demonstrating what the physical structure of British Library Cotton Vespasian manuscript D viii (the N. Town manuscript) reveals about its evolution.

These are all essays that are concerned, albeit in very different ways, with the literary and cultural implications of manuscript analysis. And they all demonstrate how much can be achieved in the hands of gifted practitioners of such techniques. Peter Meredith offers a meticulous codicological analysis, particularly of the paper and quiring of the N. Town manuscript. What is revealed is not a unified pageant cycle but an attempt to harmonize various components of such a cycle with other plays. His conclusions demonstrate the incremental expansion of the work, a process that is revealed through the various attempts to impose on it some general appearance of consistency.

The examination of Bodleian manuscript Rawlinson C. 86 by Julia Boffey and Carol Meale seeks to locate this interesting compilation within the context of London readership in the late fifteenth or early sixteenth centuries. This manuscript — or, more accurately, these four separate collections, first joined together in the late sixteenth or early seventeenth centuries — contains a wide-ranging collection of materials: Chaucer, Lydgate, romances, and other texts in prose and verse. The contents, and the process of creating the various components of the manuscript, are examined in detail with numerous parallels in form, content, and readership being adduced from contemporary manuscript compilations and early printed editions. In some respects Rawlinson can be convincingly shown to embody "the tastes of middle-class, usually mercantile, readers" (p. 160). The process of analysis through which the various conclusions are established here is elegant and convincing. As with Beadle's paper it suggests models and procedures that can be profitably applied to other sorts of late-medieval compilations.

The last two essays are concerned with particular authors, Skelton and Dunbar, figures on whom John Scattergood and Priscilla Bawcutt have established themselves as the leading authorities. Scattergood demonstrates the crucial importance of London in the audience and circulation of Skelton's works and stresses the range of that audience, one not restricted to the court but extending through the merchant class; in this respect his paper is a valuable complement to the work of Boffey and Meale. Bawcutt is primarily concerned with the textual sources for the study of Dunbar and the extent to which these have been inadequately understood or examined hitherto. She offers helpful commentary on all the relevant manuscripts of Dunbar's works and suggests some of their previously unconsidered textual implications.

Although not as homogeneous as the title might suggest, this is, nonetheless, a rich and stimulating collection. It shows both what can be done and how much remains to be done in the study of later-medieval manuscript and early printed materials. These remain extraordinarily fruitful areas for research. At a time when there seems to be a renewed interest in "historicizing" the text, one hopes that the example of this volume will be attended to very carefully. For, before the text can be profitably historicized, the circumstances of its physical survival and transmission must be understood as fully as possible. The best of these essays suggest how much can be achieved through such understanding.

I note a few minor errors: p. 107, no. 145: for "Yale University Library" read "Beinecke Library"; p. 108, under "Reynys": for "146" read "147"; p. 146 and n. 6: The claim that this *Polychronicon* translation is unique is incorrect: it appears also in Trinity College, Dublin, manuscript 489 and Cleveland Public Library manuscript W q09.92-C468: see E. D. Kennedy, *A Manual of the Writings in Middle English* (New Haven, Conn.: Yale University Press, 1989), 8, Yale University Press, 2,878 [25].

A. S. G. EDWARDS
University of Victoria

MARY A. ROUSE and RICHARD H. ROUSE. *Authentic Witnesses: Approaches to Medieval Texts and Manuscripts*. Publications in Medieval Studies, vol. 17. Medieval Institute. Notre Dame, Ind.: University of Notre Dame Press, 1991. Pp. viii, 518. $59.95.

This volume contains thirteen previously published articles written mostly by both authors together, but a few by Richard Rouse alone. The subject matter they cover consists of manuscript books and their presentation from the twelfth to the fifteenth centuries in northwest Europe. They are concerned with the history of the manuscript book, and all exhibit a similar methodology through which surviving manuscripts and documents yield as much information about this topic as possible. Most essays are very detailed in their analysis of the evidence, and this makes it difficult to provide a comprehensive overview of their findings in a short review. They are, however, arranged into groups as follows: "Form and Function," "Ancient Authors and Medieval Readers," "*Florilegia*," "Content and Structure," "Book Production: Stationers and *Peciae*," "Medieval Libraries," "Backgrounds to Print," and "Epilogue." Some of these sections contain only a single essay, but they do reveal the areas covered. There is a brief introduction; a subject index and a manuscript index complete the volume.

The first article deals with two fragments of a roll containing Reinmar von Zweter's *Sprüche* found in a binding. Reinmar was a minnesinger, and the evidence suggests that the fragments were part of a singer's or performer's roll that he carried around for use in performance. Most poems survive today in codices, produced for courtiers and often elaborately written and illustrated. Such codices may represent the second stage of the written production of poetry, the rolls being the first. If so, this has important implications for editors of medieval poetry, since rolls very rarely survive. If we try to re-create the text of the earliest codex, that may not reflect in any way the genesis of the original poem or poems.

The second group of essays deals principally with Philip of Bayeux and his library; Philip was bishop of Bayeux from 1142 to 1163. Philip was not a writer, but he had a library of 140 books, which he left to the abbey of Bec. Although most of these books have not been identified, a catalogue of them provides us with some idea of how he acquired his books and of the importance of men like him in the preservation of classical texts. One of the most important points to arise from these essays is that the survival of many classical texts was assured by copying in twelfth-century northern Europe, and it was this copying that provided the texts to Italy that promoted its renaissance. Also, the history of a particular text can often be followed by tracing the history of the other texts with which it often shared a codex.

The third group, which examines the history of the florilegia, and particularly the *Florilegium Angelicum*, has links with the second. This florilegium was written in the third quarter of the twelfth century and is a book of maxims in which beauty of expression is more important than moral sentence. It quotes from a range of texts, some of which were very rare and yet must have been available to its compiler. The authors suggest that it was made at Orléans. Since little has survived of Orléans's intellectual life or books of this time, the text is important in recreating what books might have been available there in the twelfth century and the importance of Orléans in the dissemination of classical texts. Philip of Bayeux may have had links with Orléans, which stood at the crossroads in the dissemination of classical texts in central France.

In addition to the *Florilegium Angelicum*, it is possible to link other books with Orléans, including the *Florilegium Gallicum*; several books in the library of Richard de Fournival, who at his death in 1260 was chancellor of the cathedral at Amiens; and a thirteenth-century grammarian. The

275

books produced at Orléans were often compilations that drew on other books, and so the sourcebooks must have been at Orléans for these compilers to quote from them. Equally it suggests that the intellectual life in France cannot be easily divided into the humanism of the twelfth century and the scholasticism of the thirteenth, since so many of the same texts were being read and studied in both centuries.

If the twelfth century gathered and organized the legacy of the Christian past, the next problem that arises is how one can exploit this information. Memory ceases to be sufficient, and it becomes essential to develop new finding devices. This means that a new way of setting out a page has to be found so that searching devices can be developed. Thus order on the page and then mechanical means for exploiting that order go hand in hand. This development is promoted by the growth of the schools, for discussion and elucidation mean the rapid availability of texts and ways of finding individual passages. This need led to many new devices in the layout of books and the type of book produced in the twelfth and thirteenth centuries. Tables of chapters, running heads, chapter titles in red, alternating red and blue initials, paragraph marks, cross references, and citations of authors all become regular features of texts. The whole concept of glossing a text meant that a page needed a new layout so that the text and its gloss could be put on the same page and clearly distinguished. Alphabetization itself becomes significant now, and may have been developed for preachers, who needed to find references to significant passages quickly. Indeed, works like the Glosses, the Decretum, and the Sentences are all different ways of arranging material to make finding particular passages easier. It could be said that changes in the layout of the page and the composition of a whole book presented knowledge in a different format, which in turn suggests that readers wanted a different sort of knowledge because they were reading texts in a new way. The way people read and studied may have undergone a sea change. Texts were seen not only as whole works but as storehouses of information that needed to be accessible in smaller units.

Another paper focuses on three new tools available at this time: biblical concordances, alphabetical subject indexes, and library catalogues. All are useful and were particularly designed to help preachers. Alphabetical order is neither natural nor rational, since it divides the world and its contents arbitrarily according to the initial letter of the alphabet. It undermines the concept that the world is a unified whole in which each part interacts with every other part and should be considered in its wholeness as an expression of the divine will and creation. An alphabetical index demands the breaking up of texts into smaller blocks, chapters and paragraphs, which then need to be numbered. That in turn encourages the adoption of arabic numerals. These changes promote an interest in an author's whole oeuvre and assist the growth of professions whose needs are specialized as far as information is concerned. It may result in people using secondary sources rather than the sources themselves, which could lead to a loss of vitality, and people will be increasingly influenced by the way the secondary sources arrange their material rather than how it appears in the primary sources. It will become important to seek out what secondary sources an author has used, which may be more important than the primary ones, because many will use them as a convenient shortcut. This applies as much to vernacular poets like Chaucer as to schoolmen.

In the essay on the book trade in the University of Paris, 1250–1350, the authors ask what the difference was between a *stationarius* and a *librarius*. They follow up the earlier work of Destrez by seeing what the archives reveal about the *stationarius*. They argue that a *stationarius* was a special kind of *librarius* and was a university creation for the purpose of renting out *peciae*. The system of stationers was probably developed in the 1260s and regulated about 1300. There were very few stationers because the rewards of doing this job were not extensive. The authors trace the members of the Sens family, who were the main stationers in Paris over several generations. The onus of acquiring exemplars seems to have fallen on the stationers, and the rental market was principally for new works. No one controlled whether the exemplar contained a good text, though extant exemplars contain many corrections. The stationers themselves may have specialized by faculty, for the Sens family appears to have dealt only in theology and philosophy and not in arts or medical books. The university set the rate for renting, and borrowers paid for the whole work rather than for individual *pecia*. Each *pecia* was lent out for a week, and a pledge was left by the borrower to be reclaimed at the end.

Two articles deal with libraries. The first describes the growth of the library of the Sorbonne, in which two important features emerge. The first is the arrangement of books and the production of catalogues that enable scholars to find books. The catalogues cease to be mere inventories and become vehicles for the organization of learning because they encourage the grouping of books by their contents and provide means for finding one's way to those contents. This promotes use of the books so that the library is divided into a chained and an unchained section. The former contains those books available publicly and which are in the greatest demand. They become like reference and reserved books in modern libraries. The latter are stored in a different room and are available for borrowing for private study to those who are allowed to use them. This leads naturally to the second article, which deals with access to libraries, for it focuses on the Wycliffite accusation that the friars, particularly the Franciscans, in Oxford bought up many books, which they put in their library and thus took out of general circulation because they restricted access to the library. Knowledge that should have been available to all was thus restricted to a few. The growth of universities had promoted study among secular people by taking learning out of the monasteries. The friars were trying to put it back into religious houses. The Wycliffites raised the question, which must have been important in all university towns, because they saw books as a common possession.

The final essays deal with features of the manuscript book immediately before and after the invention of printing. One is a study of the *Opus pacis*, written by Oswald, a Carthusian, in 1417 at Grande Chartreuse. The Carthusians, like the Lollards and the Brethren of the *Devotio moderna*, were eager to produce uniform texts that were identical as far as possible. Oswald was a gifted grammar master who wrote his work to show how this aim could be achieved without undue anxiety. It signals a change from the careful copying of texts to the need to provide standardized and uniform texts, a change from the early to the late Middle Ages. But this change was already well established before printing came along.

Another essay is a commentary on Elizabeth Eisenstein's work on the printing press as an agent of change. The Rouses argue that you can understand what changes the printing press made only if you understand the scribal culture that immediately preceded it. Certain features that might be attributed to the printing press were already found in the manuscript culture. These include clarity of textual presentation, the use of different scripts to highlight different aspects of a text, the accuracy and standardization of the text itself, and the introduction of ways of finding one's way around a text such as chapter headings and indexes. The production of books by such groups as the Brethren of the *Devotio moderna* was carefully organized, and they made good books accessible in good copies. Most of their production went to monasteries and religious houses, as is true of early printed books. Printed books drove out certain features of manuscripts such as glossing and the ability to break down a text into parts for copying. Printing also ended the primary medium for painters.

These essays are extremely stimulating and informative. They also carry an important message for Chaucerians. We can learn much about the intellectual life of a period by studying manuscripts in depth, and this applies as much to vernacular as to Latin writings. Modern scholars who know their Chaucer, for example, only through a modern printed edition will have a very restricted view of their author: what texts were available, how he used them, what his methods of composition were, and what he was trying to achieve. Although Chaucer is hardly mentioned in this volume, the methodology and approach as well as the questions asked by its authors can be applied to Chaucer and his work. All students of Middle English literature would profit from a careful reading of this book.

N. F. BLAKE
University of Sheffield

SARAH STANBURY. *Seeing the* Gawain-*Poet: Description and the Act of Perception*. Middle Ages Series. Philadelphia: University of Pennsylvania Press, 1992. Pp. x, 155. $22.95.

This is a useful and frequently compelling book, as much an exploration of method as a study of the Cotton Nero poems. As the title suggests, Stanbury focuses on the act of perception in *Pearl, Patience, Purity*, and *Sir Gawain and the Green Knight*; specifically, she studies the four poems' use of "focalization," the design of a descriptive passage both to illuminate the object being described and to represent dramatically the character, perspective, and situation of the viewer. Stanbury introduces the concept in a brief introduction that draws chiefly on Mieke Bal's *Narratology* (Toronto: University of Toronto Press, 1985) and on Alain Renoir's essays on description in *Sir Gawain and the Green Knight*. She then introduces the concept of the focalized scene with two examples from *Pearl*, the garden and the Heavenly City, showing that in each scene point of view and description are subtly interdependent. She then turns to detailed examinations of the four poems of manuscript Cotton Nero A.x. These discussions seek to "explore the construction of descriptive detail through ocular reception, the acts of vision that record and structure accounts of what is seen" (p. 6).

Holding to this very specific program proves to be a rather tall order. While the four chapters on the poems deal with perception and interpretation and with real and figurative acts of seeing, they do not each treat focalization in the strict terms that Stanbury sets out in the introduction. The truest applications of the method are to be found in the chapters on *Patience* and *Purity*, while the *Pearl* and *Gawain* discussions take "the

279

construction of descriptive detail" in subtly different directions. This is but an observation, not a criticism: Stanbury's liberal approach to her focus permits her a mature and flexible response to the four Cotton Nero poems, allowing her to introduce useful perspectives from philosophy and iconology without forcing her texts into frameworks that are less illuminating.

The four chapters dealing with the individual poems are unfailingly provocative, serving especially well as a corrective to intellectualizing studies that tend to treat these works as treatises and not poems. The best chapter in my judgment is "*Patience*: The Dialectics of Inside/Outside," one of the most acute and perceptive treatments of the poem that I have encountered. Focusing on the ship, the whale's belly, and the woodbine as enclosures that define Jonah's perspective as distinct from those of outsiders, Stanbury gets to the heart of *Patience*'s challenge to embrace the perceptual liberation of spiritual insight. The analysis of these enclosures as separating or defining the *viator* Jonah is original and powerful: Stanbury permits us to see them as crucial venues for Jonah's and the reader's liminality. The chapter ends with the cogent observation that the techniques of description in *Patience*

do not always comfortably fit their homiletic frame, for the poem's most successful and memorable story is not how to be patient but how difficult it is to attend to God in his apparent absence. [P. 92]

A conclusion such as this captures *Patience* as a work of art whose poet uses techniques without being driven by them.

The chapter on *Purity*, "Reading Signs: *Purity*'s Eyewitness to History" is nearly as good as the *Patience* chapter. Seeing correctly that *Purity* is in large measure a poem about signs and their interpretation, Stanbury sets out and develops a comprehensive sense of the poem's method:

By establishing a link between the reader and the spectator in the text and then by placing the witnessed scene within a homiletic and specifically eschatological framework, descriptive passages in *Purity* invoke vision as both an end and also a graphically enacted process, the "sight" of God we can attain by learning to see in this life. [Pp. 42–43]

It is here that focalization is its richest and densest as a critical framework. Along with the *Patience* chapter, this discussion not only is true to its text but can energize it for a new generation of students.

The studies of *Pearl* and *Sir Gawain and the Green Knight* are less successful than the other two, in large part because, in the final analysis, these poems are more demonstrative and narrative than strictly descriptive: *Pearl* and *Sir Gawain* depend inescapably on verbal exchanges and on actions, not on focalized descriptions, for their impact. The chapter on *Pearl*, for example, does not examine the discussion between the Pearl maiden and the narrator beyond noting that she warns him not to believe idly in the evidence of his senses. Similarly, the *Gawain* chapter does not consider either the hunts or the temptation scenes except to refer briefly to Gawain peeping at Lady Bercilak.

If Stanbury thus appears to nibble at the edges of these two poems, she does so consciously, attendant on her themes of seeing and perspective. And her insights are regularly valuable and provocative: especially compelling is her comparative study of *Pearl* and the iconology of illustrated Apocalypses. Presenting and discussing illustrations showing John's complex relationship to the details of his vision, she argues convincingly that the *Pearl* dreamer has an analogous "liminal" relationship to his dream work.

Chapter 5, "The Framing of the Gaze in *Sir Gawain and the Green Knight*," concentrates on several of the poem's scenes in which characters gaze at or visually "study" one another, thus manifesting the various value systems from which they operate. It is a fascinating exploration of the motif, which Stanbury shows to be important both literally (as characters look at and evaluate one another) and figuratively (in a poem full of ambiguous characters and scenes, which demand and bedevil evaluation).

A concluding chapter reaches out from the Cotton Nero poems to suggest some other fertile ground for studying focalized descriptions: Ricardian poetry and mysticism. The conclusion allows Stanbury to raise a number of interesting questions about description in the age of skepticism and mysticism, but the format does not permit her to give these issues the meticulous treatment she gives to the Cotton Nero poems. Examining *descriptio* in *The Knight's Tale*, *The Book of the Duchess*, *Sir Orfeo*, and *The Parliament of the Three Ages*, she finds none that involves viewer and viewed in quite the way that the Cotton Nero poems do. Of one prominent Ricardian poet, for example, she observes that

Chaucer often seems more concerned with the relationship between perception and action than he is with visual perception as a dramatization of a character's understanding. [Pp. 122–23]

I would disagree with that judgment, suggesting the descriptions in *The General Prologue*, Palamon and Arcite's first view of Emelye, and a number of passages in *The House of Fame* 3 that are strikingly definitive of the characters of Geffrey the Pilgrim, Palamon and Arcite, and the dreamer of *The House of Fame*. I am no less appreciative of Stanbury's book for this disagreement: good critics energize their readers, and more needs to be said on just how description functions in Chaucer's poetry.

In summary, this is a serious, intelligent, and perceptive work that elegantly meets the challenge of studying technique in the Cotton Nero poems. It is not a comprehensive study to compare with those of A. C. Spearing and Lynn Staley Johnson (to cite two examples), but it is not intended to be so. Stanbury has taken what is in some ways a bolder and riskier tack—to explore a closely related set of descriptive *topoi*—and her success makes this a worthwhile and valuable book.

J. STEPHEN RUSSELL
Hofstra University

TOSHIYUKI TAKAMIYA and RICHARD BEADLE, eds. *Chaucer to Shakespeare: Essays in Honour of Shinsuke Ando*. Cambridge: D. S. Brewer, 1992. Pp. xiii, 255. $70.00.

Shinsuke Ando, still in his early sixties, is representative of the middle generation of Japanese scholars of English literature. The earlier generation, represented by the revered, recently deceased Michio Masui, made important contributions to the study of medieval and Renaissance language and poetic. Ando's generation moved on to historical and critical interpretation of the literature, as represented in Ando's own bibliography, included in the volume. The younger generation, represented by the contributors to this festschrift, has moved on to psychological and theoretical study of the production and reception of the literature.

The festschrift is a collection of twenty-three very sophisticated essays, six on Chaucer, seven on Shakespeare, and the others on various medieval and Elizabethan authors and topics. One cannot hope in a review to analyze twenty-three essays individually, but let me say a word or two about those that interested me most. Ruth Morse's "Temperamental Texts: Medieval Discussions of Character, Emotion, and Motivation" is a very suggestive exploration of the movement in medieval culture from interest in action to concern about intention. Richard Axton's "Chaucer and 'Tragedy'" points up the incompatibility of Christianity and tragedy, and Chaucer's tendency to blunt tragedy with pathos. Yasunari Takada's "From the *House of Fame* to Politico-Cultural Histories" is a sophisticated discussion of Chaucer's transformation of the Boethian vision of a cosmos governed by enlightened authority to a politicohistorical macrocosm administered for "comune profit." Richard Beadle's "'I wol nat telle it yit': John Selden and a Lost Version of the *Cook's Tale*" offers interesting evidence for a lost text of *The Canon's Yeoman's Tale*, although it does not help explain the presence of *Gamelyn* in the manuscripts. John Burrow's "The Griffin's Egg: Gower's *Confessio Amantis* 1.2545" is a nice description, with illustrations, of goblets made of ostrich-egg shells, referred to by Gower and others in their poetry. Takami Matsuda's "The Presence of Purgatory in Two Debates in BL MS Addit. 37049" is astonishing in its familiarity with a broad range of medieval European religious literature.

Joerg Fichte's "The Passion Plays in *Ludus Coventriae* and the Continental Passion Plays" is likewise remarkable for the way it juxtaposes the English, French, and German Passion plays, an intercultural connection too seldom recognized. Soji Iwasaki's "Relative Values in Medieval and Renaissance Drama" goes beyond recognition of the morality-play oppositions between good and evil to point out that reconciliation of these oppositions into harmony in the ideal image of man is the Renaissance form of the medieval dichotomy. Derek Brewer's "Elizabethan Merry Tales and *The Merry Wives of Windsor*: Shakespeare and Popular Literature" finds the source of humor in Shakespeare's and others' plays in the popular Elizabethan "jest books."

My own taste obviously inclines me toward the essays on medieval topics. Barbara Hardy's "Telling the Future: Forecasts and Fantasies in Shakespeare's Narrative," Norman Blake's "*Why* and *What* in Shakespeare," Hidekatsu Nojima's "The *Vita Sexualis* of the Macbeths," the other pieces on Shakespeare and Milton, and Renate Haas on the reception of Chaucer in eighteenth-century Germany are likewise excellent, as are the essays on *Gawain*, Julian of Norwich, Sidney's *Astrophel and Stella*, and others. The essays in this collection are important in their own right, as a demonstration of the mastery of critical thought and language by the Japanese contributors, whose essays blend seamlessly with those by the British and European (interestingly, no American) contributors, and provide an impressive

283

recognition of the contribution of Shinsuke Ando and his colleagues to the appreciation of English literature.

JOHN H. FISHER
Knoxville, Tennessee

RICHARD J. UTZ. *Literarischer Nominalismus im Spätmittelalter: Eine Untersuchung zu Sprache, Charakterzeichnung und Struktur in Geoffrey Chaucers* Troilus and Criseyde. Sprache und Literatur: Regensburger Arbeiten zur Anglistik und Amerikanistik, no. 31. Frankfurt am Main: Peter Lang, 1990. Pp. 265. DM 82 ($63.80).

The need for a study of the impact of nominalism on Chaucer's works is apparent. As Richard Utz points out in this study of *Troilus and Criseyde*, until quite recently neither nominalism nor Ockhamism was indexed in any of the standard bibliographies of Chaucer studies: "It was only with the appearance of *The Essential Chaucer*, a bibliography edited in 1987, with eight entries on the subject, and the *Bibliography of Chaucer: 1974–85*, edited in 1988, with five entries, that a noticeable change and an acceptance of the area of research could be noted" (p. 41; my translation, as throughout this review). A major reason for this critical neglect is the lack of any specific textual passages that point directly toward nominalist sources. "Chaucer's literary Nominalism, thus, has to manifest itself through other means" (p. 61), and Utz must build a case for the existence of nominalist influence on an assortment of indirect evidence.

The methodological necessity of drawing conclusions based on indirect evidence of Chaucer's either conscious or passive adherence to nominalist thought is stated in chapter 1. Summaries of the history of nominalism during the Middle Ages and the critical comment on Chaucer's reception of nominalist ideas are given in chapters 2 and 3, respectively; these chapters are very general, serving primarily as introductions to the basic issues for nonspecialists.

The argument in Utz's study actually begins in chapter 4, "Das Sprichwort in Chaucers 'Troilus and Criseyde': Zur Problematisierung eines idealistisch-universalen Denk-und Sprachkonzepts." The author maintains that the "medieval extension of the Platonic idealism of Antiquity is Realism" (p. 80). The serious use or acceptance of *Sprichwörter*, or

284

proverbs, by characters in *Troilus* signals a reliance upon universals, which characterizes the mentality of the Neoplatonic realists. First, there is Pandarus, who uses a "lion's share" of proverbs in the first three books of the romance, as he brings together the eponymous lovers under relatively generalized circumstances, but who becomes "speechless" when confronted with the specific misfortunes presented in the final two books. Then there is Troilus:

[He] at first betrays a naïve belief in the authority of proverbs and then must painfully feel how, with the change of situation caused by the surrender of Criseyde, many of the metaphors, images, and other linguistic devices prove to have multiple meanings and can even act against him. [P. 100]

Chaucer's use of proverbs indicates a rejection of an earlier medieval mentality in favor of later nominalist attitudes.

In chapter 5, the use of allegory, or an extended metaphor understood with reference to an abstract system of ideas, is shown to be compatible with the principles of medieval literary realism. According to Utz, the characterization of Criseyde indicates Chaucer's rejection of allegory or typology in favor of more ambiguous, individualizing methods; Chaucer's avoidance of allegory reflects, therefore, yet another aspect of his literary nominalism.

Chapter 6 studies the "courtly idealism and radical determinism" that characterize Troilus. The characterization of Troilus is seen to be Chaucer's response to or criticism of the neorealist ideas propounded by John Wyclif, who was, of course, a contemporary of the poet and whose opinions would have been familiar to him.

Chapter 7, "Trennung der Wahrheiten," argues that the often negatively criticized palinode of *Troilus and Criseyde* is consistent with a nominalist reading of the work. The nominalist rejection of universals was not a rejection of faith in the unseen verities of the Christian religion. In a nominalist reading, the Epilogue becomes, rather than a statement of the *contemptus mundi* theme, a "sort of 'leap of faith'" (p. 211) by the narrator from the realm of specifics (*irdisch-empirische Wahrheit*) into the realm of religious categories (*Glaubenswahrheiten*), making complete on two levels the love story that Chaucer is presenting.

Chapter 8, the conclusion, explains that one possible reason for Chaucer's seeming modernity could be the elements of literary nominalism that this study elucidates. The chapter is short, but Utz's point forms a satisfactory coda to his book.

The most original material developed in this study on the subject of literary nominalism in *Troilus* comes in chapter 4. Here, in his most persuasive argument, Utz offers a plausible theory to account for the function of the character Pandarus, at times sympathetic and at times insensitive, and the seemingly endless storehouse of platitudes and proverbs upon which he draws but which fails him in the end. This chapter represents a true contribution to Chaucer studies. The least satisfying argument appears in chapter 6; Utz's drawing of parallels between Wyclif's reactionary realism, on the one hand, and Troilus's idealism and apparent determinism, on the other, does not quite convey a strong sense of dependence. In fact, this chapter seems a bit incongruous with the rest of the study: to ascribe every aspect of the story, including Troilus's peculiarities of character, to nominalist influence or to criticism of realist thought would be to allegorize the story, which is contrary to the author's thesis.

In this book careful consideration is given to radical or Neoplatonic realism. But Aristotle is mentioned only in the context of nominalism. Utz certainly did not intend to place the Aristotelian realists in the camp of the nominalists, but the danger of that reading exists. The reason for Utz's emphasis is clear, however; for *Troilus*, realism of the Neoplatonic variety was certainly most important.

As pointed out above, owing to the lack of any textual evidence, Utz's case necessarily depends on accumulating enough indirect evidence to support the claim that Chaucer was, in fact, a literary nominalist. Utz argues cogently, and his case, in general, is solid. There are points at the ends of some chapters, however, at which a momentary shift from the rhetoric of induction to that of deduction reveals the author's surprise at his own eloquence, but this is only an occasional occurrence. On the whole, the argument is skillfully and evenly presented.

This book was originally a dissertation directed by Karl Heinz Göller, submitted in 1990 in fulfillment of Ph.D. requirements at the University of Regensburg (Bavaria, Germany). In 1991 it won the Dr. Katharina Sailer Award, given by the university for outstanding work in the field of English studies. It is a well-researched and well-written study and makes enjoyable and rewarding reading.

NOEL HAROLD KAYLOR, JR.
University of Northern Iowa

SABINE VOLK-BIRKE. *Chaucer and Medieval Preaching: Rhetoric for Listeners in Sermons and Poetry.* ScriptOralia, vol. 34. Tübingen: Gunter Narr, 1991. Pp. 315. DM 86.

This is a curate's egg of a book. As the first sustained attempt to situate Chaucer's work in relation to contemporary preaching, it is set to break some new ground. Pioneering enterprises often enjoy this kind of advantage. Their drawbacks are equally familiar, however, and are not entirely avoided in the work under review. Although medieval sermons have been a terra incognita for many Chaucerians, that has not prevented some from discussing them as if they were quite at home there. This is not Sabine Volk-Birke's shortcoming; the corpus of Middle English sermons that she has familiarized herself with, while limited, is treated at length. Indeed, the inexorable taxonomies that she sets up and repeats chapter in, chapter out, though likely to exhaust all but the most dedicated of sermon readers, at least ensure a certain consistency and focus. What she is acquainted with she is evidently acquainted with through and through, and doubters of that are left with little refuge by the time they reach the end of the book. But the question remains how well prepared she was for her excursion of charting and mapping.

She has taken her bearings in a largely unpublished terrain from five published texts: the curious lucky dip of a sermon anthology that is to be found in British Library manuscript Royal 18 B xxiii, the far more homogeneous English Wycliffite sermons, John Mirk's massively popular *Festial*, the versified *Northern Homily Cycle*, and Thomas Wimbledon's tour de force preached at Paul's Cross, London, on the theme "Redde racionem villicacionis tue." A decided advantage in this choice, above the merely pragmatic one of the ready availability of these texts, is that they are all contemporary with Chaucer, nearly contemporary, or, in the instance of the *Northern Homily Cycle*, already in circulation before he was born. Volk-Birke's comparisons are therefore rendered all the more compelling from being chronologically justified. Unfortunately, though, what comparisons there are are rather severely defined—necessarily, however, because she is concerned to isolate six strictly formal categories (the stylistics of the preacher's interaction with his congregation, sermon formulas, structural organization, use of narrative, syntax, and rhetorical figures) that characterize, she believes, late-fourteenth-century sermon style.

Her book falls very heavily into the two halves that it announces: chapters

1 to 9 have nothing whatever to do with Chaucer, though they establish the preliminaries necessary for the writing of chapters 10 to 13, which discuss, respectively, the Parson, Melibee, the Pardoner, and the Nun's Priest. Historical issues, then, are largely bracketed as being beyond her remit, which is a pity, because it is here that some of the more challenging comparisons between Chaucer and preaching remain to be worked out, not merely as a supplement to the conclusions Volk-Birke derives from her formal analysis but sometimes as their corrective. Yet we must be grateful for what insights there are, because she has some good things to say.

Was the protracted labor of chapters 1 to 4 really necessary, however? Granted, her six formal categories required illustration, and the ground had to be cleared to make way for the Chaucer commentary in the second part of the book, but that could have been done in drastically less space. Chapter 1, an excursus through medieval preaching, most clearly shows the damage consequent on her relative inattention to the richness of historical considerations, even though the secondary critics whose work she distills are generally authoritative and lend her commentary workmanlike credibility. Chapter 2, in the main an analysis of the preaching techniques of modern American folk preachers, could have been dropped altogether without ill effect and its conclusions incorporated elsewhere as useful obiter dicta. This leaves us with the Chaucerian chapters.

In chapter 10 she achieves a judicious appraisal of the Parson. Lee Patterson, a critic of evident sophistication, may find himself disposed to thank Volk-Birke for her strictly accurate rescue of *The Parson's Tale* from his verdict of 1978 that the *Tale* has to be a manual for penitents rather than a sermon, partly in view of "the virtual exclusion of the great stock-in-trade of the medieval preacher, the *exemplum*." But exempla, as she has realized, are not the preacher's inevitable small change. Given the possible retrospective on Patterson's work and the upward revision of its value that is likely to follow in the wake of his current influence, Volk-Birke's modification comes apropos. On Melibee, in chapter 11, she is rather less convincing. Some of her six formal categories are, after all, the stuff that everyday speech is made of, and of themselves do not amount to indelible sermon characteristics. Not that she is claiming sermon status for Melibee — far from it — but her classification of it as "preaching disguised" does not seem to be especially revealing. She regains her stride with the Pardoner and in general provides a very worthwhile commentary, though some of her conclusions remain questionable. For example, rather than argue the distance between *The Pardoner's Tale* and sermon exempla as we know them (and it should be remembered that Volk-Birke's sample is limited), we might instead argue the *Tale's* proximity, that it courts the *illusion* of exemplum, not quite comparable to any one actual sermon exemplum, to be sure, but a rhetorically elaborated, and paradoxically therefore a quintessential, facsimile of the genre. Indeed, the sheer sensationalism of the *Tale*, an aspect that Volk-Birke neglects and that may leave a more lasting impression on the mind, bears close comparison to the violent and sordid resonance of certain of the exempla of John Mirk's *Festial*. Finally, before a two-page conclusion that recapitulates her main ideas, chapter 13 considers the sermon affinities of *The Nun's Priest's Tale*. Well might this chapter be headed "Preaching Transformed." Distinct, formal resemblances in this *Tale* to medieval sermons are nevertheless fitful, and on balance we are left thinking how little like medieval preaching it is.

In sum, I can imagine a worse vade mecum than this book, but unfortunately I can also imagine a better. A search through *Chaucer and Medieval Preaching* may well uncover the occasional florin, but not before we have also turned up many a crooked way.

ALAN J. FLETCHER
University College, Dublin

NICHOLAS WATSON. *Richard Rolle and the Invention of Authority*. Cambridge Studies in Medieval Literature, vol. 13. Cambridge: Cambridge University Press, 1992. Pp. xiv, 358. $90.00.

Rolle's standing has been far lower in the second half of this century than it was in the first, and Nicholas Watson concludes this judicious study of Rolle, whom he considers a major Latin author, with the sobering observation that Rolle's popularity "has. . . past all recovery gone" (p. 269). Watson's distaste is frequently only lightly masked in this study, yet his astringent reading of Rolle's works is to be welcomed: a new generation of scholars who maintain a skeptical religious stance is now subjecting mystical writing to the scrutiny of modern critical theory.

Building on much recent work on Rolle that has returned our attention to the text itself, through codicology, textual criticism, manuscript ownership, and the identification of some of Rolle's sources, Watson proposes a reordering and redating of Rolle's writings. He suggests that most of Rolle's oeuvre was produced in the two decades before his death in 1349 and that he was probably born between 1305 and 1310 rather than 1290–1300, as Horstman and Allen assumed (p. 278); in other words, Rolle was "probably nearer forty than fifty when he died." This partly resolves the term *iuvenis* which Rolle uses of himself in many of his Latin works. It was the presence of this term, and the experimental style, which led Hope Allen to assume that *Melos amoris* was an early work. Watson argues convincingly that *Melos* forms a culmination to Rolle's middle, apologetic, phase and forms a transition to his later, audience-directed works in Latin and English.

Watson evaluates Rolle's writing as an apprenticeship in an authorial style that proclaims by its very hypertextuality the divine authenticity of its content. Central to this process is the establishment of the ambivalent model of hermit preacher that Rolle sets up as the "I" within the text. This is the subject that Watson finds so fascinatingly audacious in its self-reflexivity. He claims that Rolle's writing has a hidden agenda: when uncovered, in *Incendium amoris*, this agenda proves to be the "canonization" of the writer as a modern *auctor* and modern master of the spiritual life (p. 196). Watson reads much of Rolle's work as "apologetic" in stance and so identifies the textual "I" with the author; another reading might treat it as a persona.

Watson does, however, challenge earlier readings of Rolle's work as corroboration of the dramatic conversion recounted in the *Officium et miracula Sancti Ricardi*, probably compiled in the 1380s as a prelude to a never-initiated process for Rolle's canonization.

Watson rightly classifies the *Officium* as hagiography, presenting Rolle as a fourteenth-century St. Francis, who left family and clothing in the fervor of religious conversion (pp. 40–42, 224, 295–96). In Watson's opinion, Rolle presented himself as the hermit- saint communing directly with God in solitude, only later recognizing his calling to address the church as a whole (p. 198). This ambivalent model may explain the unease felt by Rolle's readers. A double identity shift disorientates the reader's perspective: the "I" addressing us shuffles from one stance to another in adjacent sentences, and even more confusingly his putative addressee also changes identity within a single paragraph. Our inability to stabilize ourselves amid the changing points of view—Who is addressing us? What role are we playing now?—ought, however, to envigorate the modern reader. Rolle deconstructs the genres he adopts, merging sermon with satire, epistle with *postilla*, apology with homily, and vade mecum with theological compendium. Like Chaucer, he can play wittily with audience expectation because his chief audience was as educated as he in the techniques of university exposition (pp. 297–98). Unlike Chaucer, he chose Latin as his medium, and his fame has gone with the culture that sustained it at such a height in the 180 years between his death and the Reformation, when "he must have been deeply exciting to read" (p. 269).

Rolle had at least part of a university training, and his readers were parish clergy, Watson suggests (p. 298). Rolle must have found his position ambiguous: in the guise of poor hermit, an unseen purveyor of inspired truths about the importance of rejecting the world, he had to communicate through comfortably off, socially accepted clerical mediators to reach his intended audience of the worldly and godless. Such was the paradox of the preaching solitary. Perhaps this is the explanation for the lack of focus in so much of Rolle's writing. He is at his best and most attractive when he addresses a specific audience directly, as in the early *Judica me Deus* written for a young parish priest, and in the late works, with their "better defined readership" (p. 191), and his English works. All these were written, Watson claims, for nuns and for Margaret Kirkeby, whose intelligence was rewarded with the strenuous meditation exercise of the *English Psalter*. Watson claims, rather daringly, that manuscript Longleat 29 is directly descended from a compilation of his work that Rolle made for Margaret before she went to her anchorite cell and that it remained in the hands of solitaries for the next one hundred years (p. 248).

Although Watson rejects a biographical reading of Rolle, his organizing principle in this study follows Rolle's own attempt to structure his mystical experience in the famous triad *fervor, dulcor*, and *canor*. Watson groups his minutely discursive presentation of the Latin texts under the terms Rolle used for his mystic initiation, with *Judica me Deus*, which is about vocations (Rolle's, then his priestly patron's), forming an apologetic prelude. Rolle's scriptural commentaries, and his first original composition, the verse *Canticum amoris*, are treated under "Seeing into Heaven" (*Incendium amoris* 12), and *fervor* naturally covers *Incendium*. Less easy to explain is the presence of Rolle's treatments of "On the Twentieth Psalm," "On the Song of Songs," and *Contra Amatores Mundi* under the heading *dulcor*, since in the second of these Rolle "tries to bludgeon [his readers] with assertions of his own canonical status" (p. 158): it is the thematic image of sweetness in these works, certainly not their tone, that justifies the heading. More clearly applicable is *canor* as the covering term for *Melos amoris*: "The work is literally self-referential: it both is and is about *canor*" (p. 178), like the English lyrics (p. 233).

There is a circularity in assessing Rolle's development as writer from a redating of his work that is made on assumptions about that evolution, but

Watson just makes his case, I think. His evidence appears in an appendix called "Excursus I"; its detailed citation of Rolle's borrowings from himself would delay discussion if elevated to the main study.

By his redating of *Melos*, Watson locates in cap. 48 the transitional moment where Rolle reidentifies his function of "inspired didactic writer" (p. 187), intermediary between reader and God, who is to "save the lost and exhort the Church to virtue." From this point Rolle's writing is less "engulfed by eloquence" (p. 188), and Watson labels this new dimension, seen in *Super lectiones mortuorum, Emendatio vitae*, and the English epistles, the "mixed life." This term may not be appropriate to Rolle, who rejected Richard of St. Victor's "insatiable" stage of missionary love, but Watson is right to draw attention in this way to the change of mood and, apparently, vocation at the close of Rolle's career.

For Watson, it is the authorial role that most exercises Rolle, his status as communicator, rather than the divine truth he conveyed. Even in *Ego dormio*, where Rolle seems to address his epistle to a single recipient, Watson finds his use of the second-person singular pronoun misleading: it is a fictional "thou" who reaches heights the addressee never may (p. 228). Thus for Watson even the English works are as occupied with Rolle himself as the Latin. Rolle, in his own image of a spiritual pander, wins the soul of his reader for Christ by the sheer power and authority of his own love, not God's (p. 231). Were this true, we would be right to reject so stridently self-preoccupied a writer. But my doubts are aroused by a passage that Watson quotes from chapter 43 of *Melos* (p. 225): "I proceeded in this way so that all might learn to love the Author" ("ut omnes addiscerent Auctorem amare;" Arnould, ed., p. 132, line 34). Rolle's ultimate "authority" is God, as this phrase makes clear; his identification with biblical voices, his claim of divine authorization for his idiosyncratic displays of astounding, and admittedly domineering, Latin prose and verse can be explained as an adoption of the stance of prophet, speaking out God's, not his own, words. That he is not wholly (or perhaps mainly) successful in this is no doubt because he is uncertain of his *readership* rather than of his own authority. He shouts encouragement from the top of the spiritual ladder, as Watson says (p. 226), instead of accompanying his reader.

In this, however, Watson is quite unlike his subject, moving steadily through difficult material that he translates into appropriate English (suitably florid for *Melos*). His commentary skillfully exposes Rolle's failures in logic and reminds us of previous stages in the discussion, all essential in so multiform an author.

This is the first book-length comprehensive guide to Rolle's Latin and

English writing. Watson has cleared the ground for further study of Rolle, and his two "Excursus," on the dating of Rolle's work and on what may have been his real position in society, form the conclusion to this fine assessment of the texts and remind us of the exploratory nature of his study. Watson ends, appropriately, by demonstrating how often Rolle borrows from his own work as well as from thirteenth- and fourteenth-century spiritual and theological writers and suggests that Rolle may have had access to a network of graduates based in Oxford. A far cry indeed from the untaught hermit of the *Officium*.

ROSAMUND ALLEN
Queen Mary and Westfield College,
University of London

JAMES I. WIMSATT. *Chaucer and His French Contemporaries: Natural Music in the Fourteenth Century*. Toronto, Buffalo, and London: University of Toronto Press, 1992. Pp. xv, 378. $60.00.

James I. Wimsatt's latest study of Chaucer's relationship to the French poets Guillaume de Machaut, Jean Froissart, Eustache Deschamps, and Oton de Granson is a worthy and important contribution to Chaucer studies. *Chaucer and His French Contemporaries* significantly advances the dual project Wimsatt set himself nearly thirty years ago: publicizing the extent to which the English poet, especially in his notorious "early" period, was indebted to contemporary French models and methods (especially the hugely influential and enormous corpus of the much-celebrated Machaut), and rehabilitating the reputation of these French authors, who received little praise from the first generation of philologists (such as George L. Kittredge and Gaston Paris) and subsequently were ignored or dismissed by Charles Muscatine in one of the most widely read studies of Chaucer's sources. While it goes over much of the same ground covered by Wimsatt in a series of articles during the last decade and more, *Chaucer and His French Contemporaries* offers a useful compendium of and commentary on traditionally oriented source and influence research in this area. The study is also innovative and polemical in presenting a compelling argument that the truly important gift of Machaut and his followers to Chaucer was their concept (best articulated by Deschamps) of "natural music," the view, as

293

Wimsatt puts it, that poetry, reversing modern priorities, "puts the sense in service to the sound" (p. 10). The true importance of the French tradition, then, is not its content (the various "matters" of love) or its narrative or presentational devices (such as personification allegory or elaborate play with narrational structures); it is rather that Machaut and his followers taught Chaucer how to be a lyric poet and that this lyricism pervades much of what he wrote, including a number of works usually thought to be inspired solely by the Italian novelistic tradition, most especially *Troilus and Criseyde*.

Before discussing the book in more detail, I must register a serious reservation. Wimsatt conceives his study as a riposte to the current trend in Chaucer studies of understanding the poet as primarily a writer of narrative. It is apparently for this reason that Wimsatt either ignores or slights the kind of work that has become most prominent in Machaut studies during the last decade. This scholarship has emphasized the ludic qualities of the Machaldian text, dealing with its insistent literariness; its intricate (dis)connections to the poet's life and corpus; its often comic and celebratory representation of the shifting, complicated relations among poet, public, and patron; its self-conscious remaking or replacing of literary models. Such work has not necessarily privileged the narrative aspects of Machaut's poems (reflexivity is more a matter of presentationalism than storytelling), but it has certainly downplayed the lyric elements that Wimsatt wishes to emphasize. This emerging picture of Machaut's practice corrects the long-held misimpression that he was merely a slavish imitator of older models, particularly the *Roman de la Rose*. More important for the present purpose, it also constructs a different model for the influence of Machaut on Chaucer. From this perspective, as William Calin has written, "the greatest gift Machaut offers Chaucer is the notion of a poet writing poetry about the writing of poetry by a poet."[1] Wimsatt does not give this critical approach its proper due and therefore offers only a partial (albeit intriguing) account of the relationship between Chaucer and Machaut.

One example must here suffice. Machaut's two *jugement* poems (and their lyric continuation, the *Lay de plour*) constitute an elaborate transtextual series in which the traditional matter of love-debate poetry becomes secondary to a complexly comic portrait of the author at work. In the *Jugement dou Roy de Navarre* the narrator, named as the poet Guillaume

---

[1] William Calin, "Machaut's Legacy: The Chaucerian Heritage Reconsidered," *SLittI* 20 (Spring, 1987): 14.

de Machaut, is called to account by Lady Good Fortune for having composed an antifeminist work, the *Jugement dou Roy de Behaingne*. Guillaume then clumsily defends the opinion offered in the earlier work to a *demande d'amours* and after a debate in which he comes to espouse the view that men are superior to women in the experience of love is not surprisingly found guilty. His penance is to compose three lyric poems, one of which, the *Lay de plour*, was actually written. It has long been recognized that the *Jugement Navarre* was Chaucer's model for *The Legend of Good Women*, but what has never received adequate attention is Chaucer's borrowing of the idea of literary penance as well as the complex scheme of reading it establishes for the penitential compositions themselves (which, in the works of both poets, must be understood in the light of their authors' "conversion" to political correctness). The *Lay de plour* recycles in lyric form the woman's perspective on love sorrow from the *Behaingne*, but, because he uses a lyric form, Machaut is able to avoid actually recanting the judgment he authorized in that earlier work; in effect, he simply recycles part of what he had already written and corrects nothing. The relationship between the framing *Prologue* and the legends in Chaucer's work exploits the same opportunities for a complex, sometimes ironic tone. Yet Chaucerians, still not adequately informed about the sophisticated nature of Machaut's achievement, have not yet been able to read the English poet through his French source. The current work does nothing to further such an understanding. Wimsatt's treatment of Machaldian influence on the *Legend* is very brief, dealing almost entirely, like the classic study of John L. Lowes, with the Marguerite material of the *Prologue*.

This is typical of the book's approach to questions of intertextuality. Discussion of the literary relationships between Chaucer and his French contemporaries is limited to the matters of source analysis and literary history that occupied the first generation of philologists, a tradition to which Wimsatt significantly contributed in his *Chaucer and the French Love Poets* (1968). But these methods do not do justice either to Machaut's invention of narrative love poetry that makes a substantial place for the representation of the author and his literary (dis)contents or to Chaucer's innovative adaptation of this kind of poeticizing (which raises issues better handled by narratology than philology).

I cannot agree, then, with Wimsatt that Chaucer's lyricism is the most important gift he received from the Middle French poets he read. Much more remains to be said about these literary relationships. Yet Wimsatt's argument, first, that such lyricism is an important, sometimes dominant element within the Chaucerian corpus and, second, that this lyricism derives from the Middle French tradition, is absolutely convincing. Chapter 1 adroitly makes the case for "natural music" with a series of comparative technical analyses. Wimsatt gently corrects the modern predisposition to privilege sense over sound by demonstrating that Middle French verse counterpoints meaning and music. An important document here is Machaut's *Prologue*, an ars poetica written for the manuscripts featuring an organized collection of his works. Because the *Prologue* more or less treats poetry as an aspect of music, Wimsatt uses it to buttress his argument (though his discussion is disappointingly brief). Chapter 2 provides a useful discussion of the relatively unknown Jean de le Mote, an important presence at the English court in the early 1350s, whose works combine lyric and narrative modes while making extensive use of exempla (the major features, Wimsatt argues, of Machaut's verse; there is good evidence that Machaut, like Chaucer, felt the influence of Jean's technical innovations). It is here as well that Wimsatt proves himself an admirable and clear writer of literary history. His discussion of the literary interests of the court of Edward III is fascinating, though once again a bit brief.

In the remainder of the book three chapters are devoted to the relationship between Chaucer and Machaut, with single chapters on Froissart, Deschamps, and Oton de Granson. Machaut is the most important figure here, and Wimsatt acknowledges this through a series of analyses: a discussion of the use of lyric narrators (including the disillusioned lover so prominent in the corpora of the two poets); a section of "verse made to order" (which unfortunately offers only a partial treatment of the question of patronage, more important for Machaut, of course, than for Chaucer); a full-scale reading of the Machaldian influence on Chaucer's early poetry; and finally a tracing of the continuing importance of Machaut's poetry for the projects of Chaucer's maturity, including *Troilus and Criseyde* and *The Canterbury Tales*. These three chapters are the center of the book and constitute an important argument for the indebtedness of Chaucer to Machaut (even as they provide a better understanding of the French poet for Chaucerians unfamiliar with his work). The other chapters are too limited by traditional methods of source analysis; here it becomes more often than not a question of a shared use of conventions and matter, mostly derived from Machaut, and Wimsatt is obviously not as interested in these more indirect literary relationships. And yet these can be valuable. Chaucerians, for example, would benefit from a discussion of the separate uses made by the English poet and Christine de Pizan (who merits only the briefest of mentions in this book) of the *Jugement Behaingne* and the love-debate poetry tradition in general. As yet this more indirect literary relationship has not received the attention it manifestly deserves.

Throughout the book Wimsatt demonstrates an encyclopedic knowledge of the literary connections he proposes to analyze. His knowledge, in fact, is unique among this generation of Chaucerians. Moreover, his technical analyses will make interesting reading even for Chaucer scholars inclined to privilege the poet's structural and thematic achievements. Wimsatt's real service to students of medieval English literature, however, is that he persuades us to discover a different Chaucer, a poet whose musical interests are not confined to the works traditionally termed both minor and lyric.

R. BARTON PALMER
Georgia State University

JAN M. ZIOLKOWSKI, ed. *Jezebel: A Norman Latin Poem of the Early Eleventh Century*. Humana Civilitas: Studies and Sources Relating to the Middle Ages and the Renaissance, vol. 10, published under the auspices of the Center for Medieval and Renaissance Studies, University of California, Los Angeles. New York, Bern, Frankfurt am Main, and Paris: Peter Lang, 1989. Pp. xiv, 226. $32.95 paper.

Jezebel was a sacrilegious, blasphemous, idolatrous biblical harlot whose spectacular misconduct made her name a synonym for depravity, and yet, surprisingly, this is the first book devoted to a full discussion of her standing in the Middle Ages. Jan M. Ziolkowski has done much more than produce a magnificent edition of the poem in which she figures: he has produced a biographical resurrection of the heroine herself.

The book is divided into three parts. The first part describes the evolution of her image, from the "murderously pagan and tyrannical queen, the wife of Ahab" (p. 5) in the Old Testament to the use of her name in the New Testament as the type of false prophetess set on seducing all around her: "Whereas the Jezebel in the New Testament is sexually uncontrolled and heretical, the queen in the Old Testament is cruel and idolatrous" (p. 12). Thus the two strains of idolater and fornicator became fused, as, for example, in the writings of Ambrosius, who refers to her as "Iezabel idolatra simul et fornicaria."

The original meaning of the name Jezebel is uncertain. Jerome furnished what became the standard etymologies for her name in his *Liber interpretationis hebraicorum nominum*, and Isidore, among others, based his definition on Jerome's in his *Etymologies*: "Jezebel is a discharge of blood or a stream of blood: but it is better when the name is rendered as 'dung heap'" (p. 13). Her name became a byword for persecutor, and her picture appears frequently in medieval art as the persecutor of Elijah. Ziolkowski notes "the complete neglect she has received from historians of Christian iconography" (p. 20).

The second part of the book is concerned with the Norman Latin poem itself. The editor disputes the theory that the poet has an actual woman in mind and convincingly argues that she is "probably a fictitious character based loosely upon her two biblical forebears" (p. 26). The poem, which is 141 lines long, survives in one manuscript, Paris, Bibliothèque Nationale, lat. 8121A, dated on paleographic grounds to the second half of the eleventh century and copied in eastern France. In addition to two pieces of prose there are four poems in the manuscript, two named as satires by Warner of Rouen, and two anonymous, *Jezebel*, and *Semiramis*. The latter are similar in vocabulary, phraseology, sources, and themes and were probably composed by the same author, "either Warner himself or a member of his circle" (p. 37).

The third part of the book contains a transcription of the manuscript, an edition of the poem based on the transcription, a translation, and a commentary. *Jezebel* is written as a question-and-answer dialogue, a very popular form (cf. catechisms and colloquies). It is a wrangle between Jezebel and her interlocutor, couched in language that resembles the double-entendres of Old English riddles. The Latin is extremely difficult and full of ambiguities.

Jezebel's answers can be very direct. For instance, she is asked why she is an adulterer ("Dic cur moecharis") and she replies: "Uulue respondeat ignis" ("Let the fire of the vulva respond to that"; line 62). Often she is ambiguous, as, for example, when she says: "Poterit cognoscere luscus" (line 105), which literally means, "The man who is blind in one eye will be able to recognize." The editor explains that *luscus* may be taken as a metaphor for penis (cf. Martial 2.33.3 and 9.37.10). Hence she seems to mean, "The one-eyed (penis) will be able to get to know." Alternatively, Martial often applies the adjective *luscus* to lecherous women. If so, the Latin may mean, "And the man who is lustful will recognize (my dishonorable spirit as kin to his own)", which Ziolkowski suggests may be loosely rendered, "It takes one to know one." How he teases out the various possible meanings of *luscus* is a typical example of his superb handling of the ambiguities in the text.

Throughout, the interlocutor's words smack of self-righteousness, but in one comical exchange Jezebel seems to think he is asking for a kiss, when he says, "Basia da parie" ("Give kisses of tribute"; line 131), and she replies very ambiguously, "Non sit panis habunde" ("May you not have enough bread"). This reference to bread is most mysterious, but it may mean, according to the editor, that Jezebel, who earlier boasts that she has been fed a thousand times by her lovers ("Sum mille cibata cinedis"; line 80), turns him down because he does not have enough bread to pay her for her services.

As a help in appreciating the cut-and-thrust of the *Jezebel* dialogue, the editor provides in an appendix an edition of a similar set of exchanges between Solomon and the crafty Marcolf, the *De certamine Salomonis et Marcolphi*, also accompanied by a translation and notes. The book ends with notes, a full bibliography, indexes, and plates showing various depictions of Jezebel in bed and elsewhere. The indexes contain a list of Latin words, an index of authors and titles, and a hair-raising index of proper nouns and subjects (e.g., *penis*: "See also beam; bellows; one-eyed; pastries; phalliform; phallus; Priapus; rod; scrotal sack; spindle; sword").

This is an exemplary edition of a singularly difficult text. It is also a defense of Jezebel, a reproof to medieval scholars who have neglected her for so long, a glossary of obscene Latin, a guide to coping with riddles, an original contribution to misogynistic literature — and also a very good read.

T. P. DOLAN
University College, Dublin

BOOKS RECEIVED

Aers, David, ed. *Culture and History, 1350–1600: Essays on English Communities, Identities, and Writing*. Detroit: Wayne State University Press, 1992. Pp. 213. $29.95 cloth, $15.95 paper.

Allen, Peter L. *The Art of Love: Amatory Fiction from Ovid to the* Romance of the Rose. Middle Ages Series. Philadelphia: University of Pennsylvania Press, 1992. Pp. xi, 178. $25.95.

Atkinson, Clarissa W. *The Oldest Vocation: Christian Motherhood in the Middle Ages*. Ithaca, N.Y., and London: Cornell University Press, 1991. Pp. xi, 274. $24.95.

Baltzer, Rebecca A.; Thomas Cable; and James I. Wimsatt, eds. *The Union of Words and Music in Medieval Poetry*. (With audiocassette of music by Sequentia.) Austin: University of Texas Press, 1991. Pp. vii, 157. $40.00.

Barratt, Alexandra, ed. *Women's Writing in Middle English*. Longman Annotated Texts. London and New York: Longman, 1992. Pp. xv, 328. $45.00 cloth, $22.95 paper.

Beal, Peter, and Jeremy Griffiths, eds. *English Manuscript Studies, 1100–1700*. Vol. 3. London and Toronto: British Library and University of Toronto Press, 1992. Pp. 306. $90.00.

Beer, Frances. *Women and Mystical Experience in the Middle Ages*. Woodbridge: Boydell Press, 1992. Pp. vi, 174. $59.95.

Bland, Cynthia Renée. *The Teaching of Grammar in Late Medieval England: An Edition, with Commentary, of Oxford, Lincoln College MS Lat. 130*. Medieval Texts and Studies, vol. 6. East Lansing, Mich.: Colleagues Press, 1991. Pp. xxi, 235. $32.00.

Boitani, Piero, and Anna Torti, eds. *Poetics: Theory and Practice in Medieval English Literature*. J. A. W. Bennett Memorial Lectures, 7th ser. Perugia, 1990. Cambridge: D. S. Brewer, 1991. Pp. viii, 207. $70.00.

Bowers, Fredson, and David L. Vander Meulen. *Studies in Bibliography*. Vol. 45. Charlottesville: University Press of Virginia, 1992. Pp. 338. $35.00.

Bowers, John M., ed. *The Canterbury Tales: Fifteenth-Century Continuations and Additions*. Middle English Texts Series. Kalamazoo, Mich.: Medieval Institute Publications, 1992. Pp. viii, 200. $7.95 paper.

Brownlee, Kevin, and Sylvia Huot, eds. *Rethinking the* Romance of the Rose: *Text, Image, Reception*. Middle Ages Series. Philadelphia: University of Pennsylvania Press, 1992. Pp. x, 386. $44.95 cloth, $18.95 paper.

Buffoni, Franco. *I Racconti di Canterbury: Un' Opera Unitaria*. I saggi di testo a fronte, vol. 2. Milan: Angelo Guerini, 1991. Pp. 214. L 32,000 paper.

Cherry, John. *Goldsmiths*. Medieval Craftsmen Series. Toronto and Buffalo, N.Y.: University of Toronto Press, 1992. Pp. 72. $18.95 paper.

Davidson, Clifford, and John H. Stroupe, eds. *Drama in the Middle Ages: Comparative and Critical Essays: Second Series*. AMS Studies in the Middle Ages, no. 18. New York: AMS Press, 1991. Pp. xi, 389. $47.50.

Dean, James M., and Christian K. Zacher, eds. *The Idea of Medieval Literature: New Essays on Chaucer and Medieval Culture in Honor of Donald R. Howard*. Newark: University of Delaware Press, 1992. Pp. 354. $49.50.

de Hamel, Christopher. *Scribes and Illuminators*. Medieval Craftsmen Series. Toronto and Buffalo, N.Y.: University of Toronto Press, 1992. Pp. 72. $18.95 paper.

Diller, Hans-Jürgen. *The Middle English Mystery Play: A Study in Dramatic Speech and Form*. Trans. Frances Wessels. European Studies in

English Literature. Cambridge: Cambridge University Press, 1992, Pp. xvi, 336. $69.95.

Doane, A. N., and Carol Braun Pasternack, eds. *Vox intexta: Orality and Textuality in the Middle Ages*. Madison: University of Wisconsin Press, 1991. Pp. xiv, 289. $45.00 cloth, $23.50 paper.

Eames, Elizabeth. *English Tilers*. Medieval Craftsmen Series. Toronto and Buffalo, N.Y.: University of Toronto Press, 1992. Pp. 72. $18.95 paper.

Easting, Robert, ed. *St. Patrick's Purgatory*. Early English Text Society, o.s., vol. 298. Oxford: Oxford University Press, 1991. Pp. xciii, 338. $60.00.

Echard, Siân, and Claire Fanger. *The Latin Verses in the* Confessio Amantis: *An Annotated Translation*. Medieval Texts and Studies, vol. 7. East Lansing, Mich.: Colleagues Press, 1991. Pp. lviii, 95. $32.00.

Eldredge, L. M. *The Index of Middle English Prose: Handlist IX: A Handlist of Manuscripts Containing Middle English Prose in the Ashmole Collection, Bodleian Library, Oxford*. Cambridge: D. S. Brewer, 1992. Pp. xxviii, 164. $79.00.

Emmerson, Richard K., and Ronald B. Herzman. *The Apocalyptic Imagination in Medieval Literature*. Middle Ages Series. Philadelphia: University of Pennsylvania Press, 1992. Pp. xi, 244. $27.95.

Franzen, Christine. *The Tremulous Hand of Worcester: A Study of Old English in the Thirteenth Century*. Oxford: Clarendon Press, 1991. Pp. xviii, 229. $79.00.

Fries, Maureen, and Jeanie Watson, eds. *Approaches to Teaching the Arthurian Tradition*. Approaches to Teaching World Literature, vol. 40. New York: Modern Language Association, 1992. Pp. xi, 195. $34.00 cloth, $19.00 paper.

Glasscoe, Marion, ed. *The Medieval Mystical Tradition in England*. Exeter Symposium 5. Cambridge: D. S. Brewer, 1992. Pp. 221. $70.00.

Gower, John. *Mirrour de l'omme [The Mirror of Mankind]*. Trans. William Burton Wilson. Rev. Nancy Wilson Van Baak. Medieval Texts and Studies, vol. 5. East Lansing, Mich.: Colleagues Press, 1992. Pp. xxxi, 411. $62.00.

Hanks, D. Thomas, Jr. *Sir Thomas Malory: Views and Re-views*. AMS Studies in the Middle Ages, vol. 19. New York: AMS Press, 1992. Pp. xi, 112. $39.50.

Harwood, Britton J. Piers Plowman *and the Problem of Belief*. Toronto: Buffalo, N.Y.; and London: University of Toronto Press, 1992. Pp. xii, 237. $60.00.

Howe, Eunice D., trans. *Andrea Palladio: The Churches of Rome*. Medieval and Renaissance Texts and Studies, vol. 72. Binghamton, N.Y.: Medieval and Renaissance Texts and Studies, 1991. Pp. xv, 184. $22.00.

International Boethius Society. *Carmina Philosophiae: Journal of the International Boethius Society*. Ed. William Watts. Vol. 1. Cedar Falls, Iowa: International Boethius Society, 1992. Pp. 104. $16.00.

Jankofsky, Klaus P., ed. *The South English Legendary: A Critical Assessment*. Tübingen: A. Francke, 1992. Pp. xiii, 189. DM 68, —.

Jordan, Mark D., and Kent Emory, Jr., eds. *Ad Litteram: Authoritative Texts and Their Medieval Readers*. Notre Dame Conferences in Medieval Studies, vol. 3. Notre Dame, Ind.: University of Notre Dame Press, 1992. Pp. viii, 380. $39.95.

Keenan, Hugh T., ed. *Typology and English Medieval Literature*. Georgia State Literary Studies, vol. 7. New York: AMS Press, 1992. Pp. xii, 332. $45.00.

Kelly, Douglas. *The Art of Medieval French Romance*. Madison: University of Wisconsin Press, 1992. Pp. xv, 471. $65.00.

Kendall, Calvin B., and Peter S. Wells, eds. *Voyage to the Other World: The Legacy of Sutton Hoo*. Medieval Studies at Minnesota, vol. 5.

Minneapolis: University of Minnesota Press, 1992. Pp. xix, 222. $39.95 cloth, $16.95 paper.

Kerrigan, John, ed. *Motives of Woe: Shakespeare and "Female Complaint": A Critical Anthology.* Oxford: Clarendon Press, 1991. Pp. vii, 310. $79.00.

Kinney, Clare Regan. *Strategies of Poetic Narrative: Chaucer, Spenser, Milton, Eliot.* Cambridge: Cambridge University Press, 1992. Pp. xi, 261. $54.95.

Kruger, Steven F. *Dreaming in the Middle Ages.* Cambridge Studies in Medieval Literature, vol. 14. Cambridge: Cambridge University Press, 1992. Pp. xii, 254. $59.95.

Mandel, Jerome. *Geoffrey Chaucer: Building the Fragments of the* Canterbury Tales. Rutherford, Madison, and Teaneck, N.J.: Fairleigh Dickinson University Press, 1992. Pp. 257. $39.50.

Mills, Maldwyn; Jennifer Fellows; and Carol Meale, eds. *Romance in Medieval England.* Cambridge: D. S. Brewer, 1991. Pp. viii, 228. $70.00.

Minnis, A. J., and Charlotte Brewer, eds. *Crux and Controversy in Middle English Textual Criticism.* Cambridge: D. S. Brewer, 1992. Pp. xiv, 135. $59.00.

Mirrer, Louise, ed. *Upon My Husband's Death: Widows in the Literature and Histories of Medieval Europe.* Studies in Medieval and Early Modern Civilization. Ann Arbor: University of Michigan Press, 1992. Pp. x, 351. $42.50.

Mitchell, Bruce, and Fred C. Robinson. *A Guide to Old English.* 5th ed. Oxford and Cambridge, Mass.: Blackwell, 1992. Pp. xviii, 376. $64.95 cloth, $22.95 paper.

Monson, Craig A., ed. *The Crannied Wall: Women, Religion, and the Arts in Early Modern Europe.* Studies in Medieval and Early Modern Civilization. Ann Arbor: University of Michigan Press, 1992. Pp. x, 242. $37.50.

Nolan, Barbara. *Chaucer and the Tradition of the Roman Antique.* Cambridge Studies in Medieval Literature, vol. 15. Cambridge: Cambridge University Press, 1992. Pp. xv, 391. $69.95.

Ogilvie-Thomson, S. J. *The Index of Middle English Prose: Handlist VIII: A Handlist of Manuscripts Containing Middle English Prose in Oxford College Libraries.* Cambridge: D. S. Brewer, 1991. Pp. xxix, 198. $70.00.

Parkinson, David, ed. *Gavin Douglas:* The Palis of Honoure. TEAMS Middle English Texts Series. Kalamazoo, Mich.: Medieval Institute Publications, 1992. Pp. vii, 140. $7.95 paper.

Pearsall, Derek. *The Life of Geoffrey Chaucer: A Critical Biography.* Blackwell Critical Biographies, vol. 1. Oxford and Cambridge, Mass.: Blackwell, 1992. Pp. xii, 365. $29.95.

Pfaffenbichler, Matthias. *Armourers.* Medieval Craftsmen Series. Toronto and Buffalo, N.Y.: University of Toronto Press, 1992. Pp. 72. $18.95 paper.

Preston, Jean F., and Laetitia Yeandle. *English Handwriting, 1400–1650: An Introductory Manual.* Binghamton, N.Y.: Medieval and Renaissance Texts and Studies, 1992. Pp. xiv, 103. $12.00 paper.

Richards, Earl Jeffrey, ed., with Joan Williamson, Nadia Margolis, and Christine Reno. *Reinterpreting Christine de Pizan.* Athens, Ga., and London: University of Georgia Press, 1992. Pp. x, 310. $40.00.

Richmond, Velma Bourgeois. *Geoffrey Chaucer.* Literature and Life Series. New York: Continuum, 1992. Pp. 215. $19.95.

Scaglione, Aldo. *Knights at Court: Courtliness, Chivalry, and Courtesy from Ottonian Germany to the Italian Renaissance.* Berkeley, Los Angeles, and Oxford: University of California Press, 1991. Pp. xi, 489. $45.00.

Scott, John, and John O. Ward. *Hugh of Poitiers*: The Vézelay Chronicle *and Other Documents from MS Auxerre 227 and Elsewhere, Translated into English with Notes, Introduction, and Accompanying Material*. Binghamton, N.Y.: Medieval and Renaissance Texts and Studies, 1992. Pp. x, 402. $12.00 paper.

Shoaf, R. A., ed., with the assistance of Catherine S. Cox. *Chaucer's* Troilus and Criseyde: *"Subgit to alle Poesye": Essays in Criticism*. Medieval and Renaissance Texts and Studies, vol. 104. Binghamton, N.Y.: Medieval and Renaissance Texts and Studies, 1992. Pp. xviii, 270. $10.00 paper.

Simons, John, ed. *From Medieval to Medievalism*. Insights Series. New York: St. Martin's, 1992. Pp. ix, 161. $45.00.

Spector, Stephen, ed. *The N-Town Play: Cotton MS Vespasian D. 8*. Vol. 1, *Introduction and Text*. Early English Text Society, s.s., vol. 11. Oxford: Oxford University Press, 1991. Pp. lvii, 413. $59.00.

——, ed. *The N-Town Play: Cotton MS Vespasian D. 8*. Vol. 2, *Commentary, Appendices and Glossary*. Early English Text Society, s.s., vol. 12. Oxford: Oxford University Press, 1991. Pp. 246. $45.00.

Stillinger, Thomas C. *The Song of Troilus: Lyric Authority in the Medieval Book*. Middle Ages Series. Philadelphia: University of Pennsylvania Press, 1992. Pp. ix, 287. $32.95.

Strohm, Paul. *Hochon's Arrow: The Social Imagination of Fourteenth-Century Texts*. App. by A. J. Prescott. Princeton, N. J.: Princeton University Press, 1992. Pp. xii, 205. $37.50 cloth, $12.95 paper.

Windeatt, Barry. *Troilus and Criseyde*. Oxford Guides to Chaucer. Oxford: Clarendon Press, 1992. Pp. xiv, 414. $79.00.

Winny, James, ed. and trans. *Sir Gawain and the Green Knight*. Middle English text with facing translation. Peterborough, Ontario; and Lewiston, N.Y.: Broadview, 1992. Pp. xxi, 169. $11.95 paper.

Wirtjes, Hanneke, ed. *The Middle English* Physiologus. Early English Text Society, o.s., vol. 299. Oxford: Oxford University Press, 1991. Pp. xcv, 65. $28.00.

Zumthor, Paul. *Toward a Medieval Poetics* [translation of *Essai de poétique médiévale*]. Trans. Philip Bennett. Minneapolis and Oxford: University of Minnesota Press, 1992. Pp. xxiv, 467. $44.95.

An Annotated Chaucer Bibliography
1991

Compiled and edited by Mark Allen and Bege K. Bowers

Regular contributors:

Bruce W. Hozeski, *Ball State University* (Indiana)
George Nicholas, *Benedictine College* (Kansas)
Marilyn Sutton, *California State University at Dominguez Hills*
Larry L. Bronson, *Central Michigan University*
Glending Olson, *Cleveland State University* (Ohio)
Winthrop Wetherbee, *Cornell University*
Elizabeth Dobbs, *Grinnell College* (Iowa)
Masatoshi Kawasaki, *Komazawa University* (Tokyo, Japan)
William Schipper, *Memorial University* (Newfoundland, Canada)
Daniel J. Pinti, *New Mexico State University*
Erik Kooper, *Rijksuniversiteit te Utrecht*
Cindy L. Vitto, *Rowan College of New Jersey*
Faye Walker-Pelkey, *St. Olaf College* (Minnesota)
Richard H. Osberg, *Santa Clara University* (California)
Tadahiro Ikegami, *Seijo University* (Tokyo, Japan)
Juliette Dor, *Université de Liège* (Belgium)
Mary Flowers Braswell and Elaine Whitaker, *University of Alabama at Birmingham*
Cynthia Gravlee, *University of Montevallo* (Alabama)
Gregory M. Sadlek, *University of Nebraska at Omaha*
Thomas Hahn, *University of Rochester*
Margaret Connolly, *University of St. Andrews* (Scotland)
N. F. Blake, *University of Sheffield* (England)
Stanley R. Hauer, *University of Southern Mississippi*
Mark Allen and Denise Stodola, *University of Texas at San Antonio*
Don F. Chapin, *University of Western Ontario*
Joyce T. Lionarons, *Ursinus College* (Pennsylvania)

John M. Crafton, *West Georgia College*
Robert Correale, *Wright State University* (Ohio)
Bege K. Bowers and Lorrayne Y. Baird-Lange, *Youngstown State University* (Ohio)
Martha S. Waller, *Naples, Florida*

Ad hoc contributions were made by the following: Tim Machan, *Marquette University*; Constance Sabo-Risley, *Palo Alto College* (Texas); Gabriela Cosentino, Linda Pearl De Groot, W. Dansby Evans, Leah L. Garrett, Laura Mullins, William O'Byrne, Christine L. Smart, and Jill Williamson, *University of Alabama at Birmingham*; James Dean, *University of Delaware*; Paul Pellikka and George Wilhite, *University of Texas at San Antonio*.

The bibliographers acknowledge with gratitude the MLA typesimulation provided by Terence Ford, Director, Center for Bibliographical Services of the MLA; postage from the University of Texas at San Antonio Division of English, Classics, and Philosophy; and assistance from the library staff, especially Susan McCray, at the John Peace Library, University of Texas at San Antonio.

This bibliography continues the bibliographies published since 1975 in previous volumes of *Studies in the Age of Chaucer*. Bibliographical information up to 1975 can be found in Eleanor P. Hammond, *Chaucer: A Bibliographic Manual* (1908; repr., New York: Peter Smith, 1933); D. D. Griffith, *Bibliography of Chaucer, 1908–53* (Seattle: University of Washington Press, 1955); William R. Crawford, *Bibliography of Chaucer, 1954–63* (Seattle: University of Washington Press, 1967); and Lorrayne Y. Baird, *Bibliography of Chaucer, 1964–73* (Boston: G. K. Hall, 1977). See also Lorrayne Y. Baird-Lange and Hildegard Schnuttgen, *Bibliography of Chaucer, 1974–1985* (Hamden, Conn.: Shoe String Press, 1988).

Additions and corrections to this bibliography should be sent to Mark Allen, Bibliographic Division, New Chaucer Society, Division of English, Classics, and Philosophy, University of Texas at San Antonio, San Antonio, Texas 78249–0643. Authors are urged to send annotations for articles, reviews, and books that have been or might be overlooked.

Classifications

Abbreviations of Chaucer's Works

ABC	*An ABC*
Adam	*Adam Scriveyn*
Anel	*Anelida and Arcite*
Astr	*A Treatise on the Astrolabe*
Bal Compl	*A Balade of Complaint*
BD	*The Book of the Duchess*
Bo	*Boece*
Buk	*The Envoy to Bukton*
CkT, CkP, Rv–CkL	*The Cook's Tale, The Cook's Prologue, Reeve–Cook Link*
ClT, ClP, Cl–MerL	*The Clerk's Tale, The Clerk's Prologue, Clerk–Merchant Link*
Compl d'Am	*Complaynt d'Amours*
CT	*The Canterbury Tales*
CYT, CYP	*The Canon's Yeoman's Tale, The Canon's Yeoman's Prologue*
Equat	*The Equatorie of the Planetis*
For	*Fortune*
Form Age	*The Former Age*
FranT, FranP	*The Franklin's Tale, The Franklin's Prologue*
FrT, FrP, Fr–SumL	*The Friar's Tale, The Friar's Prologue, Friar–Summoner Link*
Gent	*Gentilesse*
GP	*The General Prologue*
HF	*The House of Fame*
KnT, Kn–MilL	*The Knight's Tale, Knight–Miller Link*
Lady	*A Complaint to His Lady*
LGW, LGWP	*The Legend of Good Women, The Legend of Good Women Prologue*
ManT, ManP	*The Manciple's Tale, The Manciple's Prologue*
Mars	*The Complaint of Mars*
Mel, Mel–MkL	*The Tale of Melibee, Melibee–Monk Link*
MercB	*Merciles Beaute*
MerT, MerE–SqH	*The Merchant's Tale, Merchant Endlink–Squire Headlink*

MilT, MilP, Mil–RvL	*The Miller's Tale, The Miller's Prologue, Miller–Reeve Link*
MkT, MkP, Mk–NPL	*The Monk's Tale, The Monk's Prologue, Monk–Nun's Priest's Link*
MLT, MLH, MLP, MLE	*The Man of Law's Tale, Man of Law Headlink, The Man of Law's Prologue, Man of Law Endlink*
NPT, NPP, NPE	*The Nun's Priest's Tale, The Nun's Priest's Prologue, Nun's Priest's Endlink*
PardT, PardP	*The Pardoner's Tale, The Pardoner's Prologue*
ParsT, ParsP	*The Parson's Tale, The Parson's Prologue*
PF	*The Parliament of Fowls*
PhyT, Phy–PardL	*The Physician's Tale, Physician–Pardoner Link*
Pity	*The Complaint unto Pity*
Prov	*Proverbs*
PrT, PrP, Pr–ThL	*The Prioress's Tale, The Prioress's Prologue, Prioress–Thopas Link*
Purse	*The Complaint of Chaucer to His Purse*
Ret	*Chaucer's Retraction [Retractation]*
Rom	*The Romaunt of the Rose*
Ros	*To Rosemounde*
RvT, RvP	*The Reeve's Tale, The Reeve's Prologue*
Scog	*The Envoy to Scogan*
ShT, Sh–PrL	*The Shipman's Tale, Shipman–Prioress Link*
SNT, SNP, SN–CYL	*The Second Nun's Tale, The Second Nun's Prologue, Second Nun–Canon's Yeoman Link*
SqT, SqH, Sq–FranL	*The Squire's Tale, Squire Headlink, Squire–Franklin Link*
Sted	*Lak of Stedfastnesse*
SumT, SumP	*The Summoner's Tale, The Summoner's Prologue*
TC	*Troilus and Criseyde*
Th, Th–MelL	*The Tale of Sir Thopas, Sir Thopas–Melibee Link*
Truth	*Truth*
Ven	*The Complaint of Venus*
WBT, WBP, WB–FrL	*The Wife of Bath's Tale, The Wife of Bath's Prologue, Wife of Bath–Friar Link*
Wom Nob	*Womanly Noblesse*
Wom Unc	*Against Women Unconstant*

Periodical Abbreviations

AdI	*Annali d'Italianistica*
Anglia	*Anglia: Zeitschrift für Englische Philologie*
ANQ	*A Quarterly Journal of Short Articles, Notes, and Reviews*
ArAA	*Arbeiten aus Anglistik und Amerikanistik*
Assays	*Assays: Critical Approaches to Medieval and Renaissance Texts*
C&L	*Christianity and Literature*
ChauNewsl	*Chaucer Newsletter*
ChauR	*Chaucer Review*
CL	*Comparative Literature*
CML	*Classical and Modern Literature: A Quarterly*
CRCL	*Canadian Review of Comparative Literature / Revue Canadienne de Littérature Comparée*
DAI	*Dissertation Abstracts International*
DUJ	*Durham University Journal*
EHR	*English Historical Review*
EIC	*Essays in Criticism: A Quarterly Journal of Literary Criticism* (England)
EigoS	*Eigo Seinen* (Tokyo)
ELN	*English Language Notes*
Encomia	*Encomia: Bibliographical Bulletin of the International Courtly Literature Society*
ES	*English Studies*
Exemplaria	*Exemplaria: A Journal of Theory in Medieval and Renaissance Studies*
Expl	*Explicator*
FCS	*Fifteenth-Century Studies*
FMLS	*Forum for Modern Language Studies*
HLQ	*Huntington Library Quarterly: A Journal for the History and Interpretation of English and American Civilization*
HSELL	*Hiroshima Studies in English Language and Literature*
InG	*In Geardagum: Essays on Old English Language and Literature: A Publication of the Society for New Language Study*
JEGP	*Journal of English and Germanic Philology*
JELL	*Journal of English Language and Literature* (Korea)

JWCI	*Journal of the Warburg and Courtauld Institutes*
L&H	*Literature and History*
L&T	*Literature and Theology: An Interdisciplinary Journal of Theory and Criticism*
LeedsSE	*Leeds Studies in English*
MÆ	*Medium Ævum*
M&H	*Medievalia et Humanistica: Studies in Medieval and Renaissance Culture*
MedPers	*Medieval Perspectives*
MinnR	*Minnesota Review*
MKNAL	*Mededelingen der Koninklijke Nederlandse Akademie van Wetenschappen, Afdeling Letterkunde, Nieuwe Reeks*
MLR	*Modern Language Review*
MP	*Modern Philology*
N&Q	*Notes and Queries*
Neophil	*Neophilologus* (Groningen, Netherlands)
NLH	*New Literary History: A Journal of Theory and Interpretation*
NM	*Neuphilologische Mitteilungen*
NMS	*Nottingham Medieval Studies*
PBSA	*Papers of the Bibliographical Society of America*
PoeticaT	*Poetica: An International Journal of Linguistic Literary Studies*
PQ	*Philological Quarterly*
QPar	*Qui Parle: A Journal of Literary and Critical Studies*
RES	*Review of English Studies*
Rev	*Review*
RMSt	*Reading Medieval Studies*
SAC	*Studies in the Age of Chaucer*
SAR	*Studies in the American Renaissance*
SCRev	*South Central Review: The Journal of the South Central Modern Language Association*
SELit	*Studies in English Literature* (Tokyo)
SHR	*Southern Humanities Review*
ShS	*Shakespeare Survey: An Annual Survey of Shakespeare Studies and Production*
SLJ	*Southern Literary Journal*
SMART	*Studies in Medieval and Renaissance Teaching*
SMy	*Studia Mystica*
SN	*Studia Neuphilologica: A Journal of Germanic and Romance Languages and Literature*

SP	*Studies in Philology*
Speculum	*Speculum: A Journal of Medieval Studies*
SSEng	*Sydney Studies in English*
TCEL	*Thought Currents in English Literature*
TLS	*Times Literary Supplement* (London)
UES	*Unisa English Studies*
UTQ	*University of Toronto Quarterly: A Canadian Journal of the Humanities*
YES	*Yearbook of English Studies*
YLS	*Yearbook of Langland Studies*
YWES	*Year's Work in English Studies*

Bibliographical Citations
and Annotations

Bibliographies, Reports, and Reference

1. Baird-Lange, Lorrayne Y.; Bege K. Bowers; and Bruce W. Hozeski, with the assistance of Hildegard Schnuttgen et al. "An Annotated Chaucer Bibliography, 1989." *SAC* 13 (1991): 293–368. Continuation of *SAC* annual bibliography (since 1975); based on 1989 *MLA Bibliography* listings, contributions from an international bibliographic team, and independent research. A total of 359 items, including reviews.

2. Bowers, Bege K. "Chaucer Research, 1990: Report No. 51." *ChauR* 26 (1991): 184–204. The 1990 report of the Committee on Chaucer Bibliography and Research; lists 304 Chaucer studies.

3. Denley, Marie, and Lucinda Rumsey. "Middle English: Chaucer." *YWES* 70 (1989): 210–35. Discursive review of Chaucerian scholarship of 1989.

4. Love, Nathan, et al. "International Bibliography for 1990." *Encomia* 14 (1992): 21–147. Annual bibliography of the International Courtly Literature Society, listing 806 items, some briefly annotated. The subject index lists thirty-two Chaucerian works and topics.

5. McAlpine, Monica E. *Chaucer's* Knight's Tale*: An Annotated Bibliography, 1900–1985*. Chaucer Bibliographies, vol. 4. Toronto; Buffalo, N.Y.; and London: University of Toronto Press, 1991. lii, 432 pp. Annotated entries are alphabetized in five chronological periods (1900–30, 1931–60, 1961–70, 1971–80, 1981–85) under two headings: Knight in the *GP* (and *Links*) and *KnT*. Additional sections include editions and translations; sources (subdivided under *Teseida, Thebaid*, and *Roman de Thèbes*); and backgrounds and general studies (subdivided under "Chaucer and Italy," "Romance and Romances," "Courtliness and Courtly Love," "Chaucer and Women," "Paganism and the Gods," "Chaucer and Science," "Estates and Social Satire," and "Chivalry"). Entries total 1,134. Also includes a twenty-seven-page chronological survey of criticism and a forty-nine-page index.

6. Oizumi, Akio, ed. Programmed by Kunihiro Miki. *A Complete Concordance to the Works of Geoffrey Chaucer*. 10 vols. Alpha-Omega. Lexica — Indizes — Konkordanzen. Reihe C. Englische Autoren, no. 1. Hildescheim, Zürich, and New York: Olms-Weidmann, 1991. Supplies every

form of every word in the Chaucer corpus of *The Riverside Chaucer*, using "Key Word in Context" format (KWIC). Presents the headword in the center of the page and provides about two lines of context for the poetry. Variant spellings are listed separately, and compounds are treated as single words. Volumes 1–4 include a concordance, a ranked word-frequency list, a reverse-word list, and a hyphenated-word list for *CT*, as well as a word index for each individual tale. Volume 5 supplies similar lists for *BD, HF, Anel*, and *PF*; volume 6, for *Bo*; volume 7, for *TC*; volume 8, for *LGW*, short poems, *Astr*, and "poems not ascribed to Chaucer in the manuscripts"; and volume 9, for *Rom*. Volume 10 is a word index of the entire corpus, i.e., a listing of all occurrences of all words without accompanying context.

7. Pearsall, Derek. *An Annotated Critical Bibliography of Langland*. Ann Arbor: University of Michigan Press, 1990. xx, 295 pp. A selective, annotated bibliography of 614 entries, indexed rather than cross-listed, covering 1900–88. Entries are arranged under descriptive and topical categories such as Bibliography, Date, Metre, Literary Relationships, Allegory, and Dream Vision. Under "Chaucer, Geoffrey," there are twenty-two entries.

See also no. 42.

Chaucer's Life

8. Bowers, John M. "The House of Chaucer & Son: The Business of Lancastrian Canon-Formation." *MedPers* 6 (1991): 135–43. Thomas Chaucer continued the lease on his father's house in the garden at Westminster Abbey to provide a repository for Geoffrey Chaucer's literary remains. His motive was to help form a Lancastrian poetic canon committed to social stability and religious orthodoxy.

9. Carlson, David R. "Thomas Hoccleve and the Chaucer Portrait." *HLQ* 54 (1991): 283–300. Hoccleve's hopes for preferment depended on his claim to personal acquaintance with Chaucer and to his "consail and reed." Hoccleve's patrons had known Chaucer by sight and could verify the image of Chaucer that accompanies Hoccleve's poems. Hence the Ellesmere-Hoccleve type portraits show Chaucer's true image.

10. Matheson, Lister M. "Chaucer's Ancestry: Historical and Philological Re-Assessments." *ChauR* 25 (1991): 171–89. An examination of Chaucer's original family name, Malyn, casts doubt on previous claims that Chaucer's family was involved in leather making. For social and commercial

reasons, Chaucer was a more acceptable surname. Chaucer used Malyn or its variations in his writing in a "self-deprecatory" way.

11. Pearsall, Derek A. "The Presidential Address: The Problems of Writing a Life of Chaucer." *SAC* 13 (1991): 5–14. Justifies writing a new biography of Chaucer despite objections that it may be impossible, useless, or superfluous. The exceptional nature of Chaucer's life and the richness of his historical context make the undertaking worthwhile.

12. Walker, S. K. "Letters to the Dukes of Lancaster in 1381 and 1399." *EHR* 106 (1991): 68–79. The letters provide a new perspective on the uprising of 1381, the usurpation of 1399, and exploitation of the language of love.

See also nos. 36, 136, 280, 285.

Facsimiles, Editions, and Translations

13. Boffey, Julia. "Early Printers and English Lyrics: Sources, Selection, and Presentation of Texts." *PBSA* 85 (1991): 11–26. A study of the "traditions of lyric publication on which Tottel built" his 1557 collection, *Tottel's Miscellany*. Discusses early English printers' "Chaucerian anthologies" — Caxton's quarto volumes among them — that combine Chaucer's lyrics and longer works.

14. Bowden, Betsy, ed. *Eighteenth-Century Modernizations from* The Canterbury Tales. Chaucer Studies, vol. 16. Cambridge: D. S. Brewer, 1991. xx, 263 pp. A collection of thirty-two eighteenth-century modernizations of *CT* by at least seventeen authors, known and anonymous. Valuable in an exploration of reception aesthetics and reader-response theory.

15. Cawley, A. C., ed. *Geoffrey Chaucer*: Canterbury Tales. Everyman's Library. London: J. M. Dent & Sons, 1990. xx, 612 pp. Reprint of 1958 edition, with slight revisions in bibliography.

16. Dor, Juliette. *Chaucer: Les contes de Cantorbéry*. Paris: Bibliothèque Médiéval, 1991. 255 pp. Introduction, bibliography, and French translations of *WBP, WBT, ClT, MerT, FranT, PhyT, PardT, ShT, PrT, NPT, SNT, CYT,* and *ManT*.

17. Higuchi, Masayuki, trans. *Chaucer's Boece*. Hiroshima: Keisuisha, 1991. ii, 238 pp. Japanese translation of *Bo* based on Larry D. Benson, gen. ed., *The Riverside Chaucer*, with notes.

18. Kemmler, Fritz, trans.; Jörg O. Fichte, ed. *Geoffrey Chaucer: Die*

Canterbury-Erzählungen: Mittelenglisch und Deutsch. 3 vols. Goldmann Klassiker mit Erläuterungen. Munich: Goldmann Verlag, 1989. 1,968 pp. Facing-page German prose translation of the *Riverside* text of *CT*. Original German apparatus includes notes, introductions to Chaucer's life and to the tales, a guide to pronunciation, a history of criticism, and a bibliography. See also no. 350.

19. Murphy, Michael. "On Making an Edition of *The Canterbury Tales* in Modern Spelling." *ChauR* 26 (1991): 46–64. Challenges existing editions of *CT* and proposes an alternative that would include the old-spelling version of Hengwrt with new spelling, glossing, and annotations.

20. ———, ed. *The* Canterbury Tales: *The* General Prologue *and* Twelve Major Tales in Modern Spelling. Lanham, Md.: University Press of America, 1991. xxvi, 388 pp. An edition of the Middle English text for nonspecialist students and general readers. Neither a normalization nor a translation, it retains—in all respects except spelling—the language of Hengwrt, with variants from other manuscripts of the Six Text edition and Manly-Rickert. Introductions, full side-page glossing, and end-page notes.

See also no. 303.

Manuscripts and Textual Studies

21. Boffey, Julia, and Carol Meale. "Selecting the Text: Rawlinson C. 86 and Some Other Books for London Readers." In Felicity Riddy, ed. *Regionalism in Late Mediaeval Manuscripts and Texts: Essays Celebrating the Publication of* A Linguistic Atlas of Late Mediaeval English (*SAC* 15 [1993], no. 30), pp. 143–69. Rawlinson C. 86 contains *ClT* and portions of *PrT* and *LGW*. Analysis of the manuscript reveals interests of the contemporary London audience and suggests that several booklets in the manuscript may have been produced on speculation.

22. Boyd, David Lorenzo. "Recapturing Readings: Middle English Literature in Its Manuscript Contexts." *DAI* 52 (1991): 909A. On the basis of insights provided by manuscripts (especially Harvard MS English 530), certain works by Hoccleve and Lydgate reveal unifying themes. To fifteenth-century readers, Chaucer's *PF* treated the relationship of common profit and individual will.

23. Correale, Robert M. "Chaucer's Manuscript of Nicholas Trevet's *Les Cronicles*." *ChauR* 25 (1991): 238–65. Because it contains the fewest emendations and corresponds most closely to Chaucer's *MLT*, the version of

Les Cronicles in the MS Paris, Bibl. Nationale, Franç. 9687, fols. 1va–114va (ca. 1340–50), will serve as a base text for the Chaucer Library edition of Trevet's work.

24. Hewett-Smith, Kathleen M. "Transcript Error and the Text of *Troilus.*" *SAC* 13 (1991): 99–119. Furnivall's printed transcriptions of *TC* manscripts have created a legacy of errors, especially in editions based on Corpus Christi College, Cambridge, 61 (Cp). Hewett-Smith identifies errors in Robinson's edition and exemplifies the transmission of error into other editions, particularly the first printing of Larry D. Benson, gen. ed., *The Riverside Chaucer.*

25. Kline, Barbara Rae. "A Descriptive Catalog of British Library MS. Harley 7333." *DAI* 52 (1991): 533A–34A. This first in-depth description of MS Harley 7333 provides textual information, lists editions, and describes relationships to other medieval texts. The contents shed light on scribal editing in *CT.*

26. Machan, Tim William. "Editing, Orality, and Late Middle English Texts." In A. N. Doane and Carol Braun Pasternack, eds. *Vox intexta: Orality and Textuality in the Middle Ages.* Madison: University of Wisconsin Press, 1991, pp. 229–45. Questions the role of orality in the recording and transmission of Middle English texts, suggesting that various attitudes and techniques of oral improvisation have left residues in these texts and that modern editors should use an oral model. Draws examples from *TC, PF,* and elsewhere.

27. ———, ed. *Medieval Literature: Texts and Interpretation.* Medieval and Renaissance Texts and Studies, vol. 79. Binghamton, N.Y.: Center for Medieval and Early Renaissance Studies, 1991. 201 pp. In addition to the introduction, this collection contains nine original essays focusing on the interrelations between textual and interpretive studies of late Middle English literature. The authors discuss the effect of editorial decisions on literary history, the interpretive information latent in medieval manuscripts, and the nature of medieval literary texts. All major genres (romance, drama, the lyric) and writers (Chaucer, Langland, Lydgate) are examined. See nos. 59, 72.

28. Owen, Charles A., Jr. *The Manuscripts of* The Canterbury Tales. Chaucer Studies, vol. 17. Cambridge: D. S. Brewer, 1991. xii, 132 pp. Chronologically surveys *CT* manuscripts, highlighting the importance of Hengwrt and the "wide difference in the number of independent textual traditions for different parts" of the work. Rejects the notion of a single Chaucerian copy text, crediting the "Hengwrt editor" with the first impulse to collect the *Tales* from fragments. Despite continued circulation of

"booklets" of tales, the early fifteenth century witnessed the standardization of two orders for the *Tales*. Manuscripts of single tales or small groups
increased steadily throughout the century, suggesting that modern notions
of "complete" texts of *CT* are misguided.

29. Pearsall, Derek, ed. *Studies in the Vernon Manuscript*. Cambridge: D. S. Brewer, 1990. xi, 238 pp. Thirteen essays by diverse hands
discuss what Pearsall describes as the largest manuscript "the student of
vernacular literature will ever be likely to have to deal with" — a "comprehensive programme of religious reading and instruction" (p. x). Five of the
essays address the manuscript descriptively or codicologically; two each
consider the romances included and refrain lyrics; and four assess other
literary forms or issues — homilies, miracles of the Virgin, verse laments,
and a tabular Pater Noster. Throughout, comparison with contemporary
materials is the dominant concern.

30. Riddy, Felicity, ed. *Regionalism in Late Mediaeval Manuscripts and
Texts: Essays Celebrating the Publication of* A Linguistic Atlas of Late
Mediaeval English. York Manuscripts Conferences: Proceedings Series, no.
2. Cambridge: D. S. Brewer, 1991. xiii, 214 pp. Eleven essays on such
topics as the theory and techniques of dialect comparison, the texts of
Skelton and Dunbar, the N-town manuscript, and specific dialects. See
nos. 21, 31.

31. Samuels, Michael. "Scribes and Manuscript Traditions." In Felicity
Riddy, ed. *Regionalism in Late Mediaeval Manuscripts and Texts: Essays
Celebrating the Publication of* A Linguistic Atlas of Late Mediaeval English
(*SAC* 15 [1993], no. 30), pp. 1–7. Explores editorial implications of the
South-West Midlands features of several London copyings of works by
Chaucer, Gower, and Langland, including four manuscripts of *CT* (HA4,
La, Cp, Pw).

32. Smith, J. J. "Spelling and Tradition in Fifteenth-Century Copies of
Gower's *Confessio Amantis*." In J. J. Smith, ed. *The English of Chaucer and
His Contemporaries: Essays by M. L. Samuels and J. J. Smith* (*SAC* 15
[1993], no. 83), pp. 96–113. Working from an "archetypal" corpus of
Gower's spelling forms, Smith explores the continuity and dissolution of
these forms in manuscript tradition, as well as the relation of the corpus
to the progress of Standard Written English and to practice in manuscripts
of *PardT*.

33. ———. "The Trinity Gower D-Scribe and His Work on Two Early
Canterbury Tales Manuscripts." In J. J. Smith, ed. *The English of Chaucer
and His Contemporaries: Essays by M. L. Samuels and J. J. Smith* (*SAC* 15
[1993], no. 83), pp. 51–69. Analyzes the dialectal *Mischsprachen* (lin-

guistic mixture) in Harley 7334 and Corpus Christi, Oxford, 198, and in products of the Gower D-scribe. Since all three show an "idiosyncratic mixture of West Worcestershire forms and the learnt form, *oughne*," they were evidently copied by the same person.

See also nos. 72, 83, 106, 150, 260–62.

Sources, Analogues, and Literary Relations

34. Bernardo, Aldo S., and Saul Levin, eds. *The Classics in the Middle Ages: Papers of the Twentieth Annual Conference of the Center for Medieval and Early Renaissance Studies*. Medieval and Renaissance Texts and Studies, no. 69. Binghamton, N.Y.: Center for Medieval and Early Renaissance Studies, 1990. vi, 425 pp. Twenty-six essays on the impact of the classics on medieval art, history, philosophy, education, and literature. Topics range widely from Coptic textiles to fourteenth-century England, from Neoplatonism to speculative grammar—all addressing the use and understanding of classical imagery, tradition, or precedent in medieval thought. See no. 283.

35. Crafton, John M. "Chaucer's Treasure Text: The Influence of Brunetto Latini on Chaucer's Developing Narrative Technique." *MedPers* 4–5 (1989–90): 25–41. Latini's *Li livres du tresor* influenced the rhetoric and structure of *CT* and *LGWP*, providing theory and models from the tradition of *ars dictaminis*.

36. Dinshaw, Carolyn. "Rivalry, Rape and Manhood: Gower and Chaucer." In R. F. Yeager, ed. *Chaucer and Gower: Difference, Mutability, Exchange (SAC* 15 [1993], no. 47), pp. 130–52. Discussions of the "quarrel" between Chaucer and Gower pose a Chaucer who was free of base, ingratiating attitudes toward his sovereign and who was the source of pure poeticality—language and aesthetics unpolluted by self-interest. In contrast, the same discussions create a Gower who was an "ingrate" and a "sycophant" at court, content to "follow" and to imitate in his moralizing, unequivocally second-rate poetic endeavors. Gower plays the lumbering "fall guy" to the nimble and free-spirited Chaucer.

37. Elliott, Ralph. "Chaucer's Landscapes: Language and Style." In Michio Kawai, ed. *Language and Style in English Literature: Essays in Honour of Michio Masui (SAC* 15 [1993], no. 80), pp. 74–95. Compares the various landscape features in Chaucer's works with the walled garden of

the *Roman de la Rose*. The merit of Chaucer's landscapes is that the poet tailored them to be part of an intimate, homey world.

38. Hertog, Erik. *Chaucer's Fabliaux as Analogues*. Mediaevalia Lovaniensia, 1st ser., no. 19. Leuven: Leuven University Press, 1991. viii, 290 pp. Explores the phenomenon of literary analogues in a pragmatic and structuralist analysis of four salient components of narrative, each illustrated with examples from Chaucer's fabliaux and their analogues in various European languages. The conclusion calls attention to two aspects that set Chaucer's fabliaux apart from the analogues: their context in *CT* and their explicit intertextuality. The study ends with reflections on the concept of analogy.

39. Mann, Jill. "Chaucer and the 'Woman Question.'" In Erik Kooper, ed. *This Noble Craft* (*SAC* 15 [1993], no. 114), pp. 173–88. For Chaucer, the literary traditions of Ovid and Jerome created a dual image of woman as predator or victim. Chaucer refines and deepens the "double-sidedness" of these traditions, bringing the polarized alternatives into complicating relation with each other. Mann discusses the mock encomium on marriage in *MerT* and the Wife's tirade against her first three husbands in *WBP*.

40. Mertens-Fonck, Paule. "The Indebtedness of the *Canterbury Tales* to the Clerk-Knight Debates." In Erik Kooper, ed. *This Noble Craft* (*SAC* 15 [1993], no. 114), pp. 189–99. Structurally, *CT* parodies the clerk-knight debate (an early type of courtly-love poem), especially *The Council of Remiremont*. The idea of a pilgrimage on horseback may derive from these debates as well.

41. Minnis, A. J. "*De Vulgari Auctoritate*: Chaucer, Gower and the Men of Great Authority." In R. F. Yeager, ed. *Chaucer and Gower: Difference, Mutability, Exchange* (*SAC* 15 [1993], no. 47), pp. 36–74. Chaucer is a poet with a highly developed sense of the relative — someone who instinctively shies away from those absolutes necessary for the creation of *auctoritas*, who denies experience in love, and who claims to be a mere reporter. This stance receives its finest and fullest expression in *CT* but is also found in *HF* and *TC*. Gower, on the other hand, implies that if one of his own poems were shown to be morally useful, it would have some claim on *auctoritas*.

42. Nicholson, Peter. *An Annotated Index to the Commentary on Gower's* Confessio Amantis. Medieval and Renaissance Texts and Studies, no. 62. Binghamton, N.Y.: Center for Medieval and Early Renaissance Studies, 1989. ix, 593 pp. Line-by-line commentary on the *Confessio* that synthesizes criticism and scholarship. The introduction surveys critical tradition, and the notes clarify details, patterns, and literary relations of the work. See also no. 362.

43. Speed, Diane, ed. *Middle English Romances*. 2d ed. 2 vols. Sydney: Department of English, University of Sydney, 1989. Correction and update of 1989 edition. Volume 1 includes a general introduction and bibliography, plus texts and introductions to *Havelok, Sir Orfeo, Chevelere Assigne, Sir Cleges, Rauf Coilyear*, and *The Grene Knight*. Volume 2 includes explanatory notes, textual notes, a glossary, and a name list. Continuously paginated. See also no. 374.

44. Wetherbee, Winthrop. "Latin Structure and Vernacular Space: Gower, Chaucer and the Boethian Tradition." In R. F. Yeager, ed. *Chaucer and Gower: Difference, Mutability, Exchange (SAC* 15 [1993], no. 47), pp. 7–35. There are significant differences between Chaucer's and Gower's appropriations of the *Roman de la Rose* and its Latin antecedents. Gower's priestly Genius is an authority figure in the tradition of Boethius's *Consolation*. Chaucer's rejection of authority figures is one of the most important signs of his modernity, giving point to the contrast commonly drawn between Gower's supposed conservatism and Chaucer's more open vision.

45. Wimsatt, James I. *Chaucer and His French Contemporaries: Natural Music in the Fourteenth Century*. Toronto: University of Toronto Press, 1991. xv, 378 pp. A comprehensive analysis of the contemporary French influence on Chaucer, exploring lyric rather than narrative features and concentrating on the impact of *formes fixes*. Wimsatt devotes individual chapters to Chaucer's literary relations with Jean de la Mote, Jean Froissart, Oton de Granson, and Eustache Deschamps. Three chapters assess the English poet's connections with Guillaume de Machaut, which are basic to all of Chaucer's verse from the lyrics and *BD* to *TC* and *LGW*. In all cases, biographical and historical information provides context for comparison of individual poems, stylistic features, and musical qualities of French and English court poetry from 1350 to 1400.

46. ———. "Reason, Machaut, and the Franklin." In Robert R. Edwards and Stephen Spector, eds. *The Olde Daunce: Love, Friendship, Sex, and Marriage in the Medieval World (SAC* 15 [1993], no. 100), pp. 201–10, 287–89 (notes). Examines "the paradigm of consoler-consolation-consolee" in *The Consolation of Philosophy, Roman de la Rose, Remède de Fortune*, and *TC*. The *Consolation* is "sub-text or perhaps super-text." The other texts mediate in Chaucer's adaptation of Boethius. Wimsatt cites a passage on marital friendship in *FranT* as a case in which the *Remède* "acts as intermediary between the *Roman* and a work of Chaucer."

47. Yeager, R. F., ed. *Chaucer and Gower: Difference, Mutability, Exchange*. Victoria, B.C.: University of Victoria, 1991. 152 pp. The seven essays assess Gower and Chaucer as joint recipients of an antique heritage, as readers of (and borrowers from) each other's works, and as writers whose

work reveals much about late-medieval attitudes toward language and about the constantly shifting interrelations of women and men. All seek new ways to understand the poetic interaction between Gower and Chaucer. See nos. 36, 41, 44, 49, 190, 192, 247.

48. ———. *John Gower's Poetic: The Search for a New Arion.* Publications of the John Gower Society, no. 2. Cambridge: D. S. Brewer, 1990. 289 pp. Examines Gower's efforts to establish his reputation as a poet. Frequently using Chaucer for comparison or contrast, Yeager explores Gower's stylistics, his concerns with audience, his relations with French tradition and particular sources, his so-called digressiveness, and his status as a social and moral writer. Yeager develops the views of previous Gower critics and considers the complete corpus of the poet, concentrating on *Confessio Amantis.* Unlike Chaucer, who casts himself as a "maker," Gower sees himself as "auctor" or "poete" — self-consciously, a "new Arion."

49. ———. "Learning to Read in Tongues: Writing Poetry for a Trilingual Culture." In R. F. Yeager, ed. *Chaucer and Gower: Difference, Mutability, Exchange (SAC* 15 [1993], no. 47), pp. 115–29. Most people who could read and write in England in the late fourteenth century were capable of doing so in French, Latin, and English. Gower's nearly 90,000 lines of extant poetry — roughly apportioned into thirds of Anglo-Norman French, Latin, and English — are a concrete sample of trilingual poetic vocabulary that can only be inferred for Chaucer and other late medieval English poets.

See also nos. 5, 7, 53, 69, 73, 77, 99, 102, 113, 115, 139, 140, 158, 164, 168, 184, 187, 188, 190–92, 194, 199, 202, 205, 206, 211, 221, 222, 247, 250, 252, 255, 267–69, 273, 275, 277–79, 283, 284, 286, 289, 290, 301.

Chaucer's Influence and Later Allusion

50. Allen, Rosamund S. "*The Siege of Thebes:* Lydgate's Canterbury Tale." In Julia Boffey and Janet Cowen, eds. *Chaucer and Fifteenth-Century Poetry (SAC* 15 [1993], no. 52), pp. 122–42. Reads *Siege* as an attempt to provide *CT* with "a sense of closure and completeness" by supplying the tale of Thebes to balance the plot, style, and themes of *KnT.* The poem capitalizes on the popularity of *CT* and acknowledges Chaucer's greatness.

51. Boffey, Julia. "Chaucerian Prisoners: The Context of *The King's Quair.*" In Julia Boffey and Janet Cowen, eds. *Chaucer and Fifteenth-*

Century Poetry (*SAC* 15 [1993], no. 52), pp. 84–102. Chaucer's various uses of the "structural, rhetorical, and metaphorical possibilities" of prison imagery reflect Boethian thought and influence later medieval English tradition, in particular *The King's Quair* of James I of Scotland.

52. ———, and Janet Cowen, eds. *Chaucer and Fifteenth-Century Poetry*. King's College London Medieval Studies, vol. 5. London: King's College Centre for Late Antique and Medieval Studies, 1991. x, 174 pp. Nine essays by various hands, eight of which assess Chaucer's fifteenth-century legacy. See nos. 50, 51, 53, 54, 62, 64, 65, 302.

53. Cowen, Janet. "Women as Exempla in Fifteenth-Century Verse of the Chaucerian Tradition." In Julia Boffey and Janet Cowen, eds. *Chaucer and Fifteenth-Century Poetry* (*SAC* 15 [1993], no. 52), pp. 51–65. Discusses exemplary uses of Medea in classical and medieval traditions, suggesting connections with Boccaccio's *De claris mulieribus* and Christine de Pizan's *Book of the City of Ladies*. Also notes comparisons among *LGW*, Lydgate's versions of the tale, Henryson's *Letter of Cupid*, and the latter's tale of Jereslaus's wife.

54. Davenport, W. A. "Bird Poems from *The Parliament of Fowls* to *Philip Sparrow*." In Julia Boffey and Janet Cowen, eds. *Chaucer and Fifteenth-Century Poetry* (*SAC* 15 [1993], no. 52), pp. 66–83. Davenport's survey articulates the formal, thematic, and verbal influences of *PF* and *HF* on a wide variety of late-medieval English bird poems, also mentioning those in which Chaucer's influence is not apparent.

55. Dean, James. "Gower, Chaucer, and Rhyme Royal." *SP* 88 (1991): 251–75. In his rhyme-royal poetry, Gower adapted Chaucerian techniques as well as techniques from his own French seven-line poetry. Dean reviews *Cinkante balades*, *Traitié pour essampler les amantz marietz*, *In Praise of Peace*, and Amans's "supplicacioun" from *Confessio Amantis* 8.

56. Fichte, Joerg O. "'Quha wait gif all that Chauceir wrait was trewe'—*Auctor* and *Auctoritas* in 15th Century English Literature." In Walter Haug and Burghart Wachinger, eds. *Traditionswandel und Traditionsverhalten*. Tübingen: Niemeyer, 1991, pp. 61–76. Chaucer's playful attitude toward authority contrasts Gower's serious one; analogously, Henryson's questioning of Chaucer's authority (*Testament of Cresseid*) contrasts Lydgate's endorsement of it (*Siege of Thebes*).

57. Flahiff, F. T. "'Mysteriously Come Together': Dickens, Chaucer, and *Little Dorrit*." *UTQ* 61 (1991): 250–68. The theme of rumor connects Dickens's *Dorrit* with *HF*; Dickens's Miss Wade capitalizes on Wade and his boat of *MerT* 1424 and *TC* 3.614; and Amy Dorrit recalls Dorigen of *FranT*, although Dorrit is not "so reckless."

58. Fleissner, Robert F. *"Much Ado* about Chaucer." *NM* 92 (1991): 75–81. Verbal echoes, connections of character, and other allusive possibilities suggest relationships between Shakespeare's *Much Ado about Nothing* and *TC* and parts of *CT*.

59. Hanna, Ralph, III. "Presenting Chaucer as Author." In Tim William Machan, ed. *Medieval Literature: Texts and Interpretation* (*SAC* 15 [1993], no. 27), pp. 17–39. English respect for vernacular authors anticipates the Renaissance. Chaucer created for our language and its literary heritage a conception of culturally significant authority based on textual correctness. More than other Middle English poets, Chaucer asserts the value of the author's *ipsissima verba* in his *CT*.

60. Hillman, Richard. "Shakespeare's Romantic Innocents and the Misappropriation of the Romance Past: The Case of *The Two Noble Kinsmen." ShS* 43 (1991): 69–79. Contrasts the characterizations of Theseus and Emily in *The Two Noble Kinsmen* and *KnT*, focusing on how the play challenges the principles of romance by manipulating Chaucerian material and perspective.

61. Johnston, Judith. *"Middlemarch*: Medieval Discourses and Will Ladislaw." *SSEng* 15 (1990): 125–39. Eliot uses Chaucerian epigraphs as part of a narrative strategy that inscribes allegory in an apparently realistic text.

62. King, Pamela M. "Chaucer, Chaucerians, and the Theme of Poetry." In Julia Boffey and Janet Cowen, eds. *Chaucer and Fifteenth-Century Poetry* (*SAC* 15 [1993], no. 52), pp. 1–14. Surveys the metafictional aspects of *TC, HF,* and *NPT*, defining narrative and stylistic self-consciousness as recurrent themes. Henryson, Dunbar, Skelton, and James I of Scotland accomplish similar ends through self-reflexive and intertextual devices.

63. McKenna, Steven R. "Henryson's 'Tragedie' of Cresseid." *SLJ* 18:1 (1991): 26–36. Explores Henryson's theory of tragedy and what is "tragic" about Cresseid, arguing for an inversion of the traditionally perceived structure of tragic action. Since Henryson anchors his poem in his audience's knowledge of *TC*, Cresseid's catastrophe (her rejection of Troilus) occurs before his poem begins. McKenna regards Cresseid's tragedy as private, with no sense of an ultimate justice at work, and notes similar ideas in *MkT* and *GP*.

64. Roberts, Jane. "On Rereading Henryson's *Orpheus and Euridice.*" In Julia Boffey and Janet Cowen, eds. *Chaucer and Fifteenth-Century Poetry* (*SAC* 15 [1993], no. 52), pp. 103–21. Explores the *moralitas* of Henryson's poem and conjectures that *KnT* was a "major shaping force" in it.

65. Twycross-Martin, Henrietta. "Moral Pattern in *The Testament of Cresseid*." In Julia Boffey and Janet Cowen, eds. *Chaucer and Fifteenth-Century Poetry* (*SAC* 15 [1993], no. 52), pp. 30–50. Considers *The Testament of Cresseid* as a "parallel text" to *TC* 5, arguing that, although Henryson echoes various Chaucerian collocations, techniques, and structures, his counterpointing of fickle and stable earthly love is unlike Chaucer's opposition of earthly and heavenly love.

See also nos. 22, 239, 272, 302.

Style and Versification

66. Barber, Charles, and Nicolas Barber. "The Versification of *The Canterbury Tales*: A Computer-based Statistical Study, II." *LeedsSE* 22 (1991): 57–83. Indicates the frequency and distribution of pronounced unelided final – *e* among the parts of speech.

67. Cable, Thomas. *The English Alliterative Tradition*. Philadelphia: University of Pennsylvania Press, 1991. x, 191 pp. Disputes the traditional view that the English alliterative poetical tradition was consistent from the seventh through the fifteenth centuries and proposes profound differences between Old English meter, early Middle English meter, and Alliterative Revival meter, with a continuing discussion of the evolution of English meters. Section 5.3, "The Decasyllabic Meter of Chaucer and Gascoigne," proposes two distinct metrical traditions in the decasyllabic line, the *alternating* pattern of Chaucer and Gascoigne and the *foot* pattern of Shakespeare and Sidney.

68. Glowka, Arthur Wayne. *A Guide to Chaucer's Meter*. Lanham, Md.; New York; and London: University Press of America, 1991. 96 pp. Designed as a supplemental textbook for college courses on Chaucer or English prosody; includes brief exercises at the end of each of seven chapters. Introduces the basics of meter and rhythm and analyzes Chaucer's verse in traditional foot scansion, exploring the regularity of his lines (pentameter and four-stress), the problems of final – *e*, and metrical substitutions.

69. Guthrie, Steven. "Meter and Performance in Machaut and Chaucer." In Rebecca A. Baltzer, Thomas Cable, and James I. Wimsatt, eds. *The Union of Words and Music in Medieval Poetry* (*SAC* 15 [1993], no. 86), pp. 72–100. Explores lyric and narrative meters in Provençal, Old and Middle French, and Middle English texts—especially Machaut and Chaucer—

showing that a poet's intuitive sense of genre affects verse rhythm more directly than does musical notation. Chaucer's embedded and free-standing lyrics show greater rhythmic variety than his narrative verse shows.

70. Markus, Manfred. "Glasnost in Middle English Prose, or, How Is Modern Text Type Theory Applicable to Medieval Texts?" In Claus Uhlig and Rüdiger Zimmerman, eds. *Anglistentag 1990 Marburg: Proceedings of the Conference of the German Association of University Professors of English*. Vol. 12. Tübingen: Niemeyer, 1991, pp. 177–94. Enumerative disjunctions, emphasizers, repetition, and variation produce the controlled style of *CT*. Chaucer's two prose tales, *ParsT* and *Mel*, have characteristics that are found less in verse (and that modern readers dislike): cohesive redundancy and repetitive verbosity, on the one hand, and a bossy and pedantic attitude, on the other.

71. Park, Doo-byung. "A Study of the Final – *e* in Chaucer." *JELL* 37 (1991): 761–82 (in Korean with English abstract). Compares several theories of Middle English pronunciation, arguing that Chaucer's rhymes require the pronunciation of final – *e*.

72. Pearsall, Derek. "Chaucer's Meter: The Evidence of the Manuscripts." In Tim William Machan, ed. *Medieval Literature: Texts and Interpretation* (*SAC* 15 [1993], no. 27), pp. 41–57. Most Chaucer criticism fails to mention that Chaucer's poetry is written in verse. The way we read that verse and respond to its musicality, whether in our heads or when reading aloud, is an important part of our interpretation of and response to its meaning. Pearsall's discussion confines itself to the pentameter couplets of *CT*.

73. Wimsatt, James I. "Chaucer and Deschamps' 'Natural Music.'" In Rebecca A. Baltzer, Thomas Cable, and James I. Wimsatt, eds. *The Union of Words and Music in Medieval Poetry* (*SAC* 15 [1993], no. 86), pp. 132–50. Applies Deschamps's concept of natural music (i.e., words in verse, from *L'Art de dictier*) to Machaut's ballade "Tout ensement," to "The Fair Maid of Ribblesdale," and to Chaucer's *Ros*, demonstrating how the rhythms of Middle French and Middle English verse differ and how Chaucer emulates the French.

74. ———. "Collections of French Lyrics Chaucer May Have Known." In André Crépin, ed. *The Medieval Imagination. L' Imagination médiévale: Chaucer et ses contemporains* (*SAC* 15 [1993], no. 98), pp. 33–51. Analyzes three manuscript collections (Pennsylvania French 15, Westminster Abbey 21, and Bibl. Nat. Nouvelles acquisitions fr. 6221) to infer their late-fourteenth-century exemplars.

See also nos. 55, 80, 155, 219, 304, 305.

Language and Word Studies

75. Brewer, Derek S. "Contributions to a Chaucer Word-Book from *Troilus* Book IV." In Michio Kawai, ed. *Language and Style in English Literature: Essays in Honour of Michio Masui* (*SAC* 15 [1993], no. 80), pp. 27–52. A word list from *TC* 4 shows that Chaucer invented new meanings by combining previously unconnected root words; however, someone else may have introduced those roots into the language.

76. Burnley, J. D. "On the Architecture of Chaucer's Language." In Erik Kooper, ed. *This Noble Craft* (*SAC* 15 [1993], no. 114), pp. 43–57. Drawing on recent socio- and ethnolinguistic insights, Burnley examines the complex stylistic associations of commonly used language in various spoken and written contexts. The structure of Chaucer's English is not neat and orderly but cumulative and diverse. The evidence for a language of the past is limited.

77. Ebi, Hisato. "A Theatre Image in Poetry: Chaucer's Tragedy." *EigoS* 137:7 (1991): 345–50 (in Japanese). Confronting the Latin world, Chaucer established his own theory of tragedy, which had not developed completely in the English vernacular. Ebi explores the meanings of "dite," "theatrum," and "scene," concluding that Chaucer used theater imagery to invent his own narrative technique.

78. Ishizaka, Ko. "Singing, Dancing and Playing in Chaucer." In Michio Kawai, ed. *Language and Style in English Literature: Essays in Honour of Michio Masui* (*SAC* 15 [1993], no. 80), pp. 277–88. Assesses how words of specific actions—such as "sing," "dance," and "play"—operate lexically and how they can help produce a courtly atmosphere by expressing the joy of love.

79. Kaufman, Janice Horner. "Original Borrowings from the French in Chaucer's Translation of *Le Roman de la Rose*." *MIFLC Review* 1 (1991): 58–67. Twenty-five percent of the Old French loanwords in *Rom* are "new to English or used with a new English meaning"; most reflect influences of aristocratic, secularized French romances. Includes chart of loanwords.

80. Kawai, Michio, ed. *Language and Style in English Literature: Essays in Honour of Michio Masui*. English Research Association of Hiroshima. Tokyo: Eihosha, 1991. x, 708 pp. Forty-two articles, including thirteen on Chaucer. See nos. 37, 75, 78, 155, 163, 213, 233, 235, 237, 253, 294, 295, 305.

81. McIntosh, Angus; M. L. Samuels; and Margaret Laing. *Middle English Dialectology: Essays on Some Principles and Problems*. Aberdeen: Aberdeen University Press, 1989. iv, 295 pp. Eighteen essays on dialects,

scribes, transmission, word geography, and related topics. Only one essay has not been previously published: Margaret Laing's "Linguistic Profiles and Textual Criticism: The Translations by Richard Misyn of Rolle's *Incendium Amoris* and *Emendatio Vitae*." See also no. 355.

82. Reichl, Karl. "Imagination: Chaucer and the Philosophers." In André Crépin, ed. *The Medieval Imagination. L'Imagination médiévale: Chaucer et ses contemporains* (*SAC* 15 [1993], no. 98), pp. 157–76. Surveys meanings of *ymaginacioun* and *fantasye* in Chaucer's time and discusses his exploitation of their ambivalence.

83. Smith, J. J., ed. *The English of Chaucer and His Contemporaries: Essays by M. L. Samuels and J. J. Smith*. Aberdeen: Aberdeen University Press, 1988. vi, 126 pp. Eight essays, six previously published, on the language, dialect, spelling, and textual tradition of Chaucer, Gower, Langland, and others. For the two newly published essays, see nos. 32 and 33. See also no. 373.

See also nos. 6, 30, 32, 33, 49, 92, 114, 126, 147, 149, 151, 180, 183, 189, 196, 204, 210, 213, 233, 253, 254, 263, 274, 295.

Background and General Criticism

84. Aertsen, Henk, and Alasdair A. MacDonald, eds. *Companion to Middle English Romance*. Amsterdam: VU University Press, 1990. 209 pp. Nine original essays on Middle English romance offer the undergraduate reader a range of critical approaches and methodologies. The essays discuss widely studied romances such as *Sir Orfeo, Sir Launfal*, and particularly *Sir Gawain and the Green Knight*. The book provides background information and reviews the general themes of love and marriage, the position of women, chivalry, parody, and psychology. See no. 162.

85. Amos, Thomas L.; Eugene A. Green; and Beverly Mayne Kienzle, eds. *De Ore Domini: Preacher and Word in the Middle Ages*. Studies in Medieval Culture, no. 27. Kalamazoo, Mich.: Medieval Institute Publications, 1989. xiv, 269 pp. Thirteen essays survey topics in the history of medieval preaching from the Carolingian period to the fifteenth century, two focusing on fourteenth-century lives of Christ and Wycliffism respectively. See also no. 308.

86. Baltzer, Rebecca A.; Thomas Cable; and James I. Wimsatt, eds. *The Union of Words and Music in Medieval Poetry*. Austin: University of Texas Press, 1991. vii, 157 pp. Five essays, an introduction, and a commen-

tary on accompanying musical selections survey the interdependence of music and poetry in Provençal and medieval French and English: in the troubadour tradition, Old English poetry, French *formes fixes*, and the works of Machaut and Chaucer. Accompanying cassette (thirteen selections) recorded by Sequentia. See nos. 69, 73.

87. Benson, C. David. "A Memoir of Chaucer's Institute." In Susanna Greer Fein, David Raybin, and Peter C. Braeger, eds. *Rebels and Rivals: The Contestive Spirit in* The Canterbury Tales (*SAC* 15 [1993], no. 148), pp. 213–21. In 1987, an NEH-supported institute titled "Chaucer's *Canterbury Tales*: Medieval Contexts and Modern Responses" addressed the concern that Chaucer's poetry was disappearing from the "standard undergraduate curriculum" and discussed ways to "revivify" approaches to teaching Chaucer.

88. Blumenfeld-Kosinski, Renate, and Timea Szell, eds. *Images of Sainthood in Medieval Europe*. Ithaca, N.Y.: Cornell University Press, 1991. vii, 316 pp. Adopting a variety of critical approaches, the fourteen essays range from detailed analyses of religious discourse to theoretical inquiries into the forces that shaped ideas of sanctity. Essays discuss representations of sainthood in the Middle Ages, the role of these representations in medieval culture and politics, and the relationship between gender and images of sainthood. See no. 238.

89. Boitani, Piero, and Anna Torti, eds. *Poetics: Theory and Practice in Medieval English Literature*. Bury St. Edmunds, Suffolk: D. S. Brewer, 1991. viii, 207 pp. Examines theory and practice of poetics in medieval English literature, including author-centered, text-centered, and modern theoretical approaches. See nos. 96, 116, 134, 147, 159, 214, 229, 270.

90. Boyd, Ian. "Chesterton's Medievalism." *Studies in Medievalism* 3:3 (1987–91): 243–55. Several references to Chesterton's *Chaucer* but no direct references to Chaucer or his poetry.

91. Brewer, Derek. "The Structure of Chaucer's Imagination in His Earlier Poems." In André Crépin, ed. *The Medieval Imagination. L'Imagination médiévale: Chaucer et ses contemporains* (*SAC* 15 [1993], no. 98), pp. 19–31. In *ABC, BD*, and *HF*, uncertainty and duality-producing irony emerge as basic patterns that can be applied to all of Chaucer's poetry.

92. Burnley, David. "Courtly Speech in Chaucer." *PoeticaT* 24 (1986): 16–38. Discusses the sociomoral and aesthetic qualities that constitute courtly speech, including social attitude, voice quality, brevity, plainness of speech, and sensitivity and understanding. Based on passages spoken "curteisly" in Chaucer, Burnley's analysis examines passages in three ways:

address, message, and attitude. Language defines the person in Chaucer's courtly world.

93. Burrow, J. A., ed. *Middle English Literature: British Academy Gollancz Lectures.* Oxford: Oxford University Press, 1989. viii, 254 pp. Includes nine Sir Israel Gollancz Memorial Lectures delivered since 1950 and one on Scots delivered in 1942. Reprints Dorothy Everett's "Some Reflections on Chaucer's 'Art Poetical'" (1950), Derek Brewer's "Towards a Chaucerian Poetic" (1974), and other essays on such topics as Langland, Hoccleve, and alliterative poetry. See also no. 321.

94. Burrow, John. "The Biennial Chaucer Lecture: Poems Without Endings." *SAC* 13 (1991): 17–37. Disagrees with modern critical arguments that *CIT, SqT, HF,* and *LGW* are intentionally open-ended. Surveys the textual history and continuations of these poems to show that recent opinions probably result from post-Romantic "taste for the fragmentary" and modern "suspicion of 'closure.'"

95. Camargo, Martin. *The Middle English Verse Love Epistle.* Tübingen: Niemeyer, 1991. viii, 220 pp. Surveys the historical, literary, and rhetorical development of the Middle English verse love epistle, tracing its precursors in Latin and Continental traditions, the roles of *TC* and Gower's *Cinkante Balades,* and the flowering of the genre in the English fifteenth century. The letters of *TC,* especially the "Litera Troili," served as seminal models of function and form for the tradition through about 1550, only to be replaced in the Renaissance by Ovid's *Heroides.* Camargo provides comprehensive description and discussion of printed and manuscript versions of love epistles from 1400 to 1568.

96. Cooper, Helen. "Generic Variations on the Theme of Poetic and Civil Authority." In Piero Boitani and Anna Torti, eds. *Poetics: Theory and Practice in Medieval English Literature* (*SAC* 15 [1993], no. 89), pp. 83–103. Examines the equation of political and poetic authority in the works of Chaucer and his contemporaries. Historical romance tends to legitimize political authority and to cite poetic authority, while the fabliau pretends to chronicle true occurrences and hence does not cite poetic authority.

97. Copeland, Rita. *Rhetoric, Hermeneutics, and Translation in the Middle Ages: Academic Traditions and Vernacular Texts.* Cambridge: Cambridge University Press, 1991. xiv, 295 pp. Traces the history and theory of vernacular translation to its roots in Latin tradition, exploring classical translation theory as a product of the academic struggle between rhetoric and grammar (or hermeneutics). Medieval translation, a kind of "vernacular appropriation of academic discourse," was affected by the tradition of commentary that has as its goal the supplanting of au-

thoritative texts. Copeland examines the reflection of exegetical tendencies in a variety of Latin and vernacular commentaries, translations, and rhetorical handbooks. *Bo* is as much a commentary as a translation; *LGW* (like Gower's *Confessio Amantis*) reflects more aggressive "textual appropriation" as part of a "native literary tradition."

98. Crépin, André, ed. *The Medieval Imagination. L'Imagination médiévale: Chaucer et ses contemporains*. Paris: Publications de l'Association des Médiévistes Anglicistes de l'Enseignement Supérieur, 1991. 203 pp. Ten essays by various hands. See nos. 74, 82, 91, 145, 171, 227, 236, 277, 278, 281.

99. Du Boulay, F. R. H. *The England of* Piers Plowman: *William Langland and His Vision of the Fourteenth Century*. Cambridge: D. S. Brewer, 1991. vii, 147 pp., map, 10 b&w illus. Introduction to *Piers Plowman* as a lively mirror of fourteenth-century English society, directed to a nonspecialist audience. Includes a synopsis, derives Langland's biography from the poem, and reads it in light of contemporary social and religious institutions, ethics and ideals, trends and practices. Du Boulay assesses the poem's notions of truth, virtuous action, and eschatology. Throughout, the historical context of the poem is a major concern. Comparisons with Chaucer's works occur occasionally.

100. Edwards, Robert R., and Stephen Spector, eds. *The Olde Daunce: Love, Friendship, Sex, and Marriage in the Medieval World*. Albany: State University of New York Press, 1991. viii, 311 pp. Thirteen chapters (six on Chaucer) by various hands, notes following text. See nos. 46, 101, 212, 226, 231, and 264 and rev. no. 333.

101. Fyler, John M. "Man, Men, and Women in Chaucer's Poetry." In Robert R. Edwards and Stephen Spector, eds. *The Olde Daunce: Love, Friendship, Sex, and Marriage in the Medieval World* (*SAC* 15 [1993], no. 100), pp. 154–76, 276–84 (notes). Argues that "Chaucer — drawing on a long tradition of Biblical commentary — is well aware of the sexual dimensions of word choice, even of the double meaning of 'man.'" He "plays on the relationship between naming and sexual differentiation"; explores the ideology of "courtly game-playing"; and "subjects all the conventional literary treatments of women by men...to a debunking examination of motive." Fyler examines motifs and language in *Mel*, *MLT*, *MerT*, *NPT*, *PhyT*, *FranT*, *WBP*, *SNT*, *ClT*, *KnT*, *MkT*, *ShT*, *SqT*, *TC*, *BD*, *LGW*, *PF*, and *Rom*.

102. Gittes, Katharine S. *Framing the* Canterbury Tales: *Chaucer and the Medieval Frame Narrative Tradition*. Contributions to the Study of World Literature, no. 41. New York; Westport, Conn.; and London:

Greenwood Press, 1991. 170 pp. In the traditions of Indian and Greek frame narratives, tensions exist between the framing story and the enclosed tales, although Western aesthetics promote tighter structure and more detailed characterization. Medieval framed narratives flourished as long as multiplicity and variety were admired. Topics discussed include *CT*, the Indian *Panchatantra*, Greek and Arabic aesthetics, Petrus Alfonsi's *Disciplina clericalis*, and works by Boccaccio, Don Juan Manuel, Gower, Sercambi, and Christine de Pizan. See no. 152.

103. Given-Wilson, Chris. "Royal Charter Witness Lists, 1327–99." *Medieval Prosopography* 12 (1991): 35–93. Discusses historical reliability of witness lists as evidence of magnate activity and relationship to the crown. Provides tabular inventory of witnesses and percentage of charters witnessed by year.

104. Gray, Douglas. "Notes on Some Medieval Mystical, Magical, and Moral Cats." In Helen Phillips, ed. *Langland, the Mystics, and the English Religious Tradition: Essays in Honour of S. S. Hussey* (*SAC* 15 [1993], no. 125), pp. 185–202. Surveys medieval treatments of cats in science, witchcraft, bestiaries, proverbs, fables, and literature. Notes Chaucer's occasional references to cats in *MilT, WBT*, and *SumT*.

105. Green, Richard Firth. "Jack Philipot, John of Gaunt, and a Poem of 1380." *Speculum* 66 (1991): 330–41. Dates the macaronic lyric "On the Times" ("Syng y wold, butt, alas!") at 1380, reading it as a commentary on events and attitudes leading to the Peasants' Revolt.

106. Griffiths, Jeremy, and Derek Pearsall, eds. *Book Production and Publishing in Britain, 1375–1475*. Cambridge Studies in Publishing and Printing History. Cambridge: Cambridge University Press, 1989. xix, 463 pp. Fifteen original essays on such topics as early book design, book purchasing and ownership, Caxton, and production of various kinds of books. Includes C. Paul Christianson on "Evidence for the Study of London's Late Medieval Manuscript-Book Trade" (pp. 87–108) and "The Manuscripts of the Major English Poetic Texts," by A. S. G. Edwards and Pearsall, with a statistical appendix (pp. 257–78). See also no. 338.

107. Halford, Donna Allard. "A Rhetorical Legacy: The Art of Memory's Place in Literature and Semiotics." *DAI* 52 (1991): 547A. Of the five parts of classical rhetoric, *memoria* (including semiotics) has been insufficiently recognized. Chaucer's dream visions reveal interaction of memory and invention; *memoria* is also significant in Renaissance and Romantic poetry.

108. Hill, John M. *Chaucerian Belief: The Poetics of Reverence and Delight*. New Haven, Conn., and London: Yale University Press, 1991. 204

pp. Chaucer's works explore and promote "cognitive credence" — belief as a way of knowing the truths reflected in fiction. In *BD*, *HF*, *PF*, and *LGWP*, the narrators' confrontations with various fictions show that belief and emotional involvement are prerequisites for approaching the truth of tales. *CT* is best understood not as a rhetorical or a dramatic variety of tellers and tales but as a series of experiments in representing effectively the feelings, beliefs, and perceptions of narrators and audience who seek to state or find truth. Fragment VII (B²) is central to understanding Chaucer's reverential epistemology of fiction, but *SNT*, *CYT*, *ManT*, *SqT*, and *FranT* also reflect his examinations. Since such an epistemology is exploratory rather than exclamatory, *ParsT* may not be part of *CT*. See also no. 341.

109. Hopkins, Andrea. *The Sinful Knights: A Study of Middle English Penitential Romance*. Oxford: Clarendon Press, 1990. x, 249 pp. Examines four Middle English romances against a backdrop of late-medieval penitential doctrine and practice and assesses the presence of penitential motifs in several more. The major penitential romances — *Guy of Warwick*, *Sir Ysumbras*, *Sir Gowther*, and *Roberd of Cisyle* — reflect little contemporary penitential theory but parallel contemporary hagiography and earlier penitential materials. The romances containing penitential motifs differ widely, although the subtle and sophisticated treatment of penance in *Sir Gawain and the Green Knight* counterpoints the hero's lack of self-awareness. See also no. 342.

110. Howes, Laura Louise. "Chaucer's Gardens: The Language of Convention in Chaucer's Narrative Poetry." *DAI* 52 (1991): 1322A. Chaucer employs traditional garden *topoi* (*locus amoenus, hortus conclusus, paradys d'amours*) to draw attention to precursors, to create discrepancy between *CT* context and tradition, to individualize narrators, and to show literary indebtedness in *BD*, *PF*, *TC*, *KnT*, *MerT*, and *FranT*.

111. Kimmelman, Burt Joseph. "The Poetics of Authorship in the Later Middle Ages: The Emergence of the Modern Literary Persona." *DAI* 52 (1991): 1741A. Mentions Chaucer among poets (Guillem IX, Marcabru, Dante, and especially Langland) who helped develop the distinction between history and fiction and who showed themselves to be individuals, not for self-promotion but to identify themselves philosophically with contemporary issues.

112. Kindrick, Robert, moderator. "Teaching Chaucer: A Roundtable Discussion." *SMART*, n.s., vol. 2 (1991): 5–22. Panelists (Larry Benson, John H. Fisher, Derek Pearsall, Alfred David) discuss recent difficulties and opportunities in teaching Chaucer, focusing on student interests and capabilities.

113. Kiser, Lisa J. *Truth and Textuality in Chaucer's Poetry*. Hanover, N.H., and London: University Press of New England, 1991. x, 201 pp. Chaucer's epistemology is skeptical: he subverts written authority, obscures traditional distinctions between history and fiction, and questions the validity and representability of experience. Analysis of narratorial voices discloses (1) that *BD* addresses how a poet can evoke the "real" without "inevitable falsification" and (2) that *HF* and *PF* mock the "authorial claims" of the "medieval visionary tradition." Through the intertextual relations of *LGW* with Dante and of *TC* with Boccaccio and Dante, Chaucer indicates that the truth-claims of historiography and fiction belie the essential falsity of human discourse, which is shaped by the social contexts of its speakers. Especially in *GP, PhyT, WBP, PardP*, and *CYP* and in the figures of the Narrator and Host, *CT*—emulating the *Decameron*—shows that human discourse cannot represent the world.

114. Kooper, Erik, ed. *This Noble Craft. . .: Proceedings of the Xth Research Symposium of Dutch and Belgian University Teachers of Old and Middle English and Historical Linguistics, Utrecht, 19–20 January, 1989*. Costerus New Series, no. 80. Amsterdam: Rodopi, 1991. vii, 221 pp. Twelve studies on historical linguistics, Anglo-Saxon studies, and Middle English literature. Includes four discussions of Chaucer. See nos. 39, 40, 76, 202.

115. Mann, Jill. *Apologies to Women: [Professorial] Inaugural Lecture Delivered 20th November 1990*. Cambridge: Cambridge University Press, 1991. 43 pp. Examines medieval literary apologies to women for use of bad language and for misogynistic remarks. More so than those of his predecessor (Jean de Meun), his contemporaries (Boccaccio, Machaut, Nicole Bozon, Jehan le Fèvre), or his followers (Lydgate, Hoccleve, even Christine de Pizan), Chaucer's apologies in *TC, LGW, MLT, MerT*, and *NPT* unmask the "ritual combination of antifeminism and apology" and effect genuine apology.

116. ———. "The Authority of the Audience in Chaucer." In Piero Boitani and Anna Torti, eds. *Poetics: Theory and Practice in Medieval English Literature* (*SAC* 15 [1993], no. 89), pp. 3–12. Chaucer's presentation of himself as a reader of literature is a metaphor for our own reading of his work, an acknowledgment of his concern with the reciprocal relationship between the reader's mind and the text.

117. ———. *Geoffrey Chaucer: Feminist Readings*. Atlantic Heights, N.J.: Humanities Press International, 1991. xiii, 222 pp. Chaucer defines "woman" as the norm against which all human behavior is to be measured, representing women in ways that undermine traditional antifeminist cate-

gories. In *HF, TC*, and *LGW*, the antifeminist theme of betrayal is recast to reflect human vicissitudes and the necessity of pity. The overt use of antifeminist authorities in *MerT* and *WBP* acknowledges their existence and confronts them. The struggle for "maistrye" in *WBT* reflects the vision of egalitarian courtship in *TC* and of egalitarian marriage in *FranT* and *Mel*. Female suffering mirrors transcendent suffering in *MLT* and *ClT*, while the heroes of *TC* and *KnT* are "feminised" in the process of idealization. *NPT* epitomizes how Chaucer's fabliaux comically undermine the "rituals through which male and female roles are constructed." See also no. 356.

118. Margherita, Gayle Margaret. "The Body Spoken: Language, Origins, and Sexual Difference in Middle English Literature." *DAI* 51 (1991): 4115A. Applies Freudian and feminist theory to three extracanonical medieval texts, presenting them as the "unconscious" of works in the literary canon. Also analyzes *BD* and *TC*.

119. Mills, Maldwyn; Jennifer Fellows; and Carol M. Meale, eds. *Romance in Medieval England*. Cambridge: D. S. Brewer, 1991. viii, 228 pp. Papers presented at the first meeting (1988) of the Society for the Study of Medieval Romance, ranging in chronological concern from the twelfth to the fifteenth centuries. Included are general discussions of editing and compilation and specific discussions of MS Ashmole 61 and the Percy Folio. Individual essays also treat such works as *Gerenides, Octavian, Sege of Melayne*, and Layamon's *Brut*; they discuss such topics as the relations of romance to history, to epic, and to hagiography and such *topoi* as deer hunting and the wooing woman.

120. Millward, Celia. "Chaucer in France." *SMART*, n.s., vol. 2 (1991): 31–36. Recounts difficulties of teaching Chaucer in France and other countries, especially in Middle English.

121. Morse, Ruth. *Truth and Convention in the Middle Ages: Rhetoric, Representation, and Reality*. Cambridge: Cambridge University Press, 1991. xiv, 295 pp. Medieval notions of historical and literary truth derive from classical rhetorical tradition and differ from modern, empirically based notions of factuality. Basing her argument on a description of education in rhetoric, Morse demonstrates that medieval imaginative history and biography were "susceptible to literary analysis" and that medieval translation is more aptly viewed, in modern terms, as transformation. Conventional notions of elegance and eloquence influenced the composition and reception of medieval works, and to understand them we must reacquire appropriate habits of thought. The study concentrates on the

High Middle Ages but ranges from Cicero to Milton; Chaucer is mentioned passim.

122. North, J. D. "Verborgen betekenissen in de dichtkunst van Geoffrey Chaucer" ("Hidden Meanings in Geoffrey Chaucer's Poetry"). *MKNAL* 54 (1991): 153–62. Derived from North's *Chaucer's Universe* (*SAC* 12 [1990], no. 101), this article argues that Chaucer's imagination was illuminated by astrological and astronomical knowledge of an unusually high quality.

123. Ostade, Ingrid Tieken-Boon van, and John Frankis, eds. *Language Usage and Description: Studies Presented to N. E. Osselton on the Occasion of His Retirement.* Amsterdam: Rodopi, 1991. viii, 200 pp. Sixteen essays encompass the interpretation of textual cruxes in Middle English, lexicography in the past and present, current and older problems in English usage, and the history of English spelling. Diana Whaley's essay discusses the flood in *MilT*. See no. 183.

124. Patterson, Lee. *Chaucer and the Subject of History.* Madison: University of Wisconsin Press, 1991. xiv, 489 pp. Chaucer approaches history as a subject and human beings as individualized subjects within history, examining the medieval view of history as degeneration from an ideal and developing the modernist, humanist view of history. In *Anel*, Boethianism transcends the recursions of the ancient past. *TC* reflects the difficulty of identifying human motivation within the limitations of aristocratic historical consciousness. *LGW* reflects Chaucer's movement toward the immediate, localized historical imagination of *CT*. *MilT* subverts the aristocratic historicism of *KnT*, each reflecting contemporary social crises. *WBPT* subverts the masculine, authoritarian construction of *MLT*, championing feminine, individual subjectivity. *MerT* and *ShT* explore commercialism as a dehistoricized ideology, and *PardPT* poses and mocks penance as a means of self-constitution, criticizing contemporary religious formalism.

125. Phillips, Helen, ed. *Langland, the Mystics, and the English Religious Tradition: Essays in Honour of S. S. Hussey.* Cambridge: D. S. Brewer, 1990. xii, 289 pp. Includes nineteen essays, an introduction, a list of Hussey's publications, and a *tabula gratulatoria.* Topics of the essays include Langland, various mystics, religious lyrics, religious drama, and handbooks of religious instruction. See nos. 104, 298.

126. Potter, Russell A. "Chaucer and the Authority of Language: The Politics and Poetics of the Vernacular in Late Medieval England." *Assays* 6 (1991): 73–91. Chaucer used English as a revolutionary gesture: ". . . the vernacular destroyed the intellectual and political control of the aristocrats

of church and state." Potter addresses several fourteenth-century English concerns: aristocratic control exercised through use of French and Latin; relationships between "power and modes of discourse" and between "literacy, gender, and social class"; and the implications of these "social and linguistic relationships" for reading Chaucer. Findings are applied to *WBP*, *SqT*, *Astr*, *BD*, *HF*, *LGW*, *CT*, and the *GP* Prioress.

127. Reuters, Anna Hubertine. *Friendship and Love in the Middle English Metrical Romances*. European University Studies, 14th ser. Anglo-Saxon Language and Literature, no. 226. Frankfurt am Main: Peter Lang, 1991. Classifies some thirty English metrical romances according to several categories of friendship or love: tales of masculine friendship, of male-female mutual love, of marriage, and of the advances of forward fairies, heroines, or heroes. These categories are related to the social and political conditions of the depicted love relation. Reuters briefly surveys courtly love in select romances and assesses Caxton as a successor to the romancers.

128. Root, Jerry. "'Space to Speke': Confessional Practice and the Construction of Character in the Works of Geoffrey Chaucer, Guillaume de Machaut, and Juan Ruiz." *DAI* 51 (1991): 2373A–2374A. Following Foucault, Root examines the theory that patristic tradition and ecclesiastical practice eventually permitted confessional self-representation, as seen especially in *WBT*, *Livre du voir dit*, and *Libro de buen amor*.

129. Rudat, Wolfgang E. H. "Reading Chaucer's Earnest Games: Folk-Mode or Literary Sophistication?" *ELN* 29:2 (1991): 16–19. Carl Lindahl's hypothesis (*Earnest Games*, *SAC* 11 [1989], no. 135) of folkloric approaches to Chaucer oversimplifies and stereotypes the poet's art. Such readings, which detract from close reading, "have a potentially distorting effect."

130. Schmitz, Götz. *The Fall of Women in Early English Narrative Verse*. European Studies in English Literature. Cambridge: Cambridge University Press, 1990. ix, 300 pp. English translation, with new preface, of *Die Frauenklage: Studies zur englischen Verserzählung in der englischen Literatur des Spätmittelalter und der Renaissance* (Tübingen: Niemeyer, 1984). Investigates the relations between subject matter and poetic form in the woman's complaint, tracing its roots in classical tradition, the influence of Continental models, and the development of the English tradition from the fourteenth through the seventeenth centuries and beyond. *LGW* and the Dido episode of *HF* are important models for Renaissance treatments, influencing form, tone, and specific subjects.

131. Sturges, Robert S. *Medieval Interpretation: Models of Reading in Literary Narrative, 1100–1500*. Carbondale and Edwardsville: Southern

343

Illinois University Press, 1991. x, 302 pp. Stressing the role of the reader in finding meaning, Sturges traces the development of a "belief in an indeterminacy of literary meaning." Alongside Neoplatonism and the "directed vision" typical of the early Middle Ages, a "new mind set emphasized a multiplicity of meanings in the world and in language." Authoritative truths no longer could be revealed through allegorical interpretation. Chrétien, for example, "rejects allegory in favor of ambiguity," and by the fourteenth century "semantic indeterminacy in love and in reading was expected, conventional, and enjoyable." In chap. 4, "Communication and Interpretation: Three States in Chaucer's Career," Sturges analyzes *BD, TC*, and *WBT*. See nos. 198, 256, 293.

132. Torti, Anna. *The Glass of Form: Mirroring Structures from Chaucer to Skelton*. Cambridge: D. S. Brewer, 1991. ix, 138 pp. Torti's introduction explores the Christian and classical precedents for mirror metaphors in late-medieval English literature and surveys medieval tradition. Subsequent chapters discuss mirror imagery in Lydgate's *Temple of Glas*, Hoccleve's *Regement of Princes*, and Skelton's *Bowge of Courte* and *Speke Parrot*. Chapter 2 addresses *TC*; see no. 296.

133. Volk-Birke, Sabine. *Chaucer and Medieval Preaching: Rhetoric for Listeners in Sermons and Poetry*. ScriptOralia, no. 34. Tübingen: Gunter Narr Verlag, 1991. 315 pp. Examines the imagery, formulas, structure, and audience appeal of a number of Middle English sermons and sermon cycles, exploring their influence on Chaucer in *Mel, ParsT, PardT*, and *NPT*. The aural element of the sermons is reflected in Chaucer's poems; stylistic features are reflected in his irony, parody, and satire. His treatments of sermon materials reflect his experiments between sermons and literature, religion and art.

134. Wallace, David. "Writing the Tyrant's Death: Chaucer, Bernabò Visconti and Richard II." In Piero Boitani and Anna Torti, eds. *Poetics: Theory and Practice in Medieval English Literature* (*SAC* 15 [1993], no. 89), pp. 117–30. The Italian city-state Lombardy and the life and death of Bernabò, its most famous tyrant, provided inspiration for the fictional realm of "Lumbardye," which functions in Chaucer's works as a spatial metaphor for tyranny.

135. Wolterbeek, Marc. *Comic Tales of the Middle Ages: An Anthology and Commentary*. Contributions to the Study of World Literature, no. 39. New York; Westport, Conn.; and London: Greenwood Press, 1991. xxvi, 243 pp. Defines and traces the development of three genres of early medieval Latin comic literature: *ridicula* ("funny stories in rhythmic verse"), *nugae* ("trifles" of learned poets), and *satyrae* (venality satires).

Such tales, especially *ridicula*, anticipate vernacular fabliaux. The appendix anthologizes fourteen examples, each translated.

136. Wurtele, Douglas J. "Treachery in Chaucer's Poetry." *FCS* 18 (1991): 315–43. Argues that a "climate" of social and political treachery prevailed in Chaucer's England, considers its effect on Chaucer's work, and surveys the poet's incorporation of the theme of treachery into his major poems.

See also nos. 12, 47, 143, 160, 241, 287.

The Canterbury Tales — General

137. Allen, Mark. "Moral and Aesthetic Falls on the Canterbury Way." *SCRev* 8 (1991): 36–49. The imagery of falling reinforces *CT*'s penitential motif at the end of *PardT*, in *NPP*, in *ManP*, and in *Ret*, affectively leading the reader "through art to morality."

138. Andrew, Malcolm, ed. *Critical Essays on Chaucer's* Canterbury Tales. Toronto and Buffalo, N.Y.: University of Toronto Press, 1991. x, 229 pp. Anthologizes twenty-one previously published essays and extracts from longer discussions. The pieces were originally published between 1809 and 1987, although all but one are from the twentieth century. Topics range from dramatic criticism to feminism and deconstruction.

139. Astell, Ann W. "Job's Wife, Walter's Wife, and the Wife of Bath." In Raymond-Jean Frontain and Jan Wojcik, eds. *Old Testament Women in Western Literature*. Conway, Ark.: UCA Press, 1991, pp. 92–107. Gregory's *Moralia in Job* not only associates Job's wife with Eve as the archetypal temptress but also links her voice to the feminine speaking of poetry, with its imagistic power to move, delight, and (mis)instruct. Chaucer refashions her in *CT* in the double form of Alison of Bath and patient Griselda, using the stories of these two Joban wives to dramatize his own troubled relationship to his literary inheritance, especially Latin clerical writings.

140. Baker, Denise N. "Chaucer and Moral Philosophy: The Virtuous Women of *The Canterbury Tales*." *MÆ* 60 (1991): 241–56. Suggests that Chaucer identifies the virtuous women in *MLT*, *ClT*, *PhyT*, and *Mel* with one of four cardinal virtues to enhance the characteristics found in his sources.

141. Biscoglio, Frances Minetti. "The Wives of the 'Canterbury Tales' and the Tradition of the Valiant Woman of Proverbs 31:10–31." *DAI* 52 (1991): 1321A–1322A. Familiar with the polarized view of women as good

or bad, Chaucer drew on the tradition of the *mulier fortis* to develop irony throughout *CT*. Wives in *MLT*, *ClT*, *Mel*, and *SNT* contrast with those of *RvT*, *MilT*, *MerT*, *ShT*, and *WBT* to counter current feminist readings.

142. Breeze, Andrew. "Chaucer, St. Loy, and the Celts." *RMSt* 17 (1991): 103–20. Traces the medieval legend and cult of St. Loy the horse smith, especially from British sources; identifies references to the saint in *GP* and *FrT*. Two gazetteers assemble artistic and cultural evidence for the legend in Europe and the British Isles.

143. Brown, Peter, and Andrew Butcher. *The Age of Saturn: Literature and History in the* Canterbury Tales. Oxford: Basil Blackwell, 1991. xii, 296 pp. Examines *CT* within the social and political life of the later fourteenth century. Chaucer had an unusually assimilative, syncretic, and integrative imagination, but he lived at a time of disintegrating social and religious forms and values. He was not a poet who chose to "rise above" such circumstances; rather, he wrote words that articulate and analyze, sometimes in coded form, the specific problems he and his society faced. His tendency was not to offer easy solutions but to provoke, air, and sustain debate, often by adopting the point of view of a Christian radical. Specific chapters discuss the Wife of Bath, the Franklin, the Pardoner, the Merchant, and the Knight.

144. Carroll, Virginia Schaefer. "Women and Money in *The Miller's Tale* and *The Reeve's Tale*." *MedPers* 3 (1988): 76–88. *MilT* and *RvT* raise the issue of "maistrie" in relation to the economic stability of the family. Women are defined as passive, in terms that equate sexual loyalty and commercial value. Wives "quyte" (repay) their husbands through financial loss and embarrassment.

145. Dauby, Hélène. "Le noyau central des *Canterbury Tales*." In André Crépin, ed. *The Medieval Imagination. L'Imagination médiévale: Chaucer et ses contemporains* (*SAC* 15 [1993], no. 98), pp. 149–56. Sees Chaucer the Pilgrim and his inverted doubles—the female image of the Wife of Bath and the male image of the Host—as three parts of Chaucer's personality. Similar unity can be found among *WBT*, *Th*, and *Mel*.

146. Eberle, Patricia J. "Crime and Justice in the Middle Ages: Cases from the *Canterbury Tales* of Geoffrey Chaucer." In M. L. Friedland, ed. *Rough Justice: Essays on Crime in Literature*. Toronto; Buffalo, N.Y.; and London: University of Toronto Press, 1991, pp. 19–51. Medieval notions of crime were broader than modern ones. Chaucer's views on justice and crime, as reflected in *FrT*, *MLT*, and *ClT*, are elusive. It appears that he was "seriously doubtful about the value and practical application of any systematic view of justice such as the 'right order' promoted by the Papal Revolution."

147. Edwards, A. S. G. "Chaucer and the Poetics of Utterance." In Piero Boitani and Anna Torti, eds. *Poetics: Theory and Practice in Medieval English Literature* (*SAC* 15 [1993], no. 89), pp. 57–67. The characters of the individual pilgrims are revealed through their speech, which often serves to underline their philosophical viewpoints. Chaucer's awareness of language and its creative powers reflects a general skepticism regarding the effectiveness of utterance through poetry.

148. Fein, Susanna Greer; David Raybin; and Peter C. Braeger, eds. *Rebels and Rivals: The Contestive Spirit in* The Canterbury Tales. Kalamazoo, Mich.: Medieval Institute Publications, 1991. xxiv, 269 pp. This collection of essays by various authors addresses the rivalry and tension among characters, themes, styles, and genres in *CT*. See nos. 87, 154, 178, 184, 185, 195, 201, 203, 209, 234, 240.

149. Felch, Susan M. "Rehearsing 'Everich a Word': Chaucer's Linguistic Investigations in *The Canterbury Tales.*" *MedPers* 6 (1991): 144–53. The realist-nominalist debate underlies Chaucer's language, which, through multiple discourses and by analogy, embodies social order. By withholding his authority, Chaucer delegates to his readers responsibility for moral decisions.

150. Frese, Dolores Warwick. *An* Ars Legendi *for Chaucer's* Canterbury Tales. Gainesville: University of Florida Press, 1991. x, 338 pp. The twofold purpose of this study is, "first, to demonstrate the originality and complexity of Chaucer's intertextual practice . . . ; second, to advance the claims of the Ellesmere manuscript as the poetic text reflecting Chaucer's final authorial intentions in the matter of narrative ordering for the *Tales.*" Frese uses the related rhetorical principles of *involucrum* and *integumentum* to reread beneath *GP* and a number of free-floating fragments to identify "the poetic matrix of number as central to Chaucer's hermeneutics in this poem"; it is this matrix that points to the correct order of *CT*. Chaucer was aware, however, of the textual contamination that *CT* suffered in transmission. In *CYT*, he describes himself as the Canon, a scribe as the Yeoman, and various textual corruptions as alchemical tricks.

151. Ganim, John M. "Forms of Talk in *The Canterbury Tales.*" *PoeticaT* 34 (1991): 88–100. Investigates the ways *CT* problematizes the medium of speech and, through its self-conscious narrators, comments on the changing value of spoken language. Though Chaucer preserves and allows resistance to the tyrannies of high literary form, his relation to the poetry of common speech is problematic.

152. Gittes, Katharine S. "*Canterbury Tales.*" Chapter 6 in Katharine S. Gittes. *Framing the* Canterbury Tales: *Chaucer and the Medieval Frame Narrative Tradition* (*SAC* 15 [1993], no. 102), pp. 109–38. Assesses the

relation of the frame of *CT* to the frame narrative tradition derived from India and Greece, focusing on how Chaucer suggests clear structure and design and then blurs their outlines. The *CT* frame retains features of Arabic origin, especially openendedness and a variety of organizing elements.

153. Goodwin, Amy Wright. "Reading the 'Canterbury Tales': The Example of Chaucer's Clerk." *DAI* 52 (1991): 533A. Analyzes how *GP* and the dramatic links in *CT* affect reader interest and narrative. Suggests that the Clerk misreads allegory for mimesis and critiques Petrarchan poetics and the narrowness of the moral, exemplary tale.

154. Jonassen, Frederick B. "The Inn, the Cathedral, and the Pilgrimage of *The Canterbury Tales*." In Susanna Greer Fein, David Raybin, and Peter C. Braeger, eds. *Rebels and Rivals: The Contestive Spirit in* The Canterbury Tales (*SAC* 15 [1993], no. 148), pp. 1–35. Mikhail Bakhtin's distinction between "carnivalesque abandon and lenten mortification" and Victor Turner's distinction between liminality and *communitas* illuminate the dual nature of the pilgrimage—of the material and the spiritual, the innkeeper and the Parson, and the Inn and the Cathedral; however, the Pardoner's complete rejection of both unites the two polarities to suggest that *CT* "is an emphatic reconciliation of the Inn and the Cathedral, which are united in the idea of the pilgrimage."

155. Jordan, Robert M. "Gothic Rhetoric in Edifices of Word and Stone." In Michio Kawai, ed. *Language and Style in English Literature: Essays in Honour of Michio Masui* (*SAC* 15 [1993], no. 80), pp. 96–107. Gothic aesthetic combines opposing propensities for regularity and for embellishment. These features are manifest in Dante's *Commedia*, while *CT* is more irregular and improvisatory.

156. Kawasaki, Masatoshi. "Chaucer's Context of 'Game' in *The Canterbury Tales*." *EigoS* 135:9 (1990): 433–35 (in Japanese). Considers the conflict between "authority," which is based on higher culture, and "experience," which is characteristic of folk mode, emphasizing the significance of "game in ernest" in *CT*. "Game" derives from the festive storytelling context.

157. Mann, Jill. "Anger and 'Glosynge' in the *Canterbury Tales*." *Proceedings of the British Academy* 76 (1990): 203–23. Anger and glossing—linked by their common "refusal to accommodate the self either to events in the world outside, or to the autonomous meaning of the text"—are evident in *SumT* and throughout *CT*. The Marriage Group centers around patience, the counter to anger, and therefore includes *FrT* and *SumT*. *ManT* suggests that the "alternative to 'glosynge'. . . is silence," but it is balanced by the "comic celebration" of *NPT*.

158. Neuse, Richard. *Chaucer's Dante: Allegory and Epic Theater in The Canterbury Tales.* Berkeley, Los Angeles, and Oxford: University of California Press, 1991. xi, 295 pp. *CT* responds to Dante's *Comedy* in a "conscious attempt" to continue its "poetic tradition" of pilgrimage narrative. Chaucer's pilgrims "comment or focus on one or more aspects of the Dantean pilgrimage," and both works define the human image and likeness to God by exploring the relations between literal and allegorical representation. *NPT*, like the Geryon episode in the *Inferno*, erases animal and human distinctions to understand the human. *KnT* and *MilT* provide the context for a deconstructionist reading of drama in *CT* and the *Comedy*, seeing them against epic and theatrical traditions. *MkT*, *FrT*, and *SumT* recall aspects of the style and themes of the *Inferno*. In Petrarchan fashion, *ClT* (except for the *Envoy*) opposes Dante's approach to allegory, and *MerT* echoes the gardens of the Song of Songs and the *Paradiso*; in these narratives, marriage is a *topos* for interpretation, a means to avoid the death of literal reading.

159. Owen, Charles A., Jr. "Fictions Living Fictions: The Poetics of Voice and Genre in Fragment D of the *Canterbury Tales*." In Piero Boitani and Anna Torti, eds. *Poetics: Theory and Practice in Medieval English Literature* (*SAC* 15 [1993], no. 89), pp. 37–55. The various fictional levels in *CT* result in a dialectic relationship between voice and genre, especially pronounced in Fragment D.

160. Ridley, Florence. "Teaching the Middle Ages: The Challenge of Chaucer." In Robert Graybill, Judy Hample, and Robert Lovell, eds. *Teaching the Middle Ages IV.* Terre Haute: Indiana State University Press, 1990, pp. 1–26. Pedagogical commentary on *CT* aligned with reader-response theory and affective stylistics.

161. Taylor, Paul Beekman. "The Uncourteous Knights of *The Canterbury Tales*." *ES* 72 (1991): 209–18. Chaucer's knights reflect three errors in their service of love: (1) the subjection of women's bodies to male wills for the sake of public order and honor (*KnT*, *FranT*, *PhyT*), (2) the rapine pursuit of women's bodies for pride or lust (*MLT*, *WBT*, *MerT*), and (3) the quest for an ideal in the absence of a person (*KnT*, *Th*).

162. Tigges, Wim. "Romance and Parody." In Henk Aertsen and Alasdair A. MacDonald, eds. *Companion to Middle English Romance* (*SAC* 15 [1993], no. 84), pp. 129–51. Examines eleven texts, dating from the late fourteenth to the early seventeenth century, that are related to the metrical romance by their metatextual commentary on one or more romance characteristics. Includes discussion of *CT*, particularly *KnT*, *MLT*, *WBT*, *SqT*, *FranT*, *Th*, and *Mel*.

163. Tripp, Raymond P., Jr. "Craft, Canonical Alchemy, and Continuity

Between *Beowulf* and the *Canterbury Tales.*" In Michio Kawai, ed. *Language and Style in English Literature: Essays in Honour of Michio Masui* (*SAC* 15 [1993], no. 80), pp. 141–58. Argues that the difference between the mechanical powers of humans and the essential power of God is central to the literary discussion of craft. Concern with craft as natural religion and with faith as the canonical craft provides a strong thread of continuity between *Beowulf* and *CT*.

164. Williams, Andrew. "Clerics and Courtly Love in Andreas Capellanus' *The Art of Courtly Love* and Chaucer's *Canterbury Tales.*" *Revista Alicantina de Estudios Ingleses* 3 (1990): 127–36. In his depiction of clerical celibacy, Chaucer may have been influenced by Andreas. The two authors approach the topic in similar fashion and reflect contemporary attitudes and turmoil.

See also nos. 6, 14, 15, 18–20, 25, 28, 31, 35, 40, 41, 50, 58, 59, 70, 72, 102, 108, 113, 124, 127, 198, 243, 245.

CT—The General Prologue

165. Braswell-Means, Laurel. "A New Look at an Old Patient: Chaucer's Summoner and Medieval Physiognomia." *ChauR* 25 (1991): 266–75. Discusses Chaucer's characterization of the Summoner in *GP* and asserts that, despite modern assumptions, it is based on the confluence of medical and astrological theories prevalent at the time.

166. Cigman, Gloria. "Chaucer and the Goats of Creation." *L&T* 5 (1991): 162–80. Although elite cultural views, such as those of theologians, set the polarities of moral judgment as good and evil, vernacular writings in Middle English — including Lollard sermons, *Piers Plowman*, and *CT*— set up instead a dialectic of sin and evil. In their neglect of social and spiritual responsibilities, the Friar, Summoner, and Pardoner of *GP*, alone among the pilgrims, show themselves "totally and immutably evil."

167. Cooney, Helen. "The Limits of Human Knowledge and the Structure of Chaucer's *General Prologue*." *SN* 63 (1991): 147–59. Argues that social identity is fundamental to the description of each pilgrim and determines how each is presented; examines how Chaucer presents himself in rhetorical terms, with particular reference to the *diminutio* of *GP* 745–48.

168. Cooper, Helen. "Langland's and Chaucer's Prologues." *YLS* 1 (1987): 71–81. *GP* was inspired by the A text of *Piers Plowman*, echoing its

concern with estates satire, its concern with social and moral cohesion, and many of its details.

169. David, Alfred. "Medieval Communities in the *General Prologue* to the *Canterbury Tales*." *SMART*, n.s., vol. 2 (1991): 23–30. Individual *GP* pilgrims represent distinct groups or organizations within medieval society, epitomizing social diversity—yet the community functions as a cohesive unity.

170. Hodges, Laura F. "A Reconsideration of the Monk's Costume." *ChauR* 26 (1991): 133–46. Places the Monk in the mainstream of medieval monastic modes of dress; his "grys," his boots, and his gold pin are not excessive in comparison to clerical fashions and practices of the period.

171. Mertens-Fonck, Paule. "L'imagination dans la conception du *Prologue général* des *Contes de Canterbury*." In André Crépin, ed. *The Medieval Imagination. L'Imagination Médiévale: Chaucer et ses contemporains* (*SAC* 15 [1993], no. 98), pp. 93–105. To Chaucer's audience, the name Eglentyne suggested the lost clerk-knight debate *Hueline and Aiglantine*. While Alice of Bath must have been the second lady of the debate, the other pilgrims stand for the qualities and defects of clerks and knights.

See also nos. 5, 20, 63, 113, 126, 142, 145, 150, 153, 154, 228–31.

CT—The Knight and His Tale

172. Bergan, Brooke. "Surface and Secret in the *Knight's Tale*." *ChauR* 26 (1991): 1–16. Chaucer manipulates devices of genre and rhetoric to achieve a highly sophisticated subtext of opacity and of perversion of order.

173. Brown, Peter. "The Prison of Theseus and the Castle of Jalousie." *ChauR* 26 (1991): 147–52. Following the example set in V. A. Kolve's *Chaucer and the Imagery of Narrative* (*SAC* 8 [1986], no. 115), Brown develops the mimetic and iconographic relations of the prison in *KnT* and the castle in *Roman de la Rose*.

174. Moore, Bruce. "'Allone, Withouten Any Compaigne'—The Mayings in Chaucer's *Knight's Tale*." *ChauR* 25 (1991): 285–301. Comparison of traditional rites to the feelings and actions of the characters shows that lack of structure does not mean disorder. Moore contends that there is no correlation between ritual and the outcome of *KnT*; in fact, a ritualistic beginning leads to a destructive end.

175. Oka, Saburo. "A Structural Interpretation of the *Knight's Tale*—

351

Chaucerian Triangle in the Global Perspective." *Medieval English Studies Newsletter* 25 (1991): 21–23. A narratological description of the love triangle in *KnT*.

176. Savoia, Dianella. "Il *Knight's Tale* di Chaucer, un *romance* tragico." *Acme* 43 (1990): 117–62. After a full review of criticism, Savoia explores Chaucer's use of motifs found in other romances. *KnT* exploits traditional romance only to transcend it, setting the "romance" of Palamon in the perspective provided by the "tragedy" of Palamon and thus presenting the traditional romance "quest" as "un assurdo e inutile vagare."

177. Woods, William F. "'My Sweete Foe': Emelye's Role in *The Knight's Tale*." *SP* 88 (1991): 276–306. Discusses Emelye's role as prime mover in *KnT*, "structurally and thematically central to the tale" and parallel to Saturn's role as mediator among the gods. Central in each of the four parts of the *Tale*, she develops from a chaste maid in the garden to the innocent devotee of Diana—one who makes "a virtue of being desired."

178. ———. "Up and Down, To and Fro: Spatial Relationships in *The Knight's Tale*." In Susanna Greer Fein, David Raybin, and Peter C. Braeger, eds. *Rebels and Rivals: The Contestive Spirit in* The Canterbury Tales (*SAC* 15 [1993], no. 148), pp. 37–57. In *KnT*, vertical movements are associated with universal cosmic cycles, while horizontal movements are associated with social containment. As Palamon and Arcite move physically and emotionally closer to Emily, each moves "toward either the periphery or the center of the chivalric world."

See also nos. 5, 50, 60, 64, 101, 110, 124, 143, 158, 161, 162, 229, 264.

CT—The Miller and His Tale

179. Fein, Susanna Greer. "Why did Absolon Put a 'Trewelove' Under His Tongue? Herb Paris as a Healing 'Grace' in Middle English Literature." *ChauR* 25 (1991): 302–17. Discusses herb paris as a premedieval symbol of Christ's passion and divine love, traces its development from religious to romantic sign, and explores its dual meaning in *MilT*.

180. Kanno, Masahiko. "A Note on the Verbal Association in *The Miller's Tale*." *Studies in Foreign Language and Literature* (Aichi University, Japan) 27 (1991): 105–16. Explores nuances of select words in *MilT* (especially lines 3187–215).

181. Malone, Ed. "Doubting Thomas and John the Carpenter's Oaths in

the *Miller's Tale*." *ELN* 29:1 (1991): 15–17. John's oaths to St. Thomas may refer to the apostle as well as to Becket.

182. Storm, Melvin. "The Miller, the Virgin, and the Wife of Bath." *Neophil* 75 (1991): 291–303. Deliberately drawn links between Alison of *MilT* and the Wife of Bath enable Chaucer to carry forward the moral and spiritual implications of the scriptural allusions in *MilT*, using them to inform and reinforce the audience's response to *WBP*.

183. Whaley, Diana. "*Nowelis Flood* and Other Nowels." In Ingrid Tieken-Boon van Ostade and John Frankis, eds. *Language Usage and Description: Studies Presented to N. E. Osselton on the Occasion of His Retirement* (*SAC* 15 [1993], no. 123), pp. 5–16. The phrase "Nowelis Flood" near the end of *MilT* has commonly been taken as a malapropism, an instance of the carpenter's complacent ignorance. Whaley tests this assumption against the evidence of manuscript readings, meter, and literary contexts; examines usage of the word and name *no(w)el* in the later Middle Ages; and explores possible associations of the word in *MilT*.

See also nos. 38, 104, 124, 144, 158.

CT—The Reeve and His Tale

184. Cowgill, Bruce Kent. "Clerkly Rivalry in *The Reeve's Tale*." In Susanna Greer Fein, David Raybin, and Peter C. Braeger, eds. *Rebels and Rivals: The Contestive Spirit in* The Canterbury Tales (*SAC* 15 [1993], no. 148), pp. 59–71. Unlike the homogeneous portrayal of the two clerks in its two closest analogues—*De Gombert et les II clercs* and *Le Meunier et les II clercs*—*RvT* not only differentiates Aleyn from John but also suggests that John dominates their relationship, mirroring the larger competition of the plot.

185. Fein, Susanna Greer. "'Lat the Children Pleye': The Game Betwixt the Ages in *The Reeve's Tale*." In Susanna Greer Fein, David Raybin, and Peter C. Braeger, eds. *Rebels and Rivals: The Contestive Spirit in* The Canterbury Tales (*SAC* 15 [1993], no. 148), pp. 73–104. Chaucer utilizes the medieval icons of the wheel, the stream, and the vessel to represent the life cycle, the passing of time, and an individual's "fluid allocation of vital spirits that gradually dries from cradle to grave." In *RvP*, the Reeve's "process of maturation has diverged from the natural course," while in *RvT* birth, aging, and death constitute a cycle of mutability of which the participants are unaware.

186. Feinstein, Sandy. "The *Reeve's Tale*: About That Horse." *ChauR* 26 (1991): 99–106. Bayard, the horse in *RvT*, is presented as a mare, a gelding, and a stallion. The stallion image represents the clerks, foreshadowing the bedroom activity; the gelding image represents the Reeve, who — though he wants to chase the mares like a stallion — is bridled by his impotence; and the mare represents human lustiness.

See also nos. 38, 141, 144.

CT— The Cook and His Tale

See no. 38.

CT— The Man of Law and His Tale

187. Archibald, Elizabeth. *Apollonius of Tyre: Medieval and Renaissance Themes and Variations, Including the Text of the* Historia Apollonii Regis Tyri *with an English Translation*. Cambridge: D. S. Brewer, 1991. xiii, 250 pp. Documents and discusses the development, influence, and literary relations of the story of Apollonius to 1609, assessing its formal characteristics and reception. Occasional mention of Chaucer, particularly *MLT*.

188. Astell, Ann W. "Apostrophe, Prayer, and the Structure of Satire in *The Man of Law's Tale*." *SAC* 13 (1991): 81–97. Chaucer's additions to Trevet's tale of Constance consist chiefly of rhetorical additions by the narrator and prayers by Custance, converting the tale to a satire of the narrator's long-winded, fatalistic views. Apostrophe and prayer, "converse" forms of address in rhetorical tradition, here pit Custance's providential outlook against that of her narrator rather than that of her persecutors in the plot.

189. Edwards, A. S. G. "'I Speke in Prose': *Man of Law's Tale*, 96." *NM* 92 (1991): 469–70. In one version of the versified *Stacions of Rome*, the word "prose" clearly designates a change of subject rather than nonmetrical writing. In *MLP*, "prose" may signal a verse tale of historical and religious significance.

190. Nicholson, Peter. "Chaucer Borrows from Gower: The Sources of the *Man of Law's Tale*." In R. F. Yeager, ed. *Chaucer and Gower: Difference, Mutability, Exchange* (*SAC* 15 [1993], no. 47), pp. 85–99. Chaucer had

two sources for *MLT*: Gower's *Confessio Amantis* (2.587–1707) and Trevet's *Chronicles*, which also served as Gower's source. Placing all three versions side by side, one can find evidence that Gower was Chaucer's principal source.

191. ———. "The *Man of Law's Tale*: What Chaucer Really Owed to Gower." *ChauR* 26 (1991): 153–74. Chaucer's primary source for *MLT* was not Nicholas Trevet's *Chronicles* but Gower's *Tale of Constance*. Chaucer found in Gower's tale a streamlined shape, a sharper focus, a greater depth of character, and a heightened moral emphasis. It was Gower who first realized the suitability of Trevet's material and who suggested to Chaucer "the directions in which it might be taken."

See also nos. 23, 101, 115, 117, 124, 140, 141, 146, 161, 162.

CT—The Wife of Bath and Her Tale

192. Beidler, Peter G. "Transformations in Gower's *Tale of Florent* and Chaucer's *Wife of Bath's Tale*." In R. F. Yeager, ed. *Chaucer and Gower: Difference, Mutability, Exchange* (*SAC* 15 [1993], no. 47), pp. 100–14. Focuses on Gower's *Tale of Florent* as a poem with its own logic and narrative beauty, using Chaucer's *WBT* to clarify Gower's purpose.

193. Bott, Robin L. "The Wife of Bath and the Revelour: Power Struggles and Failure in a Marriage of Peers." *MedPers* 6 (1991): 154–61. When describing her fourth husband, the Wife is silent on topics freely discussed with respect to her other husbands (particularly money, age, and temperament); this suggests the equality of the two in these areas. Their marriage fails because the power struggles of equals are unresolvable.

194. Charles, Casey. "Adversus Jerome: Liberation Theology in the *Wife of Bath's Prologue*." *Assays* 6 (1991): 55–71. *WBP*, belonging to the genre of the French *sermon joyeux*, "a parodic homily by women that uses biblical exegesis to endorse worldly pleasure," had a "topical resonance" for Lollards, who, "championing female literacy and lay biblical exegesis, considered widows like Alice to be specialists in the intricacies of marriage practice." *WBP* is not "just a bawdy send-up of exegetical method but a subversion of it," exposing Jerome's misogynous "power grab."

195. Hagen, Susan K. "The Wife of Bath: Chaucer's Inchoate Experiment." In Susanna Greer Fein, David Raybin, and Peter C. Braeger, eds. *Rebels and Rivals: The Contestive Spirit in* The Canterbury Tales (*SAC* 15 [1993], no. 148), pp. 105–24. *WBP* is Chaucer's attempt to formulate a

"gynocentric hermeneutic" that challenges "standard patriarchal hierarchies." Yet *WBT* demonstrates the inevitable failure of the attempt since Chaucer was a product of his time, a "fourteenth-century male poet of privilege."

196. Ireland, Colin A. "'A Coverchief or a Calle': The Ultimate End of the Wife of Bath's Search for Sovereignty." *Neophil* 75 (1991): 150–59. Chaucer's awareness of analogues to *WBT* and its theme of sovereignty may be indicated by his use of the word "calle" ("headdress"; *WBT* 1018), an early borrowing of the Irish *caille* ("veil"), a derivation of which came to mean "old woman" as well as "hag, witch."

197. Johnson, Dawn. "Some Views of Love in Chaucer." *Pleiades* 12:1 (1991): 59–63. Although the behavior of Alison and the knight of *WBT* counters the teachings of the medieval church, such behavior exemplifies a more Christian attitude toward love and marriage.

198. Sturges, Robert. "St. John, the Wife of Bath, and the Poetics of Misinterpretation." In Robert S. Sturges. *Medieval Interpretation: Models of Reading in Literary Narrative, 1100–1500* (*SAC* 15 [1993], no. 131), pp. 160–75. Of all parts of *CT*, *WBP* is most "concerned with texts, their interpretation, and their relationship with lived experience." The Wife, "a living example of the truth of the very texts" she opposes, also perceives life and people as "texts to be interpreted." In other tales in *CT*, communication does not take place; paradoxically, "only in telling tales from which they can absent themselves, and consequently in treating one another as interpretable texts," can the pilgrims "make any impression on one another." The Wife may reject texts, but she quotes them to do so. Compares *WBP* and *WBT* to *FranT* and *ClT*.

199. Wurtele, Douglas. "Chaucer's Wife of Bath and Her Distorted Arthurian Motifs." *Arthurian Interpretations* 2 (1987): 47–61. Contrasts *WBT* with its Arthurian analogues (and Gower's *Tale of Florent*) to show the Wife of Bath taking "vicarious revenge" on men through her modifications of plot and situation.

See also nos. 16, 39, 101, 104, 113, 117, 124, 126, 128, 139, 141, 143, 145, 159, 161, 162, 171, 182.

CT— The Friar and His Tale

See nos. 142, 146, 157–59, 166.

CT— The Summoner and His Tale

200. Finnegan, Robert Emmett. "The Wife's Dead Child and Friar John: Parallels and Oppositions in the *Summoner's Tale*." *NM* 92 (1991): 457–62. Textual evidence suggests that the friar may be the father of the dead child — rendering the squire Jankyn (little John, the diminutive of the friar) the projection of the central character's sinfully fathered child.

201. Georgianna, Linda. "Lords, Churls, and Friars: The Return to Social Order in *The Summoner's Tale*." In Susanna Greer Fein, David Raybin, and Peter C. Braeger, eds. *Rebels and Rivals: The Contestive Spirit in* The Canterbury Tales (*SAC* 15 [1993], no. 148), pp. 149–72. In *SumT*, exchanges between the friar and the lord of the manor illuminate the friar's bourgeois relationship with Thomas. When Thomas "pays" the friar with a fart, and the friar appeals to the social hierarchy represented by the feudal lord of the manor, the friar's social aspirations are "sharply but comically checked."

202. Hertog, Erik. "'To Parte That Wol Nat Departed Be': A Plot-Analysis of the *Summoner's Tale* and Its Analogues." In Erik Kooper, ed. *This Noble Craft* (*SAC* 15 [1993], no. 114), pp. 200–21. Based on Roland Barthes's work on the structural analysis of narrative texts, this essay assesses *SumT* and two analogues. Hertog describes a model for the recognition of similar events in fiction.

203. Ruud, Jay. "'My Spirit Hath His Fostering in the Bible': *The Summoner's Tale* and the Holy Spirit." In Susanna Greer Fein, David Raybin, and Peter C. Braeger, eds. *Rebels and Rivals: The Contestive Spirit in* The Canterbury Tales (*SAC* 15 [1993], no. 148), pp. 125–48. Examines the multiple meanings of "spirit" in *SumT* as clarified by scriptural and patristic tradition, exposing satire of friars.

See also nos. 38, 104, 157–59, 165, 166.

CT— The Clerk and His Tale

204. Booker, M. Keith. "'Nothing That Is So Is So': Dialogic Discourse and the Voice of the Woman in the *Clerk's Tale* and *Twelfth Night*." *Exemplaria* 3 (1991): 519–37. Explores the possibilities for a "woman's language" through Bakhtinian theories of discourse. Through dialogic, double-voiced discourse, both Chaucer's Griselda and Shakespeare's Viola

break into and subvert the dominant patriarchal discourse in which they are inscribed.

205. Osberg, Richard H. "Clerkly Allusiveness: Griselda, Xanthippe, and the Woman of Samaria." *Allegorica* 12 (1991): 17–27. Iconographic associations of Mary and Griselda have proved problematic in attempts to read *ClT* as allegory; however, if we hear in the "annunciation passage" a larger range of allusion — both secular and patristic — the allegorical force of the Marian imagery recedes into a background of references to other exemplary women. Like a verbal pentimento, the Samaritan woman shows through patient Griselda, so that the woman setting down her water pot at the lord's call represents "every wight, in his degree."

206. Pelen, Marc M. "Irony in Boccaccio's *Decameron* and in Chaucer's 'Clerk's Tale.'" *FMLS* 27 (1991): 1–22. Just as the themes of liberality and magnificence are treated ironically in *Decameron* 10, particularly in the tale of Griselda (10.10), so *ClT* is as "poetically and morally suspect" as are *WBT* and *FranT*. Both poets use multiple narrators and traditional material (including Scripture) to expose "contradictory or competing half-truths," forcing the reader to think critically.

See also nos. 16, 21, 94, 101, 117, 139–41, 146, 153, 158, 198.

CT—The Merchant and His Tale

207. Brown, Emerson, Jr. "The Merchant's Damyan and Chaucer's Kent." *ChauNewsl* 13:1 (1991): 5. The name "Damyan" in *MerT* alludes to St. Damian, whose healing talents support a pun on "lechour." Explores Chaucer's sources of knowledge of the saint.

208. Edwards, Robert R. "Narration and Doctrine in the *Merchant's Tale*." *Speculum* 66 (1991): 342–67. Although the Merchant's voice and attitudes are cynical and misogynistic, the "marriage encomium, Justinus's speeches, and the episode of Pluto and Proserpine" counter them. Tensions between the narrator and the material of *MerT* represent "competing views of marriage and interrogate social reality."

See also nos. 16, 38, 39, 101, 110, 115, 117, 124, 141, 143, 158, 161.

CT—The Squire and His Tale

209. Owen, Charles A., Jr. "The Falcon's Complaint in *The Squire's Tale*." In Susanna Greer Fein, David Raybin, and Peter C. Braeger, eds.

Rebels and Rivals: The Contestive Spirit in The Canterbury Tales (*SAC* 15 [1993], no. 148), pp. 173–88. Unlike its two closest analogues—*Mars* and *Anel*—the falcon's lament exceeds its own generic and linguistic constraints and functions as both narrative and complaint.

See also nos. 94, 101, 108, 126, 162.

CT—The Franklin and His Tale

210. Dane, Joseph A. "Double Truth in Chaucer's *Franklin's Tale*." *SN* 63 (1991): 161–67. Analyzes Chaucer's exploitation of the potentially contradictory meanings of "trouthe," especially (1) personal loyalty, fidelity, (2) linguistic truth, and (3) factuality.

211. Fischer, Andreas. "Story and Discourse in *Sir Gawain* and *The Franklin's Tale*." In Rüdiger Ahrens, ed. *Anglistentag 1989 Würzburg.* Proceedings of the Conference of the German Association of University Professors of English, no. 9. Tübingen: Niemeyer, 1990, pp. 310–19. Observes similarities of form and theme in *FranT* and *Sir Gawain and the Green Knight*, particularly the focus on "trawthe"/"trouthe" in each, arguing that they transcend the romance genre. Contrasts *FranT* with "Menedon's Question" in Boccaccio's *Filocolo* to clarify that Dorigen is Chaucer's protagonist.

212. Gaylord, Alan T. "From Dorigen to the Vavasour: Reading Back-wards." In Robert R. Edwards and Stephen Spector, eds. *The Olde Daunce: Love, Friendship, Sex, and Marriage in the Medieval World* (*SAC* 15 [1993], no. 100), pp. 177–200, 284–87 (notes). The controversy regarding "the moral intelligence of the narrator" of *FranT* maps the "poetic terrain" of the *Tale*, i.e., rhyme, meter, poetic structure, and complex literary plan. Gaylord examines the *Tale* by two complementary and yet contradictory methods: "reading forwards" ("unscrolling a text as if it were being compla-cently listened to") and "reading backwards" ("an activity of resistance: handling the book, releaving the progress of the narrative").

213. Kanno, Masahiko. "*The Franklin's Tale*: Transformation of Au-relius." In Michio Kawai, ed. *Language and Style in English Literature: Essays in Honour of Michio Masui* (*SAC* 15 [1993], no. 80), pp. 306–21. After examining the original, rhetorical, and contextual meanings of "gentil" and its related words, Kanno discusses how Aurelius, who is at first destitute of generosity, is transformed into a gentle squire.

214. Kolve, V. A. "Rocky Shores and Pleasure Gardens: Poetry vs. Magic

in Chaucer's *Franklin's Tale*." In Piero Boitani and Anna Torti, eds. *Poetics: Theory and Practice in Medieval English Literature* (*SAC* 15 [1993], no. 89), pp. 165–95. An illustrated analysis of moral and aesthetic issues raised by Chaucer. The rocks, garden, and study that form the loci of *FranT* carry iconographic meaning suggesting a true poetics of illusion.

215. Lucas, Angela M., and Peter J. Lucas. "The Presentation of Marriage and Love in Chaucer's *Franklin's Tale*." *ES* 72 (1991): 501–12. In seeking "blisse" and "prosperitee," Arveragus and Dorigen opt for a limited, worldly purpose for their marriage. The difficulties that arise stem primarily from Arveragus's and Dorigen's words to each other and from the nature of their relationship—and only secondarily from words spoken by Dorigen to Aurelius.

216. Lucas, Peter J. "The Setting in Brittany of Chaucer's *Franklin's Tale*." *PoeticaT* 33 (1991): 19–29. Analyzes ambiguity in the setting of *FranT*, suggesting that a distinction between the information given and what is revealed by it depends on the response of the audience. Textual clues open an ironic gap between the poet and his narrator.

217. Seaman, David M. "'As Thynketh Yow': Conflicting Evidence and the Interpretation of *The Franklin's Tale*." *M&H* 17 (1991): 41–58. No single answer to the concluding question of *FranT* is satisfactory because the *Tale's* real concern is the interpretive process itself. *FranT* emphasizes different kinds of "trouthe" and poses ambiguous promises and statements.

See also nos. 16, 46, 57, 101, 108, 110, 117, 143, 161, 162, 198.

CT—The Physician and His Tale

218. Bloch, Howard R. "Chaucer's Maiden's Head: *The Physician's Tale* and the Poetics of Virginity." *QPar* 2 (1988): 22–45. Explicates Virginia's death by reference to patristic definitions of virginity as the desired ideal veiled in substance, a state inevitably transgressed by the gaze. By extension, the ideal that virginity implies is destroyed by its articulation. In praising Virginia, Chaucer exposes her to the reader's gaze, suggesting the poet's complicity in the violence of rape. See *SAC* 13 (1991), no. 159.

219. Kanno, Masahiko. "*The Physician's Tale*: A Distorted Sense of Justice." *HSELL* 36 (1991): 1–12. Effective use of repetition solves the question of justice through obvious devices such as *polyptoton*, semantic implantation, and verbal association.

See also nos. 16, 101, 113, 140, 161.

CT – The Pardoner and His Tale

220. Dillon, Janette. "Chaucer's Game in the *Pardoner's Tale*." *EIC* 41 (1991): 208–21. The discrepancy between the vice of the teller and the moral of his *Tale* requires the pilgrim audience to revise and postpone its judgment and thus to contribute to the meaning of the exemplum.

221. Merrill, Charles, and Mary Hamel. "The Analogues of the *Pardoner's Tale* and a New African Version." *ChauR* 26 (1991): 175–83. The Baskata people of Zaire have a tale called *Mesapo* that strongly resembles *PardT*, although it was not influenced by Chaucer's work.

222. Montelaro, Janet J. "The Pardoner's Self-Reflexive Peyne: Textual Abuse of *The First Epistle to Timothy*." *SCRev* 8 (1991): 8–16. Psychological studies of pain help us understand the Pardoner's personal suffering, his abuse of others, and his "harassment" of Paul's letter in *PardP*. His intent, style, and argument subvert his biblical model.

223. Owley, Steven. "Chaucer's *The Pardoner's Tale*." *Expl* 49 (1991): 204. A dicing pun in *PardT* 6.696 foreshadows death.

See also nos. 16, 32, 113, 124, 133, 137, 143, 154, 166.

CT – The Shipman and His Tale

224. Green, Richard Firth. "Chaucer's *Shipman's Tale*, Lines 138–41." *ChauR* 26 (1991): 95–98. Lines 138–41 are authorial commentary and should be punctuated as such. The revised reading makes more immediate sense, adding parallelism and a touch of Chaucerian irony.

225. Mandel, Jerome. "*The Shipman's Tale*: VII, 204." *PQ* 70 (1991): 99–102. Removing attribution of the phrase "al stille and softe" from the monk and reading the phrase instead as narrative discourse eliminates ambiguity, enhances our perception of the monk's character, and extends the *Tale*'s thematic concerns.

See also nos. 16, 38, 101, 124, 141, 164.

CT – The Prioress and Her Tale

226. Borroff, Marie. "'Loves Hete' in the *Prioress's Prologue and Tale*." In Robert R. Edwards and Stephen Spector, eds. *The Olde Daunce: Love,*

Friendship, Sex, and Marriage in the Medieval World (*SAC* 15 [1993], no. 100), pp. 229–35. Considers whether the Prioress was capable of "love celestial," examining her invocation to the Virgin Mary and suggesting that the heaviness of Mary's pregnancy is analogous to the Prioress's need to be delivered of her tale. In *PrT*, "affective piety" is preferred to intellectualism, and speech and song, love and hate are opposed.

227. Cigman, Gloria. "Piety and Prejudice." In André Crépin, ed. *The Medieval Imagination. L'Imagination médiévale: Chaucer et ses contemporains* (*SAC* 15 [1993], no. 98), pp. 133–47. The anti-Semitism of *PrT* is not Chaucer's, and the *Tale* is less about it than about the divine power of Mary to destroy the enemies of the Christian faith.

228. Frank, Hardy Long. "Seeing the Prioress Whole." *ChauR* 25 (1991): 229–37. The Prioress's worldly graces and associations with Mary are well suited to her esteemed position of religious and social power. Frank speculates that Chaucer chose *PrT* for its associations with "the cult of Notre Dame du Puy."

229. Mertens-Fonck, Paule. "Life and Fiction in the *Canterbury Tales*: A New Perspective." In Piero Boitani and Anna Torti, eds. *Poetics: Theory and Practice in Medieval English Literature* (*SAC* 15 [1993], no. 89), pp. 105–15. Chaucer's use of the name Eglentyne in the description of the Prioress in *GP* and in a scene of *KnT* emphasizes the disparity between reality and the courtly-love tradition.

230. Saito, Isamu. "Is the *Prioress's Tale* Adapted to Its Teller?" *Doshisha Studies in English* 52–53 (1991): 8–29 (in Japanese). Discusses whether the dubious Eglentyne of *GP* is the right person to tell the pious *Tale*. Chaucer's genius makes her succeed in putting deep human and feminine emotion into the *Tale*.

231. Spector, Stephen. "Empathy and Enmity in the *Prioress's Tale*." In Robert R. Edwards and Stephen Spector, eds. *The Olde Daunce: Love, Friendship, Sex, and Marriage in the Medieval World* (*SAC* 15 [1993], no. 100), pp. 211–28, 289–300 (notes). Explores the "joining of contradictions in irony" in the *GP* portrait of the Prioress and the "joining of contraries" in "sublime paradox" in the allusion to the Incarnation in *PrT*. A further contradiction is "that the Prioress, whose faith and emotion seem so shallow and misplaced" in *GP*, "should utter so ardent a prayer at all." Spector deconstructs "the moral dichotomy in her depiction of Christian-Jewish relations" to challenge the notion of Chaucer's anti-Semitism.

232. Zitter, Emmy Stark. "Anti-Semitism in Chaucer's *Prioress's Tale*." *ChauR* 25 (1991): 277–84. Chaucer criticizes not anti-Semitism but rather the Prioress herself. The Prioress does not believe in New Testament

attitudes on accepting Jews. Despite being a nun, she is unyielding in her belief that Jews are evil.

See also nos. 16, 21, 97.

CT—The Tale of Sir Thopas

233. Nakao, Yoshiyuki. "The Language of Romance in *Sir Thopas*—Chaucer's Dual Sense of the Code." In Michio Kawai, ed. *Language and Style in English Literature: Essays in Honour of Michio Masui* (*SAC* 15 [1993], no. 80), pp. 343-60. Discusses the language of romance in *Th*, focusing on seven types of "deviation."

See also nos. 145, 162.

CT—The Tale of Melibee

See nos. 70, 101, 117, 133, 140, 141, 145, 162.

CT—The Monk and His Tale

234. Braeger, Peter C. "The Portrayals of Fortune in the Tales of *The Monk's Tale*." In Susanna Greer Fein, David Raybin, and Peter C. Braeger, eds. *Rebels and Rivals: The Contestive Spirit in* The Canterbury Tales (*SAC* 15 [1993], no. 148), pp. 223-26. Abstract of an article unfinished because of the author's death, examining the more than thirty verbal contexts for "Fortune."

235. Wetherbee, Winthrop. "The Context of the *Monk's Tale*." In Michio Kawai, ed. *Language and Style in English Literature: Essays in Honour of Michio Masui* (*SAC* 15 [1993], no. 80), pp. 159-77. Considers *MkT* complete as an experiment in a new literary form that Chaucer used to medievalize materials.

See also nos. 63, 101, 158, 170.

CT—The Nun's Priest and His Tale

236. Boitani, Piero. "Chaucer and the World of Interpretation: The Priest's Letter." In André Crépin, ed. *The Medieval Imagination. L'Imagination médiévale: Chaucer et ses contemporains* (*SAC* 15 [1993], no. 98), pp. 107–32. Discusses the conflict between the letter and the spirit in *NPT*, providing a short survey of the history of literal interpretation. Chaucer freely accepts the letter as literature without excluding the morality. The Priest makes us turn away from nonliteral exegesis while inviting us to pursue it.

237. Higuchi, Masayuki. "A Search for Chaucer's Comedy." In Michio Kawai, ed. *Language and Style in English Literature: Essays in Honour of Michio Masui* (*SAC* 15 [1993], no. 80), pp. 266–76. Examines Chaucer's use of descent and ascent, particularly in *NPT*, a successful comedy.

See also nos. 16, 62, 101, 115, 117, 133, 137, 157.

CT—The Second Nun and Her Tale

238. Sherman, Gail Berkeley. "Saints, Nuns, and Speech in the *Canterbury Tales*." In Renate Blumenfeld-Kosinski and Timea Szell, eds. *Images of Sainthood in Medieval Europe* (*SAC* 15 [1993], no. 88), pp. 136–60. By allowing the pilgrims no comment on the hagiographic discourse of the faceless, feminine "Second Nonne," and by allowing the Prioress to identify with both Word and bearer of the Word, *CT* interrogates the doctrines on which it rests: the unity of thought and language, the hierarchies of male and female, "auctoritee" and experience, speech and writing, salvific word and redemptive act.

239. Tobin, Ann Lee. "Give the Saint Her Due: Hagiographical Values for Chaucer's *Second Nun's Tale* and Graham Greene's *The End of the Affair*." *SMy* 14, nos. 2–3 (1991): 48–60. Both Chaucer's St. Cecilia and Greene's Sarah Miles are perceived as rude, disrespectful, and unbelievable. Their behavior and narratives can be appreciated only in the context of the hagiographical tradition.

See also nos. 16, 101, 108, 141, 245.

CT—The Canon's Yeoman and His Tale

240. Raybin, David. "'And Pave It Al of Silver and of Gold': The Humane Artistry of *The Canon's Yeoman's Tale*." In Susanna Greer Fein,

David Raybin, and Peter C. Braeger, eds. *Rebels and Rivals: The Contestive Spirit in* The Canterbury Tales (*SAC* 15 [1993], no. 148), pp. 189–212. *CYP* offers an earthly perspective that counterbalances the heavenly perspective in *SNT*. Moreover, the structure of *CYPT* affirms artistic striving for "something higher and more beautiful" while suggesting the "tendency to corruption that threatens each of our lives."

See also nos. 16, 108, 113, 150, 245.

CT — The Manciple and His Tale

241. Grudin, Michaela Paasche. "Chaucer's *Manciple's Tale* and the Poetics of Guile." *ChauR* 25 (1991): 329–42. *ManT* examines the kind of language by which a poet can survive. Given the historical context of Richard II's reign and the contemporary chronicle literature that warned of the necessity of suppressing one's speech, the individual must resort to guile to talk at all. Realizing that society "requires a language of poetry roughly attuned to its nature," the poet must learn to temper truth with delight, conveying passion without "threat."

242. Herman, Peter C. "Treason in the *Manciple's Tale*." *ChauR* 25 (1991): 318–28. According to the rules for infidelity in the Middle Ages, Phebus's wife is guilty of both adultery and high treason since she commits adultery with a person of lower birth and social class.

243. Pelen, Marc M. "The Manciple's 'Cosyn' to the 'Dede.'" *ChauR* 25 (1991): 343–51. *ManT* is concerned with the method by which a story is told. Emphasis on the "gods' role in human marriage" restores the relationship between word and deed, a relationship also important to the narrator of *CT*. Chaucer's numerous voices can be heard as "ironic reflections" on this central theme.

244. Schlesinger, George. "A Plug for Pluralism? A Note on the *Manciple's Tale*." *DUJ*, n.s., vol. 52 (1991): 5–8. Critical attempts to specify a single meaning for *ManT* reveal the *Tale*'s own defiance of any didactic or schematized moral.

245. Weil, Eric. "An Alchemical Freedom Flight: Linking the *Manciple's Tale* to the *Second Nun's* and *Canon's Yeoman's Tales*." *MedPers* 6 (1991): 162–70. Fragments VIII and IX are connected by opposed images of sight and blindness, idleness and work. Themes of alchemical transfor-

mation and restraints on freedom (food, mates, language) also link the fragments.

See also nos. 16, 108, 137, 157.

CT—The Parson and His Tale

246. Swanson, Robert N. "Chaucer's Parson and Other Priests." *SAC* 13 (1991): 41–80. Assesses the Parson in the context of historical records and medieval handbooks for priests, showing him to be a success of the system of patronage, education, and benefice. Identifies the social and economic advantages of his status and summarizes the rewards and responsibilities involved in his role as a beneficed member of the secular clergy and rector of his parish.

247. Wood, Chauncey. "Chaucer's Most 'Gowerian' Tale." In R. F. Yeager, ed. *Chaucer and Gower: Difference, Mutability, Exchange* (*SAC* 15 [1993], no. 47), pp. 75–84. With its focus on sin, *ParsT* is the most Gowerian and least Chaucerian of the *CT* even though Gower's presentation of sin is expository and Chaucer's indirect.

See also nos. 70, 108, 133, 137, 154, 164.

CT—Chaucer's *Retraction*

248. Travis, Peter W. "Deconstructing Chaucer's Retraction." In Peter L. Allen and Jeff Rider, eds. *Reflections in the Frame: New Perspectives on the Study of Medieval Literature*. Special issue of *Exemplaria* 3 (1991): 135–58. *Ret* is an example of a Derridean *parergon*, simultaneously marginal to and an important element of *CT*. It allows for both humanistic and exegetical readings, producing a "hermeneutic double-bind," separated by an aporetic gap that generates new meanings and interpretations while denying interpretive closure.

See also no. 137.

Anelida and Arcite

249. Favier, Dale A. "*Anelida and Arcite*: Anti-Feminist Allegory, Pro-Feminist Complaint." *ChauR* 26 (1991): 83–94. In *Anel*, Chaucer worked

out his strategy of pitting profeminist impulses (the poet assumes the voice of the betrayed women) against antifeminist allegory "in which men's betrayal of women represents poetic language's necessary betrayal of literal meaning."

See also nos. 6, 124.

A Treatise on the Astrolabe

See nos. 6, 126.

Boece

See nos. 17, 97.

The Book of the Duchess

250. Butterfield, Ardis. "Lyric and Elegy in *The Book of the Duchess.*" *MÆ* 60 (1991): 33–60. Analyzes Chaucer's treatment of bereavement and its consolation, particularly in relation to the exploitation of lyric in French narratives (both *dit* and elegy).

251. Ebi, Hisato. "Psychopathology on Melancholy and Imagination." In Hisao Turu, ed. *Reading Chaucer's* Book of the Duchess (*SAC* 15 [1993], no. 258), pp. 171–200 (in Japanese). Allegorical elements of *BD* are closely connected with the theory of melancholy in the late-medieval period. Emphasizes parallelism between mental diseases (melancholy) and the creative mind.

252. Ikegami, Tadahiro. "Chaucer's Poetic Adventure: Elegy of Love, Beauty, and Death." In Hisao Turu, ed. *Reading Chaucer's* Book of the Duchess (*SAC* 15 [1993], no. 258), pp. 119–41 (in Japanese). Examines how *BD* was influenced by the conventions of French and Latin literature. Concludes that the poet found novelty in classical authors and created his own imaginary love poem.

253. Jimura, Akiyuki. "Chaucer's Use of 'Herte' in *The Book of the Duchess.*" In Michio Kawai, ed. *Language and Style in English Literature: Essays in Honour of Michio Masui* (*SAC* 15 [1993], no. 80), pp. 289–305. Chaucer's use of "herte" for "the hart," "the heart of the body," and "the sweetheart" unifies *BD*.

254. ———. "Word Play." In Hisao Turu, ed. *Reading Chaucer's* Book of the Duchess (*SAC* 15 [1993], no. 258), pp. 221–43 (in Japanese). Considers the significance of "herte," which means (1) "dear," (2) "heart," and (3) "lover." Concludes that it contributes to the organic wholeness of *BD*.

255. Shigeo, Hisashi. "Chaucer's Innovation." In Hisao Turu, ed. *Reading Chaucer's* Book of the Duchess (*SAC* 15 [1993], no. 258), pp. 142–70 (in Japanese). Analyzes the relationship of the real world to the dream world in *BD* and surveys noncourtly innovations derived from French romances, taking account of Chaucer scholarship of the late twentieth century.

256. Sturges, Robert S. "Speech and Writing in *The Book of the Duchess*." In Robert S. Sturges. *Medieval Interpretation: Models of Reading in Literary Narrative, 1100–1500* (*SAC* 15 [1993], no. 131), pp. 127–39. *BD* "opposes interpretation to communication, favoring the latter"—a significant factor in reader response. Textuality poses a danger to communication; interpretation is unsatisfactory; and the reader "runs the risk, above all, of solipsism." In *BD*, "texts are closed and indecipherable."

257. Turu, Hisao. "Consolation and Eulogy." In Hisao Turu, ed. *Reading Chaucer's* Book of the Duchess (*SAC* 15 [1993], no. 258), pp. 201–20 (in Japanese). The Knight in Black is not John of Gaunt but his young squire, who admired and served his dear duchess.

258. ———, ed. *Reading Chaucer's* Book of the Duchess. Medieval English Literature Symposium Series, no. 5. Tokyo: Gaku Shobo Press, 1991. viii, 284 pp. (in Japanese). Japanese translation of *BD*, with introduction and notes by Haruo Harada. Includes six essays by various scholars. See nos. 251, 252, 254, 255, 257, 259.

259. Yamamoto, Toshiki. "Another Interpretation." In Hisao Turu, ed. *Reading Chaucer's* Book of the Duchess (*SAC* 15 [1993], no. 258), pp. 244–67 (in Japanese). Relates the dream vision in *BD* to the tradition of religious vision and the speeches of the Knight in Black to the Resurrection theme.

See also nos. 6, 91, 101, 107, 108, 110, 113, 118, 126, 264, 276.

The Equatorie of the Planetis

260. Edwards, A. S. G., and Linne R. Mooney. "Is the *Equatorie of the Planets* a Chaucer Holograph?" *ChauR* 26 (1991): 31–42. *Equat* is not a holograph. The careful preparation of certain aspects of the text indicates a final version, and certain deletions and corrections suggest that the copier

did not always understand the material he wrote down. The scribe was likely an inexperienced individual, writing in London, who associated the calculation for the radix with Chaucer's name.

261. Krochalis, Jeanne E. "Postscript: The *Equatorie of the Planetis* as a Translator's Manuscript." *ChauR* 26 (1991): 43–47. Numerous Latin insertions on the manuscript suggest that the scribe was translating from a Latin exemplar into English. His notations indicate that he was identifying problems with translation and guarding against them when creating his final version.

262. Robinson, Pamela. "Geoffrey Chaucer and the *Equatorie of the Planetis*: The State of the Problem." *ChauR* 26 (1991): 17–30. The Cambridge, Peterhouse MS 75.I, containing *Equat*, is a Chaucer holograph, perhaps the author's rough draft, since it contains copious revisions, both in content and in style. The manuscript's notation, "Radix chaucer," was also written by the poet, referring to the precise date of his calculations. Spelling and punctuation consistent with Hengwrt and Ellesmere confirm Chaucer's authorship.

The House of Fame

263. Jimura, Akiyuki. "Chaucer's Use of 'Soth' and 'Fals' in *The House of Fame*." *Philologia* (Mie University, Japan) 23 (1991): 11–35. Examines "soth," "fals," and various derivatives and near synonyms to suggest that Chaucer's basic question in *HF* is, "What on earth can he trust?"

See also nos. 6, 41, 54, 57, 62, 91, 94, 107, 108, 113, 117, 126, 130, 269, 276.

The Legend of Good Women

264. Edwards, Robert R. "Faithful Translations: Love and the Question of Poetry in Chaucer." In Robert R. Edwards and Stephen Spector, eds. *The Olde Daunce: Love, Friendship, Sex, and Marriage in the Medieval World* (*SAC* 15 [1993], no. 100), pp. 138–53, 272–76 (notes). *LGWP* reflects concern with poetic art, especially the notions of translation and transformation, *making*, and *enditing*. Cupid's accusations against *Rom* and *TC* privilege social over artistic meaning although Chaucer and Alceste subvert

369

this "social appropriation of poetry." Edwards assesses the relations of social and artistic meaning in *BD* and *KnT* as well.

265. McLeod, Glenda. "Al of Another Tonne." Chap. 4 in *Virtue and Venom: Catalogs of Women from Antiquity to the Renaissance*. Women and Culture Series. Ann Arbor: University of Michigan Press, 1991, pp. 81–109. Contrary to critical tradition, Chaucer did not necessarily abandon *LGW* in boredom. A reading with attention to the discrepancies between *LGWP* and the legends, and to their ordering and their figurative language, reveals a careful and purposeful structure as well as structural, thematic, and aesthetic completeness.

266. Martin, Ellen E. "Chaucer's Ruth: An Exegetical Poetic in the *Prologue* to the *Legend of Good Women*." *Exemplaria* 3 (1991): 467–90. Examines exegetical interpretations of and allusions to the story of Ruth. Chaucer's allusion to Ruth in *LGWP* expresses alienation and belatedness and asserts poetic privilege and the interpretive creativity of marginality.

267. Oka, Saburo. "Characterizations by Ovid, Gower and Chaucer of the *Tereus-Procne-Philomela* Story." *TCEL* 64 (1991): 1–15. Chaucer is consistent in keeping an unsympathetic attitude to abnormal love and boldly cuts off the "revenge" part of the story of Tereus and Procne.

268. ———. "Chaucer's Transformation of 'The Legend of Philomela' in *The Legend of Good Women*." *TCEL* 63 (1990): 79–109. The tale of Philomela involves a love triangle of one male and two females. Chaucer's narrative focuses on Philomene, whereas Gower's analogue focuses on both Philomene and Progne. Chaucer achieves his most important transformation of the story by omitting the latter part.

269. Ruff, Nancy K. "'Sely Dido': A Good Woman's Fame." *CML* 12 (1991): 59–68. Chaucer's ironic treatment of the Dido legend in *LGW* and *HF* involves a naïve narrator who erroneously sympathizes with Dido; a medieval audience would have recognized differences from the treatment of Dido in Virgil's *Aeneid* and Ovid's *Heroides*. Chaucer signals the reader to question the written word and reveals a mistrust of poetic fiction.

270. Taylor, Paul B. "Cave and Web: Vision and Poetry in Chaucer's *Legend of Good Women*." In Piero Boitani and Anna Torti, eds. *Poetics: Theory and Practice in Medieval English Literature* (*SAC* 15 [1993], no. 89), pp. 69–82. The theory that "words can reveal to the inner eye of understanding the invisible forms behind visible shapes" is rejected through repeated examples of "the complicity of sight in the tragedy of love."

271. Walker-Pelkey, Faye. "Legendary Women: Alceste and Criseyde Within 'Boundes They Oghte Keepe.'" *SCRev* 8 (1991): 19–35. Con-

structed in contrast to Criseyde of *TC*, and despite the narrator's veneration, Alceste of *LGWP* is an unacceptable model for womankind. Even though she is usually regarded as self-serving, Criseyde is a positive model.

See also nos. 6, 21, 35, 53, 94, 97, 101, 107, 108, 115, 117, 124, 126, 130.

The Parliament of Fowls

272. Fradenburg, Louise Olga. "Speaking of Love: *The Parliament of Fowls, The Kingis Quair*, and *The Thrissill and the Rois*." Chap. 8 in *City, Marriage, Tournament: Arts of Rule in Late Medieval Scotland*. Madison: University of Wisconsin Press, 1991, pp. 123–49. Identifies differences between aristocratic and lower-class desire in *PF*, exploring how endless desire establishes sovereignty in the poem. The essay also assesses the relations of the poem with Scots tradition, especially the version of the Selden Arch B.24 manuscript, which closes in unique fashion: a peacock recommends that the royal eagle win the formel eagle and that the other birds also choose permanent mates. Nature concurs, the birds choose, and the poem returns to a "still-reading dreamer."

See also nos. 6, 22, 26, 54, 101, 107, 108, 110, 113, 276.

Troilus and Criseyde

273. Anderson, J. J. "Criseyde's Assured Manner." *N&Q* 236 (1991): 160–61. *TC* 1.78–82 is based on Machaut's *Le jugement du roy de Behaigne* and his *Remède de fortune*.

274. Archibald, Elizabeth. "Declarations of 'Entente' in *Troilus and Criseyde*." *ChauR* 25 (1991): 190–213. *TC* is a drama of "entente," concerned more with *why* people do things than with *what* they do. Chaucer uses "entente" much more heavily here than in any of his earlier works and evokes its numerous meanings. As the poem progresses, there is a "slippage of meaning," focusing the reader on the "unreliability of stated intentions and the difficulty of interpreting them."

275. Benson, C. David. *Chaucer's* Troilus and Criseyde. London: Unwin Hyman, 1990. x, 226 pp. Chaucer's transformations of his sources produced a work that invites multiple and open-ended responses. Benson

contrasts *TC* and its source, Boccaccio's *Filostrato*; assesses medieval and modern readership of *TC*; and considers the story of Troy and its role in *TC*. Focusing on character, love, fortune, and Christianity, he shows that Chaucer's goal was aesthetic rather than didactic and that, even though Chaucer assumed a medieval Christian audience, his poem provoked and continues to provoke a wide variety of valid critical responses. See also no. 310.

276. ———. *Critical Essays on Chaucer's* Troilus and Criseyde *and His Major Early Poems*. Toronto: University of Toronto Press; Milton Keynes: Open University Press, 1991. ix, 246 pp. Anthologizes previously published essays and extracts from longer discussions of *TC, BD, HF,* and *PF*. Originally published between 1915 and 1986, the essays are arranged chronologically by work, most (twelve of nineteen) dedicated to *TC*.

277. Blanchot, Jean-Jacques. "Chaucer traducteur et créateur dans *Troilus*: Rhétorique et symbolisme." In André Crépin, ed. *The Medieval Imagination. L'Imagination médiévale: Chaucer et ses contemporains* (*SAC* 15 [1993], no. 98), pp. 71–80. In *TC*, Chaucer is both a translator and a creator. He combines the model of ancient authors with a mythological world and a symbolic construction.

278. Butterfield, Ardis. "Froissart, Machaut, Chaucer and the Genres of Imagination." In André Crépin, ed. *The Medieval Imagination. L'Imagination médiévale: Chaucer et ses contemporains* (*SAC* 15 [1993], no. 98), pp. 53–69. In the *Voir dit, La prison amoureuse*, and *TC*, different genres are different ways of producing meaning and possess different forms of fictionality.

279. Camargo, Martin. "The Consolation of Pandarus." *ChauR* 25 (1991): 214–28. Chaucer's Pandarus is based to a certain extent on the character of Philosophy in Boethius's *Consolation*, and his Troilus resembles Boethius. Troilus's change during the poem can be attributed to the fact that "he has experienced the consolation of Pandarus."

280. Delasanta, Rodney. "Chaucer and Strode." *ChauR* 26 (1991): 205–18. Chaucer's connection with Ralph Strode is important in shedding light on the poet's "philosophical preoccupations." His "tutorial" from Strode might have exposed him to the entire range of philosophical speculation of the day.

281. Dvorak, Marta. "'Courtly' Love in Chaucer's *Troilus and Criseyde*: Fast Track of the Seven Deadly Sins." In André Crépin, ed. *The Medieval Imagination. L'Imagination médiévale: Chaucer et ses contemporains* (*SAC* 15 [1993], no. 98), pp. 81–91. Troilus's illicit love causes his involvement with the Seven Deadly Sins.

282. Giunta, Edvige. "Pandarus: Process and Pleasure in Artistic

Creativity." *MedPers* 6 (1991): 171–77. As a figure of the writer, Pandarus embodies the perverse nature of artist as observer. Having completed his narrative in the consummation scene, Pandarus must invent another tale to make "wommen unto men to comen" and to survive as an author.

283. Huppé, Bernard F. "Plenary Lecture: Aeneas' Journey to the New Troy." In Aldo S. Bernardo and Saul Levin, eds. *The Classics in the Middle Ages* (*SAC* 15 [1993], no. 34), pp. 175–87. Surveys the typology of journeying in *Beowulf*, Abelard's *Calamities*, Chrétien's *Erec* and *Lancelot*, *Roman de la Rose*, Dante's *Vita nuova*, *Sir Gawain and the Green Knight*, and Troilus's rise through the spheres in *TC*.

284. Kellogg, Laura Dowell. "Boccaccio, Chaucer, and the Legendary Cressida." *DAI* 52 (1991): 909A. The narrators of *Filostrato* and *TC*, both selfishly motivated, create irony through their misconceptions of Cressida's traditional image. Although Boccaccio's narrator distorts Boethius and Dante, Chaucer's narrator represents Cressida's flaw as "lack of prudence" and revises the ending from condemnation of Criseyde to contemplation of mutability.

285. Kelly, H. Ansgar. "Shades of Incest and Cuckoldry: Pandarus and John of Gaunt." *SAC* 13 (1991): 121–40. Provides historical evidence that, if Pandarus was guilty of incest with Criseyde, he was also guilty of cuckolding Troilus. Similarly, if Gaunt had cuckolded Chaucer, he would not have been able to marry Chaucer's wife's sister, Katherine Swynford, although the "sororal" relation between Katherine and Philippa Chaucer was posited only in the sixteenth century. Includes Boniface IX's letter of dispensation for Gaunt and Katherine.

286. Levine, Robert. "Pandarus as Davus." *NM* 92 (1991): 463–68. The characterization of Pandarus resembles that of Davus, the slave who appears as a crafty go-between in Terence, Matthew of Vendôme, and Horace.

287. McKendrick, Scot. "The *Great History of Troy*: A Reassessment of the Development of a Secular Theme in Late Medieval Art." *JWCI* 54 (1991): 43–82. Examines tapestries dealing with the story of Troy from the fourteenth century onward.

288. Mieszkowski, Gretchen. "Chaucer's Much Loved Criseyde." *ChauR* 26 (1991): 109–32. In contrast to the strong heroines in French romances, Criseyde is a weak, passive individual who does not act but is acted upon. Chaucer creates her this way deliberately to make her "magically attractive" — she is "lovely undefined responsiveness," which is irresistible to all men. Thus she is a "flawed ideal" and under difficult circumstances will fall.

289. Ordiway, Frank Bryan. "Dante, Chaucer, and the Poetics of the Past." *DAI* 51 (1991): 2373A. Unlike Dante, who recognizes his poetic

"fathers" in *The Divine Comedy* and sees himself as surpassing them, Chaucer in *TC* adopts the stance of the translator of an ancient text but questions the value of its tradition.

290. Sanyal, Jharna. "Criseyde Through the Boethian Glass." *Journal of the Department of English* (University of Calcutta) 22 (1986–87): 72–89. Chaucer's portrayal of Criseyde had to remain true to Boccaccio's account of her as a betrayer of Troilus, both underlining and undercutting her traditional character and conveying Boethius's idea of the nature of "human felicite."

291. Stanbury, Sarah. "The Voyeur and the Private Life in *Troilus and Criseyde*." *SAC* 13 (1991): 141–58. Feminist film theory and psychoanalytic theory clarify how acts of looking and the arrangements of personal space establish power relations in *TC*. Explores how power is gained and lost in Troilus's initial gaze at Criseyde, her view of him from her chamber window, and Pandarus's involvement during and after the consummation scene.

292. Sturges, Robert S. "Ascalaphus and Philomela: Myth and Meaning in Chaucer's *Troilus and Criseyde*." *ANQ* 4 (1991): 63–67. Two allusions to birds of mythology suggest the "conflicts of signification" in *TC*; their ambiguity makes the reader "an active participant in the poem."

293. ———. "*Troilus and Criseyde*: Sexuality as Textuality." In Robert S. Sturges. *Medieval Interpretation: Models of Reading in Literary Narrative, 1100–1500* (*SAC* 15 [1993], no. 131), pp. 139–60. In *TC*, communication is "presented as a rarely attainable ideal, while the textualization and interpretation of experience remain problematic and even dangerous." The lovers are text-bound, but the reader can deal with and perhaps transcend the "alienation that textuality still implies." Presented with ambiguities, readers must choose between possible truths.

294. Sudo, Jun. "Some Notes on the Proems of *Troilus and Criseyde*." In Michio Kawai, ed. *Language and Style in English Literature: Essays in Honour of Michio Masui* (*SAC* 15 [1993], no. 80), pp. 361–73. The proem of each book of *TC* summarizes the gist of the following story and establishes a suitable mood through invocation to appropriate gods.

295. Takahashi, Hisashi. "Why Not 'This Criseyde'?" In Michio Kawai, ed. *Language and Style in English Literature: Essays in Honour of Michio Masui* (*SAC* 15 [1993], no. 80), pp. 374–91. Examines why the expression "this Criseyde" never occurs in *TC*, from the viewpoints of accent, stress, syllable, rhyme, spelling, and form. Statistically compares lines containing the words "Criseyde," "Troilus," and "this."

296. Torti, Anna. "Troilus' *Good Aventure*: Man's *Trouthe* as a Veiled

Mirror of God's *Trouthe.*" Chap. 2 in Anna Torti. *The Glass of Form: Mirroring Structures from Chaucer to Skelton* (*SAC* 15 [1993], no. 132), pp. 37–66. Analyzes the mirror imagery (and related metaphors) in *TC*, reading the work as an exploration of the relations between earthly and divine love. Criseyde's love mirrors Troilus's; Pandarus's art mirrors the narrator's. Human love and human writing are only images of divine love and divine truth. The Christian ending of the poem successfully mirrors its pagan plot.

297. Woehling, Mary-Patrice. "The Authorial Manipulation of Language in Chaucer's 'Troilus.'" *DAI* 52 (1991): 1742A. By manipulating his presumed sources and through the voices of the narrator and his characters, Chaucer develops reader-response strategy with such rhetorical devices as repetition and wordplay. The reflexive *TC* shows both love and language as subject to change.

See also nos. 24, 26, 41, 46, 57, 58, 62, 63, 65, 75, 95, 101, 110, 113, 115, 117, 118, 124, 226, 264, 271.

Lyrics and Short Poems

See nos. 6, 73, 74, 126.

An ABC

298. Denley, Marie. "Elementary Teaching Techniques and Middle English Religious Didactic Writing." In Helen Phillips, ed. *Langland, the Mystics, and the English Religious Tradition: Essays in Honour of S. S. Hussey* (*SAC* 15 [1993], no. 125), pp. 223–41. Includes brief discussion of *ABC* in light of alphabetic poems and other medieval teaching devices.

See also no. 91.

The Envoy to Bukton

299. Besserman, Lawrence. "Chaucer's *Envoy to Bukton* and 'Truth' in Biblical Interpretation: Some Medieval and Modern Contexts." *NLH* 22 (1991): 177–97. Chaucer intended to entertain and edify Bukton by means

of a network of biblical allusions that also provide an oblique comment on late-fourteenth-century biblical interpretation.

The Envoy to Scogan

300. Scattergood, John. "Old Age, Love and Friendship in Chaucer's *Envoy to Scogan*." *NMS* 35 (1991): 92–101. Explains the different strands in the poem partly through elements taken from Cicero's *De amicitia* and partly through its nature as a begging poem for Michaelmas, when annuities were renewed.

Womanly Noblesse

301. Ruud, Jay. "*Womanly Noblesse* and the Psychology of Love." *InG* 12 (1991): 15–34. In *Wom Nob*, Chaucer introduces a psychology of love new to English poetry that derives from Machaut's "'realist' scholastic epistemology" and that parallels the works of *stilnovisti* such as Dante, Cavalcanti, and Guinizella.

Chaucerian Apocrypha

302. Brown, Peter. "Journey's End: The Prologue to *The Tale of Beryn*." In Julia Boffey and Janet Cowen, eds. *Chaucer and Fifteenth-Century Poetry* (*SAC* 15 [1993], no. 52), pp. 143–74. Examines the details and style of *Beryn*, arguing that it was written to complete *CT* and that it capitalizes on several of its narrative and stylistic features. Suggests that *Beryn* was composed by a monk of Christ Church, Canterbury, perhaps in celebration of the jubilee of the cathedral in 1420.

303. Norem, Lois Elizabeth. "The Spurious Links of Chaucer's 'Canterbury Tales': Texts and Contexts." *DAI* 52 (1991): 1753A. With the inevitable variations produced by different scribes, *CT* has been edited by copyists who interpret the work variously (e.g., as ordered or unordered). A critical edition of the spurious links is here presented.

See also no. 272.

The Romaunt of the Rose

304. Feng, Xiang. "Chaucer and the 'Romaunt of the Rose': A New Study in Authorship." *DAI* 51 (1991): 4114A. Studies rhymes and rhyme words (the elements least liable to errors in transcription) and amends the traditional view that Chaucer could have written fragment A but neither B nor C: fragments A and C are equidistant from B and could be the work of a single translator.

305. Kumamoto, Sadahiro. "Some Observations on the Rhyme Words in *The Romaunt of the Rose*-A — A Comparison with the French Original Text." In Michio Kawai, ed. *Language and Style in English Literature: Essays in Honour of Michio Masui* (*SAC* 15 [1993], no. 80), pp. 322–42. Observes what kinds of words in the *Roman de la Rose* are likely to be borrowed by Chaucer as rhyme words, what alterations are made when they are transferred to *Rom*, and what sorts of words are added in the rhyme position in the translation.

See also nos. 6, 79, 101, 264.

Book Reviews

306. Aers, David. *Community, Gender, and Individual Identity: English Writing, 1360–1430* (*SAC* 12 [1990], no. 62). Rev. R. W. Hanning, *Speculum* 66 (1991): 368–70.

307. Alford, John A. *Piers Plowman: A Glossary of Legal Diction* (*SAC* 12 [1990], no. 46). Rev. David Williams, *YES* 21 (1991): 328–31.

308. Amos, Thomas L.; Eugene A. Green; and Beverly Mayne Kienzle, eds. *De Ore Domini: Preacher and Word in the Middle Ages* (*SAC* 15 [1993], no. 85). Rev. Patrick J. Horner, *SAC* 13 (1991): 159–62.

309. Baker, Donald C., ed. *The Squire's Tale.* Vol. 2, pt. 12, of *A Variorum Edition of the Works of Geoffrey Chaucer* (*SAC* 14 [1992], no. 6). Rev. Karl Heinz Göller and Richard J. Utz, *SAC* 13 (1991): 162–65.

310. Benson, C. David. *Chaucer's* Troilus and Criseyde (*SAC* 15[1993], no. 275). Rev. Helen Cooper, *TLS*, July 19, 1991, p. 5.

311. ———, and Elizabeth Robertson, eds. *Chaucer's Religious Tales* (*SAC* 14 [1992], no. 130). Rev. Elizabeth Archibald, *TLS*, Sept. 20, 1991, p. 26.

312. Benson, Larry D., gen. ed. *The Riverside Chaucer* (*SAC* 11 [1989], no. 11). Rev. Klaus Bitterling, *Anglia* 109 (1991): 485–89.

313. Blamires, Alcuin. *The Canterbury Tales* (*SAC* 11 [1989], no. 126). Rev. J. W. Nicholls, *YES* 20 (1990): 234–36.

314. Boitani, Piero, ed. *The European Tragedy of Troilus* (*SAC* 13 [1991], no. 228). Rev. J. A. Burrow, *EIC* 41 (1991): 160–66; Sally Mapstone, *RES*, n.s. vol. 42 (1991): 558–60; Derrick Pittard, *MÆ* 60 (1991): 113–14; noted in *Speculum* 66 (1991): 958.

315. ———. *The Tragic and the Sublime in Medieval Literature* (*SAC* 13 [1991], no. 45). Rev. Ronald B. Herzman, *SAC* 13 (1991): 165–68.

316. ———, and Anna Torti, eds. *Genres, Themes, and Images in English Literature from the Fourteenth to the Fifteenth Century* (*SAC* 12 [1990], no. 68). Rev. Manfred Markus, *ArAA* 16 (1991): 116–17.

317. ———, and ———, eds. *Religion in the Poetry and Drama of the Late Middle Ages in England* (*SAC* 14 [1992], no. 57). Rev. Elizabeth Archibald, *TLS*, Sept. 20, 1991, p. 26.

318. Boitani, Piero, and Jill Mann, eds. *The Cambridge Chaucer Companion* (*SAC* 10 [1986], no. 47). Rev. J. W. Nicholls, *YES* 20 (1990): 234–36.

319. Brewer, Derek, ed. *Studies in Medieval English Romances: Some New Approaches*. Cambridge and Wolfeboro, N.H.: D. S. Brewer, 1988. Rev. Robert J. Blanch, *SAC* 13 (1991): 168–72.

320. Briscoe, Marianne G., and John C. Coldeway, eds. *Contexts for Early English Drama*. Bloomington and Indianapolis: Indiana University Press, 1989. Rev. Peter W. Travis, *SAC* 13 (1991): 172–76.

321. Burrow, J. A., ed. *Middle English Literature: British Academy Gollancz Lectures* (*SAC* 15 [1993], no. 93). Rev. Bella Millett, *N&Q* 236 (1991): 94–95.

322. Chance, Jane, ed. *The Mythographic Art: Classical Fable and the Rise of the Vernacular in Early France and England* (*SAC* 14 [1992], no. 67). Noted in *Speculum* 66 (1991): 959.

323. *Chaucer*. Videocassette. Pt. 3 of Survey of English Poetry (FFH 1295). Princeton, N. J.: Films for the Humanities, 1988. Rev. Lisa Kiser, *SMART*, n.s., vol. 2 (1991): 49–53.

324. Cherniss, Michael D. *Boethian Apocalypse: Studies in Middle English Vision Poetry* (*SAC* 11 [1989], no. 70). Rev. Kathryn Kerby-Fulton, *YES* 20 (1990): 232–34.

325. Christianson, C. Paul. *Memorials of the Book Trade in Medieval London: The Archives of the Old London Bridge*. Cambridge and Wolfeboro, N.H.: D. S. Brewer, 1987. Rev. Carol M. Meale, *SAC* 13 (1991): 176–79.

326. Cooper, Helen. *The Canterbury Tales* (*SAC* 13 [1991], no. 97).

Rev. David Aers, *MÆ* 60 (1991): 116–18; C. David Benson, *SAC* 13 (1991): 183–86; J. D. Burnley, *RES*, n.s., vol. 42 (1991): 565–66; Charlotte Morse, *N&Q* 236 (1991): 203–204; Isamu Saito, *SELit* 68 (1991): 134–41 (in Japanese); Leonie Viljoen, *UES* 29 (1991): 40–41.

327. Davenport, W. A. *Chaucer: Complaint and Narrative* (*SAC* 12 [1990], no. 72). Rev. Dieter Mehl, *Anglia* 109 (1991): 191–94; Vincent Gillespie, *N&Q* 236 (1991): 359.

328. Davidoff, Judith M. *Beginning Well: Framing Fictions in Late Middle English Poetry* (*SAC* 14 [1992], no. 70). Rev. B. O'Donoghue, *MÆ* 60 (1991): 307–308.

329. Davlin, Mary Clemente. *A Game of Heuene: Word Play and the Meaning of Piers Plowman B.* Piers Plowman Studies, no. 7. Cambridge and Wolfeboro, N.H.: D. S. Brewer, 1989. Rev. Anna Baldwin, *YES* 21 (1991): 328; Mary J. Carruthers, *SAC* 13 (1991): 186–89.

330. Dinshaw, Carolyn. *Chaucer's Sexual Poetics* (*SAC* 13 [1991], no. 49). Rev. Sheila Fisher, *SAC* 13 (1991): 188–92.

331. Doob, Penelope Reed. *The Idea of the Labyrinth from Classical Antiquity Through the Middle Ages* (*SAC* 14 [1992], no. 74). Rev. Daniella Boccassini, *CRCL* 18 (1991): 600–603.

332. Edwards, Robert R. *The Dream of Chaucer: Representation and Reflection in the Early Narratives* (*SAC* 13 [1991], no. 52). Rev. Michael D. Cherniss, *Rev* 13 (1991): 131–47; R. W. Hanning, *MP* 88 (1991): 421–23; Helen Phillips, *MLR* 86 (1991): 973–74; James I. Wimsatt, *Speculum* 66 (1991): 866–69.

333. ———, and Stephen Spector, eds. *The Olde Daunce: Love, Friendship, Sex, and Marriage in the Medieval World* (*SAC* 15 [1993], no. 100). Rev. John D. Cox, *C&L* 40 (1991): 403–404.

334. Ellis, Roger, ed. *The Theory and Practice of Translation in the Middle Ages.* Cambridge and Wolfeboro, N.H.: D. S. Brewer, 1989. Rev. Helen Barr, *N&Q* 236 (1991):95–96; noted in *Speculum* 66 (1991): 705.

335. Fichte, Joerg O., ed. *Chaucer's Frame Tales: The Physical and the Metaphysical* (*SAC* 11 [1989], no. 84). Rev. Phillipa Hardman, *YES* 20 (1990): 236–37.

336. Ganim, John M. *Chaucerian Theatricality* (*SAC* 14 [1992], no. 138). Rev. Helen Cooper, *TLS*, July 19, 1991, p. 5.

337. *Geoffrey Chaucer and Middle English Literature.* Videocassette. English Literature on Video Series (FFH 906). Princeton, N.J.: Films for the Humanities, 1988. Rev. Lisa Kiser, *SMART*, n.s., vol. 2 (1991): 49–53.

338. Griffiths, Jeremy, and Derek Pearsall, eds. *Book Production and*

Publishing in Britain, 1375–1475 (SAC 15 [1993], no. 106). Noted in *Speculum* 66 (1991): 961.

339. Hanna, Ralph III, intro. *The Ellesmere Manuscript of Chaucer's Canterbury Tales: A Working Facsimile (SAC* 14 [1992], no. 8). Rev. John H. Fisher, *SAC* 13 (1991): 195–99.

340. Heinrichs, Katherine. *The Myths of Love: Classical Lovers in Medieval Literature (SAC* 14 [1992], no. 86). Rev. Helen Cooper, *TLS*, July 19, 1991, p. 5.

341. Hill, John M. *Chaucerian Belief: The Poetics of Reverence and Delight (SAC* 15 [1993], no. 108). Rev. Elizabeth Archibald, *TLS*, Sept. 20, 1991, p. 26.

342. Hopkins, Andrea. *The Sinful Knights: A Study of Middle English Penitential Romance (SAC* 15 [1993], no. 109). Rev. Dieter Mehl, *N&Q* 236 (1991): 523–25.

343. Hornsby, Joseph Allen. *Chaucer and the Law (SAC* 12 [1990], no. 85). Rev. John A. Alford, *JEGP* 90 (1991): 241–43; Marie Axton, *YES* 21 (1991): 333–35.

344. Howard, Donald R. *Chaucer: His Life, His Works, His World (SAC* 12 [1990], no. 9). Rev. Derek Pearsall, *SAC* 13 (1991): 199–203.

345. Hudson, Anne, ed. *English Wycliffite Sermons.* Vol. 3. Oxford: Clarendon Press; New York: Oxford University Press, 1990. Rev. Siegfried Wenzel, *N&Q* 236 (1991): 204–205; Edward Wilson, *MÆ* 60 (1991): 118–19.

346. Kane, George. *Chaucer and Langland: Historical and Technical Approaches (SAC* 13 [1991], no. 67). Rev. David Lawton, *YES* 21 (1991): 331–33.

347. Kaske, R. E., with Arthur Groos and Michael W. Twomey. *Medieval Christian Literary Imagery: A Guide to Interpretation (SAC* 12 [1990], no. 88). Rev. George Hardin Brown, *Speculum* 66 (1991): 176–80.

348. Kelly, Henry Ansgar. *Chaucer and the Cult of Saint Valentine (SAC* 10 [1988], no. 237). Rev. Phillipa Hardman, *YES* 20 (1990): 236–37.

349. ———. *Tragedy and Comedy from Dante to Pseudo-Dante.* Modern Philology, vol. 121. UCLA Center for Medieval and Renaissance Studies Cosponsored Publications, no. 7. Berkeley, Los Angeles, and London: University of California Press, 1989. Rev. Noel Howard Kaylor, Jr., *SAC* 13 (1991): 205–207.

350. Kemmler, Fritz, trans.; Jörg O. Fichte, ed. *Geoffrey Chaucer: Die Canterbury-Erzählungen: Mittelenglisch und Deutsch (SAC* 15 [1993], no. 18). Rev. Douglas J. McMillan, *SAC* 13 (1991): 208–10.

351. Kendrick, Laura. *Chaucerian Play: Comedy and Control in the*

Canterbury Tales (*SAC* 12 [1990], no. 129). Rev. Carl Lindahl, *Speculum* 66 (1991): 656–58.

352. Kennedy, Donald, ed. *Chronicles and Other Historical Writings*. Vol. 8 in Albert E. Hartung, gen. ed. *A Manual of Writings in Middle English, 1050–1500*. Hamden, Conn.: Archon, 1989. Rev. Lister M. Matheson, *SAC* 13 (1991): 210–13.

353. Knapp, Peggy. *Chaucer and the Social Contest* (*SAC* 14 [1992], no. 143). Rev. Derrick Pittard, *MÆ* 60 (1991): 306; Russell Potter, *Hwaet!* 2 (1991): 55–60.

354. Koff, Leonard Michael. *Chaucer and the Art of Storytelling* (*SAC* 12 [1990], no. 90). Rev. Derek Brewer, *Speculum* 66 (1991): 430–32; Winthrop Wetherbee, *SAC* 13 (1991): 215–18.

355. McIntosh, Angus; M. L. Samuels; and Margaret Laing. *Middle English Dialectology: Essays on Some Principles and Problems* (*SAC* 15 [1993], no. 81). Rev. N. F. Blake, *YES* 21 (1991): 305–306; noted in *Speculum* 66 (1991): 259.

356. Mann, Jill. *Geoffrey Chaucer. Feminist Readings* (*SAC* 15 [1993], no. 117). Rev. Helen Cooper, *TLS*, July 19, 1991, p. 5.

357. Martin, Priscilla. *Chaucer's Women* (*SAC* 14 [1992], no. 97). Rev. Joerg O. Fichte. *Anglia* 109 (1991): 205–10.

358. Mehl, Dieter. *Geoffrey Chaucer: An Introduction to His Narrative Poetry* (*SAC* 13 [1991], no. 326). Rev. J. W. Nicholls, *YES* 20 (1990): 234–36.

359. Minnis, A. J., ed. *Latin and Vernacular: Studies in Late-Medieval Texts and Manuscripts*. York Manuscripts Conference, Proceedings Series, no. 1. Woodbridge, Suffolk, and Wolfeboro, N.H.: Boydell and Brewer, 1989. Noted in *Speculum* 66 (1991): 707.

360. ———, and A. B. Scott, eds., with David Wallace. *Medieval Literary Theory and Criticism, c. 1100–c. 1375: The Commentary Tradition* (*SAC* 12 [1990], no. 98). Rev. Martin Irvine, *Speculum* 66 (1991): 451–53; T. P. Dolan, *SAC* 13 (1991): 218–21.

361. Morabito, Raphaele, ed. *La circolazione dei temi e degli intrecci narrativi: Il caso Griselda*. Atti del convegno di studi, L'Aquila, 3–4 dicembre 1986. L'Aquila, Rome: Japadre Editore, 1988. Rev. Charmaine Lee, *Medioevo Romanzo* 14 (1989): 136–39.

362. Nicholson, Peter. *An Annotated Index to the Commentary on Gower's* Confessio Amantis (*SAC* 15 [1993], no. 42). Rev. Patrick J. Gallacher, *Speculum* 66 (1991): 668–69.

363. North, J. D. *Chaucer's Universe* (*SAC* 12 [1990], no. 101). Rev. Marie Axton, *YES* 21 (1991): 333–35; Derek Brewer, *Rev* 12 (1990): 81–87;

Caroline D. Eckhardt, *Speculum* 66 (1991): 928–30; Daniel J. Ransom, *ANQ* 4 (1991): 33–37; Michael W. Twomey, *Anglia* 109 (1991): 186–90.

364. Olson, Paul A. *The* Canterbury Tales *and the Good Society* (*SAC* 10 [1988], no. 115). Rev. Lee Patterson, *CL* 43 (1991): 187–90; Derek Pearsall, *YES* 20 (1990): 230–32.

365. Patterson, Lee, ed. *Literary Practice and Social Change in Britain, 1380–1530* (*SAC* 14 [1992], no. 106). Rev. David Aers, *SAC* 13 (1991): 227–30; Gwen Crane, *MinnR*, n.s., vol. 37 (1991): 155–59.

366. *A Prologue to Chaucer.* Videocassette. English Literature on Video Series (FFH 998). Princeton, N.J.: Films for the Humanities, 1988. Rev. Lisa Kiser, *SMART*, n.s., vol. 2 (1991): 49–53.

367. Rogers, William E. *Upon the Ways: The Structure of* The Canterbury Tales (*SAC* 10 [1988], no. 120). Rev. J. W. Nicholls, *YES* 20 (1990): 234–36.

368. Rooney, Anne. *Geoffrey Chaucer: A Guide Through the Critical Maze* (*SAC* 14 [1992], no. 109). Rev. James M. Dean, *SAC* 13 (1991): 230–32.

369. Salter, Elizabeth. *English and International Studies in the Literature, Art, and Patronage of Medieval England* (*SAC* 12 [1990], no. 107). Rev. C. David Benson, *Speculum* 66 (1991): 689–91.

370. Scase, Wendy. Piers Plowman *and the New Anticlericalism* (*SAC* 13 [1991], no. 344). Rev. Robert Worth Frank, Jr., *SAC* 13 (1991): 232–35; Siegfried Wenzel, *YES* 21 (1991): 327–28.

371. Schmidt, A. V. C. *The Clerkly Maker: Langland's Poetic Art* (*SAC* 11 [1989], no. 116). Rev. J. S. Wittig, *Speculum* 66 (1991): 337–39.

372. Shoaf, R. A., ed. *Troilus and Criseyde* (*SAC* 13 [1991], no. 345). Rev. David Lawton, *YES* 21 (1991): 331–33.

373. Smith, J. J., ed. *The English of Chaucer and His Contemporaries: Essays by M. L. Samuels and J. J. Smith* (*SAC* 15 [1993], no. 83). Rev. J. D. Burnley, *YES* 21 (1991): 335–36.

374. Speed, Diane, ed. *Medieval English Romances.* 2d ed. (*SAC* 15 [1993], no. 43). Rev. Maldwyn Mills, *N&Q* 236 (1991): 522–23.

375. Strohm, Paul. *Social Chaucer* (*SAC* 13 [1991], no. 85). Rev. Alcuin Blamires, *MÆ* 60 (1991): 115–16; Mary Flowers Braswell, *SHR* 25 (1991): 174–76; P. R. Cross, *L&H*, 2d ser., vol. 2 (1991): 95–96; Britton J. Harwood, *SAC* 13 (1991): 245–50; Russell Potter, *Hwaet!* 2 (1991): 55–60.

376. Tajima, Matsuji. *Old and Middle English Language Studies: A Classified Bibliography, 1923–1985* (*SAC* 12 [1990], no. 58). Rev. Daniel Donoghue, *Speculum* 66 (1991): 482–83.

377. Taylor, Karla. *Chaucer Reads* The Divine Comedy (*SAC* 13 [1991],

no. 28). Rev. Douglas J. McMillan, *SAR* 56 (1991): 130–31; Edward Vasta, *AdI* 9 (1991): 344–48.

378. Wasserman, Julian N., and Lois Roney, eds. *Sign, Sentence, Discourse: Language in Medieval Thought and Literature* (*SAC* 13 [1991], no. 91). Rev. Daniel F. Pigg, *SAC* 13 (1991): 253–57.

379. Wetherbee, Winthrop. *Geoffrey Chaucer: The Canterbury Tales* (*SAC* 13 [1991], no. 107). Rev. Laura L. Howes, *SAC* 13 (1991): 257–59; Fritz Kemmler, *Anglia* 109 (1991): 489–90.

380. White, Hugh. *Nature and Salvation in Piers Plowman* (*SAC* 12 [1990], no. 118). Rev. David Williams, *YES* 21 (1991): 328–31.

381. Wimsatt, James I., and William W. Kibler, eds. Le Jugement du roy de Behaigne *and* Remède de Fortune (*SAC* 12 [1990], no. 33). Rev. Margaret J. Ehrhart, *SCRev* 8 (1991): 96–98; Charles Muscatine, *Speculum* 66 (1991): 879–81.

382. Yeager, R. F., ed. *John Gower: Recent Readings* (*SAC* 13 [1991], no. 94). Rev. John H. Fisher, *SAC* 13 (1991): 262–66; noted in *Speculum* 66 (1991): 962–63.

Author Index — Bibliography

385

Goodwin, Amy Wright 153
Gray, Douglas 104
Graybill, Robert 160
Green, Eugene A. 85, 308
Green, Richard Firth 105, 224
Griffiths, Jeremy 106, 338
Groos, Arthur 347
Grudin, Michaela Paasche 241
Guthrie, Steven 69
Hagen, Susan K. 195
Halford, Donna Allard 107
Hamel, Mary 221
Hample, Judy 160
Hanna, Ralph, III 59, 339
Hanning, R. W. 306, 332
Harada, Haruo 258
Hardman, Phillipa 335, 348
Hartung, Albert E. 352
Harwood, Britton J. 375
Haug, Walter 56
Heinrichs, Katherine 340
Herman, Peter C. 242
Hertog, Erik 38, 202
Herzman, Ronald B. 315
Hewett-Smith, Kathleen M. 24
Higuchi, Masayuki 17, 237
Hill, John M. 108, 341
Hillman, Richard 60
Hodges, Laura F. 170
Hopkins, Andrea 109, 342
Horner, Patrick J. 308
Hornsby, Joseph Allen 343
Howard, Donald R. 344
Howes, Laura Louise 110, 379
Hozeski, Bruce W. 1
Hudson, Anne 345
Huppé, Bernard F. 283
Hussey, S. S. 125
Ikegami, Tadahiro 252
Ireland, Colin A. 196
Irvine, Martin 360

Ishizaka, Ko 78
Jimura, Akiyuki 253, 254, 263
Johnson, Dawn 197
Johnston, Judith 61
Jonassen, Frederick B. 154
Jordan, Robert M. 155
Kane, George 346
Kanno, Masahiko 180, 213, 219
Kaske, R. E. 347
Kaufman, Janice Horner 79
Kawai, Michio 37, 75, 78, 80, 155,
    163, 213, 233, 235, 237, 253, 294,
    295, 305
Kawasaki, Masatoshi 156
Kaylor, Noel Howard, Jr. 349
Kellogg, Laura Dowell 284
Kelly, Henry Ansgar 285, 346, 349
Kemmler, Fritz 18, 350, 379
Kendrick, Laura 351
Kennedy, Donald 352
Kerby-Fulton, Kathryn 324
Kibler, William W. 381
Kienzle, Beverly Mayne 85, 308
Kimmelman, Burt Joseph 111
Kindrick, Robert 112
King, Pamela M. 62
Kiser, Lisa J. 113, 323, 337, 366
Kline, Barbara Rae 25
Knapp, Peggy 353
Koff, Leonard Michael 354
Kolve, V. A. 214
Kooper, Erik 39, 40, 76, 114, 202
Krochalis, Jeanne E. 261
Kumamoto, Sadahiro 305
Laing, Margaret 81, 355
Lawton, David 346, 372
Lee, Charmaine 361
Levin, Saul 34, 283
Levine, Robert 286
Lindahl, Carl 351
Love, Nathan 4

The New Chaucer Society
Eighth International Congress
August 1–4, 1992
The University of Washington
Seattle

Program

Saturday, August 1

7 P.M.: Welcome—William P. Gerberding (President, University of Washington)

Sunday, August 2

9–10 A.M.: Plenary Session A
  The State of Chaucer Criticism: Successes and Failures
    Presiding: Helen Cooper (University College, Oxford)
    John Ganim (University of California, Riverside)
    Jill Mann (Girton College, Cambridge)
    Linda Georgianna (University of California, Irvine)
    A. C. Spearing (University of Virginia)

10:30–12 P.M.: Concurrent paper sessions
  1) *The Legend of Good Women* in Our Time
    Presiding: *Mary Shaner (University of Massachusetts, Boston)
    Sheila Delany (Simon Fraser University): "Chaucer's *Legend of Good Women*: The Relevance of Wyclif"
    A. J. Minnis (University of York): "The World Upside Down: Gender-Games in *The Legend of Good Women*"
    Faye Walker-Pelkey (Rice University): "The Paradigmatic Paradox: Philomela's Anomalous Legend in Chaucer's *Legend of Good Women*"
  2) Exegetical Approaches to Chaucer—An Assessment
    Presiding: *Siegfried Wenzel (University of Pennsylvania)
    Richard Newhauser (Trinity University): "Avoiding the *Marlepit*: Curiosity, *Sely* John, and the Complexity of Exegesis"
    Ellen Martin (Vassar College): "Essential Exegesis in the Households of Fame and Rumor"
    David L. Boyd (University of Pennsylvania): "Exegesis and Medieval Readers: Reflections on Allegorical Interpretation and the Historical Method"
  3) Private Life in Chaucer
    Presiding: Michaela P. Grudin (University of Oregon)
    *Thomas A. Goodman (University of Miami): "Publish or Punish? Chaucer and the Fall of Public Woman"
    David Lawton (University of Sydney): "Chaucer and the Politics of Space" (paper read by John Ganim)

* An asterisk indicates the organizer of the session.

393

Sarah Stanbury (Tufts University): "Reading in the John: Privacy and the Making of the Chaucerian Subject"

4) Open Session I
   Presiding: *Robert W. Hanning (Columbia University)
   Mary Flowers Braswell (University of Alabama, Birmingham): "Judas Iscariot and His 'Tale': A Source for Chaucer's Pardoner?"
   Diane M. Ross (Lake Forest College): "Criseyde and Dido: The Implications of Widowhood"
   Thomas J. Farrell (Stetson University): "Chaucerian Monology and *The Clerk's Tale*"

5) Chaucer and French Court Culture
   *Monica McAlpine (University of Massachusetts, Boston)
   Presiding: Richard Firth Green (University of Western Ontario)
   Michael Hanly (Washington State University): "The Order of the Passion: Courtiers, Poetry, and the Peace Movement"
   Stephen Partridge (University of British Columbia): "Ideas of Authorship and the Design of the Page: Chaucer and Deschamps"
   John Bowers (University of Nevada, Las Vegas): "Chaucer's Captive Audience: Jean d'Angoulême and Charles d'Orleans"

2–4 P.M.: Colloquium sessions

C1) The Place of the *Melibee* (Debate and discussion)
    Presiding: Susanna Fein (Kent State University)
    Erik Kooper (University of Utrecht)
    Alan Gaylord (Dartmouth College)
    Gayle Margherita (Indiana University)
    *James Rhodes (Southern Connecticut State University)
    R. A. Shoaf (University of Florida)
    Peter Travis (Dartmouth College)
    Winthrop Wetherbee (Cornell University)

C2) Wife of Bath Criticism (10-minute papers)
    Presiding: *Susan Crane (Rutgers University)
    Mark Allen (University of Texas, San Antonio): "Scholarly Tradition and the Wife of Bath"
    Marilynn Desmond (SUNY, Binghamton): "Compulsory Heterosexuality and Textual Possibilities"
    Lynne Dickson (Rutgers University): "Reworking the Wife of Bath"
    Carolyn Dinshaw (University of California, Berkeley): "Loud and Queer: The Wife and the Pardoner"
    John Fyler (Tufts University): "The Wife's Romance"
    Andrew Galloway (Cornell University): "Are We Historicizing the Wife of Bath Yet?"

C3) Interpretive Cruces (10-minute papers)
    *Emerson Brown (Vanderbilt University)
    Presiding: Peter G. Beidler (Lehigh University) (substituting for Emerson Brown)

Michael N. Salda (University of Southern Mississippi): "Trojan Windows and *Roman de la Rose* Walls: An Architectural Source for *Book of the Duchess*, 321–334"

Kathryn L. McKinley (Campbell University): "Chaucer and the Fourteenth-Century Vogue for Things Roman: *Troilus and Criseyde* III.150"

Edgar Laird (Southwest Texas State University): "*Astrolabe* II.4.16–24 and an Analogue in Pelerin de Prusse"

Peter G. Beidler (Lehigh University): "Chaucer's Request for Money in *The Man of Law's Prologue*"

Beverly Kennedy (Marianopolis College): "Reambiguation of the Obvious: Alisoun's 'Chambre of Venus'"

Juliette Dor (University of Liège): "A Bakhtinian Reading of the Biblical Prayers in *The Man of Law's Tale*"

C4) Chaucer and the Texts in This Class (Debate and discussion)
Presiding: Joerg O. Fichte (University of Tübingen)
Mary-Jo Arn (Bloomsburg University)
Dolores Warwick Frese (University of Notre Dame)
Lisa J. Kiser (Ohio State University)
Peggy Knapp (Carnegie-Mellon University)
Michael Murphy (Brooklyn College, CUNY)
*Glending Olson (Cleveland State University)
Charles A. Owen, Jr. (University of Connecticut)
Julian Wasserman (Loyola University, New Orleans)
R. F. Yeager (University of North Carolina, Asheville)

C5) Readings of *Merchant's Tale* 1944–81 (10-minute papers)
Presiding: *Elizabeth Robertson (University of Colorado)
Mary E. Housum (Shepherd College): "May's Mind as a Locked Garden Without a Key"
William Woods (Wichita State University): "The Soft Privy"
Carol A. Everest (University of Alberta): "January's 'Safe Sex'"
Christine Rose (Portland State University): "Silence Is a Woman's Glory"
Robert W. Hanning (Columbia University): "Privy Thoughts: May, *Meditatio*, and the Wife of Bath"

4 P.M.: Special meetings
*Thomas Hahn (University of Rochester): "The Chaucer Bibliographies: A Session for Collaborating Authors and Other Interested Scholars"
*Siegfried Wenzel (University of Pennsylvania): "The Chaucer Library: Old and New Projects"
*Robert Correale (Wright State University): "Sources and Analogues: A Session for Collaborating Authors and Other Interested Scholars"

7 P.M.: Biennial Chaucer Lecture
"Perpetual Motion: Alchemy and the Technology of the Self"
Lee W. Patterson (Duke University)
Presiding: Anne L. Middleton (University of California, Berkeley)

Monday, August 3

9–10 A.M.: Plenary Session B
Other Disciplines and Chaucer
Presiding: Mary Carruthers (New York University)
James Boon ([Anthropology] Princeton University)
Michael Camille ([Art] University of Chicago)
Margaret Bent ([Music] All Souls' College, Oxford)
Christopher de Hamel ([Manuscripts] Sotheby's)

10:30–12 P.M.: Concurrent paper sessions
6) Chaucer and Rhetoric
Presiding: *T. P. Dolan (University College, Dublin)
Rita Copeland (University of Minnesota): "The Pardoner's Body and the Disciplining of Rhetoric"
John M. Hill (U.S. Naval Academy): "Felt Knowledge Through Subverted Mastery: The Cases of the Canon's Yeoman and the Prioress"
J. Stephen Russell (Hofstra University): "Apostrophe and the (Con)vocation of the Man of Law"
7) Chaucer, Italian Humanism, and the English Audience
Presiding: *James M. Dean (University of Delaware)
Karla Taylor (University of Michigan): "Deaf Ears: Dante, Chaucer, and the Problem of Influence"
Richard Neuse (University of Rhode Island): "Chaucer and Boccaccio: *The Monk's Tale* and *De casibus virorum illustrium*"
Leonard Koff (University of California, Los Angeles): "'Of Whom I Make Mencioun': Chaucer's Use of Petrarch"
8) Chaucer and Motherhood
Presiding: Allyson Newton (Rice University)
Louise O. Fradenburg (University of California, Santa Barbara): "Loss, Maternity, and *The Legend of Good Women*"
*Elaine Hansen (Haverford College): "Maternal Thinking About Chaucer's Mothers"
Linda Lomperis (University of California, Santa Cruz): "Maternal Practices and Political Considerations in *The Prioress's Tale*"
9) Literary Style, Political Form, and Social Justice
Presiding: David Wallace (University of Minnesota)
*David Wallace (University of Minnesota): "Chaucer, Durkheim, and the Division of Labor"
Ardis Butterfield (Downing College, Cambridge): "Anglo-French Genres and the Appropriation of Culture"
David Aers (University of East Anglia): "Social Chaucer and Langlandian Justice"
10) Piety and Devotional Practice in the Age of Chaucer
Presiding: *Gail McMurray Gibson (Davidson College)
Henry Ansgar Kelly (University of California, Los Angeles): "Sacraments, Sacramentals, and Lay Piety"

Lawrence M. Clopper (Indiana University): "From Ungodly *Ludi* to Sacred Play"

Lynn Staley Johnson (Colgate University): "Women's Ritual and *The Book of Margery Kempe*"

2–4 P.M.: Colloquium sessions

C6) Art and Chaucer (Practicum)

Panel: Michael Camille (University of Chicago), *Kathleen Scott (East Lansing, Michigan), V. A. Kolve (University of California, Los Angeles)

Ann Eljenholm Nichols (Winona State University): "Chaucer's Parody of Confession"

Michaela P. Grudin (University of Oregon): "Chaucer's Awareness of Visual Art"

Jeremy Griffiths (St. John's College, Oxford): "Illustrations of the *Troilus*" (paper read by A. S. G. Edwards)

James A. Eby (James Madison University): "Canterbury Cathedral and *The Canterbury Tales*"

Phillipa Hardman (University of Reading): "Chaucer and Images in Books of Hours"

Martha W. Driver (Pace University): "Chaucer as Cultural Artifact"

Pamela Sheingorn (Baruch College): "How Should We Discuss Art and Literature?"

Joanne S. Norman (Bishop University): "Illustrations of Vices and Virtues in GG.4.27"

Pamela M. King (University of London): "The Pardoner's Narrative and Images of Mortality"

C7) Anthropology, Religion, and Chaucer (Practicum)

Panel: *Barbara Nolan (University of Virginia), James Boon (Princeton University)

Kathleen Ashley (University of Southern Maine)

Sarah Beckwith (Duke University)

John M. Crafton (West Georgia College)

Catherine R. Haigney (St. John's College)

John F. Plummer (Vanderbilt University)

David Raybin (Eastern Illinois University)

Claire Sponsler (George Washington University)

C8) Music and Chaucer (Practicum)

Panel: *James I. Wimsatt (University of Texas), Margaret Bent (All Souls' College, Oxford)

Joseph Baldassare (Boise State University)

Thomas Campbell (Wabash College)

Steven Guthrie (Agnes Scott College)

Thomas Moser (University of Maryland)

Anne Worthington Prescott (Alexandria, Virginia)

Linda Zaerr (Boise State University)

C9) Paleography and Chaucer (Practicum)
   Panel: *Ralph Hanna III (University of California, Riverside), Christopher de Hamel (Sotheby's)
   Joan Baker (University of Washington)
   Susan Crane (Rutgers University)
   Geraldine Branca (Merrimack College)
   Kenneth Bleeth (Connecticut College)
   Carl Grindley (Wichita State University)
   Maidie Hilmo (University of Victoria)
   Barbara Kline (Florida International University)
   Suzanne Reynolds (St. John's College, Cambridge)
C10) Chaucer Studies and the NEH Seminars/Institutes (Debate and discussion)
   Presiding: Richard Emmerson (Western Washington University)
   *Lillian Bisson (Marymount University): "Chaucer and His World"
   Carolyn Collette (Mount Holyoke College): "*Troilus and Criseyde*"
   Deanna Evans (Bemidji State University): "Chaucer and Boccaccio"
   James Flynn (Western Kentucky University): "*The Canterbury Tales*"
   JoAnn Hoeppner Moran (Georgetown University): "Chaucer and His World"
   Charles Muscatine (University of California, Berkeley): "Teaching Chaucer"
   Vicki Olsen (Bemidji High School): "*The Canterbury Tales*"
   Jay Ruud (Northern State University): "*The Canterbury Tales*"
   Christie Fengler Stephany (University of Vermont): "*The Canterbury Tales* and the English Illuminated Book"
   William Stephany (University of Vermont): "*The Canterbury Tales* and the English Illuminated Book"

4:30–6 P.M.: Round Table Discussion
   "'And Whan This Book Ys Maad': Scholarship and Publication, Views from the Editors"
   Presiding: Lisa J. Kiser (*Studies in the Age of Chaucer*)
   Panel: Robert Frank (*Chaucer Review*), Thomas J. Heffernan (*Studies in the Age of Chaucer*), R. A. Shoaf (*Exemplaria*), Luke Wenger (*Speculum*)

Tuesday, August 4

9–10:30 A.M.: Concurrent paper sessions
   11) Chaucer's Popular Artistry
   Presiding: Paul Theiner (Syracuse University)
   *Carl Lindahl (University of Houston): "The Folkloric Dialect of *The Franklin's Tale*"
   Betsy Bowden (Rutgers University): "So What Else Is New? Proverbs in *The Miller's Tale*"

Nancy Mason Bradbury (Smith College): "The Rhetoric of Popular Storytelling and the Artistry of *Troilus and Criseyde*"

12) Manuscript Evidence for Chaucer's Early Readers
Presiding: *Linne R. Mooney (University of Maine)
Julia Boffey (Queen Mary and Westfield College, University of London): "Chaucer's Dream Poems in the Fifteenth Century"
Carol M. Meale (University of Bristol): "The Text and the Book: Readings of Chaucer's *Legend of Good Women* in the Late Middle Ages"
David Parkinson (University of Saskatchewan): "Chaucer Apocrypha in Sixteenth-Century Scottish Manuscripts"

13) Chaucer and Medieval Subjectivity
Presiding: *Daniel Rubey (Lehman College, CUNY)
Richard Firth Green (University of Western Ontario): "Objective Truth in Chaucer's England"
Anne L. Middleton (University of California, Berkeley): "Changing the Subject: Chaucer, Langland, and the Problem of Character"
H. Marshall Leicester (University of California, Santa Cruz): "Medieval Subjectivity Today: Comments"

14) Open Session II
Presiding: *Carolyn Dinshaw (University of California, Berkeley)
Christopher Cannon (Harvard University): "Geoffrey Chaucer and the *Raptus* of Cecily Chaumpaigne: The Use and Abuse of Biography"
Susan K. Hagen (Birmingham-Southern College): "*The Second Nun's Tale* or, Protecting the World from Rude Women"
Elisa M. Narin (University of California, Berkeley): "*The Siege of Jerusalem* and Augustinian Historians: Writing about Jews in Fourteenth-Century England"

15) Literary References to Chaucer to 1700
*Piero Boitani (University of Rome)
Presiding: Sheila Delany (Simon Fraser University)
Mark Sherman (Rhode Island School of Design): "Spenser's 'Well of English,' Time, and Defilement"
James Simpson (Girton College, Cambridge): "Statian Pessimism in Lydgate's *Siege of Thebes*"
Anna Torti (University of Verona): "Henryson's *Testament of Cresseid*: Deconstructing the *Auctoritas*"

11–12 P.M.: Presidential Address
"*Old, New,* and *Yong* in Chaucer"
Alfred David (Indiana University)
Presiding: Jill Mann (Girton College, Cambridge)

2–4 P.M.: Colloquium sessions
C11) Literature and History: *Lenvoy de Chaucer a Scogan* (Practicum)
Presiding: *Peter Brown (Darwin College, University of Kent)

399

Mark Amsler (University of Delaware)
David Burnley (University of Sheffield)
Andrew Butcher (University of Kent)
Karen Winstead (Occidental College)

C12) Spiritual Community and Social Pathology: Polemical Views of *The Prioress's Tale* (10-minute papers)
Presiding: Robert Boenig (Texas A&M University)
Miri Rubin (Pembroke College, Oxford): "Late Medieval Contexts of Anti-Semitism"
Denise L. Despres (University of Puget Sound): "Ritual Pollution and Bodily Restitution"
Gavin I. Langmuir (Stanford University): "Motives of Anti-Judaic Hostility"
Heather Findlay (Cornell University): "The Mother and the Jew: Abjection in Chaucer's *Prioress's Tale*"
Jeremy Cohen (Ohio State University/University of Tel Aviv): "Anti-Jewish Discourse and Its Function in Medieval Christian Theology"
*Thomas Hahn (University of Rochester): "Female Voice, Male Authority, and the Prioress"

C13) Chaucer and Recent Technology (Debate and discussion)
Presiding: *Thomas Bestul (University of Nebraska, Lincoln)
Robert Hasenfratz (University of Connecticut)
Dan Mosser (Virginia Polytechnic Institute)
Peter Robinson (Oxford University Computing Service)

C14) Chaucerian Source/Influence/Intertext (10-minute papers)
Presiding: *Dieter Mehl (University of Bonn)
Joerg O. Fichte (University of Tübingen): "Arthurian Literature and *The Canterbury Tales*"
Patrizia Grimaldi Pizzorno (Florence, Italy): "Intertextuality and Dialogism in *The Book of the Duchess*"
William Watts (Butler University): "Lollius on Textuality"
Martin Camargo (University of Missouri): "*Troilus and Criseyde* and *The Merchant's Tale*: Intertextuality as Resistance"
Cynthia Ho (Davidson College): "Ancient Architectures: Chaucer's Inherited Framed Tale Tradition"
Erik Hertog (Catholic University, Leuven): "Now You See It, Now You Don't: Reflections on the Concept of Analogy"

C15) Chaucer, *Piers* and Religion (10-minute papers)
Presiding: *M. Teresa Tavormina (Michigan State University)
Josephine Koster Tarvers (In*Scribe Communications Consulting): "The *Ars Orandi* in Chaucer and Langland"
Virginia A. Unkefer (James Madison University): "Same Words, Different Discourses: Langland and Chaucer's Religious Phrases"
Edwin D. Craun (Washington and Lee University): "The Manciple and Will Take Up Pastoral Discourse on Deviant Speech"

400

Lorraine Kochanske Stock (University of Houston): "Patience in Langland's C-text *Prologue* and Chaucer's *Merchant's Tale*

Kathleen M. Hewett-Smith (University of Richmond): "'Hateful Harm' or 'Hateful Good': Patient Poverty in Chaucer and *Piers Plowman*" (paper read by M. Teresa Tavormina)

Chauncey Wood (McMaster University): "Penance in Chaucer and Langland"

4 P.M.: Special meeting

*Mark Allen (University of Texas, San Antonio) and *Thomas Bestul (University of Nebraska, Lincoln): "Bibliography and Electronic Mail: Discussion of E-mail in Compiling the *SAC* Bibliography and Coordination of Several Bibliographic Projects"

Index

Adam, 6, 51, 216
Adorno, T. W., 182
Aers, David, 57n, 124n
Aiken, Pauline, 26n
Ainsworth, Peter F., *Jean Froissart and the Fabric of History: Truth, Myth, and Fiction in the Chroniques*, 147–53
Albertus Magnus, 40, 43, 47, 50n, 52
Alford, John A., 153; *Piers Plowman: A Guide to the Quotations*, 153–55
Allen, Rosamund S., 161, 241
St. Ambrose, 117, 297
Amis and Amiloun, 269
Ando, Shinsuke, 282, 284
St. Anne, 68–70
St. Anthony, 124
Apollonius of Tyre, 47
Apuleius, *Metamorphoses*, 132n
Aquinas, Thomas, 47
Archelaos, 47
Aristotle, 42–43, 47, 286; *Meterologica*, 50n
Arnobius, 117
Arnold of Villanova, 34, 41n, 47, 52, 53
Aronstein, Susan, 173
Artefius, 47
Arthur of England, 169–74
Arundel, Archbishop Thomas of Canterbury, 115–16, 162
Ashby, George, 159
Ashley, Kathleen, 192
Ashmole, Elias, 43n, 44n
Astell, Thomas, 162
Aston, Margaret, 113n
Auerbach, Erich, 185, 185n, 226
St. Augustine, 32, 111, 114, 114n, 117, 119, 120, 125, 185; *De doctrina Christiana*, 111, 111n, 113n, 114, 117, 124
Aurora consurgens, 45, 45n, 46
Avicenna, 47; *Kitâb al Shifâ*, 50n
Awntyrs of Arthure, 260
Axton, Richard, 164–65, 283
Bacon, Francis, 51
Bacon, Roger, 47, 51, 53
Badel, Pierre-Yves, 51n
Baillie, G. H., 106n

Bailly, Harry, 36, 99, 125, 126–27, 129, 133, 140, 142, 145
Baird, Joseph L., 70n
Bal, Mieke, 279
Balinas, 47
Ball, John, 213, 214
Barratt, Alexandra, 180
Barron, Caroline, 30n, 212
Barron, W. R. J., 270
Barthes, Roland, 174, 220
Bawcutt, Priscilla, 272, 273; *Dunbar the Makar*, 155–58
Beadle, Richard, 165, 232, 235, 250, 272, 273, 283
Beaufort, Henry, 160
Beaufort, Joan, 160
Bechtold, Joan, 66n, 67n
Beeson, C. F. C., 102n, 104n, 105, 105n, 106, 109n
Bell, Susan Groag, 67, 67n, 68, 68n
Bennett, J. A. W., 163, 179
Bennett, Michael, 210
Benoît de Sainte-Maure, 161
Benskin, Michael, 271, 272
Benson, C. David, 144, 144n, 163–64, 256
Benson, Larry D., 263, 272; ed. *The Riverside Chaucer*, 5n, 25n, 30n, 31n, 61n, 91n, 98n, 100n, 121n, 131n, 140n
Berger, Samuel, 115n
Berglund, Maureen N., 9, 170, 221–22, 240
Berman, Marshall, 56
Besserman, Lawrence, 126n
Betterton, Thomas, 167, 168
Bevington, David, 193
The Bible, 49, 112, 112n, 113, 113n, 114–18, 120–21, 122, 123, 127, 128, 154, 155, 224–26, 238, 297; *Deut*, 187; *Eph*, 32; *Gen*, 154; *Gospel of the Nativity of Mary*, 225–26; *Gospel of Pseudo-Matthew*, 225–26; *Judg*, 225; *Lev*, 187; *Luke*, 224; *Matt*, 187; *Ps*, 137; *Song of Sol*, 200, 246
Biblia Pauperum, 222–26, 261
Blake, N. F., 247–48, 248n, 256, 283
Blanche of Lancaster, 9